THE FIRST HISTORIANS

Other books by Baruch Halpern:

The Constitution of the Monarchy in Israel
The Emergence of Israel in Canaan

THE FIRST HISTORIANS

The Hebrew Bible and History

Baruch Halpern

1817

Harper & Row, Publishers, San Francisco

Cambridge, Hagerstown, New York, Philadelphia, Washington
London, Mexico City, São Paulo, Singapore, Sydney

Grateful acknowledgment is given for the use of the following material. Originally published as "The Resourceful Israelite Historian: The Song of Deborah and Israelite Historiography." From *Harvard Theological Review* 76 (1983): 379–401. Copyright 1984 by the President and Fellows of Harvard College. Published as "Doctrine by Misadventure" in *The Poet and The Historian*, edited by Richard E. Friedman, Scholars Press (1983): 41–74. *Harvard Semitic Studies*, 26. Copyright © the President and Fellows of Harvard College.

FIRST EDITION

Library of Congress Cataloging-in-Publication data

Halpern, Baruch.
    The first historians: the Hebrew Bible and history/Baruch Halpern.—1st ed.
        p.   cm.
    Includes bibliographies.
ISBN 0-86683-990-9 : $22.95
1. History (Theology)—Biblical teaching.   2. Bible. O.T.—Historiography.   I. Title.
BS1199.H5H34 1988
221.9'5A—dc19   87-46208
                                                                                CIP

88 89 90 91 92 RRD 10 9 8 7 6 5 4 3 2 1

To Jesse's and Orly's grandparents and Sophie

Contents

Abbreviations

AASOR	*Annual of the American Schools of Oriental Research*
AB	Anchor Bible
ABC	A. K. Grayson, *Assyrian and Babylonian Chronicles* (Texts from Cuneiform Sources 5; Locust Valley, N.Y.: J. J. Augustin, 1975)
ABL	R. F. Harper, *Assyrian and Babylonian Letters* (14 vols.; Chicago: University of Chicago, 1892–1914)
AfO Beih.	*Archiv für Orientforschung Beiheft*
AJA	*American Journal of Archaeology*
Akk.	Akkadian
AnBib	Analecta Biblica
ANET	J. B. Pritchard, ed., *Ancient Near Eastern Texts Relating to the Old Testament* (3rd ed.; Princeton: Princeton, 1969)
AnSt	*Anatolian Studies*
AOAT	Alter Orient Altes Testament
Arab.	Arabic
Arad #	Y. Aharoni, *Arad Inscriptions* (Jerusalem: I.E.S., 1981)
Aram.	Aramaic
ATANT	Abhandlungen zur Theologie des Alten und Neuen Testaments
AV	Authorized Version (King James)
BA	*Biblical Archaeologist*
BAR	*Biblical Archaeology Review*
BASOR	*Bulletin of the American Schools of Oriental Research*
BBB	Bonner Biblische Beiträge
BDB	F. Brown, S. R. Driver, and C. A. Briggs, *A Hebrew and English Lexicon of the Old Testament* (Oxford: Clarendon, 1907 [1968])
Bib	*Biblica*
BKAT	Biblischer Kommentar—Altes Testament
BMB	*Bulletin du Musée de Beyrouth*
BoSt	Boghazköi-Studien
BWANT	Beiträge zur Wissenschaft vom Alten und Neuen Testament
BZAW	Beiträge zur *Zeitschrift für die alttestamentliche Wissenschaft*
CBOTS	Coniectanea Biblica, Old Testament Series

CBQ	*Catholic Biblical Quarterly*
CRRA	Comptes rendus des rencontres assyriologiques
CTA	A. Herdner, *Corpus de tablettes en cunéiformes alphabétiques* (Mission de Ras Shamra 10; Paris: Imprimerie Nationale, 1963).
Dtr	The corpus from Deuteronomy to Kings, exilic in origin, according to Noth
Dtr₁	The Josianic author of DtrH, according to Cross
Dtr¹	The Hezekian author of DtrH, according to Peckham
Dtr₂	The exilic updater of the work of Dtr₁, according to Cross
Dtr²	The exilic revolutionizer of the work of Dtr¹ (Peckham)
Dtr(hez)	The Hezekian history produced by H(Dtr) hez
Dtr(jos)	The Josianic edition of the Deuteronomistic history by H(Dtr)
Dtr(x)	The exilic reedition of the Josianic Deuteronomistic history
DtrG	= DtrH, Smend's equivalent to Dtr₁
DtrH	The corpus from Deuteronomy to Kings, as first or finally produced
DtrN	The nomistic redactor of DtrH (Smend)
DtrP	the prophetic redactor of DtrH (Dietrich)
dss.	dissertation
E	The Elohist source in the Pentateuch
EA	J. A. Knudtzon, *Die El-Amarna Tafeln* (2 vols.; Vorderasiatische Bibliothek 2; Leipzig, Germany: Hinrichs, 1915)
EB	Early Bronze Age
E(Dtr)n	= DtrN
E(Dtr)p	= DtrP
E(Dtr)x	= Dtr₂, an exilic editor of the DtrH written by H(Dtr)
ed.	edited by
EI	*Eretz Israel*
ET	English translation
EvTh	*Evangelische Theologie*
FRLANT	Forschungen zur Religion und Literatur des Alten und Neuen Testaments
Fs.	Festschrift
G	Greek translations of HB
Gᴬ	Codex Alexandrinus
Gᴮ	Codex Vaticanus
Gᴸ	Lucianic rendition of HB

G ( ) A glossator of the text in parentheses

H ( ) The historian responsible for the primary assembly of the text in parentheses

H(Dtr) Where brought into contrast with other authors, equals H(Dtr)jos, the Josianic historian of the first edition of DtrH. Otherwise, the historian, Hezekian or Josianic, who assembled and composed DtrH in a form substantially like the one it takes today.

H(Dtr)hez The author who produced the Hezekian edition of what was to become DtrH

H(Dtr)x A hypothesized exilic historian (so, e.g., Noth, Peckham) who produced the present DtrH

HAR *Hebrew Annual Review*
HAT Handcommentar zum Alten Testament
HB Hebrew Bible
Heb. Hebrew
HSM Harvard Semitic Monographs
HSS Harvard Semitic Studies
HTR *Harvard Theological Review*
HUCA *Hebrew Union College Annual*

ICC International Critical Commentary
IEJ *Israel Exploration Journal*
I.E.S. Israel Exploration Society

J The Yahwist source in the Pentateuch
JAOS *Journal of the American Oriental Society*
JBL *Journal of Biblical Literature*
JCS *Journal of Cuneiform Studies*
JE J and E
JNES *Journal of Near Eastern Studies*
Josephus,
  Ant. Josephus, *The Antiquities of the Jews*
  Bell. Josephus, *The Jewish War*
JSOT *Journal for the Study of the Old Testament*
*JSOT*Sup Supplements to the *Journal for the Study of the Old Testament*

KAI H. Donner and W. Röllig, *Kanaanäische und aramäische Inschriften* (3 vols.; Wiesbaden, W. Germany: Harrassowitz, 1962–64)
KHCAT Kleiner Hand-Commentar zum Alten Testament

LB	Late Bronze Age
LXX	The Septuagint

M+	The stories of the major judges
M−	The list of the minor judges
MB	Middle Bronze Age
MDOG	*Mitteilungen der deutschen Orient-Gesellschaft*
MT	Massoretic Text
MVAG	*Mitteilungen der vorderasiatisch-ägyptischen Gesellschaft*

n.	Footnote
NBKI	S. Langdon, *Die neubabylonischen Königsinschriften* (Vorderasiatische Bibliothek 4; Leipzig, E. Germany: Hinrichs, 1911)
n.d.	No date
NF	Neue Folge
Noth, *US*	M. Noth, *Überlieferungsgeschichtliche Studien* (Schriften der Königsberger Gelehrten Gesellschaft 18. Geisteswissenschaftliche Klasse 2; Halle, E. Germany: M. Niemeyer, 1943)
NS	New series

OG	Old Greek rendition of HB
OIP	Oriental Institute Publications
Or	*Orientalia*
OTL	Old Testament Library
OTS	*Oudtestamentische Studiën*

P	The Priestly source in the Pentateuch
Pap.	Papyrus
PAPS	*Proceedings of the American Philosophical Society*
P.B.I.	Pontifical Biblical Institute
P.E.F.	Palestine Exploration Fund
PEQ	*Palestine Exploration Quarterly*
pl.	Plural

Qad	*Qadmoniyot*

R	The redactor (or the redactor of the sources in subscript)
4R²	H.C. Rawlinson, *The Cuneiform Inscriptions of Western Asia 4* (London: Bowler, 1864), part II
RB	*Revue Biblique*
Rdt₁	The first redactor of Judges 3–8, according to Richter
Rdt₃	Richter's third redactor of Judges

rep.	Reprinted
Richter, TUR	W. Richter, *Traditionsgeschichtliche Untersuchungen zum Richterbuch* (Bonner Biblische Beiträge 18; Bonn: P. Hanstein, 1963)
RLA	*Reallexicon der Assyriologie*
RSV	Revised Standard Version
SBLDS	Society of Biblical Literature Dissertation Series
SBLMS	Society of Biblical Literature Monographs Series
SDeb	The Song of Deborah, Judges 5
sg.	Singular
SH	*Scripta Hierosolymitana*
SOTSMS	Society for Old Testament Studies Monograph Series
Streck, Asb.	M. Streck, *Assurbanipal und die letzen assyrischen Könige bis zum Untergang Ninevehs* (3 vols.; Vorderasiatische Bibliothek 7; Leipzig, E. Germany: Hinrichs, 1916)
SVT	Supplements to *Vetus Testamentum*
Syr.	Syriac
TA	*Tel Aviv*
tr.	Translated by
TZ	*Theologische Zeitschrift*
UF	*Ugarit-Forschungen*
V	The Vulgate
VT	*Vetus Testamentum*
WdO	*Welt des Orients*
WHJP	World History of the Jewish People
WMANT	Wissenschaftliche Monographien zum Alten und Neuen Testament
WO	*Welt des Orients*
ZA	*Zeitschrift für Assyriologie*
ZAW	*Zeitschrift für die alttestamentliche Wissenschaft*
ZDPV	*Zeitschrift des deutschen Palästina-Vereins*

Preface

This volume is an attempt to rationalize an intuition: that historical narrative is not to be handled as are folklore or the elements of dramatization in historical narrative; that a historian's conviction is not formal evidence of concoction; that the ancient authors' views of their task must determine the directions from which we approach their texts.

"Text-centered" interpretation is meaningless interpretation when applied to historical literature. No historian—no interpreter of real events—writes in the expectation that the history will be divorced from the intentions that motivate it. Rather, the historian tries to communicate those intentions, to communicate information about specific phenomena outside the text, in the text. Historical texts, then, cannot speak meaningfully to those who examine what they say—as readers are wont to do—but only to those who ask what they *mean* to say. Missed communication between the author and the modern reader is the basis, in my view, of many controversies. And it is no good trying to lay the blame for this state of affairs on the ancient authors, though many of the scholarly hypotheses examined in the succeeding pages do just that: they make the authors out to be illogical, dull, or dishonest.

So far as I know, only one recent scholar, Martin Noth, has attempted to mount a systematic case to the sincerity and competence of the Israelite historian. Yet, characteristically, in the last years, those who defend Noth's work jettison this central thesis, and focus their efforts instead on his view that a single hand composed Deuteronomy and the Former Prophets. In returning to Noth's main thesis, then, I feel a little like Carlyle, in *Sartor Resartus*, discovering that Cromwell was sincere, defending Cromwell against "vulpine" imputations of cynical hypocrisy. This volume defends Noth against those who defend Noth; it champions the Israelite historian against what Carlyle, in his frustration, would have stigmatized as "vulpine" allegations of pathological fraud.

In the present climate of literary and even historical scholarship, this elementary proposition will no doubt excite a clamor of opposition. Nevertheless, I must acknowledge openly some personal debts.

Research for this volume was conducted with the support of a National Endowment for the Humanities Fellowship administered through the American Schools of Oriental Research, at the Albright Institute of Archaeological Research in Jerusalem, where Muneira Said and all the Gitins conspired to make intellectual life possible. Much to my surprise, they and many of our other friends in Jerusalem instilled me with a little (dangerous) learning in, and a deepening respect for, Syro-Palestinian, or biblical archaeology. The Institute of Advanced Studies at the Hebrew University of Jerusalem also provided support, and an environment of unparalleled vibrancy. In 1984–1985, the Alexander von Humboldt-Stiftung underwrote most of the writing of the project, during an enchanting stay at the University of Munich, where materials unavailable to me in Canada were easily accessible. The final draft was completed during a research leave generously furnished by the York University Faculty of Arts.

Chapter 4 of this volume originally appeared as "The Resourceful Israelite Historian: The Song of Deborah and Israelite Historiography." The adapted form in which the article appears also duplicates parts of my discussion in "Doctrine by Misadventure: Between the Israelite Source and the Biblical Historian," which appeared in R. E. Friedman, ed., *The Poet and the Historian* (Chico, CA: Scholars, 1983), 41–73. I am grateful to the editors of these publications for their gracious permission to reuse them here.

Chapter 3 of this volume was originally delivered in seminar at the Institute for Advanced Studies of the Hebrew University. I owe much to my colleagues at the institute—our hosts, Abraham Malamat and the late Yigael Yadin, and the team of scholars, Alan Millard, Larry Stager, Yisrael Finkelstein, Henri Cazelles, Pinchas Artzi, Ami Mazar, and Siegfried Herrmann—for their help, stimulation, and encouragement in this and in many other connections. Other sources of extra-familial aid and abetment have been Aileen Baron, Jutta Börker-Klähn, David Daube, Paul Dion, Dietz Edzard, Sy Gitin, Avigdor Hurowitz, Alan Jeude, Aharon Kempinski, Jon Levenson, Wolfgang Richter, Hayim Tadmor, David Ussishkin, and Irene Winter. I learned a great deal about the history of scholarship, and about compositional analysis, from Klaus Baltzer, whose generosity with his time and wits uniformly had the effect of sharpening or refocusing any subject under discussion.

Finally, I want to thank John J. Collins, who in editing the volume was patient with delays, liberal with ideas, and tyrannical about style!

Introduction

Darien: Vistas in the History of Israel

CHAPTER 1

The Trouble with History

For he is but a bastard to the time / that doth not smack of observation
—KING JOHN

THE TROUBLE WITH HISTORY

Reconstructing the past has been compared to detective work (mostly of the fictional variety), to woodsmanship (spotting a tiger in the bush), to writing pulp fiction, to psychoanalysis, and to various branches of the natural sciences. In one way or another, all of these comparisons are apt; but in just the same measure, they are all deceptive. History, a form of observation, reconstruction, and representation of human events, is a distinctive enterprise. This book concerns history and the Bible. It has a deceptively simple aim: to determine what ancient Israelite historians thought history demanded, to illuminate the discipline to which they subjected themselves.

The thesis of the volume is that some of these authors—those who wrote works recognizably historical—had authentic antiquarian intentions. They meant to furnish fair and accurate representations of Israelite antiquity. This argument has obvious implications for the way we use the Bible as a historical text. It would be disingenuous to claim that intentions are ever pure, or that they guarantee results. Still, insofar as history has distinctive properties, analytical operations on historical texts must take those intentions into account.

How such texts should be approached will emerge from the discussion, but it is worthwhile to explain at the start what problems in the study of Israelite history occasion the inquiry.

For believers, the history in the Bible is constitutive of a religious community. Here, as with the American myth of the Mayflower, common history is a surrogate, or emblematic, identity. Such a confessional history must be uncritical history: to question the canonized reports is to threaten the cohesion of the community. The straitjacket of doctrinal conservatism therefore prohibits critical historical analysis of the Bible.

The confessional use of the Bible is fundamentally antihistorical. It makes of Scripture a sort of map, a single, synchronic system in which the part illuminates the whole, in which it does not matter that different parts of the map come from divergent perspectives and different periods. The devotee uses it to search for treasure: under the X lies a trove of secret knowledge; a pot of truths sits across the exegetical rainbow, and with them one can conjure knowledge, power, eternity. Worshipers do not read the Bible with an intrinsic interest in human events. Like the prophet, or psalmist, or, in Acts, the saint, they seek behind the events a single, unifying cause that lends them meaning, and makes the historical differences among them irrelevant. In history, the *faith*ful seek the permanent, the ahistorical; in time, they quest for timelessness; in reality, in the concrete, they seek Spirit, the insubstantial. Confessional reading levels historical differences—among the authors in the Bible and between those authors and church tradition—because its interests are life present (in the identity of a community of believers) and eternal.

In reaction against confessional reading, critical scholars bring the principle of scientific skepticism to bear on biblical texts. For reasons explored in Chapter 2, this principle, once set loose, assumed a momentum of its own. At the extremes it became a juggernaut, generating what amounted to a negative fundamentalism, a denial of any historical value in the text—first in Chronicles and the Pentateuch,[1] and then in such historical books as Judges, Samuel, and Kings, concerning which skepticism has reawakened today.[2]

The image of the map clarifies this. The map, say of Europe, includes cities and highways of the tenth century, of the eleventh century, and so on, continuing into our own time. In effect, the confessionalist maintains that all those cities were on the map from the start, that God created Europe, and the map, in the tenth century. Critical study divulges that this is not so, that some of the cities and highways appeared later, and it is the job of the historian to determine when each town, highway, and so on, was added. Negative fundamentalists, however, date the whole map by its latest elements. Because the map reflects a view from the twentieth century, they argue, it cannot be used to get at earlier times.

A third constituency rejects historical study on philosophical grounds. These are historical Pyrrhonists, those who deny all possibility of acquiring significant and reliable knowledge of the past. Some among this group, the historicists, argue that historians write in a biased way, from culturally conditioned perspectives.[3] Others stress the relativity, not of reconstruction, but of observation: thus, Sir Walter Raleigh supposedly burned his history of the world on hearing different eyewitness accounts of an incident he had seen from his Tower window. How can one ascertain anything about the past if firm conclusions elude one even about contemporary events?

Most vocal among the Pyrrhonists, however, have been literary critics of the (post-)New Critical variety. Their rhetoric is sometimes combative. Robert Alter, for example, as recently as 1975, castigated historical-critical scholars for failing to treat the Bible as scholars treat modern literature.[4] This is the more regrettable in that modern literary study of the Bible is as old as literary study in the postclassical West, with roots in the work of Goethe,[5] Lowth,[6] and Herder.[7] It is the foundation of all other work in the field: thus source criticism was first called literary criticism, because it arose from literary study and took its mother's name; every diachronic approach to biblical texts is at heart a variety of author-centered literary study. In this enterprise historical assumptions condition literary interpretations, and literary interpretations determine historical conclusions. The relationship between the disciplines is dialectical.

Still, this is not to come to grips with the literary critics' Pyrrhonism. Some of these critics transmogrify the Intentional Fallacy—the proposition that a work's artistic merit bears no necessary relationship to what the author intended to wreak—from an esthetic into a historical principle. They deny that readers can construe what the Israelite historian meant; so all possible interpretations are equally legitimate or illegitimate. Others, much like historicists, argue that history is not falsifiable—and is therefore less than scientific—because it is literary. The historian, they say, integrates "facts" into a dramatic framework—builds a story around them, to be precise. This story is something extrinsic to the "facts", something supplied. Because it is concocted, therefore, from the imagination, and presented in the garb of prose fiction—dramatically, as a story—history is indistinguishable from "fiction". Only "text-centered" (i.e., reader-centered) approaches are appropriate.[8] To revert to the map, the historical Pyrrhonists concede the existence of towns and highways, but insist that the cartographer has merely concocted their relative size and position; and, some hold that the reader has no access to the cartographer's intentions, others that the intentions are not, in any case, binding upon the interpreter.

These critiques—those of the confessionalists, the negative fundamentalists, and the Pyrrhonists—have caught the study of Israelite antiquity in a cross fire. This has evoked a cacophony of historical approaches, a scramble to make an end run around the problem of interpreting text. Most of the methods are social scientific,[9] and call on models extrinsic not just to the text, but to the culture as a whole. They apply universal, unhistorical schematics, like those of the natural sciences, yet deal, like the human sciences, in variables (e.g., forms of society) whose components, whose atoms, are never isolated. Such tools cannot usher in a revolution in historical certainty. Their promise, like that of the positivist program of the nineteenth century, is an eschatological one.

All these responses, including the recourse to social science, betray not just an unease with history, but a naïveté toward it, a naïveté which exceeds the narrow confines of biblical studies. No treatment of Israelite historiography has yet engaged the philosophical problems involved in the study. One recent survey, in fact, sets out with the disclaimer that such contemplation is out of place, and develops a view that history is detailed, unbiased, and antithetical to religion and to religious language, but that history is not necessarily an attempt accurately to depict the past. This is like saying that a lamp has well-insulated wires and a reliable switch, and runs on alternating current, but need not provide illumination.[10] So revolutionary a proposal invites circumspection.

WHAT OUR TEACHERS NEVER TELL US

The word *history* is like a secret set of homonyms. Distinguishing them through different spellings, such as *pear* and *pair,* might help. But the lack of differentiation in the term actually reflects a lack of differentiation in popular reflection on the subject. The average schoolchild, once taxed, recognizes a difference between history as event and history as a description of event. But the finer distinctions among the types of history—and among their functions (mythic charter, and so on)—are not so self-evident.

Except insofar as they trench on the critiques of the confessionalists, negative fundamentalists, Pyrrhonists, and social scientists, the varieties of history are not material here. It must be remembered, however, that history as a program or endeavor (for simplicity's sake, we may exclude history as human events past) involves three stages, the first two dialectically related: the identification of evidence, the interpretation of evidence, and the presentation of a reconstruction from the evidence. One must take care not to apply arguments concerning one stage to the others. The literary critics, for example, focus primarily on the presentation, implying that reconstruction and presentation are identical. But reconstruction is a stage unto itself, entailing various operations, from the most local to the most general levels of problem-solving.

History produces histories, from broad, not too detailed textbooks (for example, *The History of Modern Europe*) to short notes in obscure journals about the date of a battle or of a battle-ax. In common parlance, however, history is the undertaking of rendering an account of a particular, significant, and coherent sequence of past human events. This delimits the genres of historiography—or history-writing—fairly narrowly. Thus an accounts book is not a history, in that it involves neither research into the past nor an attempt to make the past coherent. Similarly, a chronicle, or a list of events without any necessary connections among them, does not constitute a history as the term is conventionally understood: the sequence lacks coherence and particularity by definition. Nevertheless, in common with such texts, histories purport to be true, or probable, representations of events and relationships in the past. They make this claim as to particular allegations: the people they describe, the significant actions they describe, are historical, authentic.

This definition of historiography means that it always has a subject: it can be about one thing, and ignore other things; but it must always be *about something* (some sequence of events or set of relationships). In the ancient Near East, Assyrian royal inscriptions are historiography about the king's building and military accomplishments—they are concatenations of snippets about individual campaigns and public works projects. Often found in works of dedication, they never expose royal political or strategic programs, or the real politics of a governor's appointment here, a priesthood's there, and so on. Yet these texts contain historiography. Their subject is the king's service to nation and god, or the divine blessings for which the king is grateful, or the events to which the dedication is in theory a response (such as the completion of a temple).[11]

This limitation is not crucial. Historiography cannot—and should not—be infinitely detailed. All history is at best an abridgment—better or worse—of an originally fuller reality. Can one write a history of the American Revolution that follows every individual affected through a period even of twenty years? That traces crop yields and profits on every farm and in every firm in the New World and in Britain? That relates the tortured politics, economics, and logistics of French and Spanish involvement in the New World? Who would have the time or zeal to read the result? Does a textbook cover the history of the United States, or only selected economic, or social, or political aspects of it? What this textbook suppresses from the most detailed professional studies is nothing to the omissions that they all share. History is always the study of one thing, or of several things, and the exclusion of many others. Until history is brought down to the level of physical particles, until it reduces the past to beta particles and midget misuns, "as it really was," it can represent nothing more than a selective approximation. History, in sum, is a literally false but scientifically more or less useful coherence imposed by reason on reality. An infinity of sculptures lurk inside the ghostly marble of the past; only the unfashioned stone will ever be complete.

It follows that historiography need not be comprehensively accurate in order to be historiography: much can be omitted; indeed, most events must be. History is not how things happened, but an incomplete account, written toward a specific end, of selected developments. Yet normally we would say that if the author does not *mean* to be accurate in representing the past ("as it really was"), if the author does not try to get the events right and to arrange them in the right proportion, the result cannot be history.

This is an important point, ignored in the survey of Near Eastern historiography previously mentioned.[12] It is most easily illuminated through concrete illustration. Imagine the extreme case of a history of England in which there is no Tudor accession, no break with the Roman church, no rise of a middle class, no exploration on the seas, and no war with Spain: England continues Plantagenet, Catholic, medieval, and insular until the Long Parliament.

From our vantage point, such a work would share much in common with those novels, produced in the first decades of this century, that portray a world after a German victory in World War I. But under what circumstance would our book be historiography? Only if the author knew no better—if the author had no evidence of the Tudors. If this condition does not obtain, our book on England is plainly not historiography. If the author, for example, attempts knowingly to perpetrate on the reader a fraudulent reconstruction contradicted or unsupported by evidence, then the author is not engaged in writing history. Quite the opposite: the author is attempting to fob off as history a text known to be something else.

Whether a text is a history, then, depends on what its author meant to do. Consider this: when Edgar Rice Burroughs writes a book, such as *A Princess of Mars*, about inhabitants of another planet, we entertain no doubt as to its character. Yet it is as possible, historically, as the story of a known person, say Talleyrand, in a populated city in a real epoch. When Alan Grant, Josephine Tey's fictional detective, assembles the revisionist case for rehabilitating Richard III, never for a moment does the reader hesitate to distinguish the historical, evidential claims from the fictional. As readers, we identify what is historiography and what is not based on our perception of the author's *relationship to the evidence*.

It is a function of this relationship to the evidence that an untutored reader may, like the author ignorant of Henry VII, fall into confusion. In 1985, the governor of New York titillated the American press by celebrating publicly a "great American," Miss Jane Pittman. The governor had "misread" a television movie about this fictional character as a (fictionalized) biography of a historical character. Lacking an adequate acquaintance with the personalities of American social history, he was incapable of assessing what parts of the film dramatized reconstructed events, and what parts dramatized the scriptwriters' fancy: he could not draw the line between the movie and historiography. The line, then, falls not between history and fiction—all history is fictional, imaginative, as the literary critics say. The distinction is between history and romance, or fable; it is a distinction in authorial intention, in the author's adherence to sources.

Even in the particulars it does include, historiography is never accurate. It portrays the past, as portraiture must, through the imaginative lenses used to create all fictions. More: a reader who rejects this or that element of a historian's reconstruction (such as a Vatican plot against Lincoln) does not allege that the error takes the book out of the realm of history; there are books whose whole thesis one may reject (as Charles Beard's *Roosevelt and the Coming of the War, 1941*) without prejudice to their character as historiography. We call a narrative a history on the basis of its author's perceived intentions in writing, the author's *claim* that the account is accurate in its particulars, the author's sincerity.

Here, historiography departs from romance. Romance does *not* excite expectations of an accurate sketch of events or relations experienced by the particular actors named. The subjectivity of the difference explains how it is that historiography can be read as romance (as in the case of Churchill's *My Early Life*) or romance as historiography (*The Autobiography of Miss Jane Pittman* or Orson Welles's *War of the Worlds*). Indeed, in historical romance, as in Dmitri Merejkowski's *Julian the Apostate,* the two genres intermingle. Romance often makes excellent historical reconstruction, and the Claudius of Robert Graves is perhaps more authentic, more lifelike, than any other representation of the emperor, ancient or modern. Reflection excludes it from the category of historiography, because it does not claim to be accurate, or probably accurate, in its particulars. It is "true," instead, to human nature or to Roman thought in general (cf. Aristotle *Poetics* 1.9).

Thus neither its contents nor the accuracy of its contents ropes historiography off from fiction. Ancient authors, such as Thucydides and Josephus, supplied speeches for their characters, for example, on a principle once enunciated by Dickens: "If Sydney Carton had spoken, this is what he would have said" (cf. Thucydides 1.22). The speeches were a *convention*—one of many—of effective presentation, and the reader was expected to know that *in this case* no claim as to the accuracy of the particular was being lodged. But it is just that qualification—explicit in Thucydides and Polybius (2.56; 29.12),[13] among others—that illustrates to what degree such authors thought of themselves as writing history.

"Persiflage!" retorts the literary critic: there are legends and dialogues in the recitals of Herodotus, myths in the accounts of Xenophon, motivations in the biographies of Carlyle, that indulge the fictional imagination and defy credulity in no lesser measure than the poetry of Shakespearean dramas. What intrinsic feature makes Herodotus a historian, but Shakespeare a dramatist? To argue that Herodotus intended to write history and Shakespeare intended to write drama writes only a vicious close to the circle of one's thought.

Shakespeare, however, knew the difference between Shakespeare and Holinshed. Intuitively, we make the same distinction. We apply it successfully in the measure that we accurately construe the author's intent. Romance and historiography can be formally identical, the latter even dialogical at points. The perceived mix of romance and history, the perceived emphasis that makes of the dialogue a vehicle for the presentation of developments or a medium for the articulation of thematic concerns, determines how the reader assesses the genre of a work or of the passages in that work.

What is the passage about? The real and historical? Issues of historical moment? Does it conform to, or willfully contradict, or fail to engage what is known about the issues in question? Does it aim primarily to entertain and to illustrate grand truths, or does it draw principles only secondarily from the "facts", sharing information concerning which is the first object of the presentation? Does it *imitate* or *duplicate* reality?

Here is what marks Graves's Claudius dilogy or Peter Shaffer's *Amadeus* as historical romance, not history. These works are not *about* the events of the past, the events known through the evidence, even though their dramatic sequences answer to the limits of historical possibility, or even to those, liberally construed, of probability. They are imaginations of events, and whether the particulars are true is immaterial to author and reader alike. These works do not assert authority. Contrast Herodotus, who reconstructs events as, in the author's view, they probably or certainly were. In Herodotus' case, the reader accepts this intention. His history is *about* real events.

Transpose the difference between history and romance into portraiture. The historian depicts a real subject, the dramatist an imagined one. The contrast holds even for historical romance, in that the historian is corraled by observable evidence and inference, consigned to the Pale of the probable; the dramatist grazes all the pastures of the possible, where imagination transcends evidence and supplants inference as the chief forage. The techniques are identical—each copies from an ideal original (real or imaginary), and both use the same fictionalizations, concealing or stressing warts or imperfections in complexion or other features of the model. But the originals, the models, are different. One is susceptible to objective scrutiny, to examination by someone other than the artist; one is not.

At the most superficial level, this means that one cannot argue with Edgar Rice Burroughs that Tarzan or John Carter is inaccurately portrayed. One cannot reason that Homer's Achilles, Graves's Claudius, or Shaffer's Mozart thought differently than the masterworks suggest. Were Homer, Graves, or Shaffer persuaded that the historical reality deviated from the historical romance, none would incur any ethical obligation to revise his work. Filling in the silences of the romance is pointless. What is not there just is not there.

One can argue, however, with Mommsen about the real Caesar, or with Parkman about Pontiac or Frontenac. One can argue with Tey about Richard III, if not about Alan Grant. History, in sum, *is* subject to falsification, to argument as to the accuracy of its particulars and the assessment of their interrelation. The dramatic tropes in which it presents these reconstructions are, as the literary critics say, incontestable: whether Waterloo is a tragedy or a comedy is for the reader to decide, but that France was worsted there admits of no qualification. There is romance in history, and there can be history in romance. But in each case only one element invites meaningful debate, only one element has an objective, external referent, only one element is liable to appraisal on the evidence. Historiography, unlike the novel, is scientific; it is epistemologically based (more on this in this chapter and in Chapter 2).

All this means that history is an antiquarian enterprise, an attempt to get at the past. It can, of course, have ideological dimensions. Leon Trotsky's *History of the Russian Revolution,* Winston Churchill's *World Crisis,* Edward Gibbon's *Decline and Fall of the Roman Empire,* all are shot through with and dedicated to sustaining party bias. To Francis Parkman, the winning of the New World divulges the merits of individualistic, entrepreneurial Protestantism, and the defects of lockstep Catholicism. Macaulay's *History of England* is renowned as a "Whig interpretation". Even Basil Liddell Hart's military histories—much like those of Thucydides, Arrian, or Polybius—advocate doctrines dear to factions in the political hierarchy of his time.

After all, there is a curious pattern in the literatures of the nations. Greeks write for Greeks about Greeks, Britons for Britons about Britons. To adapt Xenophanes, if mad dogs wrote history, they would write about mad dogs, and exhibit the biases of their breed. Bias can *enhance* historiography, except where it runs amok, as where a writer repudiates obvious fact (such as the Holocaust), and indulges in fantasy or fraud. Historians of the lowest competence, given over to the most infuriated prejudices, have vented those prejudices constructively in selecting their subjects, in presenting causal connections, and in proportioning the thematic sinews of particular themes and episodes. Perhaps a measured, dispassionate judgment characterizes the best history. But historiography can defend high principles in a setting of high charge. There are passages in Macaulay's "Bacon" or his "Clive" that are as moving as anything in English melodrama. These essays remain historical because they are antiquarian.

The antiquarianism of historiography, its traffic in particular truths, demands author-centered interpretation. How, after all, can we straw the romantic chaff from the antiquarian wheat except by asking what the author meant? To distinguish a work's narrative conventions and fictions (the speeches of Thucydides) from its falsifiable assertions requires a judicious appreciation both of metaphoric, or fictitious, and of literal, or authoritative, discourse. Narrative history especially, the genre most common before the advent of academic journals, and the genre most prized even today, loses all meaning in the hands of a reader unable to discern what is fictitious and what factitious. This incapacity is the proprietary link between the fundamentalist and the Pyrrhonist. The former takes nothing as fictitious, and so nothing as specious. The latter takes all as fictitious, and so all as specious. Again, history is referential: historians try to communicate information about phenomena extrinsic to the text. One can exploit such literature referentially only by determining what data its author meant the reader to extract.

What tests, we ask, can we administer to determine if an author intends to write a work of history? The question sweeps us along the controverted and capricious ground of mentalist literary interpretation.

Some critics appeal to the reactions of earlier readers as a strategy to unman the aggrandized intentional fallacy—the denial that the reader has access to the author's meaning. But what is the profit in exchanging the various but equally legitimate responses of ancient readers for the various but equally legitimate interpretations of modern readers? To study readers, to study how they read a text, is to study a tradition, not the text.

Our judgment as to a historian's intentions, thus, must be passed on individual passages. The principal criterion can only be one: does the work parlay the available evidence (sources) into coherent narrative *about* events susceptible to reconstruction from the sources? In other words, did the narrator have reason to believe what he or she wrote, or did the narrator depart at will from the sources, concocting freely about matters concerning which he or she had no, or contradictory, evidence?

This question is most revealing where the sources are extant. Chapter 4 examines such a case; the sources can be isolated with some confidence in the texts examined in chapters 6 and 8 as well. But for texts whose sources are no longer isolable or extant (the bulk of Israel's historiography), ancillary tests must be devised. These center on the techniques by which a historian signals historiographic intentions to the reader.

The ancillary questions are corollaries of the principal criterion. So the historian who is digesting sources into a coherent, justifiable presentation of a reconstruction will minimize divagations extrinsic to the evidence. He or she will focus upon events, states, and persons of historical significance. The historian may so far yield to the importunities of an antiquarian conscience as to incorporate details incidental to the main themes of the work. But he or she will avoid gratuitous decorations (private miracles in a political history) whose reconstruction is *not* demanded by the evidence: the historian will not supply a Miss Jane Pittman, or intimate details of Claudius' personal life. Here is where history parts company with romance: in degree, only, the vehicle which conveys the reconstruction to a reader is stripped down, the better to serve its purpose; it is not festooned with odd transactions that the historian has no evidentiary license to reconstruct. Shakespeare's *Antony and Cleopatra* goes far beyond the evidence in its presentation of characters' mentalities, motivations, and concerns. This is the poetic, not the historical, imagination at work.

When a narrative satisfies these criteria, it is legitimate to ask, What changes, if any, would one have to introduce in order to transform it into a history? There is no formal difference betwen history and romance. But if a narrative answers to available evidence, if it avoids elaboration *unnecessary to the presentation of a reconstruction from the evidence*, then at the least it tests the limits between romance and historiography. One must approach each text warily, not to mistake stripped-down legend for history (as the ancients sometimes did: see chapters 3 and

10–11). But when a stripped-down text does not trade *primarily* in metaphoric language (as that of kinship or of divine causation; see chapters 10–11), when it treats significant events without unjustified dramatization, it deserves to be examined as history. Economy, in a political-historical narrative, is one sign of historiographic intentionality (see chapters 9–11).

The application of such criteria in no way proves what an author intended to write. It does produce evidence of those intentions. The distinction is important, for history, ultimately, is susceptible to evidence, but not to proof. This is, too, the answer to the historicist critique: a historian, conditioned by a culture, must persuade other historians, whom the culture conditions differently, that one reconstruction is accurate. Like a physicist applying a familiar rule to the unknown (Einstein's caveat was that "E = mc² may be a local phenomenon"), the historian must defend a reasoned interpretation; the reasoning will survive, it will prove formidable, only if it covers the evidence pro and con. As in theoretical physics, the compounding of subjective views is what creates scientific standards in history. The standards are those of evidence and argument, not Euclidean proof.

Historical knowledge is based upon evidence in just the way the deliberations of a jury are. We do not violate, thus, the etiquette of investigation if we expect even ancient historians to minimize fictions unjustified by evidence, unconditioned by causal axioms, uncalled for by the exigencies of narrative presentation. The reader will detect theoretical flaws in these criteria; practically deployed, they suffice to flush Homer, or Shakespeare, or Graves from the flock whose muse is Klio, whose archpriest is Herodotus, whose myrmidons are the positivists and philologians.

Literary questions dominate this discussion, because studies of Israelite historiography focus on its literary integrity, as an argument, in some cases, to concoction and insincerity.[14] But a competent presentation of history will exhibit literary integrity, however little it concocts. The questions we must address to such a work concern its reconstructive logic, its relationship to the evidence or sources. These are stringent questions, and demand extensive treatment, as chapters 3–4 will show. They preclude an abbreviated review of all Israelite historiography. This volume limits itself to the Former Prophets, Joshua, Judges, Samuel, and Kings. Even here not every text is covered. Instead it is my hope to illustrate what sorts of questions it is appropriate to ask of the historiographic literature, what sorts of authors and editors it is appropriate to hypothesize, what sorts of expectations it is appropriate to entertain about the texts' accuracy. Much of the literature in question is antiquarian in its intent, as the treatment will show. We must approach it not as fiction, and not as romance, but as historiography.[15]

Notes to Chapter 1

1. See W.M.L. de Wette, *Beiträge zur Einleitung in das Alte Testament 1. Kritischer Versuch über die Glaubwürdigkeit der Bücher der Chronik mit Hinsicht auf die Geschichte der Mosaischen Bücher und Gesetzgebung* (Halle, E. Germany: Schimmelpfennig, 1806).
2. Among others, see H.-D. Hoffmann, *Reform und Reformen: Untersuchungen zu einem Grundthema der deuteronomistischen Geschichtsschreibung* (ATANT 66; Zurich: Theologischer, 1980); J. van Seters, *In Search of History* (New Haven: Yale University, 1983).
3. See, e.g., J. M. Sasson, "On Choosing Models for Recreating Israelite Pre-Monarchic History" *JSOT* 21 (1981): 3–24. For the history of the controversy, see A. Momigliano, *Essays in Ancient and Modern Historiography* (Middletown, Conn.: Wesleyan, 1977), 365–73; n. 15.
4. R. Alter, "A Literary Approach to the Bible," *Commentary* 60:6 (December 1975): 70–77. See also H. W. Frei, *The Eclipse of Biblical Narrative: A Study in Eighteenth and Nineteenth Century Hermeneutics* (New Haven: Yale, 1974) 134–36, 151–54, 160f.; Y. Zakovitch, "Story Versus History," *Proceedings of the Eighth World Congress of Jewish Studies: Bible Studies and Hebrew Langue* (Jerusalem: World Union of Jewish Studies, 1983), 47–60.
5. J. W. von Goethe, *Sämtliche Werke* (Stuttgart, W. Germany: T. Knaur, 1902), 36.95–105. See latterly, W. Schottroff, "Goethe als Bibelwissenschaftler," *EvTh* 44 (1984): 463–85.
6. R. Lowth, *De sacra poesi Hebraeorum: Praelectiones academicae Oxonii habitae* (Oxford: Oxford, 1753).
7. J. G. von Herder, *Vom Geist der ebräischen Poesie: Eine Anleitung für den Liebhaber derselben und der ältesten Geschichte des menschlichen Geistes* (Dessau, E. Germany, 1782–83; Leipzig, E. Germany: Joh. Philipp haugs Wittwe, 1787; 3rd ed., Leipzig, E. Germany: K. W. Justi, 1825).
8. Among others, C. Lévi-Strauss, *The Savage Mind* (London: Weidenfeld and Nicolson, 1962), 258–63; Hayden White, *Metahistory: The Historical Imagination in Nineteenth-Century Europe* (Baltimore: Johns Hopkins, 1973).
9. For example, G. E. Mendenhall, "Biblical History in Transition," in G. E. Wright, ed., *The Bible and the Ancient Near East* (Fs. W. F. Albright; Garden City, N.Y.: Doubleday, 1961), 27–58; N. K. Gottwald, *The Tribes of Yahweh* (New York: Orbis, 1979); L. L. Thompson, "The Jordan Crossing: Ṣidqot Yahweh and World Building," *JBL* 100 (1981): 343–58. The method arose early, with the Bedouin model of the nineteenth century; it entered the modern era with M. Weber's *Gesammelte Aufsätze zur Religionssoziologie. III. Das antike Judentum* (Tübingen, W. Germany: Mohr, 1921), especially 47f., 93f.; Weber's influence suffuses the work of A. Alt, such as "Die Landnahme der Israeliten in Palästina" (1925), *Kleine Schriften zur Geschichte des Volkes Israel* (Munich: C. H. Beck, 1953), 1.89–125.
10. Van Seters, *In Search* (n. 2), 1 (and 77–92, 114, 146, 150f.). Ironically, the author appropriates J. Huizinga's definition of *history*, but construes it so as to exclude Huizinga's own work. Huizinga also affirms that only texts intended to accurately depict events are history, a qualification van Seters violates, in silence (n. 12).
11. See, e.g., *NBKI*, 218–20; C. J. Gadd, "The Harran Inscriptions of Nabonidus," *Anatolian Studies* 8 (1958): 35–92, and the comments of H. Tadmor, "History and Ideology in the Assyrian Royal Inscriptions," in F. M. Fales, ed., *Assyrian Royal Inscriptions: New Horizons in Literary, Ideological, and Historical Analysis* (Orientis Antiqui Collectio 17; Rome: Istituto per l'Oriente, Centro per le antichità e la storia dell'arte del vicino oriente, 1981), 13–33, especially 23, with citations, all on Nabonidus. Further, A. L. Oppenheim, "The City of Assur in 714 B.C." *JNES* 19 (1960): 133–47, especially 134,

on Sargon's Letter to the God, the fullest and most sophisticated campaign report Assyria has left us.

12. Van Seters, *In Search* (n. 2), which defines the Deuteronomistic History as the earliest work of history, but affirms that its author lacked evidence, and, where he had it, felt free to ignore it. Cf. M. Sternberg, *The Poetics of Biblical Narrative* (Bloomington, Ind.: Indiana University, 1985), 25–32, with the Aristotelian view taken here, but applied, to my mind, misguidedly, to the Pentateuch.

13. See K. S. Sacks, *Polybius on the Writing of History* (Classical Studies 24; Berkeley: University of California, 1981), 79–95. Polybius' pronouncements equally testify that the practice of inventing and restyling speeches was widely recognized and accepted.

14. As van Seters, *In Search* (n. 2).

15. A humanistic, author-centered philosophy of history is developed, under the sometimes salutary influence of Benedetto Croce, in R. G. Collingwood, *An Autobiography* (Oxford: Oxford University, 1939; rep. 1970); further, his *Idea of History* (Oxford: Clarendon, 1946; rep. Oxford University, 1961). Against the relativism to which Collingwood seems, illusorily, to give rein, and for a corrective to that "efficacious" interpretation embodied in F. Nietzsche, "On the Uses and Disadvantages of History for Life" (1874), ET in *Untimely Meditations* (tr. R. J. Hollingdale; Texts in German Philosophy; Cambridge: Cambridge University, 1983) 59–123, see E. H. Carr, *What Is History?* (G. M. Trevelyan Lectures, 1961; Harmondsworth: Penguin, 1964); further, K. Popper, *The Poverty of Historicism* (London: Routledge & Kegan Paul, 1961), especially 133–43, 154–56.

CHAPTER 2

As It Really Was: The History of the Trouble

It is precisely the hypercritical historian, the skeptic extraordinaire, who is most often compelled for his own dissenting presentation of the facts, to adopt such fantastic constructions that he himself is propelled from critical doubt into bottomless credulity.

—J. HUIZINGA

The historiographic questions raised in Chapter 1 are not all new. But their application has often been maladroit, and has never been widespread. Vestiges of an outdated view of history are to blame: these frustrate consensus on Israelite history, occasioning both the false fragmentation of biblical studies into social scientific and humanistic disciplines, and the resurgence of historical Pyrrhonism. This chapter explores how problems in the historical use of textual evidence led to the delusion that one could know history, the science of what is no longer, just as one could know chemistry.

THE BIBLE UNDER THE MICROSCOPE: REBELS FOR REASON

Thomas Jefferson once counseled a nephew, "You must read your Bible as you would Livy or Herodotus," by which he meant, without suspending the operation of your critical faculties. The Bible, he meant, recorded events past, and supplied interpretations of their interconnections—and a host of fairy stories to boot. As with Herodotus, insightful readers distinguish what is preserved and what is supplied, and free themselves to jettison or replace the latter. An elementary operation.

Jefferson wrote from the standpoint of an Enlightenment liberal, in a spirit of unabashed optimism and faith in human reason. His rationalism had roots in the Protestant Reformation. Representative of the relationship is a statement attributed by Johnson's biographer to Dr. Johnson: "If God had never spoken figuratively, we might hold that he speaks literally when he says, 'This is my body.' . . . Tradition, sir, has no place where the Scriptures are plain." Protestantism rallied the revolt against Catholicism by waving the banner of reason in the face of church tradition. Against the church, it affirmed that patristic and papal interpretation were not identical with the sacred text, but extrinsic to and later than it. One could not read the tradition as a synchronic whole, as a single map.

But reason, though sometimes unpalatable, is always in supply. It can be directed at tradition, in defense of Scripture, as Dr. Johnson thought. Or it can be directed at Scripture, in defense of reason itself. As Europe in the fifteenth and sixteenth centuries revised its relationship with the church, both strategies found play, and men such as Baruch Spinoza repudiated holy writ (and suffered for it) by arguments to its improbability, its inconsistency, and its moral bankruptcy.

By the eighteenth century, with England on the ascendant and the Protestant upheavals of Cromwell's era subsided, Enlightenment liberals, scientific rationalists, had emancipated themselves from the church's god; they adopted a god, almost a non-god, suited to their program. Thomas Paine's *Age of Reason*, written shortly after his *Rights of Man* in 1790, rehearsed the proposition that the Torah, or Pentateuch, was the product of "some very stupid and ignorant pretenders to authorship several hundred years after the death of Moses":

> Take away from Genesis the belief that Moses was the author, on which only the strange belief that it is the Word of God has stood, and there remains nothing of Genesis but an anonymous book of stories, fables and traditionary or invented absurdities, or of downright lies. The story of Eve and the serpent, and of Noah and his ark, drops to a level with the Arabian tales, without the merit of being entertaining, and the account of men living to eight and nine hundred years becomes as fabulous as the immortality of the giants of the Mythology.[1]

This was no elite theological tract with a readership restricted to seminarians. It was, like Paine's other works, a manifesto of revolution, penned for the advocates of vulgar pluralism, of relativism. If Protestantism had cured Europe of the superstition of tradition, scientific rationalism could exorcise the demon of Scripture. Paine summarizes: "It is a duty incumbent on every true Deist, that he vindicate the moral justice of God against the calumnies of the Bible."[2]

Nothing in Paine's harangue departs in substance from the program laid down in Spinoza's panegyric to another republic, the *Theologico-Political Tractate* (1670). Like all deists, Paine enjoyed twin intellectual legacies, that of the Reformation, and that of Renaissance humanism. The latter engaged the critical spirit of the scientist against faith. It created a climate in which the observation of contradictions in the biblical record, which dates at least to Clement (*Homilies* 2.52; 3.43,47), impugned at a basic level the authority of the text.

Among the earliest scholars—such as Hobbes (*Leviathan*, 1651) and Spinoza—the bill of indictment claimed that Moses had written little, if any, of the Pentateuch. Deprived of the resonance of Moses' voice, this jumble of benighted twaddle was rendered valueless as a historical document. Opponents of the heresy (largely anti-Jansenist) were almost as heterodox as the heretics. Aside from defenders of Moses' authorship,[3] Richard Simon and, later, Jean Astruc dissolved the text's contradictions in a diversity of hypothetical sources.[4] For Simon the sources began with Moses, who erected the prophetic office (Deut. 18:9–18) to provide for their ongoing production; Astruc (and, later still, J. G. Eichhorn)[5] suggested that Moses *relied* on earlier, eyewitness accounts, even in Genesis. These critics hunted the sources in order to salvage the text's status as a firsthand account, foreclosing on charges of unreliability, and implying the text's divine origin in terms acceptable to scientific rationalist thought.

This recourse no more than reacted to the challenge deists and humanists had mounted to the text's authority. But far from being limited to the Bible, the challenge was addressed to all the culture myths of Western civilization. Greek legends were the subject of special scrutiny: how could one assess their undifferentiated assertions? By the late eighteenth century, the search for Homer's sources too had entered a heyday. Friedrich Wolf's *Prolegomena zu Homer* (1796), which identified Homer's component sources, captured the intellectual atmosphere of an epoch. Homer lived later than the Trojan War, Moses later than the patriarchs. Pushing the sources each used back to the time of the events was a sort of rearguard action to defend the history.

Behind this program lay the premise that the older the source, the more reliable its claims. This remained a governing principle even after de Wette proved the Pentateuchal sources were post-Mosaic.[6] The impulse is clearest in classical history. In 1811 Barthold Georg Niebuhr reverted to a seventeenth-century method by dismissing late accounts of Roman origins; he appealed instead to supposedly early poetry and legends. The procedure, soon after applied to Greece, was reimported into Israelite history a century later without reference to its antecedents.[7] In classical studies it spawned the idea that Greek and Roman historians relied on a lost poetic epic as their central source for early times, another thesis that has enjoyed currency in biblical scholarship.[8] Early biblical scholars had solved mythic texts as though they were costumed records of real events (Genesis 3 detailed how one couple discovered sex, then fled an oasis during a storm).[9] But the first history of Israel produced under the influence of the historical-critical program, that of Heinrich G. A. Ewald, embodied Niebuhrian postulates in its repeated, often metaphoric, applications to the patriarchal legends.[10] Through ancestral legends, tortuously interpreted, early history could be recovered.

None of this work, on Israel or elsewhere, outlived the century. Its demise had three causes. First, to read folklore as history in a simple code (Abraham's movements = his descendants' movements) imposed a stiff tax on sophisticated literary sensibilities (what events were encoded in "Little Red Riding Hood"?). Second, the methods used on early history were alien to the repertoire of techniques applied to any other period; the adoption of such desperate measures reflected only a fixation on periods of origins. Myths of origins were the pacifier, the ersatz pap of nationalist German Romanticism, as their role in Wagner, Heidegger, and Nazi Aryanism illustrates.

The third factor was most crucial of all. Source criticism had been a rearguard action against Enlightenment attacks on the Bible. The oldest sources, scholars presumed, were repositories of the best information; eyewitness reports were beyond reasonable reproach. This presupposition had informed even the most critical work on Israelite history: Spinoza reposed implicit trust in the records of Judges, Samuel, and Kings; even Paine used them as a redoubt from which to assail the superstitions of the Pentateuch. These records looked historical—devoid of important supernatural elements, concerned with the fates of nations. They looked as though they had been compiled from sources contemporary with the events.

But even these works did not elude de Wette's critical scrutiny: sources or not, they were compiled late. And their authors' interest did not lie in writing history, but in expressing an irrepressible religious zeal, hamstringing the historian in their use.[11] Here was born a skepticism of the highest order, which developed through the course of the century: if one *could* uncover the sources, they were not necessarily antique; if antique, they were not eyewitness reports; if eyewitnesses reports, they were not to be relied on. How could one guarantee the reliability of the sources? No simple route offered itself around the roadblock of historical skepticism.

REASON IN HARNESS: SUBVERTING SKEPTICISM

The story of how scholars hurdled the barrier of skepticism is instructive. They took it with a surge of momentum that spent itself only after the field had achieved its present estate. The story centers on the evolution of historical method.

The most winning approach to history developed in the nineteenth century was that of the positivists, or the philologians. In the famous formulation of L. von Ranke, the historian aimed "to discover how it really was." All the evidence had to be gathered, and minutely sifted, every detail ascertained. Then the talented historian could construct a universal history.

The source critics of biblical and classical scholarship fit the positivist mold. They were, foremost, philologians, and their method was painstaking textual analysis, with the object of placing exegesis and historical research on a scientific footing. Philology plugged along tolerably for the study of medieval Europe, where access to primary documents could be had. But elsewhere, it limped: for Israel, or Greece, the main sources were all historical résumés, written well after the events; they were transmitted by untold generations of scribes, each of them suspected of odiously defacing the text, as though to mark it as a private preserve. Here, defending techniques of textual analysis was a full-time occupation.

Positivism thus forgot to frame a response to Pyrrhonists, who observed that history was built between facts, not of them, and to skeptics, who asked whether, even if one *could* isolate sources, this would produce reliable information. What good were the ancients' versions of events, if they were nothing more than biased constructs? Contemporary or not, the accounts omitted, twisted, and invented so much that their testimony was worthless, their use an oracular excursion into the mysteries of the occult.

All these critiques found a riposte in midcentury. Classical historians took shelter in treating the texts themselves as events. Texts reflect the contemporary state of society, said the Pyrrhonists, a twentieth-century map, twentieth-century Europe; then, from a text, one could draw a synchronic picture of the (relatively late) time when it was produced. This simple pirouette subverted the skeptics' most ferocious objections.[12]

The compelling breakthrough was the work of Theodor Mommsen. Integrating, in philological style, available archaeological data, Mommsen trained his eye on the history of Roman law. He exposed the system of the late republican constitution (anticipating Weber). This synchronic framework permitted him to assess the claims of his sources about politics in the past and issue a critical, diachronic political history.[13]

Jacob Burckhardt's model was honed on the anarchic political mosaic of ancient Greece, not on litigious Rome. Burckhardt used Greek texts to unlock the minds of their audiences, treating them as exemplars of the culture from which they emanated: he constructed, not political history, but *Kulturgeschichte*.[14] He, too, created synchronic pictures, but of the state of culture contemporary with each document. He then linked the successive stages in a chronological sequence.

Mommsen and Burckhardt, giant twins of (Swiss-)German learning, levered the weight of Pyrrhonism by a feat of jujitsu: if the sources were evidence primarily of the time in which they were produced, they afforded a systemic purchase on single stages in the history of Greece and Rome. Burckhardt's method was purer: the sequence of synchronic stills was itself the history; Burckhardt ransacked the texts only for data about the times in which they were written. Mommsen used the information the sources divulged about contemporary society as a ladder into earlier history—his synchronic *political* gleanings enabled him to evaluate reports texts made about the time *before* they were written. So his method was, in fact, only synchronic at the outset. He used his grasp of a synchronic system only as a fixed point around which to organize the sources. He did not rest content, as Burckhardt did, with a sequence of stills.

These advances left biblical studies lagging. The latter had been the cradle of source criticism: the Pentateuch broke like a sedimentary stone, convincingly, if not cleanly, into coextensive narrative strands; this, Homer could never be cajoled to do. Yet biblicists never weaned themselves from the unyielding breast of earliest history. Even de Wette's dating of Deuteronomy to Josiah's reign (640 B.C.E.–609 B.C.E.) was exploited to date other Pentateuchal sources more than to analyze seventh-century society.[15] These sources were used in a Burckhardtian way, to reflect stages in Israelite culture;[16] but the Pentateuchal sources were also used to fight through to Israel's origins, an endeavor incompatible with Burckhardt's methods. Scholars wanted to get at Moses or Abraham; the methods were those of Wolf and Niebuhr. So the study of Israelite antiquity labored in transition between Niebuhr and Burckhardt. Biblical studies never foreswore its confessionalist penchant for origins. Even today its lowest spires resound with studies of the patriarchs; no respectable historian would dream of taking a similar approach to Romulus.

In the autumn of the century, however, biblical studies produced its Mommsen, or its Burckhardt. Julius Wellhausen, who had studied with Ewald at Göttingen, put his signature to a work entitled *Geschichte Israels. Erster Band* in 1878. Reissued in 1883 as *Prolegomena zur Geschichte Israels,* this book furnished a common denominator for all subsequent scholarship. It consolidated an emerging consensus about the relative dating of the four Pentateuchal sources by dating the Priestly source after the fall of Judean monarchy: Wellhausen showed that the religious "stages" reflected in J, E, D, and P fall into an orderly evolutionary sequence if P comes last. His fervent prose and ready polemic rang in a new scholarly era.

In *Prolegomena* Wellhausen applied to the Bible the principles pioneered by Burckhardt. First, he interrogated his sources chiefly about the times that had produced them—the sources were his events. Second, he used his sources as sketches of single stages in the history of Israelite society.

Still, no doubt unconsciously, Wellhausen steered his *Prolegomena* on a middle course between Burckhardt and Mommsen. He created, like Burckhardt, and like other biblicists before him (n. 16), a cogent sequence of the stages of Israelite culture reflected in his documents. He maintained, like Burckhardt, and unlike Mommsen, a *purely* synchronic method. But his aim was to pave the ground for a political history (hence, *History of Israel*, and even *Prolegomena to the History of Israel);* he aimed to be another Mommsen.

Mommsen had succeeded by analyzing the Roman legal system. Wellhausen, too, dealt with law, the Law in the Bible. The difference was that Mommsen's interests and materials concerned the Roman constitution; Wellhausen's Law and scholarly tradition centered on the structure of the cult. Wellhausen's ambition to write political history had been inflamed by Ewald. His model, there is reason to believe, was Mommsen, and his method philological. But he was restricted by *his* Law to recounting religious development; he was restricted by the pure Burckhardtian assumption that sources could be interrogated only about the time in which they were written. In *Prolegomena,* therefore, he produced only a Burckhardtian *Kulturgeschichte.*

Wellhausen's link to Burckhardt, thus, was his method; his ambition tied him to Mommsen. But Wellhausen's acquaintance with Mommsen was not firsthand. He came to know him through the eyes of a colleague four years his junior, Ulrich von Wilamowitz-Moellendorf. This helps to account for the fact that Wellhausen never really embraced Mommsen's methods.

Wellhausen and Wilamowitz were together at the University of Greifswald in 1875–1882, the period when the *Prolegomena* first appeared. Wilamowitz was Mommsen's student and, from 1876 on, his son-in-law; at the time Mommsen moped that the youngster "relates to me as the second, improved edition of my *History* does to the first."[17] The ambivalence of this lugubrious comment ran deep. Wilamowitz was a Junker, Mommsen a bourgeois liberal. Wilamowitz was more a philologian than a historian. He worked first on Greece, and early immersed himself in source criticism of Homer. Gradually, too, he reverted to habits more Prussian, more aristocratic, and more racist than were consonant with his mentor's thought. On Mommsen's behalf, he polemicized against Burckhardt, and against Burckhardt's purely synchronic approach. And he steeped himself, like a biblicist, in redaction history—in the hypothetical prehistory of his texts. But he wrote always with a certain Burckhardtian zest, a flair more for culture than for politics.[18]

What divided Wilamowitz from Mommsen drew him to Wellhausen, whom he revered. Wellhausen, too, was the Kaiser's man—it was rumored that, around 1870, he chose to forgo the chance to succeed Ewald at Göttingen rather than renounce his support for a Greater Prussia.[19] Wellhausen was also a source critic, and it was fitting that to him, in 1884, Wilamowitz dedicated his *Homerische Studien.*

In 1883, the year after Wellhausen had left Greifswald for Marburg, *Geschichte Israels* was retitled *Prolegomena,* echoing Wolf's *Prolegomena zu Homer.*[20] No doubt Wellhausen's work had drawn comparison to Wolf's in the years after 1878; but it is not too much to see Wilamowitz's influence at play, the more so in that Wilamowitz offered his source-critical analysis of Homer to his friend only a year later, in the expectation of reciprocation; and in that Wilamowitz had that very year gone on to Göttingen, the school not just of Wellhausen's master, but, earlier, of Wolf. This is enough to inspire the suspicion that it was Wilamowitz who mediated the synchronist models of classical history, along with devotion to Mommsen, to Wellhausen.

A decade later the two friends were reunited. In 1892, twenty years after the contretemps with Ewald, by the offices of R. Smend, and, no doubt, at the connivance of Wilamowitz, Wellhausen joined Wilamowitz in Göttingen. Two years further on, and sixteen years after the *Prolegomena*, Wellhausen brought to light the second part of his History, *Israelitische und Judäische Geschichte*. The title, unlike the earlier *Geschichte Israels*, now resembled that of Mommsen's history, just as the name of the *Prolegomena* had been altered to echo Wolf. The book was dedicated to Wilamowitz as a *Gegengabe*, a "countergift." It was the sequel to Wellhausen's source-critical endeavors, the Mommsenian political history built to a Burckhardtian blueprint.

Wellhausen's *Geschichte* did not wear the years proudly. In comparison with the great histories of the time—those of Kittel and Stade—it was a puny thing, shorter even than its *Prolegomena*. Small wonder: the history married a grounding in theological *Kulturgeschichte (Prolegomena)* to Rankean ambitions formed in Mommsen's image. But Mommsen repudiated "theological history";[21] it was on his program that Wilamowitz had entered the lists against Burckhardt.[22] A letter of Burckhardt's illuminates the problem:

> More and more, Philology demonstrates its spiritual bankruptcy by the fact that it has still not produced a good portrait of antiquity. . . . We will yet experience the triumph that the first readable ancient history will see the light of day without the participation of the Philologians. Philology today is nothing but a second-rate science, whatever airs it may put on.[23]

Wellhausen's history was, the foreword says, scientific and positivistic. Yet it was founded on a *Kulturgeschichte* that had been conceived as the antithesis of such an exercise. *Kulturgeschichte* was a *pure* synchronic method. Positivism violated its principles by weighing the claims the sources made about the past. Mommsen had, in fact, transcended the synchronic stage of study by examining the structure of Roman politics. This enabled him to do what was anathema to Burckhardt—to determine what reports about the past were likely. Mommsen could not have written political history without abandoning synchronic methods; for him, synchronic work was really no more than a prolegomenon.

Wellhausen, in the end, was only a mediocre political historian, just because he was so accomplished a cultural historian. He never provided a basis in Israelite social structure for evaluating political history. Like

Wolf, he had produced a programmatic source analysis; but, like Wolf's, his sources' claims remained unproved. This was the very problem against which de Wette had provided ninety years before, when he dismissed the recovery of Israel's political history, and declared, "the most important aim [*Augenmerk*] for the scholar of Israelite history must be the history of religion and of worship."[24] De Wette had stopped at *Kulturgeschichte*. Wellhausen, driven by the model of Mommsen as mediated to him by the cultural historian, Wilamowitz, fell into error: he thought that a *pure Kulturgeschichte* (in which the sources testify only to the character of the culture that produced them) could ground a real political history.

Wellhausen did not so much turn traitor to his method as to attempt to get at Abraham. But the claims of German Idealism lay heavily enough upon him to extort a treatment of the Exodus. In this, and throughout, he found himself compelled time and again to get at historical events through late texts that he had formerly pronounced unfit for the purpose. Dimly acknowledging the problem, he called in his foreword for a wedding of theology and philology that he was destined never to see, and that no philologian could countenance. The insight was Burckhardtian—Benedetto Croce, soon after, wrote under Burckhardt's influence that "*philology*, joining with *philosophy*, produces *history*."[25] But Wellhausen's appeal to theology was characteristic. Nothing better captures the contrast than this: the hero and consummation of Mommsen's opus was Julius Caesar; that of Wellhausen's was classical prophecy.

Wellhausen's history enjoyed the prestige to which an illustrious sire entitled it, appearing in seven editions before his death, in 1918 (a ninth edition appeared in 1958). Never did it approach the station earned by *Prolegomena;* it is all but forgotten today. De Wette's dictum proved a "sullen presage": *Kulturgeschichte* held out promise for analyzing Israelite religion; the attempt to translate this into philological political history was foredoomed to failure.

The confusion in Wellhausen's ambitions was conditioned by Wilamowitz—*aut Mommsen aut nihil* instead of *aut Mommsen aut Burckhardt.* In consolidating gains of historians of theology, such as Vatke and Ewald, Wellhausen never reflected that, like Wilamowitz, he set the garland on Mommsen's lofty brow but meanwhile kissed Burckhardt's feet. His history was political in the flesh, but theological in the spirit.

REASON TRIUMPHANT: ISRAELITE HISTORY IN DISARRAY

Wellhausen always denied having a head for theology. At Göttingen, his orthodoxy dissolved, his imagination was stirred only by Ewald's history. Yet Wellhausen's history was shaped by de Wette, a man fixated on theology—even Ewald never clambered free of the channel de Wette had laid out, and that Gramberg, George, and Vatke had dug. This may have made Mommsen's secular genius the more appealing. But Wellhausen glimpsed the noble Roman political historian only through the eyes of the source critic and cultural historian, Wilamowitz. The notion that a *Kulturgeschichte*, the *Prolegomena*, had laid a foundation for political history was a mirage.

The delusion was widely shared. Wellhausen's success in analyzing the sources impressed itself on scholars' minds as a victory of positivism, of a natural-scientific model. It suggested that one could write a Mommsenian political history, yet maintain the theoretical purity of Burckhardt's *Kulturgeschichte*. The next fifty years saw, as the previous century had seen in the wake of de Wette's work, frenzied efforts to work out the implications. Based on a typology of theological development, these efforts yielded no mature historical fruit.

In sciences such as source criticism, which admits of no confirmation, a hypothetical edifice that is the pride and monument of one era is often razed in the next, to clear the ground for new, modern structures. Wellhausen's edifice survived the changing of the guard around the time of World War I. But it was abandoned by historians, among whom the echoes of jubilant self-congratulation died slowly in a still of hollow frustration. By the 1920s German scholars such as Albrecht Alt and Martin Noth were grasping at Weberian sociological models for Israelite geopolitics and constitutional history. In Sweden the anthropological approach to religion had taken hold, presaging a revolt against German philology. And in America William Foxwell Albright had begun to formulate a cryptofundamentalist philological program heavily laced with archaeology. These scholars sensed spontaneously that source criticism had about played itself out as a historical tool, that literary analysis could not furnish historical evidence, that it would not, after all, prove possible to get at the events described in the texts through the texts themselves.[26]

The reaction was excessive: had Wellhausen set out from the structure of Israelite politics, and jettisoned his synchronic method when it had served its purpose, as Mommsen did, he might have produced a solid history. Conversely, had Wellhausen confined his ambitions to the sort of history compatible with his *Prolegomena*—that is, to *Kulturgeschichte*—no difficulty would have arisen. The problem was Wellhausen's synthesis: he tried to graft Mommsen's diachronic history of the nation onto the antiphilological Burckhardt's purely synchronic history of the culture; he tried to base a political history on the history of theology.

The result was poetic and predictable: Wellhausen's premise that the texts testified only to the times in which they were written was roundly vindicated; those bent on recovering political history were driven to comparative materials outside the circumscribed professional field. That this development was to be correlated to Wellhausen's assumptions has not been understood. That the problems of historical testimony confronted by Wellhausen had been appreciably surmounted in the study of classical antiquity seems also to have been ignored. No responsible classical historian denies the historicity of Cleisthenes' reform. Rightly or wrongly, denying the historicity of Hezekiah's or Josiah's reform has been a reliable cottage industry.

THE SORCERER'S APPRENTICES: WELLHAUSEN'S LEGACY

For the history of biblical scholarship, the nature of Wellhausen's confusion—his attempt to write diachronic political history without violating the principles of synchronic cultural study—is less important than the impact of his success. So shining was the example of Wellhausen's *Prolegomena* that it seemed that source criticism was the last, best hope for writing history, for which his *Kulturgeschichte* was mistaken. *Kulturgeschichte* was a preoccupation to which scholars were predisposed by theological training; it formed the heart even of Ewald's political history. Wellhausen had shown that it was the *sine qua non*, the only possible prolegomenon, for historical work. The union of theology and philology for which Wellhausen pined in the prologue to his history was therefore taken by his colleagues to have been consummated already in the *Prolegomena*. The history was a disappointment; but this did not sully the synchronist principles the *Prolegomena* had enshrined.

Wellhausen's success in *Prolegomena* and failure in the history saddled the study of Israelite antiquity with a heavy freight. Among other things, the *Prolegomena* did duty for an articulated portraiture of Israel's political complexion. It encouraged scholars to pursue the history of theology while only semiconscious of political history. More often than not, Israelite ideas are traced to single events, with the result that Israel appears sometimes to have yoked its religion solely to its military fortunes.[27] This simpleminded approach betrays a lack of historical grounding.

Second, Wellhausen's success ratified the methods of source criticism, form criticism, and redaction criticism. Because source criticism in the Pentateuch yielded meaningful results, scholars tested the margin of return by applying the method to the historical books of the Former Prophets. But nineteenth-century compositional analyses were hypothetical and subjective, occasioning fraction over specific texts; their historical implications were few. For this reason other fields, in which the identification of sources remains central, have jettisoned the attempt to carve texts up with surgical precision.

This is the ramification of Wellhausen's work that will occupy us most extensively. The tendency to approach Israelite history as the history of books fostered the delusion that historical battles could be fought at the level of compositional analysis. More substantive historiographic issues—how the historians came to believe what they wrote, what they thought writing history demanded—were neglected by scholars obsessed with isolating the sources *verbatim,* even in the Former Prophets and Chronicles.

Literary sensibilities, thus, were the only arbiters of historicity, a perspective held in common with Pyrrhonist literary critics. The idea that the texts could be queried only about the time that produced them—the premise Burckhardt took from Pyrrhonism, and Wellhausen's *Prolegomena* from Burckhardt—nourished the *enfant terrible* of negative fundamentalism. An author's convictions were, by definition, biases; and, by definition, any evidence the author adduced was baseless. From this premise emerged a working sketch of the Israelite historian: a man unconstrained by the credence of contemporaries, without loyalty to fact or common knowledge. A writer rather than a historian, an editor, not a scholar, he perpetrated the wildest enormities on unsuspecting readers. Israelite historiography was less historiography than romance, because it was as romance that these critics approached it.

Wellhausen himself contributed to the skepticism. He insisted on the inaccuracy, maliciously construed, of all late sources. Authors such as P and the Chronicler distorted, fabricated, and fantasized, and had neither genuine historical concerns nor legitimate historical intentions. Catalyzing the secretion of this venom was the conviction that compositional analysis enabled the critic to strip away and discard "lifeless" Jewish "accretions" to "warm," "sympathetic" Israelite tradition. The drift of this program was as much anti-Catholic as anti-Semitic: from the Protestant perspective, the object of exegesis was to constitute oneself the New Israel, and to tar the Roman Church as the new Judaism. The hidden agenda was not lost on the church, which placed critical scholarship under the interdict.[28]

C. A. Briggs exemplified the problem, in 1901:

> The valleys of biblical truth have been filled up with the debris of human dogmas, ecclesiastical institutions . . . and casuistic practices. Historical criticism is searching for the rock-bed of divine truth . . . in order to recover the real Bible. Historical criticism is sifting all this rubbish. It will gather out every precious stone.[29]

The witch hunt for fraudulent Scripture aimed to salvage pristine revelation from (Jewish) detritus. Critics emblazoned their escutcheons with a motto from Jeremiah (8:8), about "the lying pen of the scribes" that made Torah a "lie."

Here throbs the arterial pulse of negative fundamentalism. Scribes lie, historians invent, and the Hebrew Bible is a not-so-pious fraud. Wellhausen proved that the biblical view of the history of religion was woven warp and woof on the loom of a late, doctrinaire, autocratic priesthood. Much the same was therefore to be said of the historical books.

Philosophically, too, the *Prolegomena* stoked the coals of negative fundamentalism. It reinforced the philological paradigm, molded by such thinkers as Ranke and Droysen, for pursuing historical research. In philology, one could establish almost mathematically the meaning of a term; one could decipher almost mathematically dead tongues. The same model was carried over into history: history, too, could be based on cut-and-dried proof.

In effect, philological history demanded just what Pyrrhonists demand: proof absolute. This no historian can furnish: historians describe events transacted on a physical level—in the interactions of charge, mass, and motion—in terms of human beings, even groups. The level of causation at which they trade is psychological. Further, history cannot base itself on predictability, as does natural science, because it cannot be reproduced to order in a laboratory. Lacking universal axioms and theorems, it can be based on testimony only; its standards of proof must be evidential, not algebraic, probabilistic, not absolute.

The fact is, no branch of human knowledge is immune from the Pyrrhonist-philological critique. Nevertheless, we manage to live from day to day, relying on subjective observations and culturally conditioned analyses. We do so without the objective certainty of the philologian, on the basis of a preponderance of evidence. Our understanding of human history resembles our knowledge of the contemporary world. The material implication of the Pyrrhonist and philological programs is that because that knowledge is imperfect, and never proved, it must be abandoned. Insisting resolutely on scientific certainty, both reject the claims of moral certainty. Gibbon formulates the point:

> As soon as I understood the principles, I relinquished forever the study of Mathematics; nor can I lament that I desisted before my mind was hardened by the habit of rigid demonstration so destructive of the finer feelings of moral evidence which must however determine the actions and opinions of our lives.[30]

The forensic model for history is near the mark. A defense attorney, for example, cannot get a client off by creating *unreasonable* doubt: that Martians committed the murder, that Trilateralists framed the accused. Nor can the defense succeed by flying in the face of the evidence, with the submission, for example, that the wound was self-inflicted in a case where the revolver was carried off from the scene of the crime. Evidence, whether circumstantial or direct, can be a damnably useful commodity.

Still, a murder charge is rarely proved beyond all doubt. Were the jury to demand that certainty for which the Pyrrhonist and philologian look, they could never vote conviction. Sir Walter Raleigh, who despaired of extracting truth from conflicting testimony, would hang more juries than killers; how, indeed, could he be sure of telling queens from charwomen, mud from dirt, or his own cloak from a colleague's? Rejecting the probable as unproved is tantamount to intellectual suicide, so few objects of contemplation does it leave secure. Those who advocate the course should fall silent not just about history, but, out of a decent consistency, about everything.

In biblical research, where the scientific paradigm of classical philology survived the demise of the philological philosophy of history, dire consequences ensued. Philology never furnished the proof it promised, because people were less tractable objects of analysis than words. Philology never framed an answer to Pyrrhonism, because it was predicated on the same epistemological model.

All this led to a relativization of shared professional standards. By a sort of Gresham's Law of historical research, possibility supplanted probability as the measure of a workable reconstruction. Successful theories were spun from the gossamer of philological evidence, but never matched to the pattern of political, historical likelihood.[31] Examples are common enough to be familiar to every practitioner in the field. Besieged by negative fundamentalism and Pyrrhonism, therefore, historically attuned scholars of Israelite antiquity have taken haven in social scientific models generated from data irrelevant to Israel, and in source criticism, form criticism, and redaction criticism. Social science projects an air of the laboratory. And compositional analysis is, after all, the beggar's philology: it has been the oracular tool, the Urim and Thummim, of Biblical studies, blessed by the greatest of the sybils, Wellhausen himself.

A CONTRIBUTION OF NOTH: BIBLICAL HISTORIOGRAPHY

The Wellhausen phenomenon sequestered compositional analysis from historical reconstruction, and from historiographic concerns. The principle of treating the texts only as evidence for the contemporary state of society was never strictly observed—even in the *Prolegomena*, Wellhausen tried to read an early, secular tribe of Levi out of the tales in Genesis about the tribe's eponym. But the principle was entrenched. Scholars stripped the latest layer, the plaster, from the masonry of the text, to arrive at earlier stages in the culture. Banish the editor or redactor from the text, and what remained was a *Kulturgeschichte*.

In the Pentateuch, the redactor was the fellow who had interwoven parallel narrative strands. His own contributions were scissors, paste, and an occasional marginal annotation. R was a shadowy figure whose dull intelligence led him to overlook the contradictions his conflations had created.[32] He was, in fact, a casual by-product of the source-critical hypothesis, without corporeal form, an editor who existed by definition. This concept of an editor was transferred, almost unconsciously, to the writers who shaped the historical books of Joshua through Kings.

But the climate of the historical books is hostile to the transplant. Here the compiler is unmistakably the historian who provides the text's narrative framework. In any individual case he may have recast his sources; and, none of the sources can be said to have run from the start to the finish of his work, or to have been preserved intact. The situation could not be further removed from that of the Pentateuch, whose interweaving of parallel sources abounds in doublets, discrepancies, and other invitations to compositional research. The redactor of Kings, or of Judges, is not to be mistaken for the disembodied elf who cobbled Genesis together. He is not an editor, or not solely an editor, but a historian.

This does not render compositional questions irrelevant. Techniques which have been employed to isolate redactorial (secondary) passages will be examined in chapters 5–8; to an extent, they will be seconded. But these questions must not be isolated from the historiographic ones: chiefly, what led the historian to believe what he wrote?

The historiographic questions approximate an endeavor called tradition history, which explains ideas as progressive, layered developments around some minimal original "kernel". They depart from it in limiting themselves to the historian's own time: what sources then existed, and how did the historian interpret them? The only scholar to raise the issue in a meaningful fashion has been Martin Noth. Noth concluded that Deuteronomy and the Former Prophets together composed a single historical work, the Deuteronomistic history.[33] Its author, the Deuteronomist (Noth's Dtr), "was not just a 'redactor,' but the author of a historical work," who took his sources seriously, if selectively, and rarely departed from them.[34]

Noth has, for forty-five years, had his share of detractors and defenders. The detractors, for the most part, accept the integrity of the Deuteronomistic corpus, and hypothesize one or more redactions after it was first assembled.[5] But Noth's central argument—about historiography—has been transposed, characteristically, into a discussion about compositional history. Ironically, two recent defenses of Noth's theory of Dtr's unitary authorship (they call it a "single redaction") contest incidentally Dtr's historical character, in a sort of double-defense: Dtr rarely, if ever, had real sources, and felt free to ignore or contradict them when he had.[36]

Noth had the courage to reach beyond the grasp of compositional study, of study directed at texts, and to ask about the redactor as a person. This question alone brings us to grips with R as a historian. It translates him from a historical and social void, from the status of a character in a romance, into a concrete cultural continuum. In a void, any or all of the historian's reports could be arbitrary and unbased—and his convictions conjure up suspicions that the evidence for them is concocted. In his social setting, however, the historian is answerable to the expectations of his contemporaries (see Polybius 31.22).

Noth's work proceeded from the premise that the Deuteronomist was a historian. The premise was self-validating. If Dtr was a historian, it followed that there were sources for the history's otherwise unsupported assertions. It should be added, however, that the opposite premise, that the Deuteronomist gave free rein to fancy, is also self-validating. It bases itself on the unity of the presentation, which rightly has few implications for the operations of observation and reconstruction, and hypothesizes an absence of sources. The hypothesis then works out in a form latterly exemplified by J. van Seters.[37] In one sense it is the fruit of an inexorable logic. Compositional analysts read text historically, in order to flush out sources and authors. But when the source is isolated, when an indivisible text is recovered, historical reading is sent into abeyance, and the principle that the text cannot mediate knowledge of its historical subject kicks in.

From Noth's premise one gets a plausible perspective on what it is Dtr was doing. He did not write pseudepigraphic memoir, or direct revelation; he chose instead to find meaning in Israel's antiquities, in the conviction that the course of events vindicated his views. From the opposite premise one derives a Dtr who was indifferent to his sources, indifferent to the past, and indifferent to the criticism of his contemporaries, but who was galvanized by his whimsy to construct in the face of all three a long national history. This portrait seems devised, in accord with the Commandment, to resemble nothing in the heavens above, in the Earth below, or in the waters underneath the Earth. Noth's historian fits the mold of a thinker emboldened by honest conviction to impose a meaningful order on his nation's past. Van Seters imagines him a rogue and a fraud, a distributor of taffy.

It would be an exaggeration to say that those who preserve Noth's unitary author have it in mind morally to disembowel him. This is a mere by-product of their method, an unconsidered corollary. But for just that reason, it is apposite to inquire how Israel's historians look, when our literary analysis is done, as human beings. What led them to write what they wrote, what genre of literature were they writing, what did they think were its limits, why did they choose to write it? Did they mean to write history or romance? What sorts of particular truths, what sorts of fictions, were they ready to supply?

The following pages do not assume the literary homogeneity of the Former Prophets. Because it is disputed what sources of that work were incorporated substantially intact,[38] and because the issue is more compositional than historiographic, the question of what Dtr and subsequent redactors contributed is taken up, though extensively, only in passing. Instead, the focus moves from limited specimens of Israelite historiography whose authorship is uncertain (chapters 3–4) to larger blocks of text shaped by Dtr and integrated into the ongoing narrative (chapters 6–7), and, finally, to characteristics of the corpus as a whole (chapters 8–10). The upshot is that the historian's thematic concerns most strongly affect the proportion and cast he gives to eras, and that in the presentation of individual episodes, the relationship to sources is closest. The focus, thus, is not on compositional analysis, but on how the historians interacted with their sources.

It is not my claim that this procedure enables us to get with philological certainty at the human events the texts describe. The Deuteronomist's use of sources and the Deuteronomist's conception of what it meant to write history are accessible to our inquiries; the views of those who wrote the several sources are buffered by an additional stage of remove. But asking after the historian as a person offers unwonted advantages: some control on compositional speculation, by virtue of its implications for the mentality of the authors involved; some control on assertions about the historian's own times; and some control on characterizations of those earlier times about which the historian and his contemporaries had material or literary evidence.

Such a meager harvest will not satisfy an appetite for early history. It will, I hope, make an adequate hors d'oeuvre for synchronic investigation of the historian's day, which in turn could furnish the basis for sophisticated political history. Indeed, even if it does not issue in so ambitious an accomplishment, it will at least have addressed the enigma of the Israelite historian. So long as that personality remains unsolved, so long as we form only unrealized, adventitious notions of it, all our compositional hypotheses remain only half-considered, unworked out. We confine ourselves, thus, to the purely literary questions that bedeviled nineteenth-century scholarship, and to the historical paradigms that produced them. We condemn ourselves to a Sisyphean cycle in which the historical intentionality of biblical historiography is called perpetually, and needlessly, into question.

Notes to Chapter 2

1. P. S. Foner, ed., *The Complete Writings of Thomas Paine* (New York: Citadel, 1945), 1.521, 528.
2. Ibid., 523.
3. This tradition was at least as old as Ibn-Ezra's (d. 1167 C.E.) interdict on the book of ben-Yasus for dating Genesis 36:31 to the time of Jehoshaphat. Similar assaults on Mosaic authorship come, after the Talmud, in the fifteenth century (as Alphonsus Tostatus' attribution of parts of Deuteronomy not just to Joshua but to Ezra); cf. Andreas Bodenstein, *De canonicis scripturis libellus* [Wittenberg, E. Germany: 1520]); defenses tended to concede the Talmudic reservation, e.g., Sixtus of Siena, *Bibliotheca sancta ex praecipuis ecclesiae catholicae autoribus collecta et in octo libris digesta* (Venice: 1566), defending the authenticity of everything but Deuteronomy 34:5–12; cf. Andreas Masius, *Josuae imperatoris historia illustrata atque explicata* (Antwerp, Belgium: 1574), with a somewhat more critical perspective; Bento Pereira, *Commentariorum et disputationum in Genesim* (4 vols.; Lyon, France: 1594–1600); Jacques Bonfrère, *Pentateuchus Mosis commentario illustratus* (Antwerp, Belgium: 1625) arguing isolated accretions to the Mosaic record. See further, R. E. Friedman, *Who Wrote the Bible?* (New York: Summit, 1987).
4. J. Astruc, *Conjectures sur les mémoires originaux dont il paroit que Moyse s'est servi pour composer le livre de la Genese* (Brussels: Fricx, 1753); R. Simon, *Histoire critique du Vieux Testament* (1678; rep. Rotterdam: Reinier Leers, 1685): "J'y ai inserè quantitè de principes tres utiles pour satisfaire en même temps aux objections qu'on a accoutumé de faire contre l'autorité des livres sacrés" (p. II). Spinoza, too, attributes problems in the Pentateuch to the use of sources, but by Ezra.
5. J. G. Eichhorn, *Einleitung in das Alte Testament* (3 vols.; Leipzig: Weidmanns Erben und Reich, 1780–83).
6. W.M.L. de Wette, *Beiträge zur Einleitung in das Alte Testament. 1. Kritischer Versuch über die Glaubwürdigkeit der Bücher der Chronik* (Halle, E. Germany: Schimmelpfennig, 1806). An excellent discussion of de Wette's contributions is J. W. Rogerson, *Old Testament Criticism in the Nineteenth Century: England and Germany* (London: SPCK, 1985), 28–49.
7. B. G. Niebuhr, *Römische Geschichte* (2 vols.; Berlin: G. A. Reimer, 1811–12); K. O. Müller, *Prolegomena zu einer wissenschaftlichen Mythologie* (1825; rep. Darmstadt, W. Germany: Wissenschaftlicher, 1970); G. von Rad, *The Problem of the Hexateuch and Other Essays* (New York: McGraw-Hill, 1966), 1–78, (first ed., 1938). On Niebuhr's methods, see A. Momigliano, *Essays in Ancient and Modern Historiography* (Middletown, Conn.: Wesleyan, 1977); 231–51.
8. G. F. Kreuzer, *Historische Kunst der Griecher in ihrer Entstehung und Fortbildung* (Leipzig, E. Germany: Göschen, 1803; 2nd ed., 1845); A. Kuenen, *Historisch-kritische Einleitung in die Bücher des Alten Testaments hinsichtlich ihrer Entstehung und Sammlung* (Leipzig, E. Germany: O. Schulze, 1887), 215f.; latterly, F. M. Cross, "The Epic Traditions of Early Israel: Epic Narrative and the Reconstruction of Early Israelite Institutions," in R. E. Friedman, ed., *The Poet and the Historian: Essays in Literary and Historical Biblical Criticism* (HSS 26; Chico, Calif.: Scholars, 1981), 13–39; cf. J. van Seters, *In Search of History* (New Haven: Yale University, 1983), 20.
9. See on the "Neologists" J. W. Rogerson, *Myth in Old Testament Interpretation* (BZAW 134; Berlin: Töpelmann, 1974).
10. H.G.A. Ewald, *Geschichte des Volkes Israel bis Christus* (5 vols.; Göttingen, W. Germany: Dietrich, 1843–55), especially v. 1.
11. W.M.L. de Wette, *Beiträge zur Einleitung in das Alte Testament* (n. 6), 1.4–6, 52, and

passim; on the same principle, *idem, 2. Kritik der israelitischen Geschichte* (Halle, E. Germany: Schimmelpfennig, 1807).

12. See Momigliano, *Essays* (n. 7), 297f.

13. T. Mommsen, *Römische Geschichte* (Berlin: Reimer, 1856); the interest begins earlier, as *De collegiis et sedaliciis romanis* (Killiae, Poland: Liberia Schwersiana, 1843); *idem, Die römischen Trubus in administrativer Beziehung* (Altona, W. Germany: Hammerich, 1844), and culminates in his great *Staatsrecht.* On the links between Mommsen and Wellhausen, see L. Perlitt, *Vatke und Wellhausen* (*BZAW* 94; Berlin: Töpelmann, 1965), 61ff.

14. J. L. Burckhardt, "Über Studium der Geschichte" (1868–71), issued as "Griechische Kulturgeschichte" in F. Stähelin, ed., *Gesamtausgabe* (Basel: B. Schwabe, 1930).

15. W.M.L. de Wette, *Dissertatio critico-exegetica qua Deuteronomium a prioribus Pentateuchi libris diversum* (so cited variously; 1805) rep. as "Dissertatio critica qua a prioribus Deuteronomium Pentateuchi libris diversum alius cuiusdam recentioris auctoris opus esse monstratur" in *Opuscula Theologica* (Berlin: Reimer, 1830), 151–68. This adds a late dating to Hobbes's work (*Leviathan* 3.33), which is more sophisticated in differentiating Deuteronomy 11–27 as the code found in the temple; cf. also Jerome's comment to Ezekiel 1:1.

16. See C. P. W. Gramberg, *Kritische Geschichte der Religionsideen des Alten Testaments. I. Hierarchie und Kultus* (Berlin: Dunker & Humblot, 1829); J.F.L. George, *Die älteren jüdischen Feste mit einer Kritik der Gesetzgebung des Pentateuchs* (Berlin: E. H. Schroeder, 1835); W. Vatke, *Die biblische Theologie wissenschaftlich dargestellt. I. Die Religion des Alten Testaments nach den kanonischen Büchern entwickelt* (Berlin: G. Bethge, 1835); Ewald, *Geschichte* (n.10), on which see further, J. H. Hayes, "Wellhausen as a Historian of Israel," *Semeia* 25 (1982): 37–60.

17. L. Wickert, *Theodor Mommsen: Eine Biographie* (Frankfurt: Klostermann, 1970), 4.28.

18. See the treatment of Momigliano, "Religious History Without Frontiers: J. Wellhausen, U. Wilamowitz, and E. Schwartz," 55–59 (a study I have in a copy without bibliographic data). Momigliano furnishes, too, details of the relationship between Wilamowitz and Wellhausen.

19. E. Schwartz, "Julius Wellhausen," 326–361 in *Gesammelte Schriften* (Berlin: de Gruyter, 1963), 337.

20. The coincidence is observed by Cross, "Epic Traditions" (n. 8), 23.

21. See his *Reden und Aufsätze* (Berlin: Weidmann, 1905), 1.6–10.

22. Wilamowitz omits Burckhardt from his "Geschichte der Philologie" in A. Gercke and E. Norden, eds., *Einleitung in die Altertumswissenschaft* (2nd ed.; Berlin: Teubner, 1921); ET, *History of Classical Scholarship* (London: Duckworth, 1982). He incidentally betrays great admiration for Jacob Bernays, whom he credits with introducing what amounts to redaction criticism into classical history.

23. 7 Feb 1845 to Gottfried Kinkel, in J. Burckhardt, *Briefe* (ed. F. Kaphahn; Leipzig: A. Kröner, 1935), cited in Momigliano, *Essays* (n. 7), 304, n.1. By *philology*, Burckhardt meant the program of Ranke and Mommsen. Cf. B. Croce, *History: Its Theory and Practice* (2nd ed.; New York: Russell & Russell, 1960), 26–50 (1919), denying the authenticity of philological history, which can be "correct," but not "true." This critique is articulated by Nietzsche, with whom Wilamowitz polemicized, but had much in common.

24. de Wette, *Beiträge* (n. 6), 1.4.

25. Croce, *History* (n. 23), 26.

26. So, explicitly, R. Kittel, "Die Zukunft der alttestamentliche Wissenschaft," *ZAW* 39 (1921): 84–99; J. Pedersen, "Die Auffassung vom Alten Testament," *ZAW* 49 (1931): 161–81, correctly identifying Wellhausen as recycled Vatke. This impasse is the most probable explanation of Wellhausen's abandonment of biblical for Islamic studies, though Dr. V. Hurowitz proposes an apocryphal quotation, "Too many camels pissed in my well."

27. It suffices to cite the assignment of monotheism to the exile (latterly, B. Lang, *Monotheism and the Prophetic Minority* [Social World of Biblical Antiquity 1; Sheffield, U.K.: Almond, 1983]). Nor do other models (as Y. Kaufmann, *History of Israelite Religion* [8 vols.; Jerusalem: Bialik, 1937]; M. Smith, *Palestinian Parties and Politics that Shaped the*

Old Testament [Lectures on the History of Religion NS 9; New York: Columbia, 1971]) add a strictly developmental historical dimension.

28. For a parallel situation in New Testament studies, see A. Deissmann, *Paul: a Study in Social and Religious History* (2nd ed.; New York: Harper & Row, 1957), 15f. (1927). On the Protestant program in critical scholarship, see provisionally J. D. Levenson, "The Hebrew Bible, the Old Testament and Historical Criticism," in R. E. Friedman and H.G.M. Williamson, eds., *The Future of Biblical Studies: The Hebrew Bible* (Semeia Supplements; Decatur, GA: Scholars, 1987), 19–59.

29. C. A. Briggs, *General Introduction to the Study of Holy Scripture* (1901), cited by J. L. Kugel, "Biblical Studies and Jewish Studies," *Association for Jewish Studies Newsletter* 36 (Fall 1986): 22–24, 23.

30. E. Gibbon, *Memoirs of My Life* (London: Th. Nelson, 1966), 78.

31. As H. H. Rowley's view ("Zadok and Nehushtan," *JBL* 58 [1939]: 113–41) that David's high priest, Zadoq, was a Jebusite priest: 1) Psalm 110:4 and Genesis 14 trace the priesthood to Jebus; 2) David, with no temple, must have used an old Jerusalem shrine; 3) the onomastic element *ṣdq* (Melchizedeq, Adonizedeq, Zedeqiah[!]) is Jerusalemite, and Zadoq could have been so named before David only if he was Jebusite. Rowley hypothesized Jebusite power in Jerusalem after David's conquest, minimized the use of the nominal element *ṣdq* outside Jerusalem, never considered the effects the maneuver would have among the xenophobic Israelites, and set the tone of scholarship for forty years. Comparable are the theories of P. Haupt that David introduced Yhwh from Edom ("The Burning Bush and the Origins of Judaism" *PAPS* 48 [1909]: 357f.), and of H. Gressmann that the temple was built for Baal (*Die Lade Jahves und das Allerheiligste des Salomonischen Tempels* [Forschungsinstitut für Israelitisch-jüdische Religionsgeschichte. Abt. 5; Berlin: Kohlhammer, 1920], 27f.). The misapplication of truth-testing to history is cited as a cause of historical relativism in a general way in L. J. Goldstein, *Historical Knowing* (Austin, TX: University of Texas, 1976). Goldstein, however, seems inclined toward a coherence-and-consensus theory of historical epistemology, to which I would not subscribe. I owe the reference here to P. R. Davies.

32. So already H. Hupfeld, *Die Quellen der Genesis und die Art ihrer Zusammenhang von neuem untersucht* (Berlin: Wiegandt & Grieben, 1853), 166f.

33. M. Noth, *Überlieferungsgeschichtliche Studien I. Die sammelnden und bearbeitenden Geschichtswerke im Alten Testament* (Schriften der Königsberger Gelehrten Gesellschaft 18. Geisteswiss. Kl. 2; Halle, E. Germany: M. Niemeyer, 1943), 12–18. This work is hereafter referred to as *US*.

34. Noth, *US* (n. 33), 11, 89f., 95–100.

35. Noth's refutation of this position (*US* [n. 33], 6–11) was directed at scholars spotlighting inconsistencies within the history, which he attributed either to accretion or to conflicts among sources. For the literature, see Chapter 5.

36. H.-D. Hoffmann, *Reform und Reformen: Untersuchungen zu einem Grundthema der deuteronomistischen Geschichtsschreibung* (ATANT 66; Zurich: Theologischer, 1980); van Seters, *In Search* (n. 8).

37. Van Seters, *In Search* (n. 8).

38. As 2 Samuel 9ff., on which the basic work is L. Rost, *Die Überlieferung von der Thronnachfolge Davids* (BWANT 3/6; Stuttgart: Kohlhammer, 1926); Judges 3–8, for which see W. Richter, *Die Bearbeitung des "Retterbuches" in der deuteronomischen Epoche* (BBB 21; Bonn: P. Hanstein, 1964).

Part 1

Romance and Historiography: Two Cases of Historiography in Microcosm

CHAPTER 3

A Message for Eglon: The Case of Ehud ben-Gera

"The perfect criminal is a superman. He must be meticulous in his techniques: unseen, unseeable, a Lone Wolf.
—ELLERY QUEEN

The Deuteronomistic history spans the centuries from the conquest of Canaan to the Babylonian exile. The will of Yhwh is its unity, the string on which the historian threads treatments of individual episodes. To tease from events some earnest of Yhwh's abiding disposition, the historian sweeps with a gracious coquetry across the grounds of the ages, here passing quickly; here pausing, eyes wide, in rapt attention; here dallying in an eddying dialogue with the past. As a rule, from which are exempted those texts that make the most vivid impress on the popular imagination (Joshua's invasion, Absalom's revolt, the Elijah cycle), single events are proportioned on a diminutive scale, the better to show off the pattern of Yhwh's deeds.

To articulate his themes the Deuteronomist structures the eras of his history by applying ideological tools of explanation, and by selecting the episodes he represents partly with a view to their thematic integration. Broadly, the history is most contaminated when it exposes trends, themes, and causes that transcend limited periods. In individual episodes these larger trends are less germane; here, the historian is prone to appeal to causes directly pertinent to the action, more "scientific", less theological.

The following two chapters, therefore, explore the logic by which Israelite historians constructed short accounts. In neither instance can one warrant unconditionally that the Deuteronomist did not incorporate the text verbatim from elsewhere. Still, the texts in Judges 3 and 4 illustrate how *some* Israelite historians worked with sources; they are inside the corpus of the Deuteronomist. We begin with the story of Ehud, in Judges 3:12–30.[1]

EHUD AT THE PALACE

EHUD CALLING

Eglon, the corpulent king of Moab, has occupied "the city of palms," probably Jericho, on the Israelite shore of the Dead Sea (3:13; cf. 2 Chron. 28:15; Deut. 34:3; Judg. 1:16). It is there, through Ehud's agency, that Israel sends him its tribute.[2] A "lefthanded" Benjaminite (lit., "son of the 'right' "), Ehud conceals on his right thigh a short, two-edged sword (vv. 15f.). He delivers the tribute, starts home with his Israelite porters, and then doubles back to the court. There he secures the dismissal of the king's courtiers, to confer privately with Eglon, who is sitting in the "upper chamber" (ʿaliyyâ), "which was his alone" (vv. 17–20). In private, Ehud thrusts the dagger deep enough that the king's "fat closed over the blade"; Eglon expires, and his anal sphincter explodes (v. 22, wyṣʾ hpršdnh).[3]

Locking the doors of the upper chamber, Ehud leaves by way of the misdārôn (meaning unknown). Then Eglon's servants return. The locked doors create the impression that the king is defecating (lit. "covering his feet"),[4] and they wait. When Eglon does not appear, they fetch the key and unlock the upper chamber, finding the king, alone, dead (v. 25). Meanwhile Ehud has had time to rally his troops from thie hills, and seize the fords of the Jordan (vv. 26f.). They cut down the Moabites, who have fled homeward in panic (vv. 28f.). Victory and liberation are achieved.

Not every element is transparent. The terms having to do with excretion have caused difficulties; crowded into the space of a few verses is the highest concentration of rare and unique vocabulary in the literature of ancient Israel. The minute details of the killing tumble out one upon the other like the mops that the apprentice summoned up to do his swabbing. In the Hebrew Bible (HB), only Genesis 22 and 2 Samuel 18 lavish comparable detail on killings; and, these texts, less reticent about character development, concern the deaths of favorite sons. Why does the slaughter of a porcine Moabite command the appurtenances of so pregnant a theme? Why are the mechanics of the murder of such special interest? To answer these questions, we must refine our philological and archaeological suppositions.

EHUD'S CALLING

Ehud is not "lefthanded"; rather, "his right hand was ʾiṭṭer". This adjective comes from a root meaning "to bind," and suggests that the use of the hand was somehow impeded (v. 15; cf. Ps. 69:16). The form of the adjective may imply a disability or deformity—ʿiwwēr means "blind," gibbēn means "hunchbacked," and so on. But Judges 20:16 speaks of "seven hundred picked troops," their right hands ʾiṭṭer, who "could sling a stone at a hair and not miss." This excludes physical deformity: it would be comical to invent elite brigades organized on such a principle. But "his right hand was *ʾiṭṭēr*" is not the normal term for "lefthanded." 1 Chronicles 12:2 furnishes that lexeme, *maśmîl* (lit., "to use the left hand"), used of lefthanded slingers.[5]

In all three texts the lefthanders are Benjaminites. In no other text does handedness figure. The logical inference is that Benjamin was known for producing southpaws. They could have done so as, until recently, the Maori did, by binding the right arms of young children— hence "bound as to his right hand"—and inculcating dexterity with the left. On this supposition Ehud was not, as the translations have it, "a man lefthanded." He was one of a breed of men schooled in the use of the left hand for war.

Why lefthanders? Foremost because their opponents train to fight righthanded men. The southpaw is practiced in the clash of blade on blade and shield on shield. The righthander learns to fight blade against shield, shield against blade; against the southpaw his whole tactical repertoire, and most of his martial experience, are irrelevant. Portsider pugilists confound even the finest boxers. Lefthanders enjoy a similar advantage in line combat.

Two of the three texts that mention lefthanders associate them with the sling. This cannot be coincidental, and may reflect another Benjaminite specialty (cf. Thucydides 2.81 on regional specialization in the sling), the more so in that slings do not loom large in the literature of HB. Now, the sling was state-of-the-art weaponry in Iron Age warfare. Goliath, for example, never has the chance to close with David. He lumbers forward like a peasant with a pitchfork. David, who rejects wearing Saul's heavy armor, sends him lurching to earth with the ancient version of the thirty-ought-six.[6] The story exemplifies the tactic of meeting heavily armored troops with mobile skirmishers, who withdraw in the face of a massed advance, exacting casualties as they go. These light infantry were perfectly suited to mountain terrain, where cavalry could not easily run them down, and their mobility made them immune to charges by heavy infantry. They were inexpensive to field, sparing the costs of armor, heavy weaponry, and close-order drill. The only drawback was that they could not stand in line combat without heavy infantry support.

The sling's long range and high trajectory also made it invaluable in siege.[7] Assyrian reliefs in the British Museum, for example, depicting the conquest of Lachish in 701 B.C.E., consistently place slingers to the rear of attacking columns. The sling functions as a sort of howitzer, furnishing long-range barrages and covering fire (cf. 2 Kings 3:25).

Lefthanded slingers and assault troops were specially valued. Iron Age fortifications often forced beleaguerers to expose the right side to the walls when charging the gate (Fig. 1).[8] The shield, on the left arm,

FIGURE 1: ISRAELITE GATES

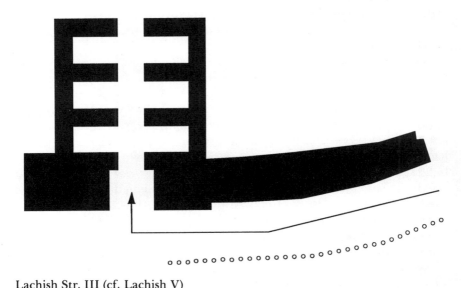

Lachish Str. III (cf. Lachish V)

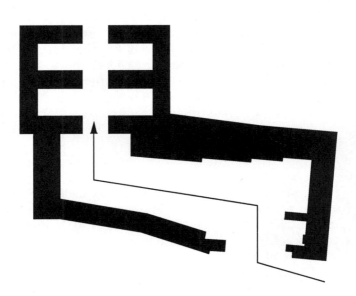

Beersheba Str. V

could not be used to fend off stones and other missiles from the walls. Thus, when the defenders launched sallies from the gate, their comrades on the parapets offered an effective crossfire. But southpaw assailants partly nullified the advantage. Their shields rested on their right arms, providing against fire from the wall; those assailants to the rear could face front, yet offer covering fire either toward the gate or against the parapets. The southpaw and the slinger were Israelite military specialists.

Early Israel's farmer-soldiers fought on foot in the hills. At first (ca. 1200–1030 B.C.E.) they rarely succeeded in storming fortresses frontally.[9] Thus, Judges 1 lists a whole series of fortified towns the Israelites (Judah excepted) cannot take; the only one they do overcome is Bethel (1:22–26), and Bethel by a postern gate. Joshua captures Ai by decoying the defenders into an ambush in the open field (Josh. 8); Abimelek succeeds at Shechem by the same tactic (Judg. 9).

As the first kings (ca. 1030–974 B.C.E.) trained heavy infantry and won superiority in the uplands, the zone of battle moved from backwater hills to the lowlands, with their major forts. Starting in this era the modern tactics and field ordnance of the standing army outmoded older forms of drill. It is striking, thus, that all three texts about lefthanded warriors refer to this or an earlier age. In the society of the premonarchic era, such warriors must have enjoyed tremendous prestige among the armies of the tribes.

In sum, to say that Ehud's right arm was 'iṭṭer is to say quite a bit. Ehud conveyed Israel's tribute to Eglon, guarding it against local bandits and kings. He was charged with this mission because he was the closest thing to a professional soldier that the Israel of his period produced. He was a seasoned samurai, or, to use a modern caricature, a sort of James Bond. Bred for combat, schooled to feats of sinister valor, Ehud was precisely the man to execute the operation that Judges 3 describes.

THE PROBLEM: EHUD'S ESCAPE

EHUD VANISHES

To this point, every detail the narrator supplies is geared toward the climax, Israel's surprise deployment at the Jordan. Ehud's lefthandedness marks him as a professional killer. Medieval exegetes already observed that, repeatedly mentioned (vv. 15b, 16, 21), it entailed his strapping his dagger on his *right* thigh. There, the blade, normally a bulge on the *left* thigh, eluded the observation of Eglon's guards.[10] The initial movement of the left hand in Eglon's presence would also have appeared innocuous,[11] as the similarly camouflaged murder in 2 Samuel 20:9–10 illustrates (cf. also 2 Sam. 2:23).

The sword, double-edged to slice cleanly into the flesh, is matched to the diameter of Eglon's belly. It is short enough for the folds of fat to engulf it.[12] This is why the tale starts with the statement that Ehud frequented the court as a tribute-bearer: the role afforded him the chance to gauge Eglon's girth. Finally, the force of the killing blow leads the king to befoul himself: Mesudat Zion suggests the element adds to the concealment; the courtiers assume that the king is relieving himself behind the closed doors of the ʿaliyyâ (v. 24), because they smell the excrement. The end result is a knife hidden in the corpse, and the corpse in a locked ʿaliyyâ. And the climax: Israel's surreptitious deployment at the river.

Surprise and concealment, concealment and surprise: the narrator drums out a cloak-and-dagger tale. The whole covert operation is conceived to achieve a grip on the Jordan fords. Nothing is left to chance. Not a detail in the story is superfluous. Form and content correspond. Yet in standard treatments, detailed through the narrative is, one cannot say the same of Ehud's escape. The Greek states that Ehud's getaway confounded Moab (reading htmhm for MT htmhmhm, v. 26), and even in the Hebrew this is the sense of it. The Hebrew describes it intricately, insistently plumbing the Moabites' befuddlement (vv. 23–26). Its presentation demands coherent treatment.

The Moabites leave their king alone with an Israelite in verse 19. When they return (v. 24), the doors of the ʿaliyyâ are locked. They surmise that Ehud is gone and that the king is relieving himself. They wait until "they blush" (v. 25). Of all things, this delay cannot be fortuitous: Ehud reckons on it for time to rally his troops. But how did he know what the courtiers would think? They had left Ehud and Eglon alone. What told them that Ehud had left? What indicated that the king had come to no harm during their absence?

The predictable nineteenth-century answer was the claim that two sources were involved: verse 20 originally had Ehud return unnoticed by the courtiers to the king's private suite; verse 19, in which Ehud requested a private audience in the servants' presence, was inserted from a parallel narrative.[13] There are no other traces of such a parallel narrative; that the editor should have elected to include a small fragment of it here, and only here, is improbable.

But the alternatives are also unpalatable. Ehud was above suspicion, it is submitted, an absurd view prima facie, and unfounded in the text. Or Ehud's egress, the misdārôn, was a rear exit of some sort. How, then, did the courtiers know he had left? Did they see him absconding out the back, and think him above suspicion? Even in the bovine breast of a Moabite, this sight would fan the embers of distrust. Yet the courtiers waited stoically. All this aside, why did the courtiers fetch a key and unlock doors the king had locked (v. 25)? Why did they not check the unlocked access Ehud had used?

Sensible of the difficulties, some exegetes suggest that Ehud left the way he entered, and used a key taken from the corpse to lock the ʿaliyyâ behind him.[14] But this involves our inventing action not narrated. The otherwise scrupulous account does not say that Ehud "fetched a key," although the reader cannot be expected to realize this; yet when the courtiers *unlocked* the ʿaliyyâ, it notes that *they* used a key, something we are apt to surmise. Did the narrator forget the key when the reader needs his guidance, and remember it when we *must* assume it was used? Too, it will be seen in this chapter's section entitled "Ehud's Iron Age Alibi" that Ehud locked himself inside the ʿaliyyâ. This is what justified the courtiers' assumption that the ʿaliyyâ had been locked from inside.

E. G. Kraeling concluded that Ehud bolted the ʿaliyyâ by pulling a thong from outside, a recourse that runs afoul of the same considerations. It further fits with no bolting mechanism so far attested archaeologically: the locks known to the Israelites could not be manipulated without a key from the outside;[15] certainly, demand for such a device would have been low, and the device itself unfamiliar to the reader.

We arrive, thus, at an impasse. Ehud does not lock the ʿaliyyâ from the outside, with a key. But if he locks the ʿaliyyâ from the inside, sinewy problems block the way: how did the courtiers know when to return? Why didn't they enter through Ehud's unlocked egress? And how did they know Ehud was gone? If they glimpsed Ehud's heels against the hills, why did they stand inactive? The solution lies in the architecture of the account.

THE LOCKED ROOM

Eglon receives Ehud in his private room, ʿaliyyat ham-meqērâ (v. 20). It is mentioned three times thereafter as the ʿaliyyâ (vv. 23, 24, 25), and once as ḥadar ham-meqērâ (v. 24). The word ʿaliyyâ means "the room over." It was a normal feature of public architecture, and occurred also in private homes.[16]

The ʿaliyyâ is ordinarily defined by what it is above (ʿly). The terms used to define it are always architectural: the room over the wall (2 Kings 4:10), the gate (2 Sam. 19:1), the corner (Neh. 3:31f.). Sometimes no more than a rooftop (2 Kings 23:12), it is most often an enclosed, upper-story space (1 Kings 17:19, 23; 2 Kings 4:10; Jer. 22:13f.; 2 Sam. 19:1 vs. 18:24 gag, "rooftop"). Except in Jeremiah 22:13f., where it appears in the plural, the noun never denotes more than a single room.[17] This is the case also in Judges 3, where the courtiers call it a ḥeder, "chamber." And this in turn explains why the servants assume that the king is evacuating himself: if the doors to this room are locked (v. 24), it can mean only one thing. There are no other rooms opening on it, and probably no rear exit.

Since antiquity the phrase ʿaliyyat ham-meqērâ has been understood as "the upper chamber of cooling"(meqērâ). But "cooling" is not an architectural term. And by the Dead Sea, where the account is situated, one does not take to upper stories to escape the heat; rather, one burrows from it as far as possible. Psalm 104:3 suggests an alternative: Yhwh "beams (*mᵉqāreʰ*) his upper chambers (*ᶜaliyyôtāyw*)". Here, we have an architectural feature. The phrase *ᶜaliyyat ham-mᵉqērâ* can mean "the room over the beams."[18]

The room in Judges 3 is the king's *ᶜaliyyâ*—"which was his alone" (v. 20). 2 Kings 1:2 mentions a king who fell from his *ᶜaliyyâ*; again, the royal *ᶜaliyyâ* is in point. Like Judges 3, this text assumes a familiarity with the structure. Thus Ehud in verse 19 begged an audience. Then (v. 20), "Ehud 'entered unto him,' " which means that he crossed a threshold of some sort, not that he merely drew near to the king.[19] Only here does the narrator interject, "Eglon was sitting in the chamber over the beams, which was his alone." Presumably it was the *ᶜaliyyâ* that Ehud entered.

The *ᶜaliyyâ* therefore verges on the audience hall. It is not another room to which the king and Ehud move:[20] hypothesizing such a transfer again leads us into the snare of supplying unnarrated action in an account distinguished by painstaking detail (cf. 2 Kings 9:5f). Further, the retinue has already left the scene (v. 19); there is no need to change rooms for privacy. And the sequence is plain: in verse 19 Ehud returns to address the king, which creates the presumption that the king remained where Ehud had left him, in the audience hall; the courtiers then are dismissed, again as though from a public hall. Finally in verse 20, the narrative is explicit: Eglon was *already* sitting in his *ᶜaliyyâ;* Ehud now enters it—which is why we first hear of it at this point. The notice is not belated, which would contrast with the author's technique of disbursing necessary particulars in advance of the crucial moment (the dagger, Ehud's lefthandedness, Eglon's girth). The information is timely: the reader must know at *this* juncture that Eglon was already sitting in his *ᶜaliyyâ*. Previously Ehud was in a different space; he enters the *ᶜaliyyâ* in order to kill the king. Thus before the retinue left, Ehud, standing outside the *ᶜaliyyâ*, addressed Eglon, who was seated in it.

These spatial relations are puzzling, because the narrator presumes the palace layout. He expects the reader to recognize the *ᶜaliyyâ* as an appurtenance of a reception hall. The notice about where Eglon sat, coming at the last possible moment, sharpens, rather than radically refocuses, the reader's conditioned imagination of the venue. To understand the role of the *ᶜaliyyâ*, therefore, an excursion into the palace is in order.

THE PALACE

THE FORM OF THE PALACE IN ISRAEL'S WORLD

Where did Israelite readers situate the Ehud account? The likeliest setting is a royal palace. Evidence concerning Israelite palaces is scant, and the archaeological data are controverted. Still, only here can we discover the possibilities for the location of the *ᶜaliyyâ*. If the following survey does less than justice to some complex questions, it is in order not to digress too far or too long from this relevant issue.

Assyrian sources testify that the most impressive palace in Israel's environs was called the *bīt ḫilāni* (É *ḫi-[il]-la-ni*). In the eighth century Tiglath-Pileser III and Sargon II boasted of building such structures from western (Syrian) models (*tamsil ekal māt Ḫatti*, Clay Tablet R 18, Display 161f.). Scholars trace the name to the Hittite *ḫilammar*, "gate(house)." Some claim that the term *bīt ḫilāni*, relates only to a (palace) gate complex, and does not denote the palace type most often found in the ground.[21] But the texts suggest that the Assyrians, at least, used the phrase to denominate such palaces as a whole, and we may retain the nomenclature here.

The Assyrian and contemporary Syrian palaces are known from single-story remains. They have in common a complex focused on two main rooms: a long, pillared portico, entered on the broad side; and, within, a throne room as long or longer, adjacent and parallel to it, entered on the long side from the portico (see Fig. 2). To one side of the portico, a stairway leads upward. This is not uniformly a feature of the Assyrian imitations, but is common in Syria during the Iron Age (ca. 1200–500 B.C.E.).

This complex formed the heart of Solomon's palace in Jerusalem.[22] 1 Kings 7:6f. describe a "hall of pillars" (i.e., the portico), bordering on "the hall of the throne . . . the hall of judgment," behind which are the living quarters. Solomon's artisans, after all, came from the north, the home of the *bīt ḫilāni*, and built a temple of a variety associated with this palace type at Tell Tayanat. Too, Y. Yadin has identified Palace 6000 at Megiddo, and D. Ussishkin Palace 1723, as *bīt ḫilānis* (Fig. 2).[23] Both structures are Solomonic. Ussishkin has gone so far as to construe Palace 1723 as a diminished version of the Jerusalem model.

These suggestions have some defects.[24] V. Fritz interprets the Israelite remains not as a combined portico and throne room, but as the offspring of a central-court palace witnessed in LB (ca. 1600–1200 B.C.E.) in Syro-Palestine.[25] Showing that some Israelite specimens (ca. 900–700 B.C.E.) conformed to this pattern, Fritz takes the throne rooms in Megiddo 1723 and 6000 as such courtyards, along with that of the tenth-century *bīt ḫilāni* at ancient Jericho[26] (all Figure 2). Still, the throne rooms of the Syrian *bīt ḫilānis* are unmistakable. Though the Israelite structures are not identical to the Syrian, they are susceptible to the same functional interpretation. And the textual testimony, as we shall see, suggests that the use of the Israelite palace conformed more or less to what one would envision from the Syrian remains.

Pending a glance at the texts, we shall not stray too wide in engaging the *bīt ḫilāni* as a guide to the features the Israelite reader associated with palaces. The *bīt ḫilāni* had roots in the soil of LB Canaan.[27] And it exercised a hold over the imaginations of Assyrian architects.[28]

In the pre-Assyrian *bīt ḫilāni* the throne room is surrounded by other,

FIGURE 2: *THE BĪT HILĀNI*

Tell Halaf

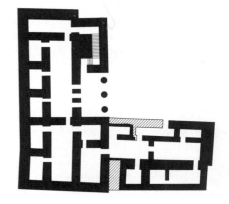

Tell Tayanat

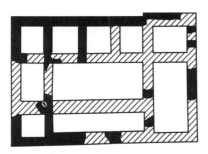

Megiddo 6000

Megiddo 1723
(As reconstructed by
D. Ussishkin)

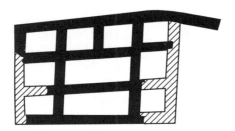

Jericho

smaller rooms. By definition the portico adjoins the throne room on one long side. Small rooms also run the length of the opposite side, though sometimes one of these rooms is interpreted as an open court (J6 or 7 at Zincirli); the only exception is the peculiar *bīt ḫilāni* I at Zincirli. Usually the small rooms continue around the throne room's short sides. At Halaf, Tayanat I, Zincirli Upper Palace (C) and K2, and Megiddo 6000 and Tell es-Sultan (Jericho), the throne room is abutted on all four sides.[29] The obvious question is, Did the king have to sit in the dark?

The throne rooms often contain large hearths. J, K, and Upper Palace C at Zincirli share this feature (cf. Building 1727 in Field VII at Shechem), and fire wagons were unearthed in the palace at Halaf. To forgo natural light is one thing, if fatal to lizards and flowers; but there is no effective substitute, when smoke rises from the coals, for natural respiration.

The nearest fund of light and air is above. To tap it the throne room must have risen higher than the surrounding rooms, permitting illumination and ventilation through upper-level windows. That is, the throne room rose two stories, and the other chambers only one. The layout is called clerestory, and explains why the *bīt ḫilāni* long sides uniformly face north and south:[30] the throne room windows in the upper story picked up steady sunlight, not the shifting illumination of an east-west exposure.

When, starting with Tiglath-Pileser III (745–727 B.C.E.), Assyrian kings adopted the *bīt ḫilāni*, their architects wedded it to local types of suites. They eliminated the row of small rooms opposite the portico, so that the throne room bordered on a courtyard. This obviated the need for the clerestory. Still, Tiglath-Pileser describes his *bīt ḫilāni* as a *bīt appāte*, probably "a house with (distinctive) windows."[31] A few decades later Sennacherib (705–681 B.C.E.), installed a *bīt ḫilāni* in the great temple of Asshur: his principal innovation, as J. Börker-Klähn has shown, was to insert a loggia "just under the roof" (*ina pān appāt uri*—KAV 42 r I 18).[32] Apparently Assyrian architects preserved the clerestory arrangement even though they had attenuated its functional value.

I. J. Winter, in a synthetic reconsideration of the problem, has revived the discarded theory that in Assyria, a combination of features distinguished the *bīt ḫilāni* from local buildings.[33] She suggests—a view corroborated by Börker-Klähn—that fenestration from above was one. Her argument draws strength from a letter written in Sargon's reign (722–705 B.C.E.), concerning "the bronze bases of the lower story of the *bīt ḫilānis*" (K 943:5–7): the upper stories, too, must have had bases and pillars, and thus a loggia. There may thus be some truth in the old suggestion that the Assyrians thought *bīt ḫilāni* meant "house of windows," Hebrew *bêt ḫallônîm*.[34]

The *bīt ḫilāni* joined a throne room at the palace core with enough air and light to make it pleasant. In Assyria, and in the West, the form was not restricted to royal halls, but was applied also to less formal settings.[35]

Like medieval cathedrals, the Jerusalem temple was built on the same pattern. Surrounded on three sides by three stories of offices fifteen cubits high in total, its nave, or central hall, and adyton (holy of holies) rose thirty cubits. It was lighted, and the hearth before the adyton was ventilated, by clerestory.[36] The story of Samson's death also presupposes such a structure: Samson pulls down the bearing pillars of a Philistine temple (Judg. 16:25f.). Yet the spectators are standing on the roof (v. 27). How does one watch from a roof the pillars supporting the roof? Did the narrator toss the story off, oblivious to the inconsistency, carelessly installing spectators atop the building Samson was in? More likely, he had a concrete building in mind. The Philistines must be standing on surrounding roofs, atop the abutting chambers, peering through windows down into a central hall. Access to the roofs would be gained from the staircase next to the portico.

The place to reconstruct the Israelite royal $^{(a}liyyâ$, therefore, is at the level of the throne room clerestory (so the reading of the scroll in Jer. 36:21f.). Royal bedrooms were located on upper stories, sometimes, like the rear tiers of Megiddo Palaces 1723 and 6000 and the palace at Tell es-Sultan (and Lachish Palace A), sitting on the city wall (1 Sam. 19:11–15; cf. Josh. 2:5–7, 15; 2 Sam 6:16; Judg. 5:28),[37] or opening onto rooftops that commanded a view of the city (2 Sam. 11:2; 2 Kings 6:26, 30; 2 Sam. 16:21f.). The staircase by the portico of the bīt ḫilāni shows that the upper reaches around the throne room were in use.[38] The suggestion is that it was at this level, inside the throne room, that the king's $^{(a}liyyâ$ sat. The king could see out from his royal seat, as several texts indicate (Wen-Amun 1, 48; 2 Kings 1:2).[39]

The elevation of the throne is a commonplace of architecture. In triple-segmented royal chapels, such as Solomon's, the adyton (holy of holies) was regularly raised.[40] This was the god's seat, or dais.[41] Just so, Yhwh's adyton stood ten cubits above the nave floor: the temple rose thirty cubits, the adyton twenty (1 Kings 6:2, 20), so that from the nave, at a maximum remove of less than forty cubits, only the carrying poles of the ark projected far enough forward from the adyton to be visible (1 Kings 8:8; 2 Chron. 5:9).[42] Toward the rear of the adyton, the wings of two cherubs, ten cubits higher still, were imagined to constitute Yhwh's throne, probably at window level; the ark was his "footstool" (Ps. 99:5; 132:7; cf. 1 Chron. 28:1f.). That both were unseen from the nave means that the holy of holies stood atop a flight of stairs at the rear of the temple. Yhwh, Isaiah tells us, sat "high and exalted" over the nave (6:1). That his description reflects a vision of Yhwh enthroned in the adyton is corroborated by the description of the temple in 1 Kings 6–8.

Not every throne rested on an $^{(a}liyyâ$: Solomon's lion throne, atop six steps (1 Kings 10:18–20; 2 Chron. 9:17–19), may not have had one.[43] But Solomon's adyton, with its double doors (1 Kings 6:31f.; 7:50; 2 Chron. 4:22), was Yhwh's alone, as the double-doored $^{(a}liyyâ$ (Judg.

3:23–25) was the king's.[44] In royal architecture only the throne is so private; its occupation by someone other than the king signals usurpation. The king's *ᶜaliyyâ* is the throne platform "high and exalted" in his judgment hall (cf. 1 Sam. 2:8; Jer. 17:12; 52:32//2 Kings 25:28; Esth. 3:1). Its elevation both expressed and concretized the idea that the king was magnified on enthronement (1 Kings 1:46–48; 1 Chron. 28:5; 29:23–25), an idea underlying the myth of the god too short for the throne (CTA 6.1:56–65, alluded to in Isa. 14:13f.).[45] Wen-Amun, too, in audience with the king of Byblos (ca. 1100 B.C.E.) in the royal *ᶜaliyyâ*, sees ocean waves breaking against the king's back. Thus, as in Israel, where a king sustains a mortal fall from it, and like the temple adyton, this throne platform probably sat high at the end of an audience chamber. At *ground* level, Assyrian thrones occupy the same position. Further, the hearth before the throne in the *bīt ḫilāni* corresponds to the altar in front of the adyton. The architecture of royal exaltation is a general one.[46]

These conclusions follow: the royal *ᶜaliyyâ*, or "upper room," was a throne platform overlooking and accessible from the audience chamber (as in the Ehud story); just as the temple adyton was placed inside the nave (and developed from the niche), it was formally inside the audience hall. Despite some evidence of wood, e.g., at Megiddo 6000, there is no archaeological reflex of it: possibly Syrian throne rooms lacked wooden platforms. But Eglon's platform rested on wooden joists, not on stone walls; and texts concerning audiences treat the *ᶜaliyyâ* as an integral component of the audience hall. So it probably stood inside the hall, a platform partitioned by a wood screen. It was not, in all likelihood, a separate room (IV on Fig. 3). In any event, windows offered access to the adjoining rooftops.[47] It was placed so as to benefit from the *bīt ḫilāni*'s clerestory light and ventilation, and from the warmth of the hearth in winter. Assyrian kings used the *bīt ḫilāni* both for residential and for state suites; Tiglath-Pileser III built one "for my recreation." In 1 Kings 7:8 the same usage is attested in Israel—the private suites of Solomon and of his Egyptian bride were patterned on his public reception halls (1 Kings 7:6f.). Evidently the form was both durable and adaptable.

THE ISRAELITE PALACE IN ACTION: SPATIAL AND STATUS DIVISIONS

The foregoing discussion trisects the royal reception suite into a portico just outside the throne room proper, the throne room or audience chamber itself, and an enclosed throne platform, or *ᶜaliyyâ*. These are labeled A, B, and C of Figure 3. The complex figures in several texts.

Indications of court protocol provide the background. In 2 Samuel 17 Absalom deliberates with the elders. Ahitophel's advice sways them (vv. 1–4); and then they summon Hushai. Absalom reviews Ahitophel's report (v. 6), and Hushai successfully rebuts it (vv. 7–14). But Hushai cannot gauge his success—after trying to win time for David, he urges the old bear to flee headlong (vv. 15ff.). Evidently he is absent from the final deliberations, and knows only what alternatives are under discussion. Nor is Ahitophel better informed. Much action intervenes before Ahitophel sees "that his counsel was not being executed" and rides home to hang himself (v. 23). Hushai and Ahitophel, thus, are present in the throne room only when arguing briefs.

1 Kings 1 correlates this usage to the tripartite layout of the court. David sits with a concubine in the $^{(a}liyy\hat{a}$ (Fig. 3C). Into this chamber comes Bathsheba (v. 15). While she is there the attendants (Fig. 3B) announce Nathan (Fig. 3A; v. 23), who enters David's presence (Fig. 3B). But when *he* finishes, Bathsheba must be called back—she has gone to the portico (3A) to wait. Bathsheba reenters the audience chamber (Fig. 3B; v. 28). But then *Nathan* must be recalled (v. 32): *he* has gone out during Bathsheba's audience. Nathan and Bathsheba are on the Hushai–Ahitophel merry-go-round. The contrast is to Abishag, who remains in the $^{(a}liyy\hat{a}$.

Three classes are in point: the king, with special retainers (in 1 Kings 1, the wife and the consort), on the dais; the entourage, who stand in the audience hall and regulate admission to it ($h\bar{a}$-$^{(}\hat{o}m^ed\hat{i}m$ $^{(}al$ ham-$melek$); and those the attendants admit (see Fig. 3). Members of the last class wait in an antechamber (Fig. 3A) and enter singly: to this custom, not to arbitrary redaction, we owe the complexities of 2 Samuel 17 and 1 Kings 1. Starting with Solomon (1 Kings 2:19), the queen mother ranks among the premier class: she has a throne of her own to the right of the king's.[48] The division of the reception suite mirrors gradations of prestige.

The same social distinctions appear, implicitly, in other texts. But the most striking confirmation comes from 2 Samuel 13.

In this text Amnon, David's son, feigns illness, to lure his sister Tamar to his home. She kneads dough and seethes it, on a hearth, before his eyes (v. 8). Amnon dismisses his servants, who leave him with Tamar (v. 9). He now tells Tamar, "Bring the dish into the room" (v. 10). Tamar had prepared the food in Amnon's sight and hearing, but in a room adjoining that in which he reclined. In the palace of Figure 3, Tamar was in Area B, and Amnon was in C.

When Tamar approaches, Amnon ravishes her. This suggests that the servants are out of sight, not in the area where Tamar had simmered the dough. But the retinue are within earshot, for after the rape, Amnon calls his aide, who expels Tamar from the house (vv. 17f.). Three spaces are in use: 1) the room in which Amnon lies, equivalent to the royal station overlooking the audience hall; 2) the hall itself, equipped with hearth, from which Tamar enters Amnon's chamber; and, 3) the space outside the complex, which is out of view, but within earshot. In this third space the servants waited.

Any complex with three such spaces would satisfy the demands of the narrative. Thus one could locate Amnon above the rear chamber of a four-room house (Fig. 4), where ovens sometimes appear in the central

FIGURE 3: EGLON'S PALACE (MOCK-UP)

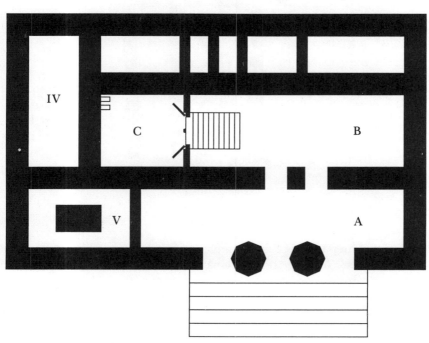

A. Porticoed antechamber
B. Audience hall
C. ʿaliyyâ
IV. Casemate room behind the audience hall
V. Stairway to upper story

FIGURE 4: A FOUR-ROOM HOUSE

(8th century, Tell en-Nasbeh)

courtyard. The palace is a more likely setting, because that is where informed readers would be likely to place a prince. Further, situating the account in a four-room house implies that the courtyard was unroofed, and that Amnon's courtiers stood in the open, waiting out the rape on the street.[49] But the functional principle is identical in any case: the royal station commands a view of a hall separate from it; in the latter stand the courtiers. The spatial and class relations in the texts about the palace make the *bīt ḫilāni* a serviceable model on which to proceed. They indicate that the palatial structures at Megiddo and Tell es-Sultan should be interpreted as fully roofed complexes with large audience halls.

Using the *bīt ḫilāni*, with an *ʿaliyyâ*, as a model, coordinates the Ehud story with the assumptions shared between the narrator and his ancient audience. As the next section shows, all evidence converges on the conclusion that the Israelite narrator had some such model in mind.

EHUD'S IRON AGE ALIBI

Locating Eglon on a podium opening on an audience hall resolves the basic difficulties in the Ehud account. It invites an interpretation not dependent on an elaborate apparatus of reader-supplied action, one that assumes only the reader's familiarity with the architecture. The narrator provides all the necessary spatial orientation in Judges 3:18–20.

When Ehud returns to the court, in verse 19, there is no notice that Eglon has left the state room in which he earlier received his tribute. He is still holding court and still receiving Israelites. The narrator therefore must have expected the reader to situate Eglon on the throne. The behavior of the courtiers, and the subsequent action, corroborate this inference.

Ehud addresses the king: "I have a secret word for you, o king!" This places the assassin in the audience hall (B in Fig. 3). The retinue, then, leave Eglon and Ehud alone (v. 19), which suggests they have been in attendance in the public chambers. But they *do not* go wandering aimlessly about town. As protocol demands, they remain on call, on duty, now, in the portico (Fig. 3A), like Absalom's retinue during the rape of Tamar.

Verse 20 begins, "Ehud entered unto him," to describe his crossing from one space to another (n. 19). Here the usage is normal: just at this juncture comes the remark that Eglon "was sitting in the chamber atop the beams, which was his alone." Had this notice come earlier or later, it might imply that the whole conversation between Ehud and Eglon took place inside the ʿ*aliyyâ*. The notice comes exactly at this point, just after the notice that Ehud crossed a threshold, to differentiate between the area in which Ehud and the courtiers had stood, and the chamber that Ehud now entered. Ehud has crossed from Area B to Area C on Figure 3.

Verse 23 carries the spatial argument further. Ehud escapes the locked ʿ*aliyyâ*. The assumption that this takes him from C to B (Fig. 3) explains why the servants return: in verse *24*, Ehud emerges from Area B and enters Area A, signaling the end of the audience. After all, had they not seen Ehud leave, they could not know when to return; and the locked doors of the throne platform should have suggested that Ehud was within. Nor is an unconventional egress a possibility:[50] as noted earlier, it would raise the specter of foul play. Rather, everything is normal: Ehud has left by the usual egress.

The courtiers waited outside the throne room: on their return (v. 24), "Behold! the doors of the ʿ*aliyyâ* were locked!" They have resumed their posts in the audience hall, but the king's throne chamber, inside the hall, is closed. It follows that during Ehud's audience, they must have stood at a remove of two doors from the king: those of the ʿ*aliyyâ*, locked by Ehud, and those of the room they entered to find the ʿ*aliyyâ* locked. They have come from the portico, their station during private audiences, to Area B.

The whole account revolves around this presupposition. The king sat in the ʿ*aliyyâ* (Area C); the courtiers left Ehud in the hall Eglon overlooked (Area B). Ehud somehow locked the murdered king in the ʿ*aliyyâ*, and made his way from the audience hall (Area B) to the portico (Area A), where the servants waited. The same logic calls for one further step:

Ehud must have locked the ʿaliyyâ from *inside,* before negotiating a passage into the audience hall.

Several considerations converge on this point. That the meticulous narrator mentions no device by which Ehud could have locked the doors from outside has been noted. Moreover, the courtiers, on their return to the audience hall, suspect nothing. The locked doors of the ʿaliyyâ suggest that the king is defecating (v. 24). This is an act Israelites performed in private (n. 4), and the inference was that Eglon had himself locked the doors: the doors appeared from without as though locked from within, and it wanted a key to work the lock from without (v. 25).

The narrator implies that there was no obvious means of egress from the ʿaliyyâ to the audience hall (Area B). The courtiers had left Ehud in Area B and Eglon in Area C. On their return there was every indication that Eglon had locked the ʿaliyyâ only after Ehud left. Were there grounds for suspicion, the concealment of the dagger in the corpse (hiding all traces of the murder, v. 25) would have no narrative function. In fact, suspicion arises only because Eglon takes too long about his private business.[51]

The Hebrew, *wyṣ ʾhwd hmsdrwnh wysgr dltwt hʿlyh bʿdw wnʿl whwʾ yṣʾ wʿbdyw bʾw* (vv. 23f.), seems repetitive: "Ehud went out through the *misdārôn.* He [had?] closed the doors of the ʿaliyyâ upon him and bolted [them]. Now, he went out, and [Eglon's] servants entered." The second notice of Ehud's exit coordinates his departure with the retinue's return; Ehud's emergence onto the portico signals the end of the private audience. But the first statement, "Ehud went out," cannot simply duplicate the action. It would be redundant and would violate the pattern of verbal forms in the narrative.[52] On any reasonable reading, the statement that Ehud "went out through the *misdārôn*" must describe his passage from the locked ʿaliyyâ to the audience hall. This is the one element of his escape that is otherwise shrouded in mystery.

If a rear exit is excluded, two possibilities come to mind. The *misdārôn* could be the audience hall itself, or even the portico. The verse, then, would say that Ehud left through the normal exit, arousing no suspicion. But if this is *all* it says, how did Ehud get out of the chamber into which he had locked himself? Assuming that Ehud locked the ʿaliyyâ from without, again, the narrator will have mentioned what he need not (the passage from ʿaliyyâ to audience hall) without describing what he should (the means by which Ehud locked the ʿaliyyâ from without). Further, *misdārôn* is a *hapax legomenon*—an expression that in all of HB occurs only here. It probably denotes an unusual feature of palace architecture.[53] For the audience hall and the portico, more workaday terms were available: an example is ʾûlām, or reception area: the ʾûlām of justice, or of the throne (1 Kings 7:7); and the ʾûlām of the pillars (1 Kings 7:6). Thus the diction would be awkward at best.

The other obvious recourse is better: the *misdārôn* could be the loggia stretching around the upper part of the throne hall. Ehud would have stepped out from the king's *ʿaliyyâ* to the adjoining rooftop, walked a few paces toward the other end of the hall, and jumped down to the floor of the audience hall, Area B. This would still leave him the opportunity to waltz through the door of Area B into Area A, as though everything were normal. He could not, of course, simply leave through the loggia: in that case, the courtiers could not know Eglon was left alone.

The argument that this course *would* risk detection is not debilitating. But the lexical problems are again discouraging. The biblical word for *palace* or *temple loggias* is consistently "window," *ḥallôn*. Nor could *misdārôn* refer to the rooftop: this is always called the "roof" (*gag*). Finally, on this reading, the narrator mentions that Ehud went *out* through the loggia, but forgets to say that he jumped back *into* the audience hall. Again, the interpretation satisfies the demands of the story's plot. But it asks, again, that the reader supply action that the narrator, for no reason, forgets.

These alternatives suggest on literary and lexical grounds that Ehud locked the *ʿaliyyâ* from within. This means that the action between "Ehud went out" and "Now, he went out" (vv. 23f.) is related out of sequence: the rhetorical resumption, or epanalepsis, frames explication that breaks the temporal continuum; here, the first member of the epanalepsis refers to an earlier, the second to a later event.[54] Thus, "Ehud went out of the *ʿaliyyâ*. He *had* closed the doors of the *ʿaliyyâ* b*ʿdw* (upon him) and bolted them" (v. 23f.). Ehud locked himself inside the *ʿaliyyâ*.

This interpretation is enhanced by the formulation, "he had closed the doors *bʿdw*" (v. 23). In every instance in which the verb "to close" occurs in association with the preposition *bʿd*, the object of the preposition is shut inside the structure being closed.[55] Commentators alive to this fact have, since Qimhi, taken Eglon as the preposition's object. Again, stylistic considerations confute them: Ehud is long since the last subject mentioned, and the reader naturally assumes that he is the object of the preposition here. He "had closed the doors of the *ʿaliyyâ* upon him."[56] The logic of the account and the style of the narrative thus triangulate on this reading.

At first glance the notice that Ehud had locked himself in with the corpse may seem awkwardly placed. But if the *misdārôn* is, as seems likely, an unexpected exit from the king's special chamber to the audience hall, then the narrator has simply followed the course he adopted when mentioning that Eglon was already seated there (v. 20). Instead of retarding the flow of the action with a circumstantial element whose relevance lies further on, he incorporates the information in a telegraphic aside when it becomes necessary. Ehud left through the *misdārôn* because "he had closed the doors of the ʿaliyyâ upon him and bolted them," from the inside: one needs to know this in verse 23 to understand both his unusual egress and the subsequent action. This accounts for the use of the *hapax*, for the other stylistic peculiarities, and for the courtiers' befuddlement.[57] Ehud locked himself in with the king.

How did Ehud escape? The clue is the character of the ʿaliyyâ. This was a room atop wooden joists. It was further a room in which Eglon evacuated himself (v. 24). It stands to reason that below was an area *under* the beams.

The indoor toilet characterizes palaces from the middle of the second millennium onward. It is well attested in the *bīt ḫilāni*.[58] At Fort Shalmaneser one stands just to the left of the royal dais in T1, which two post holes divide from the tracks of a wheeled fire wagon.[59] Three stone objects that look like toilets have been unearthed at the City of David.[60] There is also evidence of drainage from a second-story installation at Iron Age Taanach.

Here, then, is an inconspicuous—an unthinkable—avenue from the privy chamber to the audience hall. The courtiers infer that Eglon has locked his doors to *use* one; it follows that the ʿaliyyâ contained a commode. What the king deposited from above can only have fallen through the floor. And to this nether region, which will hardly have been kept locked, janitors must have had access, from a room opening onto the audience hall. Thus the term *misdārôn* should be linked not, as usual, to the Hebrew *sēder* (root *s-d-r*, "order"; hence "portico, row of pillars"),[61] but, after the suggestion of David Golomb,[62] to the Hebrew, Targumic, and Arabic root *sadira*, denoting "to be blinded, puzzled." The expression mirrors the attitude that produced the euphemism "to cover one's feet," for excretion—the motif of concealment is the same. *Misdārôn*, then, means something on the order of "the hidden place," an appropriate designation for the area under the beams. There is a philological parallel in the Yehawmilk inscription from Persian-period Byblos. There the *mistārîm*, "the hidden," is the recess under a temple floor or, conceivable, its contents.[63] It denotes a hollow, untraveled space. In the probable absence of any other access into the audience hall from the locked ʿaliyyâ, the opening leading through this cellar presents the most probable avenue of Ehud's escape.[64]

This explains why the word *misdārôn* is so recondite: the region in question otherwise plays no part in Hebrew narrative. It further explains why the narrator lays such stress on the escape: the movement through the "hidden place" completes the killing's concealment, and leads to the preemptive grip on the fords. Ehud's exit, and his complicity in a crime that is not seen to be a crime, is camouflaged from the Moabites' consciousness. Eglon's killing is a "perfect murder." A recapitulation of the account is in order.

EHUD'S ADVENTURE

Ehud ben-Gera was a lefthanded combat ace, a hardened professional warrior. Commander, for this reason, of the detachment that escorted Israel's tribute to Eglon, the corpulent Moabite king, he was a grizzled colonel, Moab's vassal-in-chief. One day he strapped a diminutive dagger, double-edged for cleaner cutting, onto his right thigh, not his left. Ehud did his obeisance, and then marched his detachment back to its point of dispersal, out of sight of the court, by the enigmatic *pesîlîm* at Gilgal. Only afterward did he double back to the court, seeming thereby to keep his second assignation with Eglon a secret from his countrymen.

At the court Ehud secured a private audience by the subterfuge of promising a sensitive disclosure (*debar sēter*)—by implication a denunciation of some fellow vassal.[65] His dirk, on the right thigh, went unnoticed; and he had just before abased himself in the submissive role of a tributary. The retinue withdrew from the audience hall (Fig. 3B) to wait in the porticoed antechamber (Area A). They left Ehud in the audience hall, and Eglon on his *ʿaliyyâ* (Area C). Once the doors to the hall had shut, Ehud sprang up the stairs of the royal podium, imparting an air of urgency to his mission. Perhaps he even bolted the doors at this point, as a final precaution against eavesdroppers. In a modern adaptation the assassin would examine the chamber for listening devices, or turn on the water taps to confound them.

Inside the *ʿaliyyâ* Ehud confronted the crapulous monarch: "It is a word of God (*debar ʾelōhîm*) I have for you!" he cried. In a single dextrous motion, innocuous at first blush, his left hand crossed his body and plucked from his right thigh a sinister shaft. The king struggled to stand in bewildered horror,[66] but the Israelite's right hand restrained him, half-bent. All his practiced strength focused in the blow, Ehud stabbed the dagger skyward from his knees, and punched it into Eglon's ample belly, driving it home deep with the heel of his palm. The uncrossed hilt buried itself in a sea of paunch.

Death was instantaneous; no blood seeped out. The sole sign of violence was the unsavory release of Eglon's anal sphincter, which expelled the contents of his intestines onto the floor. Meanwhile Ehud, having fastened the doors of the *ʿaliyyâ* from inside, swung down through the floor to the level below. He emerged, from an adjoining room, into the audience chamber (Area B) and crossed deliberately to the door. His audience finished, he appeared on the portico (Area A), and strode unchallenged out the courtyard.

Filing back into the throne room (from Area A to Area B), the Moabite courtiers looked, "and behold! the doors of the *ʿaliyyâ* were barred!" (v. 24). Possibly the odor of Eglon's final deposit wafted to the retainers through the air. In any event, the courtiers satisfied themselves he must be relieving himself, and had locked the ⟨*aliyyâ* doors to that end.

The courtiers waited. We may imagine them whiling away their time with quips on quotidian reality—the inferior Israelites, cuisine at the court, the king's constipation. As moments mounted into embarrassing minutes, the delicate matter of disturbing their liege pressed ever more on their minds. The minutes elapsed—an hour, at a guess—"and behold! he did not open the doors of the ⟨*aliyyâ!*" (v. 25). They called, then knocked, first demurely, then louder. Sure now of something amiss, they fetched the key. One of them undid the door: "Behold! There was their lord, fallen dead on the floor" (v. 25), his load dropped beside him. No blood; dagger enveloped; no sign of fiddling with the lock. Ehud's "secret word" (v. 19) remained a secret, but Eglon's "hidden things" were now exposed. To all appearances, Eglon had come a cropper during a marathon bout on the "throne."

The Moabites dallied, with their head cut off; Ehud rallied his troops from the hills. They seized the Jordan fords and then engaged the Moabites. The latter, cut off from home, retired in disorder, to be cut down at the river. The consecutive concealment of intent, weapon, assassination, body, and signs of violence issued in tactical and strategic surprise.

THE GENRE OF THE STORY

In this story Ehud bewilders the Moabites with what amounts to a locked room "howdunnit."[67] Logically, the act was impossible: the assassin must have left before the killing was done. The tale bears some similarity to the episode in which Odysseus blinds Polyphemos. Odysseus identifies himself to his victim as "No one," and, when the Cyclops' brothers inquire who was the culprit, their one eyewitness repeats, "No one." In this respect the story resembles other premodern fiction about an actor unlocking a riddle already solved for the audience.[68] A locked room murder in an archetypal locked room, among people who do not dream of murder—this is a picaresque.

Because of this Alter has asserted that the story's author enjoyed the latitude to write "an imaginative reenactment of the historical event . . . fictionalized history—history in which the feeling and meaning of events are concretely realized through the technical resources of prose fiction."[69] Because all premodern historical narrative is fictional in this sense (Chapter 1), the observation is a truism. But Alter means that the author of the account did not have it in mind to write history, but rather to write a story, a historical romance. Against this position should therefore be posed the question, What changes would make the account history?

A salient property of the Ehud story is its narrative economy. Until one comes to the playful notice in verse 29 that all the Moabites were obese, virtually no detail is superfluous. The author furnishes details not to elaborate, thus, but only to actualize his reconstruction: his interest centers on the crucial events that enabled Ehud to sever the head of the Moabite hegemony, or to deprive the Moabites of their chief warrior, and to win surprise at the fords. Indeed, the terse notices about Ehud's lefthandedness and Eglon's palace layout provide a minimum of information, just enough to follow the plot. Ehud's doubling back, as though he were double-dealing with his compatriots, realistically communicates the secretive undertones of his approach, and averts the question as to why the king was not suspicious of him. Ehud's declaration to the king maneuvers the monarch into position to be struck, and dissipates the impression of the unctuous, dark man that assassins so often create. It differentiates Ehud's daring from deceit, repudiating intimations of insinuation (cf. Joab in 2 Sam. 20:9f.). This far, the author goes. No other detail is remotely unnecessary to the plot.

Narrative economy alone cannot sustain the verdict that an account is historical literature. This can be proved only through a comparison of the account with its sources. If the narrative conforms to the data in the sources, if it digests and represents them chiefly with a view to conveying the central historical data they provide, then we may claim that the account is historical. The reconstruction and presentation in Judges 3 are driven by an inexorable logic, which furnishes grounds for suspecting an underlying antiquarian impulse. But, in contrast to those of the text examined in Chapter 4, the sources of Judges 3 are no longer extant, except within the story itself. This is the case for most of the reports in the Former Prophets, and it is as a representative of this situation that the Ehud episode is considered here. Proof that the narrative is historical cannot be adduced. But evidence that it is historical can (chapters 1 and 2). The evidence derives from the contrast between the nature of the pericope as we have it and the probable nature of the sources.

The Ehud story is not part of a continuous narrative, such as the Court History. It is a short note, integrated probably with little reworking into an episodic framework.[70] Internally it is not a vehicle for thematic or for literary development, but a relation of events. This is not to gainsay its artistry. The historian who produced the account was a masterful narrator. In the hands of a professional storyteller, however, Ehud's exploits would have spilled over the present fifteen verses of prose, and furnished the stuff of an evening's entertainment, a drama.[71] This is the source on which the author in Judges 3:15–29 drew: from the oral tradition, the evidence suggests, he extracted a reconstruction of events. What we have in Judges 3 is a boiled-down version of a long-transmitted escapade.

The nature of the oral recension is important. Ehud's is a story of daring and cleverness, which made its protagonist an object of popular accolade. The same genre of oral entertainment underlies notices in the lists of David's heroes: 2 Samuel 21:15–22; 23:8–12 record victories in single combat against champions and accomplishments in generalized battle. More vivid notices in 2 Samuel 23:14–17, 20–23 commemorate especially striking feats. In each case, the text distills drastically what must have been a colorful narrative celebration.

Treatments of such incidents are fuller when integrated with an ongoing literary context. Jonathan's rout of the Philistines, for example, is the linchpin of the account in 1 Samuel 13:2–14:45. Various Davidic adventures are strung onto the romance of his early career (1 Sam. 17; 19:11–18; 21:10–16).

One group of texts will illustrate the principle. In 2 Samuel 23:14–17, three of David's champions raid a Philistine garrison in Bethlehem. They return with water from its well. But David pours it out, exclaiming, *ḥalîlâ lî (mē-)yhwh mē-ʿáśôtî zōʾt* ("Yhwh forfend that I should do this"). This exploit probably inspired 1 Samuel 24; 26. Here Saul falls unwittingly into David's power—in Chapter 26 David raids the king's camp. In each case David appropriates a token, like the water from Bethlehem. Indeed, in 26:12, he removes Saul's water jug, along with his spear (the spear signifying the threat to Saul, the water jug perhaps from 2 Samuel 23:14–17, in oral tradition). In both chapters David refuses to kill his adversary, though urged on by his underling(s) (24:4, 6f.; 26:8–11; cf. 2 Sam. 23:16f.): his words are *ḥalîlâ lî mē-yhwh* (24:6; 26:11; "Yhwh forfend")ʾim ʾeʿéśeh ʾet had-dābār haz-zeh (24:6; "that I should do this thing"). Only in these passages and 1 Kings 21:3 is *ḥalîlâ* followed by *mē-yhwh*. Saul next recognizes that David is destined for great things, and leaves off campaigning against him (24:8–22; 26:13–25).

1 Samuel 24; 26 composes a doublet. Each text is constructed around the sort of exploit enshrined in 2 Samuel 23:14–17 (see Fig. 5), and each was inherited by the Deuteronomist with an ongoing source about Saul and David (Chapter 8). Both elements of the doublet are preserved, because differences between them implied that two separate events were involved. Yet the texts serve the same literary function: they describe the resolution of the conflict between Saul and David, and they complement traditions dissociating David from Saul's death (1 Sam. 21:11–16; 29–30; 2 Sam. 1; 1 Chron. 12:20f.). Their parallel development, and their parallel incorporation into the historiography, testify to their place in the Israelite storytelling tradition. These oral variants illustrate the sort of tradition from which the Ehud story was probably drawn.

The embellishment in characterization and in detail that marks 1 Samuel 24//26 reflects their central role in the cycle of tales about David's rise. They are integral to an evolving thematic sequence, and have the marks of romance as a result. These adventure stories establish that the feat of valor, turning on a stratagem, had a secure position in the early storytelling of the Israelites. With the arguable exception of Jehu's putsch, there are no instances of them in Kings—the genre belonged to the heroic age, and to an oral context; in the dusty records of the chan-

FIGURE 5: 1 Samuel 23-24//26//2 Samuel 23

2 Samuel 23:13-17	*1 Samuel 26*	*1 Samuel 23:19-24:22*
David in מצודה (1 Sam. 23:19; 24:22)	1 ויבאו הזפים אל שאול הגבעתה לאמר הלוא דוד מסתתר (G עמנו) בגבעת החכילה על פני הישימן	ויעלו זפים אל שאול הגבעתה 23:19 לאמר הלוא דוד מסתתר עמנו במצדות בחרשה בגבעת החכילה אשר מימין הישימון
		אוה, cf. 2 Samuel 23:15; סגר, 26:8
		conversation, unsuccessful pursuit follow; in 24:1, Saul learns that David is in the מדבר of Ein Gedi
	2 ויקם שאול וירד אל מדבר זיף ואתו שלשת אלפים איש בחורי ישראל לבקש את דוד במדבר זיף	24:2 ויקח שאול שלשת אלפים איש בחור מכל ישראל וילך לבקש את דוד על פני צורי יעלים
13 Philistines camp David and men in cave	3-6 Saul camps; David reconnoitres	3 Saul enters cave to defecate David and men present in cave
15 David calls for volunteers ("Who will . . .?" cf. 1 Sam. 26:6)	David calls on Ahimelek and Abishai for volunteers to enter Saul's camp	
15 "Heroes" enter (unguarded?) garrison	Saul sleeping (night)	Saul squats in dark cave
(v. 18) Abishai associated (?)	(v. 7) David and Abishai enter camp	
	8 Abishai advocates killing Saul:	4 David's men urge him to kill Saul:
	(cf. 1 Sam. 23:20; 24:18) סגר היום אלהים את איביך בידך	הנה היום אשר אמר ה׳ אליך הנה אנכי נתן את איביך בידך
		נתן ביד, cf. 26:23
16 "Heroes" retrieve water from Philistine camp (on water, cf. 26:12)	See no. 11f., this column	4 David cuts off edge of Saul's robe
	———	5 David regrets clipping robe!
16f. David refuses to drink ("did not allow": cf. 26:23 on Messiah)	9-11 David precludes killing Saul:	6f. David precludes killing Saul:
חלילה לי (מ)ה׳ מעשתי זאת	חלילה לי מה׳ משלח ידי במשיח ה׳	חלילה לי מה׳ אם אעשה את הדבר הזה לאדני למשיח ה׳ לשלח ידי בו משיח ה׳ הוא

2 Samuel 23:13–17	*1 Samuel 26*	*1 Samuel 23:19–24:22*
See no. 16, this column	11f. David takes water flask and spear from Saul	See no. 4, this column
	12f. David and Abishai distance themselves from camp	7 Saul leaves cave
	14–16 Taunting Abner, David calls to show evidence that he could have killed Saul ("Look!")	8–13 David calls to Saul, showing the evidence that he could have killed him ("Look!")
	17 Saul recognizes David's voice (speaking to Abner anonymously): הקולך זה בני דוד	See v. 16, this column
	18 David claims innocence: כי מה עשיתי מה בידי רעה	11 David claims innocence אין בידי רעה ופשע
16 David pours out water as libation to Yhwh	See vv. 23f, this column	11b–13 + 15: David invokes Yhwh: ישפט ה׳ ביני ובינך ונקמני ה׳ ממך
	20 David will not die an enemy: כי יצא מלך ישראל לבקש את פרעש אחד כאשר ירדף הקרא (cf. v. 18) בהרים	14 אחרי מי יצא מלך ישראל אחרי מי אתה רדף אחרי כלב מת אחרי פרעש אחד
	See 26:17, this column	16 Saul recognizes David's voice (David not speaking anonymously): הקולך זה בני דוד
	21 Saul confesses he was in the wrong, promising immunity: תחת אשר נפשי בעיניך היום הזה (see v. 23)	17f. Saul confesses David is in the right: אשר סגרני ה׳ בידך ולא הרגתני
	22 David returns spear	No equivalent
	23 David invokes Yhwh (cf. 24:11b): A וה׳ ישיב לאיש את צדקתו ואת אמנתו	19 Saul continues (cf. 11ff.): A וכי ימצא איש את איבו ושלחו בדרך טובה

2 Samuel 23:13-17	1 Samuel 26	1 Samuel 23:19-24:22
	B אשר נתנך ה' היום ביד (cf. v. 21)	B cf. 24:18
	C ולא אביתי לשלח ידי במשיח ה'	C cf. 24:18
	A' והנה כאשר גדלה נפשך היום הזה בעיני כן תגדל נפשי בעיני ה'	A' וה' ישלמך טובה תחת היום הזה אשר עשית לי
	25 Saul blesses David, who will "prevail"	20f. Saul recognizes that David will succeed him, extracts an oath not to extirpate Saul's house
	25b וילך דוד לדרכו ושאול שב למקומו	22 וילך שאול אל ביתו ודוד ואנשיו עלו על המצדה
	(imperfect–perfect verb sequence)	(imperfect–perfect verb sequence)

cellery, in the reverential idiom of prophetic tales, it had no natural life.[72]

Here, the contrast between the abbreviated note of 2 Samuel 23:14–17 (and its context, 5:17–25) and the expansive, romanticized accounts of 1 Samuel 24//26 deserves special attention: the Ehud story lacks all that the latter have—dialogue, characterization, inessential action; it is, like 2 Samuel 23:14–17, a reduction of the oral tradition. The same is true of 2 Samuel 21:19//1 Chron. 20:5 (read G), the notice that Elhanan ben-Dodo (?) smote Goliath. The story is told in expanded form in 1 Samuel 17, where it, like 1 Samuel 24//26, is displaced to David: the displacement is a typical effect of the oral tradition (Chapter 10). What characterizes the relationship between the oral romance and the literary notice is again a dramatic reduction, a reduction of the drama.

The oral version of the Ehud episode, then, had its home probably in the premonarchic or early monarchic era of Israel's history. Like the notes about David's heroes, the literary version is the fossil of a living tradition. It is self-contained, without theological or ideological implications for surrounding narratives. Driven by the logic of the reconstructed incident, the presentation focuses not on history and eschatology, but on mystery and scatology. The point of the story is to communicate the reconstruction of events.

Does all this distinguish the account from romance? Formally, there is no difference. But the diminishment of fictionalization and characterization, in contrast with comparable sources from the oral tradition, does constitute evidence that Judges 3 is a history. That physical sources (the palace, the topography) are carefully respected does not prove the author's intention is historiographic—the sewers of Vienna are accurately used in *The Third Man*. But Harry Lime is not a historical figure; he is at best a pastiche of other figures. Ehud's name, all scholars concur, was received with the tradition (and 1 Chron. 7:10, suggesting he became an eponym); and the account little resembles the sort of tale the Deuteronomistic historian can be said to have invented (see chapters 6 and 9–10). Judges 3 derives from sources. Throughout, it presents only data that the oral story and his general knowledge licensed the historian to reconstruct.

Is there a difference between Judges 3 and a historical novel? In a novel the author presents events and details for which there is no historical evidence (David struggling with Saul's armor in 1 Samuel 17:38f.). Judges 3 minimizes such elements. Ehud speaks. But he does not speak about topics irrelevant to the reconstruction of events. And, like the generals of Thucydides, he speaks only where the historian was entitled to suppose he must have done. Where is the theme-building dialogue, as between David and Saul in Samuel; where the characterization, say, of Eglon; where the subtle suggestion of a hidden divine hand behind the episode? This is not elegant, but economical, reporting; it is in shorthand. And that shorthand reflects antiquarian interest (Chapter 1), the interest of a historian intent on extracting a reconstruction from his sources. This conclusion cannot be proved. But the evidence from the storytelling tradition renders it probable. The existence of a parallel case, where the source is actually extant (Chapter 4), further bears out the conclusion.

The Ehud story is not a romance in the sense that the Iliad is. It is an attempt to extract from fictionalizations, from more elaborate presentations, the bare historical facts. This tale stands in relation to the oral "romance" of Ehud as the historical credo of Deuteronomy 26:5–9 stands to that of the Hexateuch, as Thucydides' summary of the Trojan War stands to the Iliad; it is as densely historical as the Thucydidean epitome, much more so than that in Deuteronomy. The Ehud account is not "fictionalized history," in the sense of historical romance. It is history defictionalized.

It has been a staple of scholarship that the sources of the book of Judges were recollections about tribal heroes achieving local triumphs. The redactor generalized these accomplishments to imply the succor of all Israel.[73] The Ehud story, all on Benjaminite ground, is a parade case. Yet even the all-Israel redaction is not willful. Embedded already in Ehud's bearing (all) Israel's tribute to Eglon (vv. 15, 27), it reflects rather the forum in which the tale was preserved: the redaction took place over generations of recitation among Israelite audiences; these identified with the protagonist not because they were denizens of Benjamin or the central hills, but because they, too, were Israelites. When our historian rendered the account in writing, he respected this aspect, too, of the oral tradition.

That the account comes from the storytelling tradition, yet exhibits the features of a précis, affords an indication that the author wrote it down to preserve what he thought was a historical memory, all-Israel redaction included. At the same time the historian, or the story he inherited, made painstaking use of other sources: the layout of the palace, as known to Israelite audiences; the protocol of the court concerning private audiences, the stations of the courtiers, and interrupting the king *in camera;* and the military-topographical realities of the Jordan Valley. This application of knowledge is what drives the reconstruction, makes it work: historiography always represents a refraction of what the author believes happened once through what he or she thinks happens generally.

Other biblical narratives make comparable use of architectural data or court protocol to reconstitute the past. Among their number, the cases of Tamar's rape, Absalom's consultation with Ahitophel and Hushai, and Solomon's designation as heir have been touched on in this chapter's section entitled "The Palace." In no case does the historian indulge in fanciful rearrangement of familiar facilities or of recognized custom. These accounts, and the Ehud account in particular, presume the reader's predictable knowledge, instead of providing elaborate explanations of an author's imaginative departures from reality. This has the obvious implication that such narratives are reliable in their incidental details. In concert with the evidence that Judges 3 is a historical reduction from the storytelling tradition, it means further that the historian grounds his reconstruction as far as possible in the reality of Israelite life. His interest lies in recreating events experienced by real people in real time. The Ehud account, so bare, so terse, is as close as the ancient world comes to modern historical narrative. What must one add or subtract to convert it into history? Hardly a word.

The historian's reliance on sources does not certify that his account is accurate. He may have imposed the wrong usage or the wrong palace layout on an earlier Moabite court. His oral sources may not have been historical in orientation, as he thought, but may have been shaped instead by xenophobia vis-à-vis Moab (as Exod. 15:13f.). These are not, however, limitations that preclude the account's being history (Chapter 1). Its aim is to communicate to the reader an allegedly accurate record of physical and mental transactions. It is a meticulous, efficiently crafted, minimal, antiquarian reconstruction,[74] a contribution to the history of premonarchic Israel.

The case of Ehud involves selection, representation, mentalism—"fictionalization," as addressed in Chapter 1. Ehud speaks! But the reader must take care not to interpret such actualization more literally than its author intended. If we reproached the historian, "Those were not Ehud's words!" he would perhaps smile at our naïveté—one cannot argue that the romantic elements of the narrative should be amended. If we taxed him, "None of that occurred," his reaction would be more vigorous. History, as already noted, is all fictionalized, and yet history. An art, mediated by language, it differs from romance in degree and in intention—it is less metaphorical, more literal, and more often meant to convey accurate information at the literal level of discourse. Mark Twain wrote, "The difference between the right word and the almost-right word is the difference between lightning and the lightning bug." *Fictionalized* history is the almost-right word. This is history, historical narrative, intended by reenactment to communicate antiquarian data.

Notes to Chapter 3

1. With W. Richter, *Traditionsgeschichtliche Untersuchungen zum Richterbuch* (BBB 18; Bonn: Hanstein, 1963), vv. 12–15a, 30 are a formulaic framework. See Chapter 6. Hereafter Richter's book is referred to as *TUR*.

2. The setting in Cisjordan is disputed; but the Moabite path homeward crosses the Jordan in v. 28, which is why the framework mentions "the city of palms," and why it says Moab "occupied" (*yrš*) it, not "conquered" or "smote" it. Cf. W. Nowack, *Richter* (HAT; Göttingen: Vandenhoeck & Ruprecht, 1902); A. Malamat, "The Period of the Judges," in B. Mazar, ed., *Judges* (WHJP 1/3; (Tel Aviv: Massada, 1971) 154f.; M. Garsiel, "The Ehud ben-Gera Episode (Judges 3:12–30)," in *Sepher Ron* (Tel Aviv: Don, 1974), 61f. (Hebrew); Richter, *TUR* (n. 1) 9f., with vv. 15–26 in Transjordan (but the geographic details in vv. 19, 26, should then center on the river, not some feature near Gilgal).

3. Older versions render "and the excrement came out" (V *cibus/stercus eius eiectus;* T *ʾwklyh špyk*); cf. Heb. *prš*, read by K. Budde (*Das Buch der Richter* [KHCAT 7; Freiburg: Mohr, 1897], 31), arguing corruption from *msdrwnh*. It is difficult to see what other rendering could be appropriate. RS 24.258 (*Ugaritica* 5:546–51) also mentions this commonplace of death. Cf. C. F. Burney, *The Book of Judges* (2nd ed.; London: Rivingtons, 1920), 72f.; O. Gläser, "Zur Erzählung von Ehud und Eglon. (Ri. 3,14–26)," *ZDPV* 55 (1932): 81f., with *pršydnh* parallel to *msdrwnh* as Ehud's avenue of egress ("a place of excrement"), followed by W. von Soden, "Zum akkadischen Wörterbuch. 61–66," *Or* 24 (1955): 136–45, with lexical evidence (CT XIX 27a I 5; MSL XII 109:174, Akk. *parašdinnu* equals [. . .]HABRUD.DA) and a supposed Hittite etymon. This theory would demand the formulation *wysʾ ʾhwd hpršdnh*. If the Sumerian equivalent is "hole," read "It came out at the anus."

4. In 1 Samuel 24:3 the phrase denotes something Saul seeks out the privacy of a cave to do, from which he afterward "arose," in the course of which David could, undetected, cut a corner from his (limp) robe. Defecation is indicated. According to Josephus (*Bell.* 2.148f.), the Essenes shielded themselves when defecating, which probably reflects an application of this expression to the prohibition against exposing excrement to Yhwh's sight in Deuteronomy 23:13–15. Cf. Y. Yadin, *The Temple Scroll* (Jerusalem: I.E.S., 1977), 1.233–35 (Hebrew); Hesiod, *Works and Days* 727–732. On the element of privacy, cf. Herodotus 2.36.

5. G^AB and V see ambidexterity here, and carry it into Judges 3:15; 20:16. These passages are not, however, comparable.

6. The joust in Mark Twain's *Connecticut Yankee in King Arthur's Court* translates the incident aptly. On the sling's accuracy, note A. Christie, *An Autobiography* (N.Y.: Ballantine, 1978), 46.

7. Y. Yadin, *The Art of Warfare in Biblical Lands* (London: Weidenfeld and Nicolson, 1963), 64, 296f. Cf. M. Korfmann, "Die Waffe Davids. Ein Beitrag zur Geschichte der Fernwaffen und zu den Anfängen organisierten kriegerischen Verhaltens," *Saeculum* 37 (1986): 129–49.

8. Yadin, *Art* (n. 7), 68f. (Middle Bronze example); M. Gihon, "The System of Fortifications in the Kingdom of Judah," in J. Liver, ed., *The Military History of the Land of Israel in Biblical Times* (Israel: Maarkhot, 1964), 415; E. Stern, "The Fortified City Gate and the Struggle for it under the Monarchy," ibid., 400–407 (both Hebrew). Examples include Iron II Tell en-Nasbeh, Tel Miqneh, and MB II Shiloh. The connection to the Ehud story was made, in conversation, by S. Talmon (1971).

9. A. Malamat, "Early Israelite Warfare and the Conquest of Canaan," *Fourth Sacks Lecture* (Oxford: Centre for Postgraduate Hebrew Studies, 1978), 13–19. On tactics, see

further J. H. Breasted, *The Battle of Kadesh: A Study in the Earliest Known Military Strategy* (University of Chicago Decennial Publications 3; Chicago: University of Chicago, 1903), 81–126; S. Yeivin, "Canaanite and Hittite Strategy in the Second Half of the Second Millennium B.C.," *JNES* 9 (1950): 101–107.

10. Rashi, Qimhi; P. M.-J. Lagrange, *Le Livre des Juges* (Paris: V. LeCoffre, 1903), 52.

11. Yadin, *Art* (n. 7), 254f.

12. So G. F. Moore, *A Critical and Exegetical Commentary on Judges* (ICC; New York: Scribner's, 1910), and, effectively, Gersonides.

13. H. Winckler, *Alttestamentliche Untersuchungen* (4 vols.; Leipzig, E. Germany: E. Pfeiffer, 1893–1906), 1.55–57; Moore, *Judges* (n. 12); Burney, *Judges* (n. 3); Budde, *Richter* (n. 3).

14. As Garsiel, "Ehud" (n. 2), 70f.

15. See B.-Z. Eshel, "*tyqym, sdrwt* and *msdrwn* in Biblical Usage," *Leshonenu* 37 (1972–73): 10; A. Salonen, *Die Türen des alten Mesopotamien* (Annalen Academiae Scientarum Fennicae B/124; Helsinki: Suomalainen Tiedeakatemia, 1961), 74ff. M. Waelkens, *Die kleinasiatischen Türsteine* is unavailable to me. Cf. E. G. Kraeling, "Difficulties in the Story of Ehud," *JBL* 54 (1935): 205–210. Kraeling's example does not relate to a double door, and confuses a latch with a lock. See latterly, A. Malamat, " 'Doorbells' at Mari—A Textual–Archaeological Correlation," *Cuneiform Archives and Libraries* (CRRA 30; Istanbul: Nederlands Historisch-Archaeologisch Instituut te Istanbul, 1986), 160–167, especially 167, n. 30.

16. The former in 2 Samuel 19:1; 2 Kings 1:2; 23:12; Jeremiah 22:13f.; 1 Chronicles 28:11; 2 Chronicles 3:9; 9:4; Psalm 104:3; Nehemiah 3:31f. The latter in 1 Kings 17:19, 23; 2 Kings 4:10.

17. Note also Proverbs 8:3; 9:3, 14; 11:11; Job 29:7.

18. So Garsiel, "Ehud" (n. 2), 62; Yadin, *Temple Scroll* (n. 4), 2.19. See now the *byt qwrh* with an *(ªliyyâ* near the Dead Sea in M. Broshi and E. Qimron, "A House Sale Deed from Kefar Baru from the Time of Bar-Kokhba," *IEJ* 36 (1986): 201–14, especially 206:2.

19. For which one expects Heb. *ngš* or *qrb*. The expression "enter unto someone" (*bôʾ ʾel*), when not metaphorical (Gen. 6:13; 42:21; 43:23, and use with impersonal subjects), denotes entering someone's presence from somewhere else (Judg. 13:6, 10; 1 Sam. 23:27; 25:5), and generally implies entry into a structure or private room, whence its occasional sexual overtones (as Gen. 16:4; 29:21, 23, 30; 30:4, 16; note Gen. 19:33; 39:14, where the use is not extended, with 39:17). Often the structure is not mentioned (Gen. 27:18; Judg. 4:22; 6:19; 1 Sam. 5:5; 14:29–33; 28:8; 2 Sam. 6:9; 19:6, and so on), and the verb alone has the same meaning (as 1 Sam. 3:10; 4:14; 26:7). Particularly clear is 2 Samuel 4:4–7. The most important parallels to the Ehud account occur in 2 Samuel 13:10ff.; 19:1–9; 1 Kings 2:13–22 (note v. 14 in contrast to v. 20); 2 Chronicles 29:18; Esther 6:5 (in a *bīt hilāni*?); especially 2 Kings 9:5f. (cf. also 2 Kings 9:1f.; Num. 8:22; Ezek. 44:2; probably Gen. 7:9–15, 16; 19:5, 8; Josh. 2:2–4 [entry to the house]; perhaps 1 Kings 1:47). In Judges 4:21 Yael reenters the tent from the doorway (v. 20) after collecting the peg and hammer. Only in 1 Samuel 28:21 are the bearings unclear: is Saul in a courtyard or an antechamber?

20. So Kraeling, "Difficulties" (n. 15), 205–210; Garsiel, "Ehud" (n. 2), 70. Cf. Burney, *Judges* (n. 3), 67f., with a two-source theory; on which C. Steuernagel, *Lehrbuch der Einleitung in das Alte Testament* (Tübingen, W. Germany: Mohr, 1912), 294.

21. See I. Singer, "Hittite *hilammar* and Hieroglyphic Luwian *hilana*," *ZA* 65 (1975): 69–103; cf. *RLA* 4.404–409; S. Alp, *Beiträge zur Erforschung des hethitischen Tempels. Kultanlagen im Lichte der Keilschrifttexte. Neue Deutungen* (Turk Tarih Kurumu Yayinlari 6/23; Ankara: Turk Tarih Kurumu, 1983), 325–32.

22. See H. Weidhaas, "Der *bīt hilāni*," *ZA* 45 (1939): 108–68, especially 115; D. Ussishkin, "King Solomon's Palace and Building 1723 at Megiddo," *IEJ* 16 (1966): 174–86. Attempts to find the designation in 1 Kings 6:4 or Jeremiah 22:14 have not been compelling.

23. Yadin, *Hazor* (Schweich Lectures, 1970; London: Oxford University, 1972), 154; on the dating, cf. Y. Aharoni, "The Stratification of Israelite Megiddo," *JNES* 31 (1972):

302–11; W. G. Dever, "Late Bronze Age and Solomonic Defenses at Gezer: New Evidence," *BASOR* 262 (1986): 9–34, 32, n. 34, with bibliography. For 1723, Ussishkin, "Palace 1723," (n. 22); *idem*, "On the Original Position of Two Proto-Ionic Capitals at Megiddo," *IEJ* 20 (1970): 213–15; "King Solomon's Palaces," *BA* 36 (1973): 78–105.

24. Solomon's portico would have the lowest length:width ratio (1.66:1) known (Tayanat IV is closest; a room with this ratio was found in 1986 at Tel Batashi, but the context is not yet exposed). It would probably have required internal columns to bridge the thirty-cubit width. Moreover, no *bīt hilāni* occurs to date in association with a structure like the House of the Forest of Lebanon.

25. "Paläste während der Bronze- und Eisenzeit in Palästina," *ZDPV* 99 (1983): 1–42; also, *idem*, "Die syrische Bauform des Hilani und die Frage seiner Verbreitung," *Damaszener Mitteilungen* 1 (1983): 443–58. Cf. Ussishkin, "Building IV in Hamath and the Temples of Solomon and Tell Tayanat," *IEJ* 16 (1966): 104–110, and note that the palace at Hamath, with a temple resembling Tayanat's and Solomon's (but with broadrooms), exhibits no features of the *bīt hilāni:* E. Fugmann, *Hama: Fouilles et Recherches 1931-1938* II.1 (Copenhagen: Nationalmuseet, 1958), 234, Fig. 308. Nor has such a structure appeared at Samaria or Ramat Rahel VB. In LB, note the elevated rooms off the pillared court in G. Loud, *Megiddo II: Seasons of 1935–39* (OIP 52; Chicago: University of Chicago, 1948), 23–28, 113f., with drains, esp. 4084. For Shechem and Amman, see R. C. Boling, "Bronze Age Buildings at the Shechem High Place," *BA* 32 (1969): 82–103; E. F. Campbell and G. E. Wright, "Tribal League Shrines in Amman and Shechem," *BA* 32 (1969): 104–116, but G.R.H. Wright, "Shechem and League Shrines," *VT* 21 (1971): 572–603. These are probably palaces, Shechem Stairway B and room B laid out as at Megiddo.

26. H. and M. Weippert, "Jericho in der Eisenzeit," *ZDPV* 92 (1976): 139–45.

27. L. Woolley, *Alalakh* (London: Society of Antiquarians, 1955), 113, Fig. 44; 92, Fig. 35; *Ugaritica* 4, Fig. 21; latterly, J. Margueron, "Un ⟨hilāni⟩ à Emar," *AASOR* 44 (1979): 153–76. Note also the palace of Shamshi-Adad I, and the western "reception suite" of Megiddo 2041. See H. Frankfort, "The Origin of the Bît Hilani," *Iraq* 14 (1952): 120–31.

28. Especially Khorsabad F; cf. Room H of Asshurnasirpal's NW Palace at Nimrud. In the West, R. Amiran and I. Dunayevsky, "The Assyrian Open-Court Building and its Palestinian Derivatives," *BASOR* 149 (1958): 25–32; G. W. van Beek, "Digging Up Tell Jemmeh," *Archaeology* 36 (1983): 12–19; R. S. Lamon and G. M. Shipton, *Megiddo I. Seasons of 1925–34. Strata I–V* (OIP 48; Chicago: University of Chicago, 1939), Fig. 89, Building 1369, with room 509 (cf. 1052); O. Tufnell, *Lachish III: The Iron Age* (London: Oxford, 1953), pl. 119. For a Babylonian derivation, see V. Fritz, "Die Paläste während der assyrischen, babylonischen und persischen Vorherrschaft in Palästina," *MDOG* 111 (1979): 63–74, emphasizing the courts. But the forms are mixed: see generally G. Turner, "The State Apartments of Late Assyrian Palaces," *Iraq* 32 (1970): 177–213.

29. At Sakcagözü, Zincirli Upper Palace I and *bīt hilānis* II, III, and IV, and Megiddo 1723 (with Ussishkin), one short side of the throne room is unabutted: J. Garstang, *The Hittite Empire* (London: Constable, 1929), 266, Fig. 29; F. von Luschan, *Ausgrabungen in Sendschirli* 4 (Königliche Museen zu Berlin. Mittheilungen aus den orientalischen Sammlungen 14; Berlin: Reimer, 1911). The throne rooms in Zincirli J (Kilamuwa's palace) and Tayanat Palace IV are unabutted on both short sides: R. C. Haines, *Excavations in the Plain of Antioch* 2 (OIP 95; Chicago: University of Chicago, 1958). On Halaf, F. Langenegger, K. Müller, and R. Naumann, *Tell Halaf* 2 (Berlin: de Gruyter, 1950).

30. Except Zincirli III and Alalakh. Zincirli Upper Palace A and H divide the light between northern and southern exposures. Note Fritz, "Paläste während Vorherrschaft" (n. 28), 69.

31. Tiglath-Pileser, Clay Tablet R18; Sargon, Display 161f.; Sennacherib in D. D. Luckenbill, *The Annals of Sennacherib* (OIP 2; Chicago: University of Chicago, 1924), 97:82.

32. "Der *bīt hilāni* im *bīt šaḫūri* des Assur-Tempels," *ZA* 70 (1980): 258–73 and Fig. 4.

33. "Art as Evidence for Interaction: Relations between the Assyrian Empire and North

Syria," in H.-J. Nissen and J. Renger, eds., *Mesopotamien und seine Nachbarn* (Berliner Beiträge zum Vorderen Orient 1; Berlin: Reimer, 1982), 355–82.

34. Ibid., 363f., and n. 50; B. Meissner and P. Rost, *Noch einmal das bît hillâni und die assyrische Säule* (Leipzig, E. Germany: Pfeiffer, 1893), 7; Meissner, "Das bît hilâni in Assyrien," *Or* 11 (1942): 251–61.

35. See Winter, "Art as Evidence" (n. 33), 363, especially 362 on Sargon. Tiglath-Pileser claims to have built a *bît hilâni* "for (his) leisure," *ana multaʾûtiya.*

36. 1 Kings 6:2, 5f., 10; 2 Chronicles 3:3; windows in 1 Kings 6:4. See T. A. Busink, *Der Tempel von Jerusalem 1. Der Tempel Salomos* (Studia Francisci Scholten Memoriae Dicata 3; Leiden, Neth.: Brill, 1970), 180–92 and Fig. 52. For clerestory illumination, see also the Israel Museum's clay model shrine (*IMJ* 82.24.415). Note *CTA* 4.7.13–47 on the window in Baal's palace, which, in light of the foregoing feast, is probably installed to ventilate smoke. This text at least suggests that the "windows" of 1 Kings 6:4 are windows, not pier-and-rubble construction. Note that 1 Kings 8:12 is corrupt (see OG), and *ʿrpl* there not tenebrousness, but a local environment of Yhwh (cf. Exod. 20:18). For identification of the temple with the *bît hilâni*, see E. Grant and G. E. Wright, *Ain Shems Excavations V* (Haverford: Haverford College, 1939), 68–69, with bibliography.

37. So 2 Kings 9:30–32; cf. Genesis 26:8, with Isaac and Rebecca out of town; note Jeremiah 22:13f. Also *bît hilâni* III and L of Palace K at Zincirli.

38. Tayanat I, IV (staircase only to top of portico unless the user crossed the upper level of the throne room), Zincirli K (4 or 5), J10, Megiddo 1723M (public stairs in 1723G, Zincirli J GK), probably Zincirli III, I, Upper Palace C (B), Megiddo 6000.

39. Both with *ʿaliyyâ*. For Wen-amun, however, cf. G.P.F. van den Boorn, "*Wdʿ-ryt* and Justice at the Gate," *JNES* 44 (1985): 1–25, which links the term used here with judgment, which would bring it into line with the "hall of judgment" as the denomination for Solomon's throne room, presumably with an *ʿaliyyâ;* W. A. Ward, "Late Egyptian *ʿr.t:* the So-Called Upper Room," *JNES* 44 (1985): 329–35, arguing that the Wen-Amun is in a throne room, and that these are on the ground floor (the problem is, upper stories do not survive; and Wen-Amun has a clear view of the sea, below). Also Genesis 26:8, looking down from above (the verb, *šqp*).

40. See A. Mazar, *Excavations at Tell Qasile* (Qedem 12; Jerusalem: I.E.S., 1980), 68f., for instances; F. Langenegger, et al., *Tell Halaf* (n. 29), 2.349–57; Fugmann, *Hama* (n. 25), II.1, 235, Fig. 309, and Ussishkin, "Building IV at Hamath" (n. 25); M.E.L. Mallowan, *Nimrud and its Remains* (London: Collins, 1966), 1.236, 262, 263, figs. 199, 242, 244; Y. Aharoni, "Arad: Its Temple and Inscriptions," *BA* 31 (1968): 19; *idem, IEJ* 34 (1984): 34. Contrast Busink, *Tempel* (n. 36), 199–207, 397ff.; but note the elevation at Beth-Shean, and his comments on Lachish. In temple 2048 at Megiddo (*Megiddo* [n. 25] 2. Figs. 402–404), the bench in VIIB reflects a dais in the niche in VIII.

41. See T.N.D. Mettinger, *The Dethronement of Sabaoth* (CBOTS 18; Lund, Sweden: Gleerup, 1982), 19–22; Akk. *parakku*, Ug. *ʾlt ṭbt*, Heb. *mākôn*. Further, J. W. and G. M. Crowfoot, *Early Ivories from Samaria* (London: P.E.F., 1938), 11.

42. The carrying poles sat 1.5 cubits above the adyton floor (Exod. 25:10), and the front of the ark, therefore, about 9 cubits recessed. Contrast Busink, *Tempel* (n. 36), 201–203, 283f., with the poles unnecessarily sideways. That the poles were unseen from outside the temple has to do with the steps leading to it, which Busink, too, reconstructs.

43. Assyrian thrones stood at ground level, despite the clerestory, and may have had no upper chamber. Busink (*Tempel* [n. 36], 284f.) would place Yhwh on a Solomon-like platform. For cherub throne, with footstool, see G. Loud, *The Megiddo Ivories* (OIP 52; Chicago: University of Chicago, 1939), 4:2a, b. Note further the illustration on the Ahiram sarcophagus.

44. Tripartite temples have double-doored adytons at Tayanat (C. W. McEwan, "The Syrian Expedition of the Oriental Institute of the University of Chicago," *AJA* 41 [1937]: 8–16) and Hazor (Y. Yadin, *Hazor 3–4* [Jerusalem: Magnes, 1961], 126:2–3, 101f., with sockets in front of the niche). At Lachish, Tufnell describes (*Lachish* [n. 28], 3.141f.) "a small circular hole in the plaster to act as a drain" in the center of the adyton doorway, "with another drain near the recess or cupboard to the left of the door-

way." The drain to the left contained various fragments of objects, the "small circular hole" none. The latter probably received the vertical post that anchored the double doors when closed. Note Mallowan, *Nimrud* (n. 40), 1.42.

45. Note especially 2 Kings 9:13, where some steps form the platform for a makeshift "throne," and such texts as 1 Kings 1:37, 47; Isaiah 22:23; Jeremiah 17:12; Ezekiel 1:26; 10:1; Isaiah 66:1; Psalm 11:4; 1 Samuel 2:8. See further, K. Kenyon, *Royal Cities of the Old Testament* (New York: Schocken, 1971), 50–66. Solomon's lion-throne was, in fact, probably on a platform.

46. The layout is paralleled in the Stratum VI temple at Beth Shean, for which see A. Rowe, *The Four Canaanite Temples of Beth-Shan* (Philadelphia: University of Pennsylvania, 1940), 6–21. See further, D. Ussishkin, "Levels VII and VI at Tel Lachish and the End of the Late Bronze Age in Canaan," in J. N. Tubb, ed., *Palestine in the Bronze and Iron Ages. Papers in Honour of Olga Tufnell* (London: Institute of Archaeology, 1985), 213–30 on the Level VI Area P temple at Lachish, with further comparisons and literature. Cf. a temple type podium in what may be a residency, *IEJ* 34 (1984): 34. Busink (*Tempel* [n. 36] 199ff.) hypothesizes an unraised adyton in Jerusalem, which, apart from falling afoul of 1 Kings 8:8 (above, and n. 42), and of the layout at Arad and Lachish, demands that the nave be considered as separate from the adyton. But the adyton, which develops from the cult niche, is part of the nave, and the throne platform a part of the audience hall. On both points V. Fritz ("Der Tempel Salomos im Licht der neueren Forschung," *MDOG* 112 [1980]: 53–68) lines up with Busink's position, but based largely on etymology. Note that von Luschan (*Sendschirli* [n. 29], 4.296–99) thought that the hearths served a sacramental function. They are not solely for heat, as they appear in the summer and winter palaces (J and K) at Zincirli. For heat, braziers were employed.

47. So 2 Kings 1:2; 6:26, 30 (the king with a cloak thrown over his sackcloth). Saul's *môšab qîr* (1 Sam. 20:25) could be either atop the wall (1 Kings 4:10) or against it. The Assyrian remains shed no light, because the better first-story lighting there and the absence of a strong tradition of raised daises (Mazar, *Qasile* [n. 40], 68f.) attenuate the impulse to elevation. There is a parallel in the raised adyton of the Arad temple, inside the nave. For this, and for a putative wood screen (as of a throne platform), see Y. Aharoni, "The Solomonic Temple, the Tabernacle and the Arad Sanctuary," in H. A. Hoffner, ed., *Orient and Occident* (Fs. C. H. Gordon; *AOAT* 22; Kevelaer: Butzon & Bercker, 1973), 1–8, with bibliography, and indications of priestly offices surrounding the temple, as in Jerusalem. Note that Busink (*Tempel* [n. 36], 208) has the adyton in Jerusalem built on wood. It should be added that heavy concentrations of wood found in throne rooms, as, e.g., at Halaf or the Hama temple, are not sufficient evidence of an upper chamber: see M.E.L. Mallowan, "The Excavations of Nimrud (Kalhu), 1956" *Iraq* 19 (1957): 1–25, especially 15, with much wood found by a throne dais in Ezida, with "stone tram lines" for a fire wagon leading up to it.

48. See Chapter 9, n. 28, and E. Weidner, *Politische Dokumente aus Kleinasien* (BoSt 8–9; Leipzig: Hinrichs, 1923), 18:60–61 ("Let no one sit with her") for the import of the queen's (or queen mother's) throne station.

49. Cf. 2 Kings 4:21, 32–37: the Shunamitess waits outside, at a remove of two rooms from Elisha's *ʿaliyyâ*. Gehazi is in the four-room-house courtyard. But the resonance of zones of holiness may be in play. Cf. also 2 Samuel 21:13f. On the roofing of the courtyard, see the forthcoming study of J. S. Holladay, "The Stables of Ancient Israel," in Fs. S. Horn.

50. As Lagrange, *Juges* (n. 10), 56, 60, citing Bonfrère, presumably *Josue, Judices et Ruth commentario illustrati* (Paris: 1631), unavailable to me; Budde, *Richter* (n. 3); C. Rabin, "Etymologica-Miscellanea," *SH* 8 (1961): 394; Eshel, *"ʾtyqym"* (n. 15), 3–12, equating *msdrwn* with a reconstruction of *ṡdrwt*.

51. Cf. R. Alter, "Sacred History and Prose Fiction," in R. E. Friedman, ed., *The Creation of Sacred Literature: Composition and Redaction of the Biblical Text* (Near Eastern Studies 22; Berkeley: University of California, 1981), 19f., suggesting that the account makes a butt of Moabite stupidity. But Ehud's tactics shine only against a realistic background, in which the Moabites, if plodding, are not preternaturally obtuse.

52. Here the suffix conjugation is used 1) in subordination (vv. 18, 22); 2) in negation (28, 29); and 3) to start units of narrative (19, 20, 24, 26; on v. 23, see n. 57). Thus the perfect-imperfect, as in v. 26, is the expected sequence.
53. Narrators use the *hapax* chiefly to denote unusual qualities or items. See H. R. Cohen, *Biblical Hapax Legomena in the Light of Akkadian and Ugaritic* (SBLDS 37; Missoula: Scholars, 1978).
54. See S. Talmon, "The Presentation of Synchroneity and Simultaneity in Biblical Narratives," *SH* 27 (1978): 9–26; C. Kuhl, "Die 'Wiederaufnahme'—ein literarkritisches Prinzip," *ZAW* 64 (1952): 1–11; B. O. Long, "Framing Repetitions in Biblical Historiography," *JBL* 106 (1987): 385–99. The similar epanalepsis in v. 26 (perfect-imperfect *mlṭ*) frames action occurring while the courtiers dally. See also the progressive epanalepsis of Genesis 15:12, 17.
55. Genesis 7:16; Isaiah 26:20; Judges 9:51; 3:22; Job 9:7; 2 Kings 4:3, 5a, 33, 4a *bis*, 21, all clear. The preposition implies enfolding (57 of 102 occurrences involve intercession on someone's behalf, which is linked to the connotation of physical shielding, as Job 1:10; Lamentations 3:7; Psalm 3:4; Jonah 2:7, and 6 other references). Note Amos 9:10 (preventing flight). Genesis 20:18; 1 Samuel 1:6 thus describe Yhwh sealing wombs from outside. The preposition otherwise implies defenestration or peering down from a window (the exception is Joel 2:9). The expression for locking someone *out* of a room is to close *ʾhry* (2 Sam. 13:17, 18). Note Joshua 2:7; Ezekiel 46:12; Genesis 18:10, with Yhwh outside the tent.
56. So Gersonides, AV, Bonfrère (Lagrange, *Juges* [n. 10], 55); Eshel, "ʾtqym" [n. 15], 10. The sequence of subjects from v. 23 on is: Ehud, Ehud, x, Ehud, Eglon, and any alternation could only cause confusion.
57. Though v. 23 suggests ongoing action (imperfect *wysgr*), *wnʿl*, "he bolted (them)" suggests action out of sequence. This is sometimes emended (Moore, *Judges* [n. 12], 99), but 2 Samuel 13:18 furnishes a counterexample. *wnʿl* could be infinitive absolute, neither adverbial nor simultaneous (Exod. 8:11), suggesting circumstantiality. Genesis 41:43 exemplifies the use, where the clause with infinitive absolute parallels the preceding two verses, linking to the Pharaoh's commission.
58. See A. Parrot, *Le Palais: Architecture* (Mission Archéologique de Mari 2; Paris: Geuthner, 1958), pl. XLVI: 2, 3, 224f.; Winter, "Art as Evidence" [n. 33], 360–62; Turner, "State Apartments" [n. 28], 192–94, with seat fittings; *ABL* 487. For elaborate plumbing at LB Ugarit, including some for upper stories, see Y. Calvet, "Ougarite. Une maison bien aménagée," *Le Monde de la Bible* 48 (March-April 1987): 15.
59. Mallowan, *Nimrud* (n. 40), 2.442. That the posts shored up the roof is unlikely; probably they helped screen off the king's end of the hall. Note also the toilet on the royal podium in MB IIC-LB I Megiddo Palace 4031 (and cf. LB I Palace 2134 above it).
60. One by Kenyon, two by Y. Shiloh (seventh century). Compare the furniture fitted with chamberpots at Versailles. Contrast M. Kochavi, "The Canaanite Palace of Aphek and its Inscriptions," *Qad* 10 (1977): 62–68, especially 67.
61. See AV. G^A translates *prostada*, "porch," G^B *diatetagmenoi* (equals *mᵉsuddarim*?). G^B doubles its translation of the term to make Ehud lock the doors after his departure (cf. Qimhi). All these renderings are tentative. No early evidence links the root with pillars.
62. "The Root SDR, 'Blindness' and Two Old Testament Hapax Legomena," forthcoming. Golomb points to Job 10:22 and the Targum to Genesis 19:11, as well as to Arab. *sadira* ("to be blinded").
63. For the parallel, see *KAI* 10:14f., the fragment in the Beirut Museum, but joined in M. Dunand, "Le Stèle de Yehavmilk," *BMB* 5/5 (1941): 57–85. For the context, see Dunand, *Fouilles de Byblos I: Texte* (Bibliothèque archéologique et historique 24; Paris: Paul Geuthner, 1939), 81–84, 87. Cf. Jeremiah 49:10; Isaiah 45:3.
64. See especially R. H. Kennett, *Ancient Hebrew Social Life and Custom as Indicated in Law, Narrative and Metaphor* (Schweich Lectures 1931; London: Oxford University, 1933), 28, hypothesizing egress through a sewer in an outer wall; also, Gläser, "Erzählung" (n. 3), 82; cf. Kraeling, "Difficulties" (n. 15) 208: "It is difficult to treat the suggestion seriously!"

65. Budde, *Richter* (n. 3), 30; Kraeling, "Difficulties" (n. 15), 206f. This excludes the suggestion that Ehud went to Gilgal for an oracle, a view based on the declaration of v. 20, *after* Ehud has gained privacy with Eglon.

66. Not, as commonly held, to receive an oracle. There is no Israelite tradition of kings rising for prophets. In K4310 1.30 (4R² 61), an oracle of Ishtar of Arbela to Esarhaddon ends, *atabbe uššab*, "I shall rise up; you sit!" This is not a reversal of a custom of standing to receive oracles, but an order to Esarhaddon to remain still, so that Ishtar can work alone (cf. Exod.14:13, 14). On the physics of Eglon's death, see LXX.

67. So Malamat, " 'Doorbells' at Mari" (n. 15), n. 30.

68. So Hamlet and Oedipus. Modern specimens of the genre mystify the reader instead, and Agatha Christie Mallowan's *Murder of Roger Ackroyd* (1936) is a sort of counterpart to Oedipus. Christie probably drew inspiration from Israel Zangwill's *Big Bow Mystery*, the first true locked-room mystery (the locking is incidental in "Murders in the Rue Morgue"): it, too, plays on the opportunities of a principal investigator. *Big Bow* is the earliest modern equivalent of the Ehud escapade.

69. Alter, "Sacred History" (n. 51), 20.

70. See Richter, *TUR* (n. 1), and Chapter 6, on the assembly of Judges 3ff.

71. This insight comes from Professor J. Meagher (oral communication).

72. Some heroic tales may have been reframed when reduced to writing—Hushai at Absalom's court, for example. The literary form of a story need not mirror its character in oral transmission.

73. E.g., Noth, *Überlieferungsgeschichtliche Studien* (Halle: Niemeyer, 1943), 89–92, where the "all-Israel" redaction is seen as the work of the second editor, Dtr.

74. For comparable perspectives on the historiography, see M. Liverani, "Memorandum on the Approach to Historiographic Texts," *Or* 42 (1973): 178–94; A. R. Millard, "The Old Testament and History: Some Considerations," *Transactions of the Victorian Institute* 110 (1983): 34–53.

CHAPTER 4

Sisera and Old Lace
The Case of Deborah and Yael

With regard to the people of past time, we are in the same position as
with dreams to which we have been given no association—and only a
layman could expect us to interpret such dreams as those.
—FREUD TO L. STRACHEY (TR. W. KENDRICK)

The historian who recounted Ehud's exploits drew on several sources
to do so. He used the architecture of the palace, probably as it was in his
own day. He applied a familiarity with the Jordan Valley. And he depended on an old story, orally transmitted. It is unlikely that a literary
recension underlies his account. To judge from the treatments of Gideon, Jephthah, and Samson (Judges 6–16), and from 1 Samuel 24//26,
embellishment inherited in writing would not have been eliminated.
Still, the case of Ehud ben-Gera is one in which history was extracted,
successfully or not, from a source that was a romance.

The text addressed in this chapter presents an instance of the same, or
a similar, historian working with a written source. Again, the source is
not historical— it is a lyric celebration, not an attempt to describe an
event coherently. Again, the account exhibits a certain economy, and
other historiographic traits of the Ehud story. It does not plumb expan-
sively, as a novella on the subject might, either the characters of the
principals or the dramatic possibilities the materials offer.[1]

THE PROBLEM OF DEPENDENCE

Judges 4 and 5 reflect in parallel on the same event, a victory in the
Jezreel over a Canaanite field force commanded by Sisera. Judges 4, the
prose treatment, proceeds through the course of things as seen from the
Israelite side. Judges 5, the Song of Deborah (SDeb), is the lyric; impressionistic and episodic, it culminates in an icily sardonic portrait of Sisera's mother awaiting his return.

The analysis of this diptych starts from the relationship of the texts.
This presents the most formidable hurdle. Thus it is possible that they
represent independent variants. Whatever their polemical relationship

to one another, for example, the creation accounts in Genesis 1 and 2–3 reflect wholly skewed traditions. Similarly, the Deuteronomic premise that Moses expounded the Law only as Israel poised to cross the Jordan (and Amos 5:25; Jer. 7:22) bears no genetic relation to P's claims, surely traditional, that the Aaronic cult was erected whole in the wilderness (Exod. 25–Num. 10, with a "deuteronomy" in Num. [27:12ff.], 28–36, esp. 36:13).

Where differences between two variants are less severe, scholars most often appeal to relative dating to determine the direction of dependence. Passages shared by Kings and Chronicles, for example, are universally thought to come from Kings, because Chronicles is dated later. This is a weak argument: it does not exclude the possibility of a common source, and few biblical texts can be dated firmly. Thus nineteenth-century scholars determined that J reinterpreted an earlier P; their successors deftly reversed the relationship between these sources when they reversed their relative dating. This is not even to consider instances in which mutual infection makes parallel texts *interdependent*, or in which an author harmonizes disparate sources (Deut. 11:29f. with Deut. 27; Josh. 8:30–35 and Josh. 1–6).[2]

Short of secure dating, only one circumstance permits confidence as to the relationship between parallel texts: there must be substantive points of difference, preferably several, such that one text only could be derived from the other. In practice, this means that the author of the derivative version must have interpreted the source in a manner with which the modern analyst takes issue: if the two agree, no basis for arbitrating priority remains.

A simple instance is David's capture of Philistine idols in 2 Sam. 5:21//1 Chron. 14:12. In the first, "he bore them off" (*wyś'm*). In Chronicles, however, "David commanded that they be burned with fire." Qimhi (amplified in Mesudat Zion) clarified the conflict: he pointed *wyś'm* in 2 Samuel 5:21 as a causative (*way- yaśśî'ēm*, denominal from *maś'ēt*, "bonfire," instead of the normal *way-yiśśa'ēm*). By harmonizing, Qimhi recreated the thought of the interpreter. Chronicles read *wyś'm* as a causative, "He caused them to be set alight," a reading inspired by a hagiographic view of David. To resolve the ambiguity of the consonants, *wyś'm*, which might mislead the reader to think that David had actually taken Philistine idols home, Chronicles then introduced a fuller formulation. The text in Chronicles can have derived from Samuel, but the defective *wyś'm* in Samuel cannot reasonably be derived from Chronicles.

F. M. Cross has made a similar argument about the relationship between the Song of the Sea (Exod. 15) and the P account in Exodus 14. Neither the Song nor the J account in Exodus 14 has Israel crossing the sea, between walls of water or otherwise. Cross suggests that the cosmogonic motif of Sea's dissection influenced P's presentation, which is indisputable. It should be added, however, that P found a warrant for his reading in the source. He seems to have seen in Exodus 15:16 a crossing of the Reed Sea, instead of the Jordan (as Ps. 78:53ff.) The "heaped," "congealed [churning?]" waters of Exodus 15:8 suggested a pathway, by association with the tradition that Israel crossed the Jordan dry-shod (Josh. 3:14–4:11). The point is that the P account could have come from the Song; but the Song, with no walls of water, no Israelite crossing, could not have come from P. The relationship between the Song and J in Exodus 14 is similar.[3]

JUDGES 4 AND 5: THE DIFFERENCE

Judges 4 and SDeb are susceptible to the same sort of analysis. Two disparities between the accounts have, since the nineteenth century, provoked comment. First, the prose version asserts that only Zebulun and Naphtali participated in the battle against Sisera (vv. 6, 10). SDeb (vv. 13–18) claims that at least six tribes fought—Ephraim, Benjamin, Machir, Issachar, Zebulun, and Naphtali. The other difference concerns the manner of Sisera's demise. In the poem Jael the Qenite complies with Sisera's request for a drink. While he quaffs she sneaks up behind him and bludgeons him, so that he collapses at her feet (5:24–27). The prose is more elaborate; Sisera falls asleep, *after* drinking, in Jael's tent. Jael then creeps up with a mallet and pounds a tent peg through his skull and into the ground. There is no question of his falling after the blow (4:17–22).

Because of its implications for the extent of Israel's premonarchic league, the issue of which tribes participated has had pride of place in scholarly discussions. Some scholars side with the poem, on the ground that it is older. Others champion the prose, claiming somewhat perversely that it attributes victory to fewer tribes and is therefore more modest, hence more believable.[4]

A. Malamat has proposed that the prose and SDeb refer to two different stages in the conflict, the former to the battle, the latter to the pursuit. He compares the parallel accounts to the prose and poetic renditions of the battle of Qadesh.[5] The difficulty with this more sophisticated approach is that the poem situates the tribal muster *all* in the stage before the battle (5:9–18, and consecutive)$\bar{a}z$, "then," in v. 19). It portrays the Canaanite flight as mounted (v. 22) and, accordingly, makes no suggestion of pursuit by the Israelite infantry. Moreover, it, like the prose, sees the battle as climactic and decisive, the only part of the confrontation worth celebrating. If anything, it is from the prose that one should expect an enumeration of those who joined in afterward (cf. Judg. 7:24–8:3; 12:1–6).

Malamat stressed that SDeb seems to single out Zebulun and Naphtali as the tribes who risked most in the field (v. 18). A. Weiser also made this a critical juncture in an attempt to harmonize the versions. Weiser argued that the Song represents a liturgy from "the covenant renewal festival." The relevant section runs:

11d	Then the people of Yhwh came down to the gates.
12	Wake, wake, Deborah! Wake, wake, sing a song!
	"Arise, Baraq, and capture your captives, son of Abinoam!"
13	Then Israel came down as mighty ones;
	The people of Yhwh came down to him with warriors:
14	Out of Ephraim—their root is in Amaleq;
	After you (Ephraim), Benjamin, among your contingents;
	Out of Machir, rulers came down,
	And from Zebulun, those who wield the sceptre;
15	The officers of Issachar with Deborah,
	So [with] Baraq, dispatched to the valley at his command; . . .
18	Zebulun, a people who taunted death,
	And Naphtali, on the heights of the field.[6]

On Weiser's reading, verse 11d describes a procession to the sanctuary gates, to which tribes "came down" to celebrate the triumph. This explains why the name Zebulun is repeated (vv. 14, 18; on Naphtali, which Weiser adds, see n. 6): verse 18 refers not to the festival, but to the fighting. Meroz (v. 23) is cursed for not joining the fray; what appear to be gentle rebukes in verses 15c–17 address tribes whose lapse was a failure to attend only the celebration.[7] Like Malamat, therefore, Weiser distinguishes between the role of Zebulun and Naphtali (v. 18) and that of the other tribes.

Weiser's view, too, has weaknesses. The martial language of verses 11d, 12f., 14b, and 15b–c belies a context in purely cultic celebration, as does the absence of any marked transition between verses 11–17 and verse 18. One could read verses 9–11 with Weiser as a call to panegyrize the victory; but the following exhortation (v. 12b), "Arise, Baraq, and capture your captives," indicates that a battle, not a bacchanal, is brewing. There is no signal that the action in verses 11ff. is cultic (contrast Ps. 68:25–30).[8] Indeed, were there no Judges 4 to raise the question of which tribes participated, it is doubtful that either Malamat or Weiser would have proposed his interpretation of SDeb. Both have exploited the impressionistic quality of the poem to interpret it in line with the less malleable prose.

JUDGES 4 AND 5: THE DIRECTION OF DEPENDENCE

The methods applied to Judges 4 and SDeb, like Qimhi's treatment of 2 Samuel 5:21//1 Chronicles 14:12, have considerable value: the effort to harmonize provides a key to how the ancients resolved disparities between accounts; sometimes, as in Qimhi's case, it explains the derivation of one of the ancient texts. Harmonization in Judges 4 and 5 yields similar results: it reproduces not the intent of the poet, but that of the prose author interpreting the poem.

Judges 5:13–18 affirm that at least six tribes appeared on the field. Literally, however, their claims are modest: "the people of Yhwh came down to the gates" (v. 11d), "came down to him with warriors" (v. 13b); Ephraim, Benjamin, and Machir "came down" (to the gates, with warriors), as did Zebulun and Issachar (vv. 14f.). Thus, only verse 18 states unequivocally that Israelites actually fought—Zebulun and Naphtali, the combatants of Judges 4. The prose version can be seen to arise from a certain reading of the Song. The inverse relationship does not obtain.

Two factors probably conditioned the prose interpretation. First, after the list of participants in 5:13–15b comes a segment that appears to rebuke tribes who did not appear (5:15c–17). The Song, so read, supplied two classes of favorable mention: one, in verses 13–15b, with a counterpoint in 15c–17, and one, in verse 18, comprising the combatants. Zebulun's names appeared in *both* positive segments. This suggested that the action in verses 11–15b was not identical to the warfare in verse 18.

Second, it is not crystal clear what the tribes of verses 13–15b did. It is said that they "came down to the gates." Possibly the historian in Judges 4 read verses 10–11 as Weiser did, as a summons to celebrate the victory. Alternatively, he may have reckoned the tribes of 5:13–15b as being at the ready, but not, like Zebulun and Naphtali, on the field: the implication of military organization by tribe was that some units (i.e., tribes) were early committed to battle, while others were maintained, at the theater of war, in reserve (as Judg. 1:1–4; 20:18–21). This seems the most appropriate interpretation of SDeb, but is not reflected in a universal Israelite muster in the prose. Most probably, therefore, the historian understood the quiescent tribes anxiously to have awaited the outcome at the gates of their towns. This is the function of the gate, for example, in 1 Samuel 4:13–17; 2 Samuel 18:24–28. Thus verses 13–17 all related to those still at home: the tribes of verses 13–15b (including some of Zebulun) suspended all activity, awaiting tidings; those of 15b–17 did not gather anxiously.

This argument for the historian's use of the poem draws strength from the numbers furnished in the two chapters. Judges 4:10, 14 assign Baraq ten thousand troops (or ten brigades). The figure is not, as one might first expect, plucked from thin air. SDeb names ten tribes, of which, according to the prose, two fight (5:13–18). Judges 5:8 mentions forty thousand troops (or forty brigades), which are *unarmed*. If the prose author identified the unarmed citizenry with his eight idle tribes, simple division would produce the proportion of five thousand troops (or five brigades) per tribe, and the troop count for Zebulun and Issachar (ten thousand, or ten brigades) would result.[9] Again, the implication is that the prose understands the tribes of 5:13–17 to have remained at home. Again, the prose could have derived from the poem, but the reverse is unlikely indeed.

The hypothesis that the prose relies on SDeb also accounts for the discrepancies arising over Sisera's assassination. Even on its own merits, the prose version (4:17–22) is incongruous, with Jael steadying her spike on Sisera's skull and, taking careful aim—so as not to smash her thumb—hitting it on the head. What occult, atavistic impulse evoked such elaborate measures? Here is the Song:

24   Of women, Jael is most blessed,
     The woman of the Qenite community;
     Of the women of the tent she is blessed.
25   Water he asked;
     Milk she provided;
     In a lordly crater she proffered ghee.
26   She sent her hand to the peg,
     Her right hand to the workers' smiter.
     She smote Sisera;
     She smashed his head;
     She splintered, she broke through his gullet.[10]
27   At her feet, he kneeled, fell, stretched out.
     At her feet, he kneeled, he fell.
     Where he kneeled, there he fell, slain.

More epicurean relish over Sisera's collapse could not be expressed.

That there is some relationship between the prose and the Song here is clear. Judges 5:25 describes Sisera's request for a beverage and the hospitality it elicited; the prose in 4:19 has the same sequence. The discrepancy surfaces in the matter of whether Sisera stretched out before or after Jael's blow. But this is only the visible symptom of a discrepancy in the mechanics of the murder. The bizarre killing, with hammer and spike, in 4:21, is explicable, perhaps uniquely, on the assumption that the prose historian used SDeb as a source: as Wellhausen observed, he took 5:26a, b to describe two different hands and two different implements.[11] The historian construes some couplets figuratively, as synonymous statements in parallelism: "Milk she provided; in a lordly crater she proffered ghee" has as a reflex the offering of only one beverage in the prose; similarly, the prose transposes the poem's ceramic vessel into a pastoral wineskin, in accordance with the setting in Jael's tent. Conversely, the couplet in 5:26 is taken literally, as a description of successive actions.

Probably the author of Chapter 4 did not recognize the fact that one could strike an effective blow with a *yāted,* here "(tent) peg." In nine of its eleven other occurrences in HB (only Deut. 23:9 and Zech. 10:4 sugget it would make an adequate blunt instrument), this noun denotes a sort of rivet (as Exod. 27:19; Isa. 22:23; Judg. 16:14). A spike wanted a hammer to propel it, and the historian found the hammer in 5:26b. He must have seen 5:26e as confirmation: *ḥlph rqtw,* "she broke through-/pierced his gullet" could be taken to show that the "spike" penetrated through the head; Judges 4:21 duly reports that Jael "drove the 'spike' into his gullet" (*rqtw,* n. 10).

From this point, all the other differences in the two accounts follow logically. After all, Sisera could not have stood still and aware, as in SDeb, while Jael leveled a tent peg against his skull and reared back with the hammer. Physics and verisimilitude demanded that Sisera be lying down before Jael struck the blow (4:18c, 19b, 21g). This led to a difficulty—Sisera could not fall *after* the blow, as he does in 5:27. But this was a minor problem, easily dismissed (see the following section), compared with that of having him posing upright to receive the tent peg. The timing of Sisera's fall is different in the two versions, because the killings are different.

In theory, an inverse dependence, of the song on the prose, is possible. The poet could have represented Jael's taking up her hammer and tent peg in a single parallel couplet (v. 26). But the poet could have no reason to make Sisera collapse after the blow. There is every reason, contrariwise, for the prose historian to put Sisera on the ground *before* the blow: even in the face of the poetic sequence, sensible reconstruction demands it. As in the matter of which tribes fought, the prose can be derived from the verse, but not vice versa. In each case there seems to be a close relationship between the prose and the song. This hypothesis will be worked out in the remainder of the chapter. The focus, however, will be on the mechanics of the historian's reconstruction and its intent.

THE HISTORIAN AT WORK

The hypothesis of dependence is ringingly corroborated by its extensive explanatory power. Virtually no detail in Judges 4 is without an identifiable source; nearly all of them come from the poem, and from the historian's reconstruction of the event, based on a painstaking analysis of the poem. This case offers an exceptional opportunity to dissect the construction of a Biblical historical account.

THE MURDER, THE QENITES, AND THE GEOGRAPHY OF SISERA'S FLIGHT

The impediments to his reconstruction of Sisera's death did not escape the historian's notice. He confronted them in a way that illustrates just how answerable he felt both to his source and to questions an audience familiar with it might raise. Given, for example, that Sisera could not fall in Judges 4, what could be the meaning of 5:27? Here, a sequence of three verbs (*krʿ npl škb*) founds the description of Sisera's collapse; this formulation comes, appropriately in SDeb, at the end of the assassination account. The prose author provides a reading of the verse in a corresponding position, at the end of his own account of the killing, in 4:21g. He mirrors the poem's three successive verbs (5:27a) with a similar sequence of his own. But his report is out of place: he interprets 5:27 as *foregoing* action—Baraq "*had* slumbered, for he was tired, so he died" (*whw' nrdm wy'p wymt*). Judges 4:22, "and there was Sisera, fallen, dead" (*npl mt*), next corresponds, back in proper order, to 5:27c ("there he fell, slain") (*npl šdwd*).

The prose interpretation was conditioned in part by the use of *škb* as one of the verbs in 5:27; normally it means "lie down" (to sleep), so that the historian reconstructed from it Baraq's having dropped off earlier. Indeed, R. Boling, who perceived that the prose author discovered his hammer and peg in a literal reading of 5:26, actually reads 5:27 in accordance with the prose.[12] This course violates the poetic sequence; it also distorts the nuance of the verb *npl*, "he fell" (5:27 *tris*), which implies a collapse. Once again the prose provides guidance not for the meaning of the song, but for the prose interpretation of the song. But this interpretation is only a first step in a chain of implications, all following from the introduction of the double-weapon murder, that the historian, quite properly, feels driven to pursue.

The impressionistic poem does not furnish a reason for Sisera's applying to Jael. It suggests that he stopped outdoors, for a drink, and momentarily relaxed his guard (5:25). The prose author, however, had a fresh problem: how did Sisera come to lie down, and where?

The only logical place for Sisera to lie down was inside Jael's tent. Because the Canaanite had not yet reached safety (so 5:28–30), his only logical motive for entering the tent was to elude pursuit. He was, that is, in headlong flight, desperate for refuge. The wording of 5:24c (lit., "of women *in the tent*") may have added fuel to the reconstruction.

With this deduction, Sisera's drink lost the function it had served in SDeb. There it distracted the Canaanite while Jael crept up behind him. In the prose, however, Sisera enters the tent, instead of pausing outside, out of fear instead of thirst. The prose retains the drink, adding a motive: "for I thirst" (4:19). But the placement is awkward. Because Sisera has come to hide, Jael places him under cover (4:18). Now she must uncover him, serve the drink, and cover him up again (4:19). Commentators have long speculated that Jael employed milk as a soporific. There is no evidence that the Israelites cherished it for this quality. Quite the reverse, Sisera slumbers because the drug of exhaustion has overcome the adrenalin of fear (*wy'p*, 4:21g). But the commentators' urge to find a function for the drink expresses a sense, first, that the narrative is otherwise tightly drawn, and, second, that this element is now otiose. The historian has taken the element from SDeb (5:25) in order to include all the relevant action relayed by his source.

Once Sisera is ensconced in Jael's tent, the question is, How did she collect her tool kit without being espied? Here the historian is at his best. Jael has maneuvered Sisera under a coverlet, ostensibly to protect him

(4:18f.), but really because she is plotting his demise. This precludes his catching sight of her lurking sinisterly with the lethal spike. Moreover, Sisera himself stations Jael at the tent door, to deny his presence should any pursuers come calling (v. 20). The expedient carries no insinuations of cowardice, as identical devices in Joshua 2:4–7 and 2 Samuel 17:17–20 show. Rather, it is an integral part of hiding, which furnishes Jael the chance to secure from outside the tent the means for a killing (verse 21, with "she 'entered unto him,' " implying she had been outside, Chapter 3, n. 19). All this suffices to explain how Jael got into position. That Sisera did not feel the spike being steadied on his head is explained by his falling asleep (v. 21g), an element won from the historian's reading of 5:27.

If Sisera was to cower under Jael's carpet in hopes of avoiding capture, the historian had to provide pursuit. Thus he brings Baraq onto the scene right on the heels of the killing (v. 22). In the poem the Canaanite flight was mounted; this would prohibit pursuit by the Israelites (5:22), who lacked chariotry.[13] Here is the reason that the undoing of Sisera, who seemed to have escaped (5:22), is such a focus of the Song (vv. 24–30): it is a stroke of unforeseeable providence (5:31).[14]

The author of Judges 4 is not insensible of these limitations. He explicitly describes the Israelites as infantry: Zebulun and Naphtali "ascended [to Tabor] on foot" (brglyw) (4:10). Judges 5:15b describes Issachar as "dispatched brglyw"; the poet probably means that Issachar was "under [Baraq's] command" (cf. Exod. 11:8; Judg. 8:5; 2 Sam. 15:16–18). But the historian uses brglyw to mean "on foot" in 4:15, 17, as distinct from $^{\gamma}$hryw (v. 14) for "under his command." He probably construed the poetic reference to sustain his general outlook; AV (Issachar "was sent on foot into the valley") takes it the same way.

How could Israelites, on foot, overtake Canaanites? The prose historian tempers the vehicular retreat of 5:22 with a dose of military reality. He distinguishes the Canaanite chariotry from the camp. Baraq pursues both all the way to base; but only the camp is overtaken and exterminated (4:15f.). Because chariotry always operated in conjunction with other arms, the reconstruction of a mixed flight was almost demanded. At the Egyptian battles of Megiddo and Qadesh, too, the rout of the chariot arm led to pillage in the camp and pursuit. But the introduction of unmounted fugitives presents an opportunity to send Sisera scurrying from his chariot on foot, a fact that the historian stresses (4:15, 17). Now it is not so remarkable that his cohorts do not lift Sisera onto one of their own chariots: there are many men on foot. Nor is it remarkable that he so distances his pursuers as to find time to slumber beneath the winding that became his shroud. Baraq catches up with him just after the murder (4:22). His occupation with the stragglers accounts for any delay.

To this juncture, the logic of the account is as follows. The hammer-and-peg assault implied that Sisera must be lying, covered, in the tent.

This posture meant that he was hiding, and hiding implied pursuit. But for there to be pursuit, Sisera must have fled on foot, with Baraq far enough behind to allow Jael adequate leeway, but close enough to impel Sisera into her tent (4:22). Finally, Sisera's flight on foot implied that the rout was a mixed one, of both cavalry and camp. Everything in the prose follows from Jael's modus operandi. The poem, with its single murder weapon, mentions only mounted flight, and no pursuit.

One last question arises from the killing. What led Sisera to think he would find refuge with Jael? The Song poses no such question, because Sisera pauses, outdoors, for a drink. The Israelite of the prose histori-an's time, however, thought of the Qenites as friendlies (or sympathiz-ers: Judg. 1:16; 1 Sam. 15:6; 27:10; 30:29). Their pasturage, too, was in Canaan's southernmost reaches. Jael's role thus raised political and geo-graphic issues.

A logical inference satisfies the geographic problem. Reading 5:24 to identify Jael as "the wife of Heber the Qenite" (it could also be read, "the woman of the Qenite community"), the historian was compelled to deduce that Heber migrated north, outside the normal range of Qenite transhumance, to the vicinity of the battle.[15] Judges 4:11 provides a spe-cific location, Elon Bezaananim (*lwn bṣ'nnym*). The choice of this, as against other possible sites, may be a playful attempt to link the two heroines in the prose version—Deborah, with her tree (4:5), and Jael, at an *lwn* (cf. this chapter's section entitled "Deborah" for the link to Deb-orah) associated with spoil (*bṣ'*, 5:19d; cf. LXX in 4:11). But Elon Bezaan-anim was a real town in northern Naphtali (Josh. 19:33). The historian must have reckoned it as standing on Sisera's route home from the scene of battle. So the geographical data serves to orient the reader, in much the same way as does the architectural data in the Ehud story. The detail thus has two obvious valences: to explain how Jael happened to be on the path of Sisera's flight, a specific location was desirable; faced with this necessity, the author chose a site whose name served the structure of the narrative. A third, and more specific, reason for the choice remains.

Given the political realities known to the prose author, the question of why Sisera would seek refuge among the Qenites (and how Jael knew him well enough to hail him— 4:18), was a more taxing one. One expla-nation squires Sisera on his arrival: "There was (a treaty of) peace" be-tween Jabin, Sisera's overlord, and the "house of Heber the Qenite" (v. 17). The inference seems modest enough, reasoned in its way: "Heber" was a Canaanite friendly!

There is, however, a complication. Heber's encampment is set at Elon Bezaananim in verse 11. Six verses, and the battle, intervene before we learn of Heber's treaty with Hazor, when the issue of where Heber camped becomes relevant. Where verse 11 stands, it seems purely inci-dental to the narrative; it could just as well come in verse 17.

Verse 11 stipulates that Elon Bezaananim was "by Qedesh," where

Baraq musters his troops. The succeeding verse relates, "*They told* Sisera that Baraq ben-Abinoam had ascended Mt. Tabor." Formally, the verb could be impersonal. In context, though, the implication is that it was the house of Heber who informed on the Israelites (so G^A?). This is why Heber's encampment is mentioned in verse 11—not a verse before, nor in verse 17, but just where Heber first *acts* in the narrative. It explains the choice of a locale "by Qedesh." And it adds the final geographic factor: Heber had to camp near Baraq's muster, and on the route Sisera would take north from the site of the battle; Baraq's muster, therefore, had to be placed at some logical point in the same line, and Qedesh, for reasons some of which are explored in the following text, commended itself. Finally, all this serves to explain why Sisera sought refuge with Jael—the Qenites (verse 12) had provided intelligence when Baraq was mustering his troops.

It may seem on casual inspection that here the prose historian enters the realm of notional reconstruction. The song does not even hint that Sisera's arrival at Jael's tent was anything but fortuitous; and the treaty of verse 17 would alone have sufficed to explain it. But the historian had deduced that Israel and Yhwh had taken the initiative, and chosen the ground for the encounter at Tabor. This conclusion was founded on references in the Song: the exhortation to Baraq to "capture captives" (v. 12) implied that the encounter was planned; to Deborah herself is imputed the readying of Israel for the battle (vv. 7, 12); the role of the Qishon (v. 21) suggested divine manipulation; the elaborate treatment of the muster (vv. 11ff.) could be taken to reflect long and leisurely preparation; finally, the notice that "the kings came, they fought, then the kings of Canaan fought" (v. 19), coming after the long muster (vv. 11–18), implied both by the consecutive "then" and by the fact that the "kings *came*" that the Israelites had earlier assembled to await them. From all this it followed that Israel drew the Canaanites to the Qishon—and this becomes a centerpiece of Deborah's battle plan (4:7).

Baraq must have lured Sisera into the trap. To this end, however, Sisera must have been provided with intelligence (cf. 1 Sam. 23:19; 24:1; 26:1). An Israelite informant is not, in the circumstances, suitable; a Qenite itinerant is. In order to give Sisera reason to trust Jael, and on the principle of narrative economy, the historian accords Heber's household this second function. The image of the Qenite as an Israelite friendly leads both to an expansion of the Qenite role and to a location near Baraq's home. But the verisimilitude of the incident is substantial: the Hittite king, Muwatallis, similarly made use of itinerants to disinform Ramses II before the battle of Qadesh.

From the foregoing, it should be clear that the attempt to reconstruct a historical sequence out of the poetic source has determined the shape of the prose narrative. Every component of the murder account derives from the logic of the reconstruction (4:17–22). Sisera's slumbering under cover, Jael's watching, Heber's treaty, Baraq's pursuit, stem from the interpretation of Judges 5:26. Moreover, this segment of the narrative dictates as well some of the preceding action. The stress on unmounted flight, the location and role of the Qenite band, the region of Baraq's muster, all follow ultimately from the murder. Each of these has in turn its own links to the surrounding text, which deserve, briefly, to be identified.

OTHER ELEMENTS OF THE RECONSTRUCTION

There are a few other places where the prose historian was more or less driven to his representation of the event by evidence in the song. The instances involving association with other written sourses are treated in the next section. Three, however, reflect the further operation of pure exegetical logic.

The presentation of the Israelite victory is the first. Here, the prose does not spotlight the natural cataclysm that according to the verse struck Sisera at the Qishon.[16] One factor in this decision may have been theological: it was a tenet of Deuteronomistic dogma that the stars, cited as participants in the battle (Judg. 5:20), belonged to the nations, not Israel (Deut. 4:19), and were to be demythologized (Jer. 10:1ff.). If he shared it, this conviction would have compelled the prose historian to take 5:20–21 as figurative. In any event, the historian meant to focus on the flight, and therefore on the military, not the natural, discomfiture of the Canaanite host. A brief notice of Yhwh's intervention, using the verb *hmm*, "discomfit," to evoke associations with Yhwh's other great triumph involving water, that at the Reed Sea (4:15; cf. Exod. 14:24), is the result.[17] As in the Ehud story, the logic of the tale drives the historian along. The object is to render into the language of historical narrative, and acceptable historical causation, information inherited from another medium. The report emphasizes the human consequences of Yhwh's aid, deftly translating the religious metaphor of the ode into historiography. Throughout, this is the palpable motive underlying Judges 4.

Similar is the prose treatment of Deborah. Judges 5:7, 12, and 15 accord her the place of honor in reversing Israel's fortunes. It is her rise, not Baraq's, that alters the state of affairs. Correspondingly, in Judges 4, she is the one who takes command—she is the oracle (4:4a) who formulates Israel's battle plan (vv. 6f.), consistently instructing Baraq at crucial junctures (4:6–9, 14). Further, it is Deborah who tells Baraq, "Rise!" and sends him forth to fight (*qwm*, v. 14). The word, and the element, are drawn from SDeb. Judges 5:12a ("Wake, wake, Deborah! Wake, wake, speak a song!") is interpreted as the introduction to a direct speech by Deborah in 5:12b ("Rise, Baraq! . . ."). Immediately following, in 5:13 and in 4:14, the Israelite troops descend into the fray.

This explains several elements in the prose. If Deborah initiated the conflict (see this chapter's section entitled "The Murder, the Qenites, and the Geography of Sisera's Flight"), Israel must have baited Sisera to the battlefield. But Baraq could not have chanced into Deborah by the Qishon, then spontaneously summoned his troops: Deborah must have gotten in touch with Baraq to communicate her strategy to him. Here is the reason that Deborah summons Baraq to her residence in the central hills, before the muster of troops (4:6–9). And if Deborah ordered Baraq directly into battle, as the historian understood 5:12f. to imply, she must also have escorted him from the scene of their initial consultation to the lines. She had, thus, to be present at Tabor to stipulate the propitious moment for attack, and Baraq accordingly requests her accompaniment (4:8, read G).

Thus, having reconstructed an initial contact and subsequent collaboration between Deborah and Baraq, the historian had to supply a transition between the two. This line of reasoning produced the transactions in 4:6–9, 14. The scenario there was perhaps not the only one possible. But it was based on surmise, and fleshed out by the urge to have Deborah explain that Baraq's hope of capturing Sisera was to be disappointed (4:9; 5:12). Idle fancy was not involved. The same is true of the report that Baraq mustered his troops outside the theater of operations, and then disposed them to win surprise, before enticing Sisera into the snare (4:10–13; on Qedesh, see the section on "Baraq"). Whether the muster in Qedesh also responds to the Song's summons to the "gates" (i.e. towns, 5:11–13) is unclear.

There is one last instance revolving around a visible discrepancy between the prose and the poem. SDeb speaks of a confrontation at the Qishon, "at Taanach, on the waters of Megiddo" (5:19), on the southern side of the Jezreel. Judges 4:14 (and vv. 10, 12) situates the struggle at the foot of Mt. Tabor, on the northern rim of the Jezreel directly across from Megiddo. What evoked the reading of the prose?

SDeb describes the conflict as having occurred "on the heights of the field" ('al merômê śādeʰ), v. 18. Whatever the original (metaphoric?) import of the phrase, the historian was surely justified in seizing on this basis the high ground for the disposition of Baraq's troops. The Israelites, after all, had charged downhill into the affray (5:13; 4:14). The highlands bordering the Jezreel from the south were excluded, because, according to the prose reconstruction, the tribes of those regions did not fight. Mt. Tabor, however, stands on Qishon. It is, furthermore, the southernmost point common to the combatant tribes, Zebulun and Naphtali. For all these reasons, it was a logical selection.

Moreover, Israel had to be placed on a mountainside if the episode was to conform to premonarchic reality as the historian understood it. Israel mustered 10 brigades of foot soldiers (or 10,000 troops: 4:10, 14). Against this infantry the Canaanites could dispose a substantial body of chariotry, whose presence is all but explicit in the song (5:22).[18] The Canaanites' affinity for this arm has been remarked in this chapter's section entitled "The Murder, the Qenites, and the Geography of Sisera's Flight." Sisera accordingly fields "iron chariots," a term that appears only in Judges 1:19; Joshua 17:16, 18, to explain why Israel could not conquer the lowlands. Where their number (900) comes from is uncertain (4:13); a possible source is the 892 (923) chariots captured by Thutmosis III from the kings of western Asia (cf. SDeb, "kings of Canaan") at the battle of Megiddo.

To neutralize Sisera's shock force, the historian felt the need to have Israel join the issue before the chariotry formed up. A surprise charge from the concealment of a wooded height, in line with 5:18 and 5:13, fills the bill. This is the trap, thus, into which Sisera had to be lured (see this chapter's section entitled "The Murder, the Qenites, and the Geography of Sisera's Flight"). In sum, the selection of Tabor as the crucial site had much to recommend it, involving only a mild extension of the inexact parallelism in Judges 5:19.[19] Indeed, flooding in the Qishon claimed a number of Arab lives during the battle of Tabor in April 1799. Again, SDeb and historical and topographical sensibilities have shaped the historian's presentation. And once more, the reconstruction is based largely, perhaps wholly, on intelligent surmise.

IDENTIFYING CHARACTERS: LOCATION BY ASSOCIATION

To this point the analysis has exposed the logic that the prose historian, sometimes in concert with general historical knowledge, applied to Judges 5. But there are aspects of the prose reconstruction that reflect a less direct dependence on the song. The method in these instances is similar.

SISERA

Sisera is a Canaanite conundrum. SDeb is silent as to his antecedents and home. He leads the enemy host (5:20), the allied army of "the kings of Canaan" (v. 19). His mother has a retinue (śārôt, v. 29), and awaits his homecoming at an upper-story window, undoubtedly of a palace (28f.). Even if presciently, the image calls to mind the iconography of the "woman at the (palace) balustrade," a motif familiar to the historian.[20] Sisera, in all, seems to be a king, as scholars have long maintained.

The historian, however, does not explicitly identify Sisera as a king. He takes him, instead, to be "commander of the army" (4:2, 7) of "Jabin, king of Hazor" (v. 17; cf. 23f.). Some exegetes deny that this association is original to the "first edition" of Judges 4; but the probelm remains even if a redactor introduced Jabin.[21] Further, the prose required some introduction for Sisera, and the comments on Jabin's relations with Jael, as already noted, are integral to the author's reconstruction; this creates a presumption that the identification of Jabin as Israel's oppressor is of a piece with the rest of the tale.

It is patent what has conditioned the prose: Jabin, king of Hazor, was the only king of the kings of Canaan known to later Israel. Specifically, Joshua 11:1–10 records the defeat of a coalition of city-states under Jabin's direction, "for Hazor," it says (v. 10), "was the head of all those kingdoms." Sisera's leading the armies of the kings of Canaan made him Jabin's captain, and 4:2, 23f. emphasize the equation by calling Jabin, "king of Canaan." Jabin's function in the narrative is the passive one of identifying Sisera.

Geopolitical considerations had an influence here. By situating the battle on the northern fringes of the Jezreel, and excluding the Rachel tribes of the central hills from the action, the historian limited his scope for choice. Hazor was the only Canaanite city-state of the northern hills with a record of domination. With its sprawling Early Bronze lower city, it was the only tell in Naphtali with the look or giant proportions that to Israelites, as in the legends of Joshua 10–11, signaled ancient power.[22]

Oddly enough, the historian does not identify Sisera himself as king of Hazor, or identify him with Jabin. Loyal instead to the tradition, he comes to a reconstruction less economical in narrative terms. The image of Sisera's mother in a palace (5:28–30), however, compels him to make Sisera reside as king in some other town, rather than as an underling in Hazor, much like David serving Achish of Gath from Ziklag. Why he selected Haroshet-Haggoyim is unclear (but see this chapter's section entitled "Baraq"). The name itself, with an intimation of the involvement of the nations, and the physical location of the town, unknown to us, presumably both played a role. In any event, the prose reconstruction again conforms to historical dictates.

There is evidence that this reconstruction was in fact inherited by the prose historian. Joshua 11 seems to depend to some extent on SDeb. Thus both concern a climactic northern battle, which Joshua 12, like Judges 5, ties to Megiddo, Taanach, and Qedesh (these follow in vv. 21f. the enumeration of Hazor and Meron[?] in 12:19f.). Further, Judges 5:18f. sets its clash "on the heights of the field" (ʿal merômê śādeh) and "on the waters of Megiddo" (ʿal mê megiddô). Joshua 11:7, with a confrontation "on the waters of 'The Height' " (ʿal mê mērôm), reads like a deliberate conflation of the two.[23] Jabin of Hazor is in both the head of Canaan's kingdoms.

It does not seem likely that the author of Judges 4 drew on Joshua 11 because in that account, Hazor is already razed and Jabin slain (vv. 9–11). Even locating Sisera outside Hazor does not quite resolve the tension created by linking him and Heber alike to a dead sovereign.[24] The reconstruction is defensible only if it drew on a tradition of a battle with Jabin's Hazor, with which Joshua's name had not yet been associated. The identification of this encounter with Deborah's victory would be natural, but must for these reasons be assigned to the preliterary stages of the tale.[25] This, in turn, yields consistency in the historian's hermeneutic: he did not lift Jabin from another chronological context (nor did his informants, for that matter). Some of Judges 4 derives, in fact, from traditional explication of SDeb. Two other cases will be seen to bear this conclusion out.

DEBORAH

The historian locates Deborah, an Issacharite in Judges 5:15, at "the palm of Deborah between Ramah and Bethel in Mt. Ephraim" (4:5). Genesis 35:8 associates an "oak [ʾlwn] of mourning" located downward from Bethel with the burial of Deborah, Rebecca's nurse. Richter argues that the "oak of Tabor" (ʾlwn tbwr) found on the way up to Bethel from Rachel's tomb (1 Sam. 10:3) is also an "oak of Deborah" (ʾlwn dbwrh); the "palm" of Judges 4:5 represents a failed, late appropriation to our prophetess.[26]

On the face of it, the historical technique here seems identical to what would be involved had Jabin been lifted out of Joshua 11. In each case the historian would have displaced an element from another context in order to flesh out the narrative. But at the literal level, to which the prose author has shown himself to be sensitive, it is possible that Deborah the prophetess should sit beneath a tree named for another Deborah; it is impossible that Baraq should make war against a man Joshua had killed who was king of a city Joshua had razed. Second, the substitution of the palm for the oak is not an error that a historian stealing a literary tradition makes. Are the trees the same or are they not? Finally, the logical explanation for the tradition is that the prose narrator (or a source) knew of a tree named for Deborah; oblivious to the etiology in Genesis 35:8, he assumed the tree commemorated the activity of a major historical figure. In other words, Deborah's location arose from (possibly older) deduction, in line with the other elements of the reconstruction in Judges 4.[27]

BARAQ

One of the principal characteristics of the prose version is its single-minded preoccupation with the central events celebrated in SDeb. Jabin's role, for example, is not even developed to the point of having the king dispatch his commander: the leak of Baraq's whereabouts is made to Sisera; Sisera acts on his own. Thus even though the relationship between Sisera and Jabin appears to have come into his hands with the transmission of the Song, the historian works almost entirely from SDeb. He restricts his imagination to the circumstances whose representation his reconstruction demands.

There is one other detail possibly taken over from the oral tradition; and it might seem to be developed more than the elements of Sisera's affiliation with Hazor or Deborah's Palm. This is the site of Baraq's home.

SDeb associates Baraq, along with Deborah, with Issachar (v. 15). Issachar, however, is a tribe that on the prose reconstruction does not fight. In the case of Deborah, a noncombatant, this is not problematic. But Baraq was the field commander of Israel's troops. His relocation, therefore, was a desideratum. He had to be linked either with Zebulun or with Naphtali.

As in the cases of Jael, Sisera, and Deborah, the historian places Baraq in a specific locale—Qedesh, in the north of Naphtali (4:6). From this town Deborah summons Baraq (4:6). To it, on his return, she accompanies him (4:9). Hard nearby is the encampment of Heber and Jael (4:11). And here Baraq calls out his forces, bent on battle at Tabor (4:10, 12).

Scholars have had difficulty fathoming this concentration of events. Qedesh of Naphtali is too close to Hazor, they maintain, for Baraq to have mustered his forces there. And Heber's location near Qedesh means too long a flight for Sisera from Mt. Tabor. Two major solutions have been proposed. Kaufmann suggests that the Qenites moved south to the Jezreel between 4:11 and 4:17, a notion that involves supplying action the reader could not be expected to imagine (in another account in which detail is rather full).[28] This, however, leaves the first problem, of Baraq's proximity to Hazor, unaddressed. Most other commentators therefore claim that a different Qedesh, that in Issachar (Khirbet Qadis), originally played this role in the story. The (late) introduction of Hazor into the story led to its identification as Qedesh of Naphtali.[29]

These arguments appeal to historical, not historiographic, logic. If the prose author had reason to place Baraq in Qedesh Naphtali, the improbability either of the muster there or of Sisera's long flight northward need not have deterred him. Both were within the realm of the possible: indeed, the longer Sisera's flight, the easier to understand how he sufficiently widened the gap between himself and Baraq to attempt to hide, and to be murdered, in Jael's tent; and, if the Israelites could live in Qedesh, in an apparent state of hostility with Hazor, then they could also muster there.

More to the point, Baraq's location had to fulfill several functions, as sketched out in this chapter's section entitled "The Murder, the Qenites, and the Geography of Sisera's Flight." It had to be near the Qenite camp, so that the Qenites could act as Sisera's informants. With the Qenite camp, it had to verge on Sisera's route homeward, so that he could meet Jael. It had to be far enough from Tabor, too, to allow Sisera to outrun the horizon of his pursuers. Qedesh is an impressive site, commanding the defile leading northward from Hazor, presumably toward Haroshet Haggoyim. Judges 4:16 states that this was the direction of the rout; and 4:22a, an epanalepsis ("rhetorical resumption") that resumes the thread of 4:16a after a break in the account of the rout, situates Baraq, Jael, and Sisera all on this line, near Qedesh (4:11). Sisera was the last (4:16, 17a) among the crowd of fugitives whom Baraq was chasing.

Without a notice that he adopted a roundabout line of retreat, and without a notice that Baraq broke off the pursuit after the camp in order to dog Sisera alone, the account reconstructs the rout (and the prebattle disinformation) as economically as possible. Qedesh Naphtali is now integral to the narrative's geographic logic.

This does not preclude confusion with Qedesh in Issachar. It means only that it must antedate the prose reconstruction. Qedesh stood in the shadow of Tabor, and near a town, Daberat, whose name evokes that of Deborah (Josh. 19:12, 20f.). It seems to be twinned with a town, Qishion, whose association with the Wadi Qishon may be organic.[30] Thus the role of the river in Judges 5:21 could have produced an early tie between the Issacharite Baraq and Qishion/Qedesh; or one might speculate about a historical affiliation. Either hypothesis would supply an additional motive for the location of the battle at Tabor: this, too, would have reached the historian amid the contextualizing lore transmitted with SDeb.

Some scholars think that Qedesh was transposed to Naphtali in a redaction of an earlier prose account.[31] But Baraq is assigned to Naphtali because of the prose view of which tribes fought; Heber's northern location hangs together with Baraq's (4:10f.) and with Sisera's line of retreat. These elements are constitutive of and integral to the prose narrative. To reconstruct a literary form of Judges 4 without them is to hypothesize a version bearing no resemblance to the one we have.

In light of this, speculation about preliterary traditions may seem superfluous. But it helps to explain why the historian elected to associate Sisera with Haroshet-Haggoyim, and Baraq with Qedesh so far to the north. It was necessary that Baraq come from Zebulun or Naphtali. The specific sites chosen, however, could have lain much farther south. Qedesh Naphtali had much to recommend it, as previously noted. It even furnished a town comparable to Hazor in its strategic significance. Still, if transmitters of SDeb thought of Baraq as a son of Qedesh in Issachar, the transposition to the far more important Qedesh Naphtali, probably in the transition from oral to literary history, wins an easier explanation.

One other factor may have had an influence. Thutmosis III's melee at Megiddo shares several elements with Judges 4–5: the site (Megiddo), the 900 (923) chariots, the united Canaanite opposition (the parallel to the use of itinerants for disinformation comes from Ramses II at Qadesh). The principal in the Canaanite coalition is the king of Qadesh (probably Qadesh on the Orontes), and the association of his name with a key battle in the Jezreel may have made itself felt, unconsciously, in the traditional identification of Baraq.

Whichever of these explanations holds, the process by which Baraq was furnished with a home will have resembled that which yoked Sisera to Hazor (see this chapter's section entitled "Sisera"). Consistently in Judges 4, exegesis of the Song combines with practical, sincere, ultimately defensible historical associations. The historian indulges his imagination insofar as is necessary to answer questions arising from a close reading of SDeb; he gives no rein at all to idle fancy.

THE PROSE HISTORIAN AS CONDUIT AND AS HISTORIAN

The cases in the preceding three sections indicate that the prose historian is a conduit of tradition. His work, naturally enough, synthesizes traditional with personal understanding, traditional with personal representation of the episode. How much of his reconstruction he gleaned from oral sources we shall never know. The same applies to the historian of the Ehud account: whether he inherited or deduced the element of Ehud's lefthandedness will be a perpetual mystery.

What can be said about Judges 4, as about the Ehud account, is that it was composed as a unit from the sources available. One cannot scrape off a late veneer in hopes of finding fixed older text smothered like a hunk of meat under a redactorial brown sauce. The whole chapter, geography included, is an organic reconstruction. It is so carefully appointed because the reconstruction, shaped by antiquarian interest, demands it—exactly the pattern that provokes the lavish furbishment of the Ehud story.

D. F. Murray has, in effect, recently argued the reverse. The tale's art, he asserts, stems from purely thematic interests: it is misguided, for example, to expect Jael's encampment to have any logical geographical coherence with Sisera's path from Tabor to Haroshet- Haggoyim.[32]

This is inverted thinking. The use of *ascend* and *descend* in verses 10–15, for example, is, against Murray, at best secondarily bound up with the symbolic resonance of the verbs; Baraq must ascend and descend from Tabor for tactical reasons, and topological ones; Sisera must descend from his chariot because that is how one gets off one to flee on foot. The art functions steadily *within* the confines of the reconstruction, serving the historian's intention, rather than shaping it. Similarly, the historian (or even a redactor) does not supply details such as the name Elon Bezaananim (Jael's camp) without thought or reason. Why should he choose this place, not Cleveland? It is a historical context that he is trying to construct, rather than fanciful, purely literary, thematic relations unrelated to reality. Otherwise, among other points, he would have felt no need to translate the battle from Taanach to Tabor, or to remove Baraq and Deborah from Issachar, or to work out Baraq's troop-strength.

Its use of and reasoned divergence from SDeb is thus cogent evidence for the character of the prose version. The historian relies consistently and closely on the poetic source. He may, by our lights, occasionally have misconstrued it. This does not mitigate the case either for dependence or for his historical intent; rather, it is a function of his distance from and reverence for his source.[33]

Virtually every element of the prose account stems directly, or by a dialectical process, indirectly, from SDeb. The mode of the killing dictates Sisera's posture, this in turn the motive for his presence in the tent, and this in turn his unmounted flight, the description of the engagement, and the nature of Heber's relations with Hazor.[34] The status of the Qenites vis-à-vis Israel conditions their double role, as providers of intelligence and as those who kill Sisera. The conviction that Zebulun and Naphtali were the only combatant tribes determines Baraq's location in Naphtali; probably a traditional association with Qedesh dictates the specific town picked; this in turn determines Heber's location, the direction of Sisera's flight, and the place of Sisera's home. Sisera's position as a pan-Canaanite leader makes him the officer of Jabin; but the Song demands that he be king of a town in his own right. The Canaanite chariots, a sense of military reality, the role of the Qishon, and some words in SDeb ("went down," "heights of the field") imply a dust-up at Tabor instead of at Taanach. This, and the portrait of Deborah in the Song, mold Deborah's transactions in the prose with Baraq. The association of her name with a tree places the "prophetess" in Mt. Ephraim.

Every facet of the prose account can be derived from a reading of SDeb. Wellhausen, who, based on a comparison between the assassination accounts, first diagnosed the relationship between the chapters, concluded accurately that the prose furnished only one independent detail—the name of Deborah's husband.[35] Yet the song presents virtually none of the *prose's* detail. The historian arrives at locations, numbers, and relationships based overwhelmingly on an interrogation of the source. The character of the process indicates that his aim was to reconstruct history—to recount the events whose memory underlay the song in concrete, historical terms. The wrinkles of the prose are not gratuitous, but follow the veins that the historian mined in SDeb. Excise a detail, and one must invent another to supply its place: a treaty between Heber and Sisera, instead of Heber and Hazor; a new town for Sisera, or home for Baraq; a new site for the battle; new agents to inform the Canaanites of Baraq's muster. The text is almost as economical as the reconstruction.

Much of the song has no reflex in the prose. The muster of the tribes is omitted (vv. 7–11c, 14–17), though the number of Baraq's troops indicates that it was actively pondered. The muster, on the prose interpretation, was irrelevant to the course of events. The curse of Meroz (5:23) goes untreated: it belongs to a stage of reflection on Deborah's accomplishment, after the triumph, which the prose does not cover. The final scene with Sisera's mother (5:28–30) is also passed over in silence, though, again, the reconstruction of Sisera as king of a small town takes it into account. For the prose historian, although not for the poet, Sisera's demise was not an unexpected windfall from Providence (n. 14), but a predictable fruit of dogged Israelite pursuit (4:9). The exultation of the poet gives way to prosaic explication. The historian restricts his art, restricts his presentation, to elements that serve the reconstruction.

There are claims in the prose, of course, that were not entirely demanded by the reconstruction: the dialogue, generally; Jael's premeditation; the number of chariots; the specific loci of Sisera and Heber. What changes, then, would one have to make in the prose in order to make it history? As in the story of Ehud, the answer depends on how literally we take each word in the text. Do we identify the dialogue as an element of the reconstruction, or as a convention of the presentation? If, in light of the canons of ancient historiography, we take it as an expedient of actualization, then no changes in the prose are necessary to remove it from the realm of romance to that of history.

After all, if Sisera did not dwell at Haroshet-Haggoyim, if Heber did not camp at Elon Bezaananim, the reconstruction *did* demand that they dwell in proximity to them. If Jael did not say, "Turn aside to me," or Sisera, "I thirst," the sense must have been the same. If Baraq did not beg Deborah's company—whatever the implications (the topos conforms to the genre of the commission in HB generally)—she must in any case have come along, and have sung at Tabor, "Rise, Baraq!" Similarly (4:6f.), she must have instructed him in his course of action. This applies to all the dialogue (4:6–9, 12, 18f., 22): all of it is functional (except Sisera's drink, taken from SDeb), none fanciful. There *is* art in the presentation, as there is in Carlyle. There is even art in the reconstruction, if only in its elegant economy. Still, the main lines of the reconstruction, the main interest of the author, were antiquarian in nature. Again, characterization is not thrust forward; the tension in the plot does not approach that of Pentateuchal narratives; the dialogue is never out of hand, the reportage—unlike that of SDeb (esp. vv. 28–30), which is not historiographic in intent—never includes symbolic or trivial detail. There is none of the elaboration that one expects from a romance. All the evidence, thus, comes down on the side of the prose's historical character.

The histories of Ehud and Deborah relay inherited materials. In one case the primary source is oral, a verbal accordion liable to prolongation or abridgement, and to infinite variation. In the second case, the source is literary, a poem long canonized, with antique linguistic elements posing knotty problems to the interpreter.[36] Its form is fixed, and it is doubtful that the staid prose companion piece ever enjoyed an organic oral circulation comparable to that of the Ehud story. Nor could the tropes of the two sources be more different. The oral version of the Ehud account is a picaresque, a romance. SDeb is a lyric, a joyous, triumphant exultation.

However substantial the differences between the sources in Judges 3 and Judges 4, there is one important point of similarity. In neither case is the chief source historiography. Neither is archival. Yet in each case the written version is a historical one. Each treatment wrings from romance a prosaic reconstruction of events. The historian's sources carry the events aloft, soaring on the wings of poetic fancy. He fixes the events in the sights of history, and brings them to solid earth.

The accuracy of the historian's representations can with profit be questioned. So can his interpretation of his source.[37] But the antiquarian character of the reports—their historic intentionality—should be clear. In each case the historian identifies the protagonists, situates the action, and provides the information necessary to follow the mechanics of his reconstruction. Art plays a role in the choice of words and names and even in the largely implicit characterizations. The historian's culture and convictions also make themselves felt—marginally, in the reconstruction (e.g., Baraq asking for Deborah's accompaniment as a response to his commission), more so in the integration of the tales into their literary contexts (chapters 6, 9). The gists of the reports, however, their logic, their structural coherence, are molded by a concern to reconstruct the past, by antiquarian interest.

Art and ideology influence the form of the reports in Judges 3 and 4. The motive for rendering a written account of the tradition may even, primarily, be political. But the idea that these are incompatible with history betrays, as noted in Chapter 1, only a naïveté about history from Greece to Gibbon, from the monastery to Mumford or Namier. Art and elements of romance are integral to the presentation of history, especially narrative history. Other biblical narratives, even in the historical books, are far more liberal with them, a problem considered in Chapter 10. But the Ehud story and Judges 4 rein in art and fancy, harnessing them to the exigencies of the reconstruction. In these accounts, as the correspondence between reconstruction and presentation shows, the historical events themselves are the focus of attention; only within this context, if at all, are thematic concerns elaborated. These chapters are modestly ornamented works of history, not historical romance.

FIGURE 6:   THE LOGIC OF JUDGES 4

The logic of the account may be represented, very roughly, as follows:

I.

1. 5:26 > 4:21 (hammer and peg) > new reading of 5:26b,d
2.   > 4:18d, 19c (Sisera under cover)
3.   > reading of 5:27 in triple verbal sequence of 4:21g based on $\check{s}kb$, and reinterpretation of npl in 4:22
4.   > 5:25 > 4:19ab
5.   > duplication in 4:18d, 19c
6.   > 4:18abc (reading 5:24, "in the tent")
7.   > 4:22 (Baraq arrives in pursuit)
8.   > 4:15b, 17a (Sisera on foot, so reading 5:14)
9.   (so 5:14 > 4:10b [Israel afoot] > 4:15b, 17a)
10. 4:15b, 17a [8, 9] > 4:15b, 16 (mixed flight)
11. 4:18, 19c, 21 [1, 2, 5, 6] > 4:20 (Jael on watch)
12. 4:15f., 18 [7, 8, 9, 2, 6] > 4:20 (Jael watching for pursuit)
13. 4:21 (Sisera dead in tent [1, 3, 4, 5, 6]) > 4:22 (Jael calls to Baraq)
14. 4:18 (flight to Jael [6]) > 4:11 (Heber in north)
     (and 4:5, palm, 5:19 $b\bar{s}^{\varsigma}$, 4:10, Qedesh > 4:11 Elon Bezaananim)
15. 4:18 [6, 14] > 4:17 (treaty with Heber)
16. 4:18, 17 (refuge, treaty [6, 14, 15]) > 4:12 (Qenites inform)
17.   > 4:11 (Heber near Qedesh) = [14]

II.

18. 5:7, 12, 21 (Israel initiates) and 11ff. + 19 (muster, "then" "kings came")
     > 4:7 (Deborah's plan, luring Sisera)
19.   > 4:11f. (Qenites [can't be Israelites] inform Sisera) = [17]
20. 5:20 (weather) > 4:15a (Yhwh discomfits, as Exodus 15 and J in 14:24)
21. 4:7 (Deborah's initiative [18]) > 4:6f. (Deborah starts process)
22.   > 4:6–9, 14 (Baraq's commission)
23.   > 4:10–13 (Baraq starts outside zone of battle, then readies for Sisera)
24. 5:12b (" 'Rise, Baraq' ") > 4:14 (" 'Rise' ") = [22, and 21, 18 (Deborah's initiative)]
25. 5:13 ("went down") > 4:14 (Israel going down from Tabor)
26. 5:18 (heights), 21 (Qishon) > 4:10, 12, 14 (Tabor, with southern hills excluded = [25]
27. 5:22 (chariots), 18 (heights), 13 ("went down") > 4:10, 12, 14 (surprise charge from wooded hill) = [25, 26]
28. 5:18 (Zebulun and Naphtali) > 4:10, 12, 14 (Tabor) = [25, 26, 27]

III.

29. 5:19f. (Sisera and kings of Canaan) + Josh. 11:10; 12:21f. > 4:2, 7, 17,
23f. (Jabin)
30. Gen. 35:8; 1 Sam. 10:3 > 4:4 (Palm of Deborah)
31. 5:21 (Qishon) > Qedesh Issachar (Qishion)
32. Thutmosis III at Megiddo, with 900 chariots, anti-Qadesh > Qedesh
33. 5:18 (Zebulun and Naphtali) + Qedesh Issachar [31, 32] > 4:6, 10, 11
(Qedesh
Naphtali)
34. 5:3 (40,000) + 5:18 (Zebulun and Naphtali) > 4:6, 10 (10,000)
35. 5:2–30 > 5:1

Notes to Chapter 4

1. Much of this chapter is drawn from my essays "Doctrine by Misadventure," in R. E. Friedman, ed., *The Poet and the Historian* (HSS 26: Chico, CA: Scholars, 1983), 41–73; "The Resourceful Israelite Historian," *HTR* 76 (1983): 379–401.
2. On interdependent text, see E. Tov, "The Composition of 1 Samuel 16–18 in the Light of the Septuagint Version" and J. H. Tigay, "Conflation as a Redactorial Technique," in J. H. Tigay, ed., *Empirical Models for Biblical Criticism* (Philadelphia: University of Pennsylvania, 1985), 97–130, 53–95, respectively. On the reversal of the J–P relationship (J. G. Eichhorn, *Einleitung in das Alte Testament* [Leiden, Netherlands: Weidmanns Erben und Reich, 1780] postulates a common source), see the response to earlier scholars in H. Hupfeld, *Die Quellen der Genesis und die Art ihrer Zusammensetzung von neuem untersucht* (Berlin: Wiegandt und Grieben, 1853), 165–67; H. Holzinger, *Einleitung in den Hexateuch* (Freiburg, W. Germany: Mohr, 1893), 355; C. Steuernagel, *Lehrbuch der Einleitung in das Alte Testament* (Tübingen, W. Germany: Mohr, 1912), 54; latterly, R. E. Friedman, *The Exile and Biblical Narrative* (HSM 22; Chico, CA: Scholars, 1981), 44–119.
3. See F. M. Cross, *Canaanite Myth and Hebrew Epic* (Cambridge: Harvard University, 1973), 123–44; B. Halpern, *The Emergence of Israel in Canaan* (SBLMS 29; Chico: Scholars, 1983), 32–43. Cf. B. Peckham, *The Composition of the Deuteronomistic History* (HSM 35; Atlanta: Scholars, 1985), 86f., n. 92.
4. For the poem, among others stretching back beyond Wellhausen (for whom, see below), R. de Vaux, *The Early History of Israel* (Philadelphia: Westminster, 1978), 729f.; for the prose, M. Noth, *The History of Israel* (2nd ed.; New York: Harper & Row, 1960), 150f.; M. Vernes, "Le cantique de Débora," *Revue des Études Juives* 24 (1892): 52–67, 225–55, adducing verbal parallels to show SDeb depended on the prose. In other works Vernes applied the same logic to date Deuteronomy, JE, and all prophetic literature to the postexilic era.
5. A. Malamat, "Israel in the Period of the Judges," in B. Mazar, ed., *Judges* (WHJP 1/3; Tel Aviv: Massada, 1971), 137–40. For a brilliant effort to ground this hypothesis in the poem, see Y. Ikeda, "The Song of Deborah and the Tribes of Israel," in *Fs. M. Loewenstamm* (Jerusalem: Kiryath-Sepher, 1979), 65–79 (Hebrew).
6. For the rendition see Halpern, "Israelite Historian" [n. 1], 384–86, reading MT in v. 12, conjecturing *yśr'l* for *śryd* in v. 13 (and reading *lw* with G), and taking v. 14b to apostrophize Ephraim. Omit v. 15b "and Issachar" with G^AB. There is no reason to replace it with "Naphtali," as urged first by G. L. Studer, *Das Buch der Richter, grammatisch und historisch erklärt* (Bern, Switzerland: J. F. J. Dalp, 1835).
7. A. Weiser, "Das Deboralied: Eine gattungs- und traditionsgeschichtliche Studie," *ZAW* 71 (1959): 67–97. The "rebukes" are more likely affirmations of participation, for which see my "Resourceful Historian" (n. 1), 381–84.
8. See further, W. Richter, *Traditionsgeschichtliche Untersuchungen zum Richterbuch* (BBB 18; Bonn: P. Hanstein, 1963), 104 (hereafter, *TUR*).
9. The topos of unequipped Israelites saved by a divine stroke recurs in 1 Samuel 13:22–14:31. Jonathan, with arms, accomplishes the rout there alone. Applying the parallel to SDeb would lead to the interpretation I have already suggested.
10. For the rendition see my "Israelite Historian" (n. 1), 388. *Rqh*, v. 26, is related to *rqq*, "expectorate" (thence to *yrq*, "green-yellow"). In Cant 4:3, it is scarlet, in or around the mouth (cf. 6:7). It is not the temple but more probably the interior of the throat or mouth, hence "gullet" here.
11. See J. Wellhausen in F. Bleek, *Einleitung in das Alte Testament* (4th ed.; Berlin: Reimer, 1878), 187–89. From this observation Wellhausen deduced the complete dependence

of the prose on the poem, an idea that enjoyed a vogue around the turn of the century. See, e.g., B. Stade, *Geschichte Israels* (2nd ed.; Berlin: G. Grote, 1889), 1.178, n. 1. I imagine that Wellhausen developed this idea in his lectures, and anticipated much of the work here.

12. Boling, *Judges* (AB 6A; Garden City, NY: Doubleday, 1975), 98. Conversely, R. Alter (*The Art of Biblical Poetry* [New York: Basic, 1985], 42–45), who denies any difference between the prose and the poem, reads the poem to say that Sisera fell.

13. Judges 1:19; Joshua 17:16, 18; cf. 1 Samuel 13:5f., 19–22; 2 Samuel 8:4; and Exodus 14–15; Joshua 24:6. On the need to bring Baraq in pursuit, contrast D. F. Murray, "Narrative Structure and Technique in the Deborah–Baraq Story (Judges IV 4–22)," in J. A. Emerton, ed., *Studies in the Historical Books of the Old Testament* (*SVT* 30; Leiden, Netherlands: Brill, 1979), 159. Murray suggests the historian could have shifted to Sisera's mother; but that scene in its entirety is precisely irrelevant to the course of events. See the section entitled "The Prose Historian as Conduit and as Historian" later in this chapter.

14. Thus the digression after the notice of the flight, in 5:23, followed by the introduction of Jael to be "blessed," followed by her providing beverage, all call attention away from Sisera. The first sense of dissonance creeps in in 5:26, when she picks up the poker, and the first mention of Sisera comes at a crescendo in 5:26c. The triumph at Sisera's mother's anxiety over Sisera's reaching home is a mirror of the anxiety created for the Israelites by 5:20–21 that Sisera might escape. The conclusions are all foregone: that Sisera will triumph (5:29f.), and that once away on horse (5:22), he will get home.

15. See Y. Kaufmann, *The Book of Judges* (Jerusalem: Kiryath-Sepher, 1962), 124f. (Hebrew). On "Heber," cf. G^A in 4:11 (*plesion*), G^B with double reading in 4:17 (*chaber hetairou tou Kinaiou*), Hosea 6:9, the town name Hebron, and Mari *hibrum*, with Malamat, "Period" (n. 5), 140.

16. For the weather as a factor, see A. Malamat, *Israel in Biblical Times* (Jerusalem: Bialik and I.E.S., 1983), 95 (Hebrew).

17. Note also 2 Samuel 22:15–19//Psalm 18:15–19, with echoes of Judges 4f.: 15 *brq wyhmm;* flood waters in 16; 17 *mrwm,* cf. Judges 5:18; 19 *yqdmny,* cf. Judges 5:21 *nhl qdwmym;* resonance with Exodus 14f. includes vv. 15, *hmm;* 16, *)pyqy ym, g^{c}rh, n^{s}mt rwh)pw;* 17, *mym rbym. Hmm* is used primarily of divine discomfiture. Cf. *m^{e}hûmâ* in 1 Samuel 5:9, 11; 14:20.

18. Note that, unlike P in Exodus 14:9b, 17, and so on, misinterpreting 15:1, Judges 4 does not introduce light cavalry.

19. For attempts to harmonize the versions, see K. Budde, *Das Buch der Richter* (KHCAT 7; Freiburg, W. Germany: Mohr, 1897), 34 (cf. K. Budde, *Die Bücher Richter und Samuel, ihre Quellen und ihr Aufbau* [Giessen, W. Germany: J. Ricker, 1890], 105); Malamat, *Israel* (n. 16), 95. On antichariotry tactics, note Pap. Anastasi I 23:8–25:1, the hesitation of Thutmosis' officers at the Wadi ʿAra, and Malamat's reconstruction of the attack in a longitudinal side-valley (*loc. cit.*).

20. The motif is attached to the queen, Jezebel, in 2 Kings 9:30f. Even if the poem does not invoke it, it will have come to the historian's mind. A mold for busts resembling the Nimrud "Mona Lisa" was found at Tell Batashi in 1984; the balustrade from Ramat Rahel is also well known.

21. This has been the consensus since Wellhausen, in Bleek, *Einleitung* (n. 11), 187f. See Kaufmann, *Judges* (n. 15), 115ff., for a rebuttal. Richter (*TUR* [n. 8], 58) thinks a redactor introduced Jabin when he applied a tradition about Heber's relations with Hazor. But "Heber" and his treaty with Hazor were never independent of the account in Judges 4. Moreover, it is unlikely that R had a fragmentary tradition about relations between Heber and Jabin. Who would have preserved such a tradition, and who would have listened to it?

22. The Joshua compaigns (especially 10–11) are reconstructions built around the vision of the huge, old EB tells as the residences of the Amorite giants whom Yhwh overthrew, as I argue in "Canaan, Conquest of" in D. N. Freedman, ed., *Anchor Bible Dictionary* (Garden City, NY: Doubleday), forthcoming.

23. For earlier cliams that Joshua 11 infects Judges 4, see Stade, *Geschichte* (n. 11), 1.178, n. 1; W. Richter, *Die Bearbeitung des "Retterbuches" in der deuteronomischen Epoche* (BBB 21; Bonn: Hanstein, 1964), 7f. Richter's view turns on the thesis (*TUR* [n. 8], 57f.) that were there no Joshua 11, "Heber's" Jabin would have been seen as a neutral in Judges 4. As a neutral, however, Jabin would never have been mentioned, because his function is to identify the enemy general. On kings of Canaan, cf. *EA* 30.

24. On the texts' incommensurability at the historical level, see, e.g., M. Noth, *Überlieferungsgeschichtliche Studien* (Halle, E. Germany: Niemeyer, 1943), 51; Malamat, *Israel*, (n. 16), 88–90 (with suggestions on Haroshet–Haggoyim). If one takes the Joshua materials as metaphor for the Israelite occupation, they could depend on Judges 4.

25. But the Hazor tradition, stemming from LB (Y. Yadin, *Hazor* [Schweich Lectures, 1970; London: Oxford University, 1972], 108f., 132ff.), could have come only secondarily into association with SDeb.

26. *TUR* (n. 8), 39–42. Richter assigns the reference to a redactor. But why would a redactor provide her with a locus, when the author did not? Why is the slip a redactor's slip, not an author's? The similar treatment of Baraq will suggest that this element fits the pattern of the historian's concerns.

27. The confusion over the tree's genus and attribution (Deborah, Tabor) is a trait of oral tradition (cf. Budde, *Richter* [n. 19]). It does not imply any relative priority among the attestations. Note that Genesis 35:8 may attach to a prehistorical figure traditions first associated with our historical one: is the "wetnurse of Rebecca," as the timing of her death would suggest, a subjective genitive, meaning the woman who suckled Jacob? In that case she would be a "mother of Israel," commemorating through the glass of eponymic folklore the "mother of Israel" of SDeb (5:7).

28. *Judges* (n. 15), 117.

29. E.g., Budde, *Richter* (n. 19), 36. Cf. Richter, *TUR* (n. 8), 36, on the removal of Qedesh to a "Jabin source."

30. The two lists of Issachar's Levitic cities runs as follows:
    1 Chronicles 6:57:   *qdš*ᵛ   *dbrt*   *rᵓmwt*   ⁽*nm*;
    Joshua 21:28:   *qšᵛywn*   *dbrt*   *yrmwt*   ⁽*yn gnm*.
    The variation in the first name is not scribal. Cf. Qishion in Joshua 19:20f.: *hrbyt* (read *hdbrt* with 19:12, Gᴮ), *qšᵛywn*, *ᵓbṣ* (cf. Judg. 12:8, Ibzan), *rmt* (equals *rᵓmwt*//*yrmwt*), ⁽*yn gnym* (equals ⁽*yn gnm*//⁽*nm*, where haplography of -*gn*- after ⁽*n* has produced the form). Note that Daberat is on Issachar's border with Zebulun.

31. See n. 29. One might adduce the immediate ascent from Qedesh to Tabor (4:10, 12) as the residue of a recension that did not identify Qedesh as Naphtalite. The absence of any other substantial hint of such a narrative, and the other connections to Qedesh Naphtali in the narrative (especially Heber's informing) should caution us about reliance on such a delicate hint. Note that Richter's approach *presupposes* an earlier, integral prose account.

32. Murray, "Narrative Structure" (n. 13), especially 186.

33. On distance and history, note H.-G. Gadamer, *Wahrheit und Methode: Grundzüge einer philosophischen Hermeneutik* (2nd ed.; Tübingen, W. Germany: Mohr, 1965), 279. On the problem in Israel, see further, Halpern, "Doctrine by Misadventure" (n. 1).

34. The narrator naturally brings the husband, not the wife, into treaty with Hazor (indeed, the "house," named properly for the husband). So the argument that v. 11 is late because it does not mention Jael is specious. The same applies to Murray's notion ("Narrative Structure" [n. 13], 180f.) that the historian is reserving Jael as a surprise for vv. 17ff. She is just not material in v. 11.

35. In Bleek, *Einleitung* (n. 11), 189. Wellhausen implies a semantic derivation from Baraq, on which compare Gersonides (and Nah. 2:5; Exod. 20:18). B. Peckham suggests (oral communciation) a tie from Deborah's Lapidoth to the *lappidîm*, "torches" of Judges 7:16, 20, arguing key-word linkage from one episode to the next in Judges (cf. also 3:13, "city of palms" with 4:5, "palm of Deborah").

36. On the dating, see F. M. Cross and D. N. Freedman, *Studies in Ancient Yahwistic Poetry* (SBLDS 23; Missoula, MT: Scholars, 1975); D. N. Freedman, *Pottery, Poetry, and Prophecy* (Winona Lake, IN: Eisenbrauns, 1980), 77–129, with a valuable typology of divine

epithets; esp. D. A. Robertson, *Linguistic Evidence in Dating Early Hebrew Poetry* (SBLDS 3; Missoula, MT: Scholars, 1972). *Bʾšr*, which Robertson treats as the late elment in SDeb, is not the prose relative, but the earlier locative ("the place where"), which developed, like Bavarian *wo*, into the relative. The antique *ša*-relative (5:7) deserves special note. And the extensive use of the suffix conjugation differs from Standard Hebrew poetic dialect. On *lmh* (vv. 16, 17), and for further bibliography, see my "Resourceful Historian" (n. 1), 383f.

37. One case in Judges 4, hitherto unmentioned, is the use of 5:13 to elucidate the battle scene ("came down," see the section in Chapter 4 entitled "The Murder, the Qenites, and the Geography of Sisera's Flight") in conjunction with the view that the tribes of 5:14–17 did not fight. On the redaction of the chapter, see Chapter 6.

Part 2

Redaction and Historiography:
''The Lying Pen of the Scribes''

CHAPTER 5

The Glass Key:
The Problem of Redaction in
the Deuteronomistic History

For no thought is contented. The better sort, / As thoughts of things
divine, are intermix'd / With scruples, and do set the word itself / against
the word.

—RICHARD II

Examining all of the Former Prophets in the detail devoted to the
Ehud and Deborah stories would require many volumes. Part 2, therefore, adverts to longer treatments—of the premonarchic period and of
Solomon's reign—that are cruxes for scholarly theories of the history's
composition. The object is to clarify how the history's antiquarian aspect
affects its presentation of whole periods, and to illustrate the interplay
between ideology and antiquarianism in the corpus (see the Chapter 6
section entitled "Historian and Redactor in Judges"). Chapter 8 illustrates how the historian used sources. All this has an impact on what
sorts of compositional processes may legitimately be hypothesized.

Before renewing our consideration of the book of Judges, it is worthwhile to review how scholars have analyzed the Deuteronomist's work in
general. This chapter catalogues and classifies the scholarly methods
that have been applied to the literature, and considers the views of the
ancient authors that have arisen from them.

THE TROUBLE WITH EHUD AND DEBORAH

The studies in Part 1 depart from the mainstream in three ways. First,
they argue that Judges 3:15–30; 4 serve political or theological goals
only within the confines of an antiquarian program. The narratives em-
body convictions—concerning the proper relationship between Israel
and Yhwh, and so on. But the narrator did not write philosophical trea-
tises on these subjects, or concoct pure works of fancy. He elected instead to work from evidence, according to rules of reconstruction whose

operation and rigor are open to our inspection. A virtuoso poet transforms the restrictions of the sonnet form into advantages. But the limitations remain. In the cases of Ehud and Deborah, the restrictions are
those of an antiquarian genre.

For this reason the two accounts are realistic both in their reconstructions and in their presentations of events. Their causal logic is mundane;
they adduce technical data; and, in presentation, they concentrate on
the course of crucial events. They do not indulge in an elaboration of
details or characterization, as, say, the *Iliad* does. The presentation reflects nothing more than the concerns of reconstruction.

Turn this argument on its flank: what if the author was writing
streamlined romance? Although the case with Judges 3 is similar, Judges
4 is clearer: the demonstrable relationship between the prose account
and its source invalidates the objection. Equally, it is most natural to take
the Ehud account as historiography: even if he concocted parts of the
tale, the historian presents it as such. As observed in Chapter 1, it is this
perceived intention that distinguishes historical from fabulous
literature.

How does the Ehud story differ from that of Joseph's sale, or even P's
creation account in Genesis 1? In written transmission, it is true, these
texts came increasingly to function as history. But they appear in a context whose overarching concern is with the *overt* actions of Yhwh. And
they do not relate the witnessable past of a nation or group. Any claim
that they depict literally human transactions is contaminated by their
use of eponyms as symbols for the later people. Too, these texts came to
be regarded as historical when the folklore they contained was detached
from its original context—when its genre was liable to be misprized
(chapters 10–11). In Ehud's case the probability is that the folkloristic
version was, in fact, rejected in favor of a historical distillation of it; the
operation resembles what a Niebuhr or an Eichhorn later practiced on
ancient lore (Chatper 2).

The second idiosyncrasy of Part 1 is related. The accounts are treated
as units, without intrusive additions. The stories' internal consistency
speaks against ham-fisted redaction. But this conclusion does not reckon
with the question of how the stories were knotted together with the
longer work of which they form a part.

A third difficulty also follows: the Ehud and Deborah accounts have
been treated in isolation, without attention to the context. The authors
of the stories have an antiquarian curiosity, or they would not reconstruct and present the events in such detail. But how do the accounts
serve the themes of the larger work? How were they redacted into the
book of Judges, and how was Judges redacted into the Deuteronomistic
history (DtrH)?

All three issues turn on the question, What is redaction? This is the
oldest, and least conspicuous, issue in biblical research. It was observed

in Chapter 2 that the regnant models for identifying the earmarks of redaction derive from the source criticism of the Pentateuch. There the
redactor (R) emerged as a by-product of literary hypotheses: at times he
created awkwardness by preserving reverently the tiniest fragments of
sources; at other times he ruthlessly suppressed whole sections of the
same sources. R was too erratic to make much sense as a historical individual. But the power of the source hypothesis to alleviate otherwise intolerable complications rendered such scruples marginal.

The problem can be transposed as follows. Imagine that a student has
devised a harmony of the Gospels (much like Tatian's *Diatesseron*) such
that most of Luke and all of Matthew and John have been preserved verbatim. Then we may sort out the separate Gospels, using duplication and
convolution as signposts; the recovery of two intact sources and the remains of a third homogeneous source will guarantee the rough accuracy
of the analysis. But take the case in which the same student works exclusively from Matthew: without some independent access to Matthew, no
two scholars will agree on just how much of the work is the student's,
and how much comes from the source, or even whether several generations of students performed successive operations on the version left by
the previous generation. Now the only criterion for judging the analysis
is what it implies about the way a student uses a written source.

This is the situation in DtrH. DtrH has no extensive parallel sources.
So analysis is limited only by its implications about the redactor; these
alone link compositional speculation based on internal evidence to the
real world and culture in which the literature was produced. In effect,
redaction critics discover the composition of a text from the text. They
employ a method halfway between those of author-centered and text-
centered literary study. But to isolate the authors of a text, one must
break the textual vacuum, and imagine them as human beings with human aspirations, not as by-products of a hypothesis. To get at textual
history, at the history of composition, one must read historically, for the
intention of the authors. To this point I shall revert later in the text.

REDACTION IN DtrH: A CACOPHONY OF SCHOLARS

In the Pentateuch contradictions are explained on the assumption
that the Redactor approached divergent sources with equal deference.
He took the sources to be "true," and worked *in good faith* to combine
them. What role, then, could R play in the Former Prophets?

R in the Former Prophets, like R in the Pentateuch, emerged by definition as scholars identified internal contradictions. Ostensibly, R added
to a finished history (DtrH) or to extensive sources (of DtrH) all those
elements that would have implied that an original author was illogical.
To an extent this is justifiable: J. H. Tigay has observed that a redactor
working with inherited matter is less free to avoid contradiction than is

the author of first instance. But Tigay largely cites cases of stylistic, not logical, inconsistency, in the Epic of Gilgamesh, a text less history than romance.[1]

Few scholars correlated R's general objects to the nature *and* placement of his specific additions. Backhandedly, thus, they impugned his intelligence: R was isolated in whatever texts seemed incongruous; then anything resembling what was first isolated was imputed to him. Sometimes the result could be persuasive—as when inconsistency converged with distinctive and repeated trajectories of vocabulary and thought. But R was first defined as a source of incongruities. The procedure was literary and linear, and furnished no means of assessing the probability of the results.[2]

Yet every editorial analysis is, willy-nilly, a historical reconstruction, just as every historical reconstruction entails a view of the sources. Editorial analysis has implications for a redactor's aims and prowess, and the redactor must make sense as a historical figure: all his contributions must be measured against all the alternatives, of location and content, he rejected. This is a test that has never been applied rigorously to any redactor hypothesized by scholars (Chapter 8).

Redaction analysis in the Former Prophets has been, in a word, fragile. It has never approached that level of consensus reached already in the mid-nineteenth century on the source criticism of Genesis. What has not been observed is that scholars today bring to DtrH utterly different models of what redaction is. The methods, thus, as well as the results, are distinct. The concepts of redaction fall into four categories, which repay consideration.

NOTH'S SINGLE REDACTION OF CONTRADICTORY SOURCES

Since 1943 Noth's treatment has been the cornerstone of the discussion. Noth felt that DtrH's chronological unity implied authorial unity.[3] He claimed that the author (his Dtr) had derived nearly all his data from sources. Two properties account for the view's longevity: it was simple; and it availed itself of the most natural explanation for inconsistency—conflicts among the sources, rather than R's intellectual fogginess or carefree invention. Noth tried to document the historian's good faith, a stance that made for a workable picture of R as a person. Dtr was not, as A. Rosenberg's *Mythos des zwanzigen Jahrhunderts* might suggest, a manufacturer of myths, but an honest antiquarian.

Like his predecessors, Noth tried to isolate the language and thought of his historian. The corollary of his analysis was signal: Noth was driven, in those cases where he thought Dtr composed freely, to excise contradictory material as secondary. For example, Noth identified Joshua's valediction in Joshua 23 as Deuteronomistic. Another farewell address appears in Joshua 24. Noth removed the latter: Dtr would not have composed a second speech had he already had one to hand. Similarly, Noth excised Judges 1:1–2:5. This text, "after the death of Joshua" (1:1; Josh. 24:28–31), precedes a reprise of that event (Judg. 2:6–9). Noth probably reckoned that Dtr would have inserted the material in sequence, after the death notice in 2:6–9. The epanalepsis from Joshua 24:28–31 to Judges 2:6–9 may also have signaled an insertion to him.[4] Overall, Noth wound up with one redactor-historian, his Dtr, and an amorphous set of post-Dtr accretions.

Currently those who champion Noth's literary views jettison his historiographic ones—they depreciate Dtr's reliance on sources and deny his antiquarian bent. This has the paradoxical implication that Dtr tolerated formal contradictions without having any overt motivation (such as conflicting sources) to create them.

This approach necessitates dire assertions. J. van Seters, for example, describes inconsistency as a hallmark of Deuteronomistic thought. H.-D. Hoffmann, conversely, furnishes literary explanations for the problems. He reads Joshua 23–24 as a diptych, looking backward and forward respectively. Flawed in that both chapters program for the future, the argument is more sophisticated than that of van Seters: it resolves the tension without postulating that Dtr was illogical or illiterate (Chapter 6). Like Noth, Hoffmann also avoids the trap of imputing to a redactor (of a finished DtrH) willful contradiction of a respected text: Noth had recourse to the awkward view that the redactor had inherited Joshua 24 separately from DtrH (context unspecified) and then combined them— the contradiction arose from conflicting sources. In any event, even Hoffmann and van Seters allow for redactional accretion to the unified DtrH.[5]

TWIN OR TRIPLE REDACTIONS DETECTED IN CONTRADICTIONS

R. Smend and his disciples have developed another approach. Where Noth refined the history to eliminate "additions," these scholars recover redactors from the dross. Smend set the trend by positing a basic history (his DtrG equals DtrH, Noth's Dtr), and a "nomistic" redactor, DtrN, responsible for Joshua 23 and Judges 1, among other passages.[6] W. Dietrich and T. Veijola added a DtrP (prophetic redactor) between DtrH and DtrN.[7] These scholars base themselves on internal contradictions. Since the original DtrH was free of such problems, they impute one component of each contradiction to a redactor.

Methodologically, little distinguishes this group from the first. Veijola, for example, assigns 1 Samuel 12 to DtrN on the familiar ground that if it stems from (Noth's) Dtr, Dtr would here have contradicted his sources: 1 Samuel 12:12 sees a threat from Ammon as Israel's motive for adopting monarchy, where 8:5 cites Samuel's sons' dereliction, and 9:16; 10:1 cite Philistine oppression.[8] The principal difference between these scholars and Noth is that they see the "additions" as unified, and dignify them with sigla (DtrN, DtrP) to indicate systematic editing.

Smend, however, now denies the unity of DtrN, which he characterizes as a set of accretions arising during transmission.[9] This represents a movement back to Noth.

These analyses posit significant "additions" in a work whose use of sources they do not dispute. "Additions" are identified by isolating the historian's style (Noth's Dtr, Smend's DtrH); contradictions of passages exhibiting that style then imply subsequent redaction (as by DtrN). Here stylistic analysis assumes a significance that exceeds its probable accuracy. Can we in every case confidently distinguish DtrH from its sources? If the historian (Noth's Dtr) sometimes rephrased sources, the signs of his style do not imply free composition. Did the historian sometimes draw style and thought, the relationship between which is often narrow, from the sources? If either alternative holds, how can we differentiate between the historian's preservation of variant traditions and later redactorial activity? And there is evidence that the alternatives hold.[10]

Nor does Smend's approach completely explain the contradictions. Why did the redactor create the problem? If he meant to reverse the intention of the source, why did he not carry the enterprise through by rewriting the offensive passage in its entirety? Tigay has shown that editors of the Gilgamesh epic introduced variant vocabulary and variant techniques of narration; he has shown how the doctrine that Moses revealed the Ten Commandments on Mt. Gerizim led to an inconsistency in the Samaritan Pentateuch (an entry into the land in Samaritan Exodus 20:17d, h before Joshua). But, as E. Tov observes, the editing that we can isolate based on early manuscripts consistently mutes any contradictions it entails.[11] Tigay's examples, too, are fairly tame.

It was safe enough to ignore such issues in the source analysis of the Pentateuch. In DtrH they are the only whetstone for redaction criticism. Where stylistic observations indicate wanton, willful, or wildly inconsistent redaction, it is an argument that the models being applied want correction.

TWIN REDACTION BASED ON HISTORICAL EVIDENCE

A third dissection of DtrH resembles the second in its results. Its chief modern exponent has been F. M. Cross. Cross's thesis, of a history (Dtr$_1$, cf. Noth's Dtr, Smend's DtrH) written under Josiah and updated in the exile (Dtr$_2$), has been consolidated in several substantial studies.[12]

Cross's key point is in nature identical to those of Noth and Smend. What Cross calls the "unconditional" guarantee of David's dynasty in 2 Samuel 7 seems to conflict with passages in Kings that condition ongoing dynasty on fidelity to Yhwh. Again, the issue of style is paramount: 2 Samuel 7 is of a piece with Dtr$_1$ (Dtr, DtrH), because the verbiage is typical. Dietrich and Veijola make the same assessment, and assign the so-called conditional promises to DtrN (Cross to Dtr$_2$).[13] The logic is that the "conditional" warrants of dynasty belong to the exile, when the dynasty lost Judah. Perhaps also implied is the idea that Dtr_1 (Dtr) would not have composed an unconditional covenant (2 Samuel 7) if his sources contained conditional ones. None of this precludes three alternatives: 1) that the unconditional dynastic guarantee is a late attempt to drum up support for a Davidic restoration (van Seters?); 2) that DtrH (Dtr_1, Dtr) inherited both the conditional and the unconditional formulations (Noth); or 3) that Dtr resolved the seeming contradiction between conditional and unconditional promises by taking them to refer to kingship over different entities (Chapter 7). Cross's arguments here, in short, are of just the same sort as those of Smend.

Nevertheless, Cross also injected a different sort of reasoning into the discussion. Anticipated by C. Steuernagel,[14] he made the dates of the editions a central factor in analysis. Dtr_1, whose chief concerns are cult centralization and the glorification of Josiah (as 1 Kings 13), must be pre-exilic. The observation is appealing: Dtr_2 attributes the exile not to a proliferation of high places among Josiah's successors, but to the depravity of Josiah's predecessor, Manasseh. This recourse trivializes Josiah's reform, the values of which infuse the whole of Kings (and all the Judahite regnal formulae up to Josiah), by implying that it had no power to alter Judah's fate. One can speak, thus, of a Josianic history meant to glorify Josiah and defend centralization. Had an exilic historian, with the same concerns, written the history, he would presumably have blamed the exile on reaction among Josiah's successors. This is, in fact, the strategy adopted in 2 Chronicles 36:13ff., and by Ezekiel.

Cross provides a motivation for his exilic redaction: the exile seemed to refute Dtr_1's idea that Josiah's reform was the tonic for Judah's ills; Jeremiah 44:15–19 illustrates that this was a popular attitude ("It was only when we *desisted* from burning incense . . . to the Queen of the Heavens that we . . . perished by the sword and by famine!"). Dtr_2 blames the exile on Manasseh (2 Kings 21:9–16; 23:25–27; 24:2–4, 19f.; cf. Jeremiah 15:4); this is an expedient to salvage the theology of the reform without claiming (falsely) that the state afterward reversed Josiah's measures. As a redactor of a history already lying before him, Dtr_2 in these passages makes sense as a historical individual concerned with a historical present.

Still, the further one extends this analysis, the thinner the hypothesis is stretched. Take the scheme:

conditional dynastic promise::exilic
unconditional dynastic grant::pre-exilic.

Three unexcluded alternatives are sketched out in the preceding. Further, such a dire step as Josiah's cult centralization presupposes a radical sense of doom, for the dynasty as well as the nation. Deuteronomy, so closely tied to the reform, makes Judah's corporate existence, let alone the kingship, completely contingent on conformity to the Law. In the exile or before, the tension between 2 Samuel 7 and the conditional promises of dynasty arises from formulations directed toward different political and theological contexts. The association of the doctrine of conditional dynasty with the end of the dynasty is possible. But it is inherently no more probable than the view that a pre-exilic history incorporated materials with different views on the subject.[15]

There are times when Cross's supporters are justified in looking beyond the account of Manasseh's reign for traces of Dtr$_2$. When indications cluster together, where vocabulary and disruption in the narrative sequence and the introduction of alien concerns all go hand in hand, as R. E. Friedman argues, there is evidence of redactional interference.[16] But the identification of texts as additions based on individual affinities with Dtr$_2$ is more hazardous. In cases where exile is predicted, for example, scholars regularly overreach the evidence (as Josh. 23:13; 1 Kings 8:44–51; 9:6–9).[17] Exile was a reality in Israel from the mideighth century onward; and the threat of losing the land followed from the story of its gift (Hos. 8:3; 9:3; 11:5; cf. Amos 1:5; 9:7 on Aram brought from and exiled to Qir). Neither the word *exile* nor the recurrent nightmare was invented in the era after 586 B.C.E.

The attempt to find Cross's Dtr$_2$ in such passages—still more in texts such as Judges 1 or Judges 19–21—moves away from Cross's insight concerning doctrines of present moment to the redactor (the causes of exile, the import of Josiah's reform). It reverts to the sorts of criteria employed by Noth and Smend. In light of evidence that redactors wrote in the language of their sources, and Tigay's admonitions in this regard,[18] it endows lexical evidence with an exaggerated importance: one cannot confidently isolate a redactor's contributions by style alone. Finally, the ideological whipping posts Cross's students detect in these texts are at best obliquely related to any issues in the life of the community. The quest for Dtr$_2$ in the corpus before 2 Kings 21 is a risky venture, and will probably never achieve the estate at which one group of scholars can persuade the next.

DtrH AS REDACTION: HISTORIES BEFORE DtrH?

The last major approach to the problem is not entirely incompatible with the others. Using Noth's methods, W. Beyerlin, W. Richter, H. Weippert, A. Lemaire, and, in a slightly different vein, B. Peckham, have all made the argument that extensive historical works underlay DtrH, so that the main frame of the history was, in fact, among its latest elements.[19]

These studies, based again on usage and inconsistency, return to Noth's first principle: the inconsistency stems from a historian's use of sources. This eliminates the proposition that the redactor was perverse or a blockhead. Further, it implies that Dtr was built on *blocks* of narrative sources. Here is an explanation of how the sources reached the historian: they were transmitted as coherent wholes. It seems unlikely, for example, that the Ehud story ever existed in isolated literary form: it assumed written shape only when integrated into a longer work; the transmission of the longer work, then, made it available for detectable redaction by a later historian.

Nevertheless, a legitimate question remains.[20] Who first assembled the diverse literary sources from a jumble of scrolls into an ongoing history? Did the earlier historical work resemble the present DtrH? Or was it entirely revolutionized (so Jepsen, Peckham) by the historian?

Beyerlin, Richter, Weippert, and Lemaire suggest that behind DtrH (Dtr$_1$, DtrG) lurk works, of a similar compass, with a history of redaction of their own. Noth himself accepted this principle in treating Samuel, which he thought was incorporated almost verbatim into his Dtr.[21] But if Dtr simply copied out inherited materials, the practice of identifying as his handiwork the overall shape of the history is inadmissible. Richter and Beyerlin (Chapter 6) argue that the frameworks of the book of Judges antedate Dtr. Yet their theology is so close to that of the historian—for a century they were unquestioningly identified as Deuteronomistic—that if these texts could stem from a source, virtually anything could. H. Weippert, Peckham, and Lemaire, too, trace the rhetoric on the high places in Kings to a pre-Josianic edition. This is the thematic focus of Kings as a whole: if it antedates the historian, no scholar yet has isolated the historian's own major thematic impact on his work!

A HARMONY OF MODELS

The variations in analysis chiefly reflect the variety of questions scholars ask. Except in the matter of which text to assign to what author, disputed within as well as across the schools just identified, the differences are those of observers adopting complementary perspectives on the same object. Noth underscored the unity of DtrH, but allowed both for sources and for accretions. Smend focused on the accretions, with Noth's unified history in the background. Cross considered the disagreement between the unified history and the additions. Finally, Richter and Weippert dealt neither with the unified history nor with the additions, but with the sources of the unified history. At a basic level there is no dispute!

For all that, the collocation smacks of disharmony. The suggestion is nourished by the welter of sigla to which the discussion has given birth. Noth's Dtr (the unitary exilic composition) is Cross's Dtr$_1$ (the unitary Josianic composition) and Smend's DtrH—all designate the (author of the) unitary Deuteronomistic history, but purged of additions. Cross's Dtr$_2$ and Dietrich's and Veijola's DtrN and DtrP are all redactors of Dtr$_{(1/G/H)}$. Beyerlin has a pre- Dtr redaction: Richter calls the first edition in Judges Rdt$_1$ (Rdt equals redactor), where Rdt$_3$ is Noth's Dtr.

Weippert has three redactors in Kings (number 2 equals Cross's Dtr_1, number 3 equals Cross's Dtr_2), Lemaire even more. And Peckham has a Hezekian Dtr^1, like Weippert's first redaction, with Dtr^2 (equals Noth's Dtr), in the exile, revolutionized.

The terminological confusion has created the impression of deep rifts in the professional community: was the first redactor Hezekian or exilic? In fact, the differences are matters of detail. But widely different activities are subsumed under the rubric of redaction. Noth, for example, dismissed the secondary materials in Dtr; like Smend's DtrN, these were the products of transmission, the marks of scribal industry. Noth and Smend call them redaction, just as they do the work of $Dtr(G/H/_1)$.

Is composing an extensive history the same thing as inserting a scribal gloss into a received text? The mental processes have points in common; they are by no means identical. And the activities that one may attribute to a historian need not be those in which a glossator is free to indulge. A historian must supply reconstructions (Judg. 4) and transitions (Judg. 2:6–3:6, Chapter 6); what may realistically be postulated about this process cannot be applied to an annotator, on whom the received text imposes an ideological and historical framework.

What scribal operations do scholars hypothesize? First, they posit pre-Deuteronomistic sources—self-contained documents, varying in length, which a historian integrated into the panorama of DtrH. Even the most negative reconstructions allow that the historian did work with *some* sources. These had themselves been compiled, and undergone secondary redaction in the course of transmission. Richter's "Retterbuch" (Judg. 3–8), the product of his Rdt_1, is an example.

All the mainstream analyses also posit that a single author (Noth's Dtr, Smend's DtrH, Cross's Dtr_1, Peckham's Dtr^2) assembled the sources into a comprehensive history. Three different activities are attributed to this character: 1) in the absence of sources (Noth's frameworks of Judges), or in contradiction of them (Noth's 1 Sam. 12), free composition; 2) rephrasing and epitomizing sources in a new historiographic framework (chapters 3–4; or Deuteronomy 1–3);[22] and 3) loyal recopying of sources (Noth on Samuel).

These three processes are best characterized as historiographic (Chapter 1). Indeed, not even van Seters demurs from the proposition that the author of DtrH was a historian. If the work is a Deuteronomistic *history*, it seems best to distinguish the historian responsible for it as such—with the nomenclature H(Dtr) to reflect the function he performed.

Cross posits another form of redaction for Dtr_2, as Veijola and Dietrich do for DtrN and DtrP. These sigla stand for whole strands of minor revisions. The revisions amplify, clarify, or defend claims in a received text. This activity differs from writing history in the first instance: if the reviser wished to subvert the text, he would either have subverted it systematically or written a different text. That the reviser transmitted the text largely intact suggests that he or his community regarded it with reverence. It is a logical corollary that the scribe's insertions must have been consonant with his reading of the text: they reconcile difficulties in the text or difficulties arising from the application of the text to changed realities. Thus Cross's Dtr$_2$ blames the Babylonian exile on Manasseh in order to explain why Josiah's righteous reforms failed to rescue Judah. The reviser fleshes out, but does not invent, a paradigm for construing the past.

What DtrN, DtrP, and Cross's Dtr$_2$ represent are editions of DtrH. They should be so called—E(Dtr)n, E(Dtr)p, and E(Dtr)x (for exilic editor), respectively. One ought not lightly introduce yet another set of designations into the discussion. But the activity of, for example, H(Dtr), differs from that of E(Dtr)x. That of E(Dtr)x differs in turn from that of Noth's and Smend's scribal glossators (Smend's DtrN equals G[Dtr]n). A terminology that distinguishes the several functions involved eliminates some clumsiness.

This terminology also helps delineate what the historian or editor might have hoped to do, producing a standard against which to judge the results of literary study. Have inappropriate properties been assigned to an editor? Take Nelson's recapitulation of E(Dtr)x: he imputes to him Deuteronomy 4:19f; 31:14f., 23; Joshua 23:4(5), 7, 12f.; 24:1–24; Judges 1:1–2:5; 6:7–10; 1 Kings 8:44–51; 9:6–9; 2 Kings 17:7–20, 23b–40; and the segments leading up to the Babylonian exile.[23] Other authors arrive at different conclusions, depending on the mix of lexical and thematic crowbars in their bags. But Nelson's is by no means atypical: it is a regulation product of redaction criticism.

What induced E(Dtr)x, as a human being, to retouch exactly and only where he did? Why did he skip Deuteronomy and most of Joshua, then suddenly introduce a long valediction and a list of unconquered towns (Josh. 24; Judg. 1)? Why did he add a second valediction for Joshua after editing the first (Chapter 23)? Why did he not express his concerns inside the first address, as he did with Solomon's speech at the temple dedication?

Nelson sees Judges 1:1–2:5 as E(Dtr)x's attempt to install a different theology into the conquest accounts. But E(Dtr)x did not reshape the book of Joshua. Supposedly E(Dtr)x wanted to blame the exile on fraternization with the Amorites (Judg. 1; 6:7–10); but, after a reference in the Gideon story, the issue lapses into a limbo freckled only with passing allusions. If the theme is worth developing, why doesn't E(Dtr)x develop it; why does he not tie the exile to miscegenation; if it was in his sources (1 Kings 21:26), how can we be sure it is E(Dtr)x's theme? Nelson works outward from the treatment of Manasseh (2 Kings 21:9–11). Assume that the vocabulary was not purloined from H(Dtr):[24] what impels E(Dtr)x to cultivate the theme so unevenly?

These questions do not invalidate the analysis. They identify a concern scholars have not been compelled to confront. What does an editor do: three verses here, three there, a chapter in the middle; has the editor an ideological program to execute? If he means to attenuate the unconditional grant of 2 Samuel 7, why does he forget to change 2 Samuel 7?

One answer to the problem is that the editor is inconsistent. But in that instance, the question arises, Is there a single editor at all? Noth's amorphous set of accretions, Smend's DtrN, make attractive alternatives to a systematic redaction that in detail proves to be sporadic, inconsistent, or lackadaisical.

The editor cannot have been unaware of his problems (Noth, for example, claims H [Dtr] did not notice the conflict between Judges 4 and the story of Hazor's destruction in Joshua 11).[25] True, scholars sometimes stumble onto problems H(Dtr) or E(Dtr) missed (for the most part, when they find riches in the text that the authors never intended). But it is a point of sound method to assume that the authors were conscious of nearly all the difficulties. The alternative is that they were foolish, culpably lazy, or dishonest.

The Israelite historian was ideologically motivated. But the historian and the editor also respected their sources, and drew heavily on them for language, thought and ideological vindication. Reconstructions of their work must reckon with their sincere belief that history could be *interpreted*, not distorted, to vindicate their views, with the fact that the editors channeled their ideological commitments into research into the past. The editors' antiquarianism goes far to explain their inconsistent interventions in the narrative; the interventions come where, and only where, they are called for, both by politics and by the logic of reconstruction. This proposition is worked out in the remaining chapters of this book.[26] The view of DtrH it produces is perhaps not the only one that answers the questions I have posed: it is, however, the only one so far that has been subjected to them.

Notes to Chapter 5

1. See J. H. Tigay, *Empirical Models for Biblical Criticism* (Philadelphia: University of Pennsylvania, 1985), 45. Cf. the reference in n. 10.

2. Already, J. J. Stähelin (*Kritische Untersuchungen über den Pentateuch, die Bücher Josua, Richter, Samuel und der Könige* [Berlin: Reimer, 1843], 103ff.) adumbrates the method, which is full-blown in Wellhausen, in F. Bleek, *Einleitung in das Alte Testament* (4th ed.; Berlin: Reimer, 1878), 181–266.

3. M. Noth, *Überlieferungsgeschichtliche Studien* (Halle, E. Germany: Niemeyer, 1943), 18–27 (hereafter, *US*).

4. Noth, *US* (n. 3), 51 and n. 1. The logic is implicit, because Noth is trying to prove Dtr's consistency, which is the argument for his analysis. But note the movement away from his posture on Joshua 23 that this entails.

5. J. Van Seters, *In Search of History* (New Haven: Yale University, 1983). See pp. 258, 269 for his characterization of inconsistency as a Dtr technique, a position that frees van Seters from confronting inconsistencies in his own analysis. Cf. H.-D. Hoffmann, *Reform and Reformen* (Zurich: Theologischer, 1980), allowing a second hand in 2 Kings 17:34–41.

6. R. Smend, "Das Gesetz und die Völker. Ein Beitrag zur deuteronomistischen Redaktionsgeschichte," in H. W. Wolff, ed., *Probleme biblischer Theologie* (Fs. G. von Rad; Munich: Chr. Kaiser, 1971), 494–509, adding Joshua 1:7–9; 13:1b–6; Judges 2:1–9, 17, 20f., 23.

7. W. Dietrich, *Prophetie und Geschichte. Eine redaktionsgeschichtliche Untersuchung zum deuteronomistischen Geschichtswerk* (FRLANT 108; Göttingen, W. Germany: Vandenhoeck & Ruprecht, 1972); T. Veijola, *Die ewige Dynastie. David und die Entstehung seiner Dynastie nach der deuteronomistischen Darstellung* (Annales academiae scientarum fennicae B/193; Helsinki: Suomalainen Tiedeakatemia, 1975); idem, *Das Königtum in der deuteronomistischen Historiographie. Eine redaktionsgeschichtliche Untersuchung* (Annales academiae scientarum fennicae B/198; Helsinki: Suomalainen Tiedeakatemia, 1977).

8. T. Veijola, *Königtum* (n. 7) 83ff., 5; cf. Noth, *US* (n. 3), 54, 57–60, with Dtr here contradicting his sources.

9. R. Smend, *Die Entstehung des Alten Testaments* (Stuttgart: Kohlhammer, 1978), 115.

10. See E. Tov, "The Literary History of Jeremiah," in Tigay, ed., *Empirical Models* (n. 1), 211–37, especially 233. To the same effect, see Tigay, "The Stylistic Criterion of Source Criticism," ibid., 149–73, especially 170–72; A. Rofé, "Joshua 20: Historico-Literary Criticism Illustrated," ibid. 131–47.

11. Tigay, *Empirical Models* (n. 1), 45, 47; on Samaritan, 81, 82, n. 67 (there is no real contradiction either in this case or in that of the association of Exodus 20:24f. with Deuteronomy 11:29f.; 27:2–7: the stone altar is already a possibility in Exodus, which the culture as a whole had adopted); Tov, "Literary History" (n. 10), 226.

12. F. M. Cross, *Canaanite Myth and Hebrew Epic* (Cambridge: Harvard University, 1973), 274–89; J. D. Levenson, "Who Inserted the Book of the Torah?" *HTR* 68 (1975): 203–33; R. E. Friedman, "From Egypt to Egypt: Dtr[1] and Dtr[2]," in B. Halpern and J. D. Levenson, eds., *Traditions in Transformation: Turning-Points in Biblical Faith* (Fs. F. M. Cross; Winona Lake: Eisenbrauns, 1981), 167–92; idem *The Exile and Biblical Narrative* (HSM 22; Chico, CA: Scholars, 1981), 1–43; R. D. Nelson, *The Double Redaction of the Deuteronomistic History* (JSOTSup 18; Sheffield, U.K.: JSOT, 1981). A. Jepsen (*Die Quellen des Königsbuches* [Halle, E. Germany: Niemeyer, 1953]), working on Noth's model about sources, comes to a conclusion midway between Noth's and Cross's.

13. See Dietrich, *Prophetie* (n. 7), 19f., 28f. on Jeroboam; Veijola, *Ewige Dynastie* (n. 7), 134ff. Note especially T. N. D. Mettinger, *King and Messiah. The Civil and Sacral Legiti-*

mation of the Israelite Kings (CBOTS 8; Lund, Sweden: Gleerup, 1976), 276–78.

14. C. Steuernagel, *Lehrbuch der Einleitung in das Alte Testament* (Tübingen, W. Germany: Mohr, 1912), 245–49; also, N. Lohfink, "Die Bundesurkunde des Königs Josias," *Bib* 44 (1963): 261–88; see further Wellhausen, in Bleek, *Einleitung* (n. 2), 263.

15. See Chapter 7. For a typology of the dynastic covenant that reverses Cross's, but is more consistent, see Mettinger, *King and Messiah* (n. 13), 276–78.

16. Friedman, *Exile* (n. 12), 21.

17. See Nelson, *Redaction* (n. 12), 69–76, with bibliography. See also Chapter 7, with additional bibliography.

18. N. 10. Cf. further, Y. Kaufmann, *The History of Israelite Religion* (8 vols.; Jerusalem: Bialik, 1937), 4.358; Friedman, *Exile* (n. 12), 10.

19. W. Beyerlin, "Gattung und Herkunft des Rahmens im Richterbuch," in E. Würthwein, ed., *Tradition und Situation: Studien zur alttestamentlichen Prophetie* (Fs. A. Weiser; Göttingen: Vandenhoeck & Ruprecht, 1963), 1–29; W. Richter, *Die Bearbeitung des "Retterbuches" in der deuteronomischen Epoche* (BBB 21; Bonn: Hanstein, 1964); H. Weippert, "Die 'deuteronomistischen' Beurteilungen der Könige von Israel und Juda und das Problem der Redaktion der Königsbücher," *Bib* 53 (1972): 301–39; A. Lemaire, "Vers L'histoire de la Rédaction des Livres des Rois," *ZAW* 98 (1986):221–36; B. Peckham, *The Composition of the Deuteronomistic History* (HSM 35; Atlanta: Scholars, 1985). See further, M. Weippert, "Fragen des israelitischen Geschichtsbewusstseins," *VT* 23 (1973): 415–42. Against these approaches, apart from the scholars enumerated above, cf. S. Timm, *Die Dynastie Omri* (FRLANT 124; Göttingen: Vandenhoeck & Ruprecht, 1982), 28–40; W. Boyd Barrick, "On the 'Removal of the "High Places" ' in 1–2 Kings," *Bib* 55 (1974): 257–59.

20. See Noth, *US* (n. 3), 89 and n. 3; Wellhausen, in Bleek, *Einleitung* (n. 2), 186f.

21. Noth, *US* (n. 3), 61–66, following L. Rost, *Die Überlieferung von der Thronnachfolge Davids* (BWANT 3/6; Stuttgart: Kohlhammer, 1926).

22. See Noth, *US* (n. 3), 27–37, especially 32–35; cf. the more complicated, and less probable, treatments of G. I. Davies, "The Wilderness Itineraries and the Composition of the Pentateuch," *VT* 33 (1983): 1–13 (Deut. 2:8, 17, 26, 28f. is a harmonization of Numbers 33, in which Israel goes through Moab, and Judg. 11:18, in which they skirt it); Nelson, *Double Redaction* (n. 12), 139, n. 20 (totally skewed traditions); cf. the remarks of B. Peckham, "The Deuteronomistic History of Saul and David," *ZAW* 97 (1985): 191; Peckham, *Composition* (n. 19), 1.

23. 2 Kings 21:3b–15; 22:16f.; 23:4b–5, 19f., 24; 23:25b–25:30: Nelson, *Double Redaction* (n. 12), 120, and *passim*.

24. For the theme as one inherited from H(Dtr), see chapters 6, 7, 9.

25. Noth, *US* (n. 3), 51. Cf H. Hupfeld, *Die Quellen Genesis und die Art ihrer Zusammensetzung von neuem untersucht* (Berlin: Wiegandt & Grieben, 1853), 165–67 on RJEP.

26. The coverage, again, is of keys for isolating H(Dtr)'s and E(Dtr)x's work. Chapter 6 treats Judges and some of Joshua, Chapter 7, 1 Kings 1–11 and the issue of exile, Chapter 8, 1 Samuel 8–15 (the key to the books of Samuel). I examine Joshua in "Canaan, Conquest of," D. N. Freedman, ed., *Anchor Bible Dictionary* (Garden City, N.Y.: Doubleday), forthcoming. Part III deals with the history as a whole. Sigla are H(Dtr) for the Josianic historian who assembled DtrH (the history as a unified whole); H(Dtr)hez for the author of the Hezekian source (Dtr[hez] // Dtr[jos]); E(Dtr)x for the exilic editor of Dtr(x) (also E[Dtr]n/p), and so on.

CHAPTER 6

The Brass Ring:
The Redactional Carousel of
the Book of Judges

A prodigy of fear and a portent of broached mischief to the unborn times.
—HENRY IV

REDACTION IN JUDGES: A CONSENSUS

For testing the ideas laid out in the preceding chapter, no book offers more fertile ground that that of Judges. Judges is exoskeletal. Its editorial history has attracted reasoned hypotheses since the past century. Yet its literary history is as complex as that of any other work in DtrH.

THE FRAMEWORK OF M+

M+ denominates the body of Judges, the stories about the major judges, Othniel, Ehud, Deborah-Baraq, Gideon, Jephthah (and Samson). Framing M+ from the front is Judges 1, a catalogue of regions conquered by Judah and regions not conquered by other tribes, and Judges 2:6–3:6, a general introduction to the period after Joshua. After M+ come two stories about tribal relations (17–21). And interspersed with M+ is a document called the list of minor judges (10:1–5; 12:7–15)—M−.

There has been agreement since the past century that the stories of M+, except that of Othniel, were drawn from sources.[1] In two cases (chapters 3–4), this verdict has been confirmed. There are verbal indications in other accounts, such as the use of the antique ša-relative in the Gideon narratives.[2] The received materials were relayed with some of their verbiage intact.

What unifies the sources of M+ is a redaction, a formulary formidable in its consistency. In its fullest form it embraces the following elements:

1. The Israelites "did/continued to do evil in the sight of Yhwh": 3:7, 12; 4:1; 6:1; 10:6; 13:1 (3:7; 10:6 amplify with notices of apostasy; cf. 8:33f.).

2. Yhwh gave Israel into the power of an oppressor, whom they served for a specific term of years:
   3:8; 3:12, 14; 4:2f.; 6:1; 10:7–9; 13:1 (Judges 3:8; 10:7 add that Yhwh was angry. Judges 3:12–14; 4:2f.; 6:1; 10:7–9 add further information).

3. The Israelites cried out to Yhwh:
   3:9, 15; 4:3; 6:6; 10:10 (no notice for Samson; that in 4:3 comes before part of Element 2, and uses a different verb).

4. Yhwh raised up a savior:
   3:9, 15; 4:4–9; 6:7–10, 11–24; 10:11–16; 11:1–11; 13:2–24 (only 3:9, 15 put this simply; the others have call narratives, negotiations, or, in Samson's case, a birth narrative).

4A. The savior saved Israel:
   (Othniel, Ehud, Baraq, Gideon, Jephthah; no such claim for Samson; but note investment with the spirit in 3:10; 11:29; 13:25; 14:19; 15:14; cf. 4:8G; 7:9ff.; 16:28).

5. The foe is subdued:
   3:10, 30; 4:23f.; 8:28; 11:33 (no claim for Samson; only 3:10 does not use the root *kn'*; it is otherwise similar to 4:24).

6. "The land was quiet" for a specified term of years:
   3:11, 30; 5:31; 8:28 (eighty years in 3:30, forty elsewhere. No claim for Jephthah or Samson, who "judged Israel" for specific terms—12:7; 15:20).

FIGURE 7: M+ FORMULAE

I.

3:7	ויעשו בני ישראל את הרע בעיני ה' וישכחו את אלהיהם ויעבדו את הבעלים . . .	
3:12	ויספו בני ישראל לעשות הרע בעיני ה'	
4:1	ויספו בני ישראל לעשות הרע בעיני ה'	
6:1	ויעשו בני ישראל הרע בעיני ה'	
10:6	ויספו בני ישראל לעשות הרע בעיני ה' ויעבדו את הבעלים . . .	
13:1	ויספו בני ישראל לעשות הרע בעיני ה'	
2:1	ויעשו בני ישראל את הרע בעיני ה' ויעבדו את הבעלים . . .	

II.

3:8	ו יחר אף ה' בישראל וימכרם ביד . . . ויעבדו ב"י את RN 8 שנים	
3:12–14	ויחזק ה' . . . על ישראל . . . ויעבדו ב"י את RN 18 שנה	
	וימכרם ה' ביד . . . (Element III+)	
4:2–3	ויתנם ביד . . . והוא לחץ את ב"י בחזקה 20 שנה	
	7 שנים	
6:1	ו יחר אף ה' בישראל וימכרם ביד . . . ותעז יד מדין על ישראל . . .	
10:7–9	ויתנם ה' ביד . . . וירעצו וירצצו את ב"י בשנה ההיא 18 שנה . . .	
13:1	40 שנה	
2:14	ויתנם ביד שסים וימכרם ביד אויביהם	

III.

3:9	ויזעקו בני ישראל אל ה'
3:15	ויזעקו בני ישראל אל ה'
4:3	½ Element II+ . . . ויזעקו בני ישראל אל ה'
6:6	ויזעקו בני ישראל אל ה'
10:10	ויזעקו בני ישראל אל ה' לאמר . . .
13:1	. . .
2:18	כי ינחם ה' מנאקתם מפני לחציהם ודחקיהם

IV.

3:9	ויקם ה' מושיע לבני ישראל ויושיעם את PN . . .
3:15	ויקם ה' להם מושיע את PN . . .
4:4–9	Deborah, a prophetess (אשה נביאה), calls Baraq
6:7–10	prophecy + וישלח ה' איש נביא אל בני ישראל
6:11–24	call of Gideon
10:11–16	prophecy + repentence
11:1–11	call of Jephthah
13:2–24	prophecy + birth of Samson
2:16	ויקם ה' שפטים ויושיעום מיד שסיהם

V.

3:10	ויתן ה' בידו את כושן רשעתים מלך ארם ותעז ידו על כושן רשעתים
3:30	ותכנע מואב ביום ההוא תחת יד ישראל
4:23f.	ויכנע ה' ביום ההוא את יבין מלך כנען לפני בני ישראל
	ותלך יד בני ישראל הלוך וקשה על יבין . . .
8:28	ויכנע מדין לפני בני ישראל . . .
11:33	ויכנעו בני עמון מפני בני ישראל . . .
13–16	. . .
2:6–3:6	. . .

VI.

3:11	ותשקט הארץ ארבעים שנה
3:30	ותשקט הארץ שמונים שנה
5:31	ותשקט הארץ ארבעים שנה
8:28	ותשקט הארץ ארבעים שנה בימי גדעון
12:7	. . .
15:20	. . .
2:18	When Yhwh raised them up judges, Yhwh was with the judge, and saved them from their enemies all the days of the judge.

Notes to Figure 7

1. Element I in 8:33 is shaped by 8:27b; "They did not remember Yhwh" (who took them from Egypt = 6:7–10; 2:1f.) = 2:13; 3:7; 10:6 ("They did not serve him")
2. The syntax of 6:7 ("and when the Israelites cried out") in relation to the formula ("the Israelites cried out") is the same as that of 2:18 ("and when Yhwh raised them up judges") in relation to 2:16 ("Yhwh raised up judges")
3. Divine spirit or accompaniment for 3:10; 4:8G; 6:16, 34; 11:29; 14:19 + 15:14 + 13:25; cf. 9:23. There is no notice for Ehud. In the prologue, 2:18.

Almost all scholars regard this framework as imposed secondarily on an existing *collection* of the tales (see nn. 1, 2).

This view is not patent. The framework has several functions: it names the oppressor, describes the oppression, and furnishes other data. It is the framework (3:13), for example, that situates the Ehud story in the Jordan River valley, in anticipation of 3:19, 26, and 28; the framework (6:2–6) provides background concerning the Midianite oppression on which the Gideon account draws (6:13). It is possible, thus, that M+ was first assembled by the author of the framework, who integrated into the framework essential story elements.

Was there a preframework M+? If so, the editor who added the framework reworked the introduction and conclusion of each episode, but left the body of the stories untouched: no related redaction has been found inside the M+ accounts. This uneconomical hypothesis is particularly weak in connection with Judges 4. Chapter 4 has disclosed not just the derivation of this chapter from the poem, but also its intellectual unity and antiquarian thoroughness: probably it belonged from the first to an ongoing history of the premonarchic era. But the chapter never existed without its framework: Deborah can command Baraq to engage Sisera (4:7) only if the context stipulates that Jabin, Sisera's liege, had dominated Israel (4:2f.). The other accounts in M+ describe Israel's straits *after* the framework introduction as well as in it (3:15b; 6:11–13; 11:1–5). Judges 4 does not introduce the oppression even obliquely, except in the framework.[3] At the end of the account, circumstances are similar: other saviors in M+ all rout the oppressors in the body of the account (3:29; 7:22–25; 8:11f., 21; 11:32f.); Baraq, who does destroy Sisera's field force in the body of the narrative (4:16), undoes the oppressor, Jabin, only in the framework (4:23f.). More than for any other episode in the book, the framework is indispensable to Judges 4.

Only one effective argument sustains the view that the frameworks were imposed on an earlier M+:[4] the framework is adapted to fit the narratives. Thus the formula (number 4), "Yhwh raised up a savior" (3:9, 15) vanishes where the narrative reports the savior's vocation (4:6-9; 6:11-24; 11:1-11; cf. 13:2-24); similarly, the rest formula is missing in the Jephthah account, because an entry from M— (the list of minor judges) supplies Jephthah's term (12:7).[5]

This line of reasoning establishes only that the frameworks were devised with the stories in mind. Similarly, Polybius' evaluations of Cleomenes or Hannibal hardly imply that someone else wrote the narrative history to which the evaluations are adapted. Indeed, if M+ existed without the frameworks, it did so without Judges 4, which is to say, in a substantially different form. H(M+), the historian who collected the stories of the major judges, is therefore on the principle of economy and in light of the substantive evidence to be regarded as the author of the frameworks.

THE LIMITS OF M+: THE SCHOLARLY VIEWS

It remains to find the limits of the original M+. Scholars generally claim that it must have set out from 3:12, with the story of Ehud (or 3:7, with that of Othniel). Judges 2:6–3:6, they maintain, stems from another author, who in 2:11–19 summarized the period by abstracting elements of the M+ frameworks. On this scenario Judges developed as follows:

sources (> M+) > M+ with framework > M+ with framework and introduction.

Judges 2:11–19 depicts the period as an iterative sequence of apostasy, oppression, and salvation. But it does not include the remarks, "The Israelites cried out to Yhwh" (framework element number 3) or "The land was quiet" for a term of years (number 6). Further, 2:11–13 explicitly identify Israel's evildoing as apostasy, and state that Yhwh was angry; in M+ only 3:7f.; 10:6–9 use similar language. These passages, therefore, are traced to the (Deuteronomistic) author of 2:11–19.

More important still, 2:11–19 identify the saviors that Yhwh raised up as judges—the figures who accomplish military victory in M+ are assigned ongoing office in 2:11–19. Likewise, 2:18 identifies the term of relief with the judge's lifespan, a connection drawn more loosely in the framework (but cf. 4:1). And 2:17 asserts that Israel's apostasy continued even during the period of relief (the judge's lifetime), an assertion without a basis in the framework. In all, there is a strong case to divide 2:6–3:6 from M+,[6] the particulars of which are discussed in the succeeding sections of this chapter.

The same scholars shear off the Othniel account from M+. This pericope is almost all framework, with the names of the savior and the oppressor plugged in. But it identifies Othniel as a judge (v. 10), identifies Israel's evildoing as apostasy (v. 7), and refers to Yhwh's wrath (v. 8), all as in 2:11–14; 10:6–9. It also adds the element of Othniel's investiture by Yhwh's spirit (v. 10). It lines up with 2:11–19, against M+, which is therefore thought to have begun with Ehud in 3:12.[7]

Where M+ ends is more disputed. Samson is generally excluded: he does not rescue Israel, there is no popular outcry on account of the oppression, and there is no rest formula. The Abimelek story (8:30–9:57), which on the same logic should also be excised, is conceded a close connection to the Gideon account. Richter excludes Jephthah: the introduction to his story in 10:6–16 resembles 2:11–19 in that it explicitly describes Yhwh's wrath; and the notice of Ammon's subjugation (framework element number 5, 11:33) does not come, as usual, at the end of the account. The rest formula (element 6) is also displaced by a notice from M− (12:7).[8] This leaves Richter with an M+ running from Ehud to Abimelek, where the introduction of M− (10:1) marks its limit.

This sort of analysis has drawn from D. W. Gooding a protest typical of most assaults on redaction criticism. Gooding insists on the literary unity of Judges. Thus 2:11–19 introduces 3:7–16:31. The two differ in detail, but broadly agree. So if Israel does not "cry out to Yhwh" in 2:11–19, 2:18 does say that Israel's "groaning" induced Yhwh to "raise up" saviors. Judges 2:18 even provides for a period of "rest" corresponding to that of M+. The variations, thus, between 2:11–19 and the M+ framework are too minor to justify the hypothesis of a second hand.

Gooding also correlates 2:11–19 with the M+ stories. Judges 2:19, "at the judge's death, they would revert to depravity worse than their fathers'," implies, in his view, a continual deterioration in behavior. This manifests itself as follows: Othniel (the first savior) has a faithful Israelite wife (1:11–15), and Samson (last) has unstable foreign liaisons (the motif links 1:11–15; 3.5f. to M+). Ehud (second) kills Moabites at the river, and Jephthah (second from last) kills Israelites. Women kill two leaders in Judges 4 (third) and 9 (third from last), the first Canaanite, the second Israelite. Gideon is at the center, and it is Gideon who degenerates from a savior to a pimp of apostasy (8:27, 33). Gooding finds other, similar schemes. Together, he maintains, these prove a unity of authorship.[9]

Finally, Gooding links Judges 1:1–2:5; 17–21 to the rest of the book; these materials lack the M+ framework because they are not savior accounts. They may have been included, out of antiquarian interest, regardless of the fact that they did not fit the scheme of the framework.[10]

Gooding's argument has three main flaws. First, the key text, Judges 2:19, does not speak of persistent moral deterioration, but of apostasy ("They were more depraved than their fathers *in going after other gods*"). The framework cites apostasy in 3:7f. (Othniel) and 10:6–9 (Jephthah); it is mentioned in 6:10 and at the start of the Abimelek story (8:33). But the theme is absent from the stories themselves. Nor does a cycle of apostasy culminate with Samson: at worst, foreign women are the issue. If 2:19 articulates a program for M+, its author forgot to carry it through.

Second, Gooding has virtually to advertise in order to discover coherence. His "deterioration" is not progressive: the first judge matches up to the last, the second to the second from last; is the book to be read with the aid of a pogo stick? Nor does the deterioration have a single standard, let alone the standard—apostasy—of 2:19. The issues are wives, killings at rivers, and killings of leaders (leaders are also killed in Judges 3; 8, without Gooding bringing them into reckoning). How is one to relate these issues to one another so as to arrive at a picture of progressive decay?

Finally, literary coherence is not an argument against multiple revisions of a text. Editors are capable of producing it, and, indeed, aim to produce it. Readers, at least those of Gooding's acuity, can also find it, even where unintended. Divorced from the logic of a plot, a literary pattern is no more an argument against editing than an argument for it.

This point can be proved by extending Gooding's thesis. Thus the framework begins to disintegrate with Deborah: she, not Yhwh, designates Baraq (4:6–10). Then Gideon's call is mediated, and must be tested by a sign (6:11–24). At the end Gideon actually usurps priestly authority (8:22–27).[11] Next, Abimelek promotes himself to a kingship. Human initiative has supplanted divine, and the minor judges follow in an orderly succession, with no note that any of them was raised by Yhwh. Jephthah is explicitly raised on human initiative (11:1–11), so that now the community as a whole has taken control of the elevation of leaders. Correspondingly, the framework formulary ruptures: Jephthah's cycle lacks the rest formula (framework element 6), which is replaced by a notice from M− (12:7). In Samson's case only the introduction to the framework cycle remains (13:1). Then, with the cycle altogether abandoned, Judges 17f. describe how a tribe chose, rather than received, an icon. And Judges 19–21 show how Yhwh must choose sides, for some Israelites and against others. Finally, Israel drags Yhwh into battle without sanction, so that he sides with aliens (Philistines) against the tribes (1 Samuel 4).

Does this progression imply that the cyclical, mythic era of the judges gave way to a linear, historical, monarchic time? Is the turning to Yhwh in Judges 13–21 (Nazirite, Yahwistic icon, ark) a sign of amelioration? Or are all these patterns coincidental, by-products of other authorial concerns? The difference between intended and unintended patterns of coherence is crucial to resolving questions of authorship.

Gooding's study is valuable as a corrective. Formal variation— in language—between 2:11–19 and the M+ frameworks does not justify assigning these texts to different hands. The imperfect application of the M+ framework to Samson may reflect, as Gooding cautions, a difference in content rather than in authorship. Historians adopt different perspectives on different episodes—Samson is not Jephthah, Jephthah not Gideon—and desist from a literary pattern when the period to which the pattern applies comes to an end. Thus content determines form: historians and editors use the words that say what they mean. Any other approach to the text oversimplifies the issues. The question, then, is how far historiographic concerns dictate the pattern of and variation in usage and thought in Judges.

REDACTION IN JUDGES IN HISTORIOGRAPHIC PERSPECTIVE

The redaction critics and their opponents have devoted insufficient attention to the antiquarian logic of Judges. This sheds considerable light on the questions under discussion.

THE LOGIC OF THE M+ FRAMEWORKS

That the M+ frameworks are infused by cultural assumptions is clear enough to demand no extensive defense: Yhwh punishes infidelity; where Israel is faithful or repentant, Yhwh provides for it so that human political structures are unnecessary (cf. 8:22–23; 1 Sam. 12:6–12). Still, whether these reflections fashion the frameworks, or whether the frameworks make use of them as an assumption, is an issue that warrants consideration.

The M+ frameworks fill a historiographic and literary void. They bridge the gaps between the individual M+ accounts, and interpret the events those accounts describe. That is to say, they shape a collocation of otherwise isolated reports (Ehud and Moab, Deborah and Sisera, Gideon and Midian, and so on) into a continuous history of an era. The frameworks furnish the only literary unity that the book of Judges possesses.

In this capacity the frameworks provide a chronology. Only Ehud's successor, Shamgar ben-Anat (3:31), lacks a specific term of years. But Shamgar was inserted after M+ was assembled: 4:1 attributes Jabin's oppression to the aftermath of Ehud's death, not Shamgar's. The insertion was motivated by a desire to illuminate the comparison of Shamgar to Jael in SDeb (5:6); but the awkward syntax of 4:1 ("The Israelites continued to do evil . . . for Ehud was dead") prohibited, on pain of substantial reworking, Shamgar's placement after the notice of Ehud's death.[12]

Except for Shamgar, M+ assigns a period of rest to every savior in the collection. This chronology, as Noth observed, is properly the property of an ongoing historical work; it could have no meaning unless linked to the chronology of eras that succeeded it. Thus M+ treats the premonarchic era as a chapter within a larger history.

The distribution of M+ frameworks confirms this inference and clarifies their function. The frameworks occur only in the period between Joshua and Eli. What the peripheral eras—of Joshua and Eli—have in common is chronological continuity, particularly continuity in leadership. By contrast, the M+ stories carry no implications of continuity: there is no inherent sequence from one account, one judge, to the next. H(M+)'s cycle of apostasy, oppression, and rest thus supplies continuity or an explanation of political discontinuity in the era between two periods of orderly succession. Judges is a sort of historiographic Intermediate Period. It could so serve only as part of an ongoing national history.

The frameworks do not impose their polemical purpose upon recalcitrant sources, but, as observed in this chapter's section entitled "The Limits of M+: The Scholarly Views," repeatedly break down: "Yhwh raised up a savior" (framework element number 4) vanishes where a vocation is reported; the rest formula (6) yields to a citation from M− (12:7). The Samson story lacks the element of Israel's outcry (3), probably because the birth narrative of 13:2ff. would not suggest a speedy divine response. It also jettisons the elements of subjection (4A, 5) and rest (6): Philistia dominated Israel into the dawn of the monarchic period. H(M+) adapted the frameworks to the content they were devised to frame.

The framework disappears completely in Judges 17–21, which deals neither with oppression nor with salvation. The same applies to the Abi-melek interlude. Judges 8:33f. interpret the episode as a punishment for apostasy.[13] But the account lacks a foreign oppressor; and the chronological continuity with Gideon (9:1–3) made invocation of the framework scheme inappropriate. The cycle breaks down in all these cases, not because of derangement in a second edition, but because of attention to content in the first. In short, the M+ formulary does not delimit the work of H(M+): the formulary appears only where appropriate.

Diagnostic is the treatment of M−, a text integrated into the book by H(M+) (see this chapter's section entitled "The Logic of the Cycle: 2:11–19"). To the minor judges, the framework cycle is not applied. A lack of details did not prohibit imposing the cycle: the case of Othniel illustrates how the frameworks might have been leveled through. Instead the cycle of oppression and rescue is suspended until M− has run its course (10:1–5; 12:7–15, followed by Jephthah and Samson respectively). Like the history in Genesis–Joshua, and like Samuel–Kings, M− implied continuity in succession; Jephthah's role in it determined its location.[14] Thus the historian abandons the cycle of discontinuity and resumes it only after M−, when discontinuity is again indicated. Whatever the theological program of M+, the content of the sources conditions its development. M+ is not overly schematic, but adaptive and antiquarian in its interpretation of the historical process.

The sequence of the accounts also seems to display antiquarian reflection. Othniel belonged just after Joshua (1:11–15). Samson dealt with Philistia, still ascendant in the monarchic era; and Dan's migration to the north (17–18) could not precede Samson's activity in Dan's earlier territory near Philistia. These accounts therefore belonged at the end of the book. Jephthah fought with Ammon, another power active in Saul's day (1 Samuel 11; cf. 10:7): this episode took place just before Samson. And Deborah's triumph against the remnants of the Canaanite city-state system belonged before the Gideon account: the Midianite incursions to which Gideon responds logically supposed the system's demise. Gideon may have been fixed already: M−, which includes Jephthah (12:7), begins with Abimelek (10:1) or perhaps even Gideon himself (8:30, 32). Alternately, Gideon's contretemps with Ephraim (8:1–3) may have suggested proximity to Jephthah (12:1–6). In any case the sequence, 1) Deborah; 2) Gideon; 3) Jephthah; 4) Samson; 5) Danite migration, left room for Ehud and Judges 19–21 only at the ends of the corpus. Ehud, a savior, came at the beginning; Judges 19–21, a tale of civil war, belonged at the end.

The ordering of the accounts, like the distribution of the frameworks, thus suggests a concern with the content of the sources. Further, the very cut of the framework theology is tailored to the literature available. The sources do not appear to have been selected with a view to advancing the theology in question: M−, Judges 9, and Judges 17–21 all appear, although unbroken to the bridle of the frameworks; further, no surviving reference to the premonarchic era suggests that a significant source was omitted.[15] H(M+) seems to have incorporated all available information. Certainly he did not shy away from including materials the framework scheme would not fit.

H(M+) applied the frameworks to the vast preponderance of his sources in sheer bulk. Not every story implied a period of foreign oppression: SDeb is silent as to Canaanite dominance; Jephthah could be taken to have met a mere threat (11:4f., 12). But overall the view was tenable and, in some cases (Ehud, Gideon, Samson, even SDeb), moderately probable.[16] Stories of deliverance implied the need for deliverance, and for these stories (not for M−), H(M+) concretizes that need in the form of foreign oppressors.

For a sequence of oppressions, it was desirable to furnish an etiology. The traditions of enslavement in Egypt afforded no satisfactory model: they give no reason, and the oppressions of Judges occur *after* Yhwh has fulfilled his promise to enfranchise Israel in the land. In this era a divine assurance of plenty and security had theoretical force.

What, then, could account for Israel's repeated straits? Only Yhwh's wrath. What called down on Israel such drastic, repeated punishment? Evildoing was the logical surmise. But if oppression was caused by evildoing, say by apostasy, only one thing would occasion a reprieve: repentance, appeal to Yhwh, the abjuration of alien gods.

The aftermath of a reprieve had to be a period of respite. Any other recourse would trivialize Yhwh's intervention. Nonetheless, the rhythm of the cycle of oppression and rescue demanded that the respite be limited. The time assigned to rest therefore coincides, schematically, with the savior's lifetime. Through Israelite ritual, liturgy, and historiography runs a consistent mythos associating the achievement of leadership with the rescue of the nation;[17] in Judges 11:1–11, Jephthah makes ongoing leadership a condition of his aid. The culture's pattern for leadership thus suggested that the savior became a national figure in the wake of his achievement.

As it stands, the whole causal logic of the theological cycle arises from the materials it frames. Just so, the particulars in the frameworks are inseparable from the accounts. The historian molds the framework to the sources in particulars and in theme, in the matter of discontinuity of leadership, and in the application of the framework scheme to M+ but not M−, to Othniel, but not Abimelek.

The M+ frameworks answer to H(M+)'s political and personal concerns. But the cycle also explains particular events. It is not recklessly imposed. It is, instead, applied where the sources afford it most leverage. In the framework (see the following section and Chapter 9), a strong polemical interest is present. Nevertheless, the analects of premonarchic history include episodes that do, and others that do not, fit the frame-

work scheme. H(M+) in the instance exhibits the sense that characterizes all reasonable historians: he confines his tendentious interpretation
to the evidence that justifies it. M+ is not a version of events concocted
to justify a schematic view of the past.

THE LOGIC OF THE CYCLE: 2:11–19

The antiquarian restraint that characterizes M+ extends also to
2:11–19. This text summarizes the whole era as one of discontinuity.
The Israelites sinned, and were subjected, and, at "their groaning,"
were rescued. They excelled in apostasy even during the judge's lifetime
(2:17f.). At the judge's death they grew worse still (v. 19).

This summary mainly recapitulates the frameworks. It exceeds them
chiefly with the idea that apostasy continued even when the judges
brought rest to the land. The conclusion may have been won from the
report of idolatry (construed as apostasy) under Gideon (8:27).

From the introduction of apostasy during the periods of rest follows
another detail in which 2:11–19 nuances the interpretation of M+. The
"crying out" of the frameworks (framework element number 3) cannot
signal repentance: apostasy continued, after all. The outcry assumes instead the aspect of pitiable moaning (v. 18), like that of Israel in Egypt.
The exception is the case of Jephthah (10:6–16), where, against 2:19,
apostasy is specifically ended. Read in place, this text caps the M+ cycle,
and no apostasy or rescue thereafter occurs. Accurate or not, the interpretation in 2:11–19 embodies a sharp reading of the texts.

A third peculiarity of 2:11–19 is that it synchronizes the period of respite
that followed each rescue with the lifespan of the generation rescued (cf.
2:10) and of the judge (2:16–19). This element is implicit in the frameworks, which report the deaths of every savior except Shamgar (who is secondarily inserted) and Deborah-Baraq (who are a pair). The placement of
Othniel's death (3:11) suggests the sort of connection that 2:16–19 infer;
the reports on Ehud (4:1) and Gideon (8:33) are even clearer (see this chapter's section entitled "The Logic of the M+ Frameworks").

That the agent of Israel's rescue remained a leader his life long was a
logical deduction on this basis. It was implicit, too, in M− and in the use
of M− instead of the M+ rest formula (6) for Jephthah (12:7). Nevertheless, the cultural pattern informing M+ is not in evidence in
2:11–19. M+ describes the calls of deliverers, who were saviors first,
and leaders only thereafter. Judges 2:11–19 makes the saviors judges,
insinuating that they occupied defined positions when they rescued their
nation. This followed from the inference in 2:11–19 that Yhwh provided judges even when Israel was apostate.

Here is the fourth and most striking property of 2:11–19. It calls the
saviors judges. As a title this nomenclature is alien to the M+ accounts
(the verb applies, once, to Deborah, 4:4). In the M+ frameworks the
verb appears in Othniel's case alone (3:10).

The use of the title judge is important. It was clear from 1 Samuel 8–12 (and Judg. 8:22–27; 9) that the saviors were not kings. Neither was their jurisdiction restricted to a single tribe. To this rule, Jephthah may be construed as an exception; but if the author of 2:11–19 took Gilead (11:8–11) as a geographic term, even Jephthah would have enjoyed a supratribal constituency. These strictures, and the fact that the deliverers' children did not, as a rule, succeed them, made the choice of the title *judge*—a royal appointee outside the structure of the tribal system (as Deut. 17:9; 19:17; 2 Chron. 19:5–11; esp. 2 Sam. 15:4; 2 Kings 15:5)—peculiarly appropriate.[18]

Stronger still was an influence pointed out by Noth. M− described each of its figures with the clause, "He judged Israel." Jephthah appeared both in M+ and M−, and the narrative itself implied his ongoing tenure in office (11:8–11). From this followed an equation of the figures in M+ with those in M−: all judged.[19] Noth held that the formulation, "He judged Israel" implied a national office, and inspired the all-Israel redaction in M+.[20] In this matter, however, M− was a more marginal factor (see the section entitled "The Genre of the Story" in Chapter 3).

All this establishes that 2:11–19 adeptly epitomizes the portrait in M+. Exposing their literary relationship will demand technical argument. As in the case of Judges 4 and 5, the presentations differ, such that 2:11–19 could be derived from M+, but the M+ frameworks could not be derived from 2:11–19. Thus the interpretation of Israel's "outcry" (3) as unrepentant "groaning" (2:16–19) follows from the generalization of apostasy to the period as a whole. Read alone, M+ creates the opposite impression—that the outcry expressed repentance. This is explicit in 10:6–16: here the start of M− (10:1–5) has rung in a dawning continuity in leadership; after Israel reforms, the M− formulary ceases to begin, "There arose" (10:1–5), suggesting increased continuity (12:7–15). But 10:6–16 may deliberately reverse 2:11–19, rather than contradict it. In any event, the other M+ frameworks sit ill with 2:11–19. They should not be assigned to the same hand.

Most clearly the term *judge* distinguishes 2:11–19 from M+. No indisputably early tradition attaches the appellation to the M+ figures (1 Sam. 12:11; Isa. 9:3; 10:26, e.g.; the referent in Isa. 1:26; Mic. 4:14 is not plain). There is a reference to the "judges" in 2 Samuel 7:11 (1 Chron. 17:10; also Ruth 1:1). And Samuel's term of office (he "judged Israel all the days of his life") is stated after he delivers Israel (1 Sam. 7:2ff., 15–8:3). But these texts (like 1 Sam. 4:18 on Eli) are widely imputed to H(Dtr)—to the same editorial stratum as Judges 2:11–19. If the author of Judges 2:11–19 had composed, rather than interpreted, the M+ frameworks, we should expect framework element 6 ("the land was quiet") to mention the deliverer's judging.

A related issue is the status of M− in the collection. If the author of

2:11–19 assembled M+, he must have included M—, on which he draws (as we have seen). But it is more likely that he inherited an M+ already combined with M—: Jephthah's rest formula (framework element 6) has been suppressed in favor of M— (12:7); yet Gideon's was left (8:28) in proximity to notices resembling those of M— (8:30, 32), and to a story about his son (Chapter 9) that did not belong forty years after his own exploits. This is understandable in the work of H(M+), whose concern with continuity in succession leaves us with a distinction between major judges, in an era of episodic leadership, and minor judges, in an era of orderly succession (Jephthah falling between). But the author of 2:11–19 identifies the major with the minor judges: they were judges all. This author experienced no difficulty in joining the rest formula to the savior's judging in Othniel's case: Othniel was a judge first, and a savior thereafter (3:10), in line with the view of 2:11–19 that the judges were first elected as such, and not, as in M+ (especially 11:1–11), in consequence of their deeds.[21] Had he assembled, therefore, the Jephthah account, the author of 2:11–19 would not have omitted the rest formula: the least unnatural explanation for its omission is that H(M+) had already incorporated M— before the author of 2:11–19 set to work on the text.

Finally, 2:11–19 includes the figures of M— in the cycle of apostasy and punishment. Were it the author of 2:11–19 who first introduced M—, we should expect him to continue the cycle there: the technique by which the Othniel account was constructed from framework elements alone could easily have been practiced on M—. Judges 2:11–19 reads, thus, as though its author had M— in the text he was interpreting, and *understood* the cycle to have operated in connection with the minor as well as the major judges. This is another difference between 2:11–19 and M+: M+ desists from imposing the cycle where continuity in succession is indicated. In any event, M+/M— antedates 2:11–19.

These observations all suggest that 2:11–19 was secondary to the work of H(M+). With 2:11–19, one must associate Othniel ("he judged Israel"). Judges 4:4b–5, Deborah "was judging Israel," may also belong to this author, although Deborah is not Israel's military deliverer. And it is possible that the accusations of apostasy in 8:33f.; 10:6, 10b–16 are part of this layer. The latter in particular bear a close resemblance (with 10:17) to 1 Samuel 7:3–7. Both texts punctuate a transition from discontinuity to partial continuity in leadership (Abimelek follows his father, Gideon; Jephthah is already in the sequence of M—). But this is unsure: the preceding argument intimates the separate authorship of 10:6–16 and 2:11–19; and the evildoing of the M+ frameworks is most probably to be identified as apostasy. On this scenario 1 Samuel 7:3–7 will have been constructed on the model of Judges 10:6–16 (cf. also Gen. 35:2–5). In any event, the resultant picture coincides in outline with Richter's view of H(Dtr)'s work:[22] H(Dtr) added little more than an introduction.

As Chapter 9 will show (and the next section), however, he made the introduction a pivot in the presentation of Israel's history.

The reconstruction, with Richter, of a pre-Dtr M+ (here, an M+/M−) implies the existence of a pre-Dtr historical work stretching from the period of the judges into the monarchic era. This inference correlates with the hypothesis of H. Weippert as to the existence of a Hezekian national history.[23] Even if one attributes M+ to the author of 2:11–19, however, both M+ and 2:11–19 thoughtfully construe the historical data they present. Judges 2:11–19 in particular will be shown to conform utterly to H(Dtr)'s propaganda aims. Nevertheless, these aims are carefully channeled through the sluice gates of antiquarian interpretation. The promotion of political goals motivates H(Dtr)'s work, and dictates its larger form. The sources, and an antiquarian logic, govern its content.

THE LOGIC OF JUDGES 1–3

Judges 2:11–19 does not, as the discussion may suggest, stand in a vacuum. It forms part of a longer introduction to the period in 2:6–3:6. This complicated text is often regarded as composite. In it, the author, H(Dtr), plumbs the sources of Israelite apostasy. H(Dtr)'s interest in the matter is bound up intimately with the doctrines of Josiah's reform. Nevertheless, the argument is a historical one, governed by historical logic.

Before Israel entered Canaan, Israel "knew" only Yhwh (as Hos. 13:4), an interlude at Baal Peor excepted (P in Numbers 25). Yhwh was "Israel's god," and, in Josianic theology, all other gods were "foreign" (Deut. 4:19; 17:3), "the gods of strangers" (*ʾlhy nkr* of Baals and Ashtarts in Judg. 10:6–16; 1 Sam. 7:3f.). The *bāmôt*, or "high places," themselves, loci of rural Yahwism (2 Kings 18:22), were treated as centers of alien worship: Deuteronomy 12:2–5 and other texts interpret them as Canaanite relics.[24]

This was a logical perspective. If Israel knew Yhwh alone in the wilderness, foreign gods in the land could have come from two sources only: from Canaanites Joshua had failed to eradicate (Josh. 9; 1 Kings 9:20–22; 2 Sam. 5:6–9), whose cults remained in place, and from surrounding peoples unsubdued until David's time. Contact with either could explain the contamination. This inference conditioned the convictions of H(Dtr).

The identification of Israel's early evildoing as apostasy thus affected how H(Dtr) (and H[M+]) understood Joshua's legacy. The Canaanites, never eradicated, were the source of Israel's sin; the surrounding peoples, unreduced, were the agency of Yhwh's punishment, and supplementary suppliers of gods (10:6). Here unfolds a theme that runs from Judges to the end of H(Dtr)'s work. H(Dtr)'s research confirms the Deuteronomic view that the *bāmôt* were Canaanite relics.

These ruminations molded the presentation in Judges 1–3, and their illumination throws the unity of these chapters into sharper relief. Judges 2:6–10 ascribes Israel's earliest infidelity to the generation after Joshua, "who did not know Yhwh, and the deeds he accomplished for Israel." The reasoning is often applied today to politicians or voters who, not having lived through the last great war, forget that "war is hell" (cf. Polybius 2.21). This reasoning also produced the equation of the period of rest with the generation of the "savior" in M +. Thus unfamiliarity with Yhwh's activity predisposed Israel to assimilate Canaanite culture. This claim founds the cycle for the whole period: 2:11–19 sketches out how Israel's predisposition manifested itself.

Judges 2:20–3:6 reports that Yhwh, angered by apostasy, ceased supplanting the nations Israel was fated to succeed. The rationale is complex: the nations remaining—Philistines, Canaanites, Sidonians, and the northern Hivites (3:3)—are unconquered until David (4:24 furnishing an arguable exception). They are spared "to test Israel," "all who did not know the wars of Canaan," "to teach them war, only those who did not know it earlier."

The foreign nations thus erase one of the causes of Israelite apostasy—ignorance of Yhwh's power at war. Their presence documented in Israel's experience, the view of them modeled on the premonarchic oppressors, they serve, so to speak, to keep Israel honest. It is not with the gods of these peripheral peoples that Israel indulged its talent for apostasy. Rather, the peoples *among* whom the Israelites dwelled supplied the foreign gods, by the medium of fraternization, and, of course, intermarriage (3:5f.). This historical deduction entails the adduction of Judges 1: Judges 1 catalogues the regions in which the Israelites failed to eradicate (although they did dominate) Canaanites in the interstices of their territory.

In order, the argument develops so: After Joshua's death the generation of the conquest failed to supplant the proscribed populations of the interior. The failure was willful: against Joshua 15:63; 17:11–13, 18, which say that Israel "could not" displace the Canaanites, Judges 1 reports that it "did not" displace them; the sequel in 2:1–5 condemns Israel for the lapse.[25]

Accommodation with the Canaanites called down upon Israel the curse of their continued presence (2:2f.; cf. Num. 33:55; Josh. 23:13). This, in turn, entailed the constant temptation to foreign worship. When Joshua's generation passed away, unfamiliarity with Yhwh's intervention disposed Israel to yield to the temptation (contrast 2:4f. with 2:10). And this human weakness precipitated them into the cycle of oppression and rescue (2:10–19).

The cycle itself implied that Yhwh preserved peripheral peoples from Israel's domination, as agencies through which to chasten his wayward folk (2:20–3:4). So the sparing of the banned Canaanites (Judges 1) and intermarriage with them induced the sufferings of the premonarchic era, and the labors of the judges. This argument moves to an elegant close at 3:5f., reverting to first causes (the remnant interstitial peoples) just on the brink of the first savior account (Othniel) (3:7–11).

Commonly, scholars dismember this passage by removing Judges 1:1–2:5 and 2:20–3:6 as secondary.[26] Judges 1:1–2:5 is excised because it comes between two near-identical notices of Joshua's death in Joshua 24:28–31; Judges 2:6–9. Judges 2:20–3:6 describes Yhwh's preservation of the peripheral enemies *after* the cycle in which they figure is laid out. It seems to come, thus, after a text it should precede. Both texts essentially raise problems in narrative sequence.

It should be noted from the outset that attributing the two texts to a second hand (E[Dtr]x) does not solve the problem. Why, composing freely, was the redactor so clumsy? If the problems in narrative sequence are not attenuated by the expedient, the justification for dating the texts after H(Dtr) (H[2:11–19]) is deficient.

Moreover, the preceding reading indicates that these chapters exhibit an organic and intelligible logic. Their argument is complex, coordinating a source of alien worship (Judg. 1) with the disposition toward it (2:10) and with a conditioning factor (3:6). But complexity does not mean composite authorship. In fact, the argument's complexity itself explains why breaks in the narrative sequence were necessary.

Judges 1 sets out "after the death of Joshua" (1:1) because H(Dtr) concludes that Joshua left territories unconquered (cf. Josh. 13:1ff.; 15:63; 17:11–18; 23:1–5): Joshua had eradicated some peoples, subdued (but not eradicated) others, and not engaged those on Israel's peripheries. Judges 1 repeatedly mirrors these distinctions: Judah conquered Jerusalem (v. 8) but Benjamin failed to supplant its inhabitants (v. 21); Judah subdued, but did not supplant, the inhabitants of the Philistine coast (vv. 18f.).

These notices are commonly taken to be contradictory.[27] But to assign the contradictions—some in adjoining verses (18f.)—to a redactor is to level fine distinctions ("conquer," *lkd;* "supplant," *hwrš*); it reckons the redactor a fool, incapable of recognizing the contradictions, or a knave, intent on ignoring them, into the bargain. The reality is the reverse of the appearance: the notices reflect nice discernment by the historian. Likewise, Ammon and Moab, two of Israel's M+ oppressors, do not figure in the list of peoples Yhwh left to chastise Israel (Judg. 3:3), because Ammon and Moab were, like Israel, successors of the Amorites, and not themselves supposed to be supplanted. Judges 1–3 pigeonholes the neighbors consistently: peripheral or interstitial; immigrant or aboriginal; unsubdued, subdued, or supplanted.

The thread of Judges 2:11–3:6 could not be joined directly to 1:1–2:5. That prologue provided that some Canaanites survived, a precondition of apostasy. It remained, however, to explain Israel's *predisposition* to apostasy. The argument, which traced the flaw in the nation's character to ignorance of Yhwh's work, started from the premise that Joshua and his generation were dead. Thus the reprise of Joshua's death in 2:6–10 (after Josh. 24:18–21) coordinates two factors with that circumstance: the cycle of 2:10ff. and the presence of the interstitial peoples. As elsewhere (cf. R_{JE}'s use of Gen. 37:36; 39:1), the epanalepsis marks Judges 1:1–2:5 as data whose relation to the following narrative is not sequential, but simultaneous.[28] First, alien gods are available (1); next, Israel resorts to them (2:10–19): the two are logically coordinated.

The seemingly awkward placement of 2:20–3:6 reflects similar thinking. This text resumes the thread of the argument after a prolepsis in 2:14–19. Again, the problem was one of coordinating several concerns. Yhwh's immediate response to a specific instance of apostasy (2:11–13) was oppression (and the whole cycle). Judges 2:11–19, which trace the consequences of oppression through the cycle, belonged together here.

To implement the oppressions, Yhwh must spare the peripheral nations (2:20–3:4). Yet the sparing (2:20ff.) and the oppression (2:14–19) both derived from Israel's apostasy (2:11–13). The sparing responded to (the prospect of?) repeated apostasy. Thus though they could not be formulated as simultaneous, the two elements were logically coordinated. The complexity of the argument demanded atemporal treatment. H(Dtr) flags the circumstance with another epanalepsis: "And the anger of Yhwh flared against Israel" introduces both results of the apostasy of 2:11–13: oppression, the immediate response to particular provocations (2:14f.); and the sparing of the peripheral peoples, a policy adopted against apostasy in general (2:20). Loosely, 2:20–3:6 (the peoples remaining) can be taken to follow 2:11–19 (the cycle). Formally, however, the texts are parallel segments of the argument.

Overall, 1:1–3:6 introduces the era of the judges by a subtle appeal to historical circumstance. It methodically appraises M+, M−, and the fact of foreign millets in the Israelite hill country. It explores the origins of Israelite apostasy or of Canaanite cultic survivals (Chapter 9) on the basis of inherited data. In this exploration lies its polemical intent: fraternization with Canaanites led the Israelites astray; Israelite heterodoxy, in the Josianic view, stems from Canaanite influence.

This does not mean that when the text was composed intermarriage was a burning issue. No more was Deuteronomy composed by Cromwell, for all the use he made of it in attacking the Irish (his Canaanites). Nor is the text primarily promonarchic or antimonarchic: such questions enter only obliquely into issue. Judges 1:1–3:6 and the M+ frameworks, like the Ehud and Deborah stories, address themselves to the past. Insofar as the past has implications for the author's time (heterodox practices are damned by their derivation from Canaanites), the text embodies theological and political goals. But the object of the author's scrutiny is the past, as past, interpreted in light of evidence concerning the past. Political goals, doctrinal convictions, are pursued within the confines of an enterprise whose parameters are antiquarian.

HISTORIAN AND REDACTOR IN JUDGES

Redaction did, on occasion, create logical difficulties (Shamgar) and linguistic inconsistencies.[29] Still, there is a lesson in the example of Judges: H(M+) and H(Dtr) redact delicately—H(M+), who introduced the frameworks, restricts their formulary to the outskirts of the M+ narratives, all the while he constructs accounts such as those of Ehud and Deborah; H(Dtr) inserts an introduction and, in 2:11–19 and in the story of Othniel, uses the language of his sources (M+). Any other editorial activity is difficult to sort out, and difficult to sort out from glossation. And the redaction conforms to the sources for the era. Like the reading of SDeb in Judges 4, it sometimes departs from the sources ("judges" applied to M+ in H[Dtr]'s 2:11–19). But it does not contradict them; in most cases the historian(s) read sharply. What changes must we make to convert this into history? As usual, none are necessary. Arbitrary contradiction, arbitrary invention, characterize neither H(M+) nor H(Dtr), except possibly in the case of Othniel (H[Dtr]).

A realistic construction of the editors of Judges must recognize their intent to construe history—history, to be sure, on a broad horizon, but history whose first frame of reference is the events and causes being narrated. On this understanding it would be an error to attribute, say, Judges 1 in isolation, or even a small smattering of passages, to an editor whose main interest lay in updating an early, Josianic work to include the exile. These texts are not about the exile, but about the remote past. They are integral with their contexts.

The dialectic of ideological motivation and historical interest is always intricate. Still, the past in DtrH is treated as the past. Oblique lessons for the historians' present haunt the presentation. The author's concerns lie in a concrete political context. But the work itself is historical, and historical logic dictates its understanding. The historian or redactor recasts history in order to persuade an audience: history is the testing ground for policy; the argument to policy is therefore adjudicated on the basis of evidence about the past itself. As Polybius observed (31.22), the fund of shared knowledge restrains the historian from falsification. It limits him, instead, to the realm of persuasive interpretation.

Biblical studies has a tradition of tralatitious or metaphorical interpretation. "This refers to the Wicked Priest," says the Qumran Habakkuk Pesher. Isaiah's "virgin" is Mary, runs the exegesis in Matthew. Finding E(Dtr)x in Judges 1 means working in this tradition: the text has nothing to do with updating a Josianic history to the exile, so the only explanation for its insertion is that, obliquely, it refers to events other than those it describes. It speaks to readers of the exile, as though somehow the reader was expected to divine that here, suddenly, the object of discussion was not the past, but the present, swaddled in symbol. The Canaanites of Judges 1, then, are not the Canaanites of the premonarchic era. They must be archetypes of later enemies.[30] There is no evidence, of course, that the history is meant as an analogy. But where we hypothesize redaction, our conviction that redaction was ideological disqualifies the possibility of antiquarian interest, of antiquarian logic, or of a legitimate concern, contextualized in politics, with history.

Metaphorical understandings of texts do fall within the realm of the possible. Analogies, oblique allusions *do* occur in Israelite literature: Exodus 32 denounces, via a story at Sinai, the cult of the golden calf at Bethel. But such conclusions can be sustained only where evidence shows that the text in question, taken as historical (as Exodus 32 later was), made first and unmistakably a poignant comment about the historian's own time.[31]

In the absence of such evidence, the literal sense of texts such as Judges 1–3 is prima facie argument to a concern with the past. The historical logic of Judges—parts (Chapters 3, 4) and whole (see the section in this chapter entitled "Redaction in Judges in Historiographic Perspective")—has been exposed already. The historians are creatures of party bias. But they rationalize and present their views based on the evidence. Under the circumstances, oblique implications divined from metaphorical interpretation or later exploitation (Cromwell and Deuteronomy) have no admissible bearing on a theory of authorship. Appeal to these expedients implies editors who wrote history, but in bad faith; redactors who amended the text only to disable it; polemicists who disguised polemic in a literary genre that made it unrecognizable to an audience. Such hypotheses are only a final refuge for readers who cannot contrive a coherent reading: like Hupfeld's R in the Pentateuch, oblivious to all the problems that combining sources entailed, they are unconscious by-products of literary, not historiographic, analysis; they imply stupidity or dishonesty in an ancient author, but call down doubt only upon themselves.

In the work of H(M+/M−), and in Judges 1–3, antiquarian and factional factors come to grips. Reform politics stigmatize heterodoxy as Canaanite. Theology (pre-Dtr in Isaiah 2:6–8) dictates that intermarriage is the culprit. The whole apparatus of the religion ties disaster to infidelity. Still, Judges applies its theology to the period of the judges. H(M+) assembles the frameworks by painstaking consideration of the stories. H(Dtr) deduces the introduction from contemplation of M+. The reconstruction exhibits the operation of historical logic. The logic serves political conviction, as it does in the work of Macaulay, or of Christopher Hill, or a hundred other historians. But because solipsism is unpersuasive—"Liberty is grand because I like it"; "Economics determines policy because I say so"— the historian builds a case from the past. The past furnishes a common ground for contemporary debate, as we can see from the periodic rehabilitation of this or that dead Soviet politician; simultaneously, it poses problems relating only indirectly to the present. In Israel as in Europe, the historian's logic, the language in which conviction is defended, the object upon which the historian or redactor practices, are all historical.

Analysis of Judges 1–3 and M+ thus confirms what the investigation of the Ehud and Deborah tales suggested: the historian—and the redactor—executed his literary agenda in careful relation to the evidence, and in good faith. This is the reason scholars have found no sign of H(Dtr) or even H(M+) inside the M+ narratives: the historian stuck largely to his sources. And this is the reason editorial history is so difficult to sort out. The editors, or historians, molded their additions to the evidence on hand.

Whether H(Dtr) applied to an earlier M+/M− the questions that generated Judges 1:1–3:6 (and 3:7–11, 31, and so on), or whether he produced Judges whole cloth, the process remains the same. H(Dtr)'s enterprise makes sense on Noth's scenario that his redaction was undertaken in good faith. He wrote to elaborate and defend a construction of the past, to forestall objections to it.[32] These concerns are not those of folklore, of romance, which are realms of arbitrary imagination: one argues about the accuracy of historical elements only (Chapter 1). Nor does Judges indulge itself in attention to minutiae or character, or in digressions of lyric or symbolic import. The long argument about the causes of Israel's apostasy in Judges 1:1–3:6 plumbs precisely the issues of detail and deep background that occupy the authors of the Ehud and Deborah stories; the same is true of the M+ frameworks.

Judges 1:1–3:6 and the M+ frameworks supply a mortar to cement together the building blocks of a history. They join the accounts of the major judges, M+ to M−, and M+/M− to the story of the period as a whole. The mortar, judiciously mixed, parlays a collocation of individual traditions into historical narrative. Concern with the literary aspects of the narrative, with its history of composition, has deflected scholarship from appreciating its antiquarian component. Instead of debating Noth's insight that the literature is historical, scholars focus on his argument to unitary authorship. But the insight about the genre is crucial: it disqualifies the supposition that an E(Dtr)x might have inserted Judges 1 as a comment on the exile. Like the work of H(Dtr) on M+/M−, even redaction can observe the niceties of historical discourse.

The implications of this position are worked out in Part 3. It remains first to ground it more fully, using two other treatments, of Solomon's reign and of the introduction of the monarchy, in which the hand of E(Dtr)x is often detected.

Notes to Chapter 6

1. See G. L. Studer, *Das Buch der Richter, grammatisch und historisch erklärt* (Bern: Dalp, 1835), 439; J. Wellhausen, in F. Bleek, *Einleitung in das Alte Testament* (4th ed.; Berlin: Reimer, 1878), 186f.; M. Noth, *Überlieferungsgeschichtliche Studien* (Halle, E. Germany: Niemeyer, 1943), 89 (from here on, *US*).
2. Judges 6:17, 7:12; 8:26: see C. Rabin, "The Emergence of Classical Hebrew," in A. Malamat, ed., *The Age of the Monarchies: Culture and Society* (WHJP 1/5B; Jerusalem: Massada, 1979), 71–78. For the history of traditions, see W. Richter, *Traditionsgeschichtliche Untersuchungen zum Richterbuch* (Bonn: Hanstein, 1963), hereafter *TUR;* idem, "Die Überlieferungen um Jephtah. Ri 10, 17–12, 6," *Bib* 47 (1966): 485–556.
3. Richter (*TUR* [n. 2], 12f.) sees the nominal sentences of 3:15b; 4:4a as old preframework narrative openings. But nominal sentences also introduce new characters in continuing narrative (1 Kings 11:26; Ruth 2:1; Gen. 16:1 after 15:1f.; probably 1 Sam. 17:12, among the ten instances Richter cites).
4. The argument that the frameworks are Deuteronomistic presumes that Dtr vocabulary is peculiar to H(Dtr), and that there was a preframework M+. See especially K. Budde, *Die Bücher Richter und Samuel* (Giessen: Ricker, 1890), 92–94. R. Boling (*Judges* [AB 6A; Garden City, NY: Doubleday, 1975], 36) finds no trace of Dtr language here.
5. Cf. W. Richter, *Die Bearbeitung des "Retterbuches" in der deuteronomischen Epoche* (Bonn: Hanstein, 1964), 1f.
6. Cf. Richter, *Bearbeitung* (n. 5), 28–35, with verbal criteria; Noth, *US* (n. 1), 48–50. Richter excises 2:17 (see 33f.), but does not explain the logic behind its insertion. Cf. R. Smend, *Die Enstehung des Alten Testaments* (Stuttgart: Kohlhammer, 1978), 116. Verses 17–18 are a unit (despite v. 17, nevertheless v. 18), culminating in v. 19. Cf. Richter, *Bearbeitung*, 28, on v. 13.
7. Compare Budde, *Richter und Samuel* (n. 4), 93; Noth, *US* (n. 1), 50f. Richter (*Bearbeitung* [n. 5], 23–26), excising the notice of "judging" as tertiary, assigns 3:7–11 to an Rdt$_2$ found only here. See n. 21.
8. Richter, *Bearbeitung* (n. 5), 13–23, with further formal arguments.
9. So Judges 17f. (an idol adopted without Canaanite influence) portrays a worse state than 2:6–3:6; chapters 19–21 (Israelites fighting Israelites) stands in the same relation to Chapter 1 (Israelites fighting Canaanites). Further, there is religious deterioration from Gideon (idolatry) through Abimelek (Baal Berit) and Jephthah (human sacrifice) to Samson (violating Nazirite vows). I suspect, however, that the ranking of these peccadilloes arises from, rather than gives birth to, the theory. See D. W. Gooding, "The Composition of the Book of Judges," *EI* 16 (1982): 70*–80*.
10. Gooding, "Composition," (n. 9), 71*, against R. Smend, "Das Gesetz und die Völker," in H. W. Wolff, ed., *Probleme biblischer Theologie* (Fs. von Rad; Munich: Chr. Kaiser, 1971), 494–509 on 1:1–2:5 and 2:20ff.; Boling (*Judges* [n. 4]) on 19–21; and, A. G. Auld, *JSOT* 1 (1976): 41–46 on 1:1–2:5; 17–21.
11. See B. Halpern, "The Rise of Abimelek ben Jerubbaal," *HAR* 2 (1978): 167–190.
12. The glossator avoids suppressing any of the context. Otherwise, eliminating "for Ehud was dead" in 4:1 would have cleared up the central problem. Nor did the glossator introduce a full M+ cycle, like that for Othniel. Note that some G codices locate Shamgar with Samson in 16:31. But 5:6 implied a time before 5:31 and after 3:30. Cf. Noth, *US* (n. 1), 51; Richter, *Bearbeitung* (n. 5), 92–96 (equals Rdt$_3$, H[Dtr]) with bibliography; esp. B. Mazar, "Shamgar ben ʿAnat," *PEQ* 66 (1934): 192–94.
13. See Richter, *TUR* (n. 2), 335–39.
14. On the limits of M−, see further the next section; cf. Richter, *TUR* (n. 2), 236f.
15. The only reference to the era without a correlative in Judges is the name of a savior,

bdn, in 1 Samuel 12:11. *Bdn* could have been treated within the context of the framework cycle. G reads Baraq (*brq*). Cf. T. N. D. Mettinger, *King and Messiah. The Civil and Sacral Legitimation of the Israelite Kings* (Lund, Sweden: Gleerup, 1976), 82.

16. It was conventional to portray wars as defensive, as Assyrian exemplars show. See A. L. Oppenheim, "Neo-Assyrian and Neo-Babylonian Empires," in H. D. Lasswell, D. Lerner, and H. Speier, eds., *Propaganda and Communication in World History. I: The Symbolic Instrument in Early Times* (Honolulu: University of Hawaii, 1979), 111–44, especially 121.

17. See my *Constitution of the Monarchy in Israel* (Chico, CA: Scholars, 1981), 111–23, 138–46.

18. The logic may have been even more elaborate. Hosea 7:7; 13:10 (alluding to 1 Sam. 8:6, 20) set king(s) and judges in parallel. The king's juridical function may have been abstracted for premonarchic leaders. Note that Judges 3:10 (Othniel "judged Israel and went out to war") echoes 1 Samuel 8:20 (a king "will judge us and go out before us to fight our wars"), in line with the thought of Judges 8:22f.; 1 Samuel 12:6–12.

19. Noth, *US* (n. 1), 49. This may be the source of the notice for Samson in 15:20, which resembles M − in form, and that on Eli (1 Sam. 4:18).

20. Noth, *US* (n. 1), 49f. On Ehud, see Chapter 3. How literally the "all-Israel" language is meant is obscure. H(M+) underscores, if anything, the limited scope of foreign domination and tribal participation in Judges 4. Presumably he used Israel often as a synecdoche (not in 10:8f., however, since a purely Transjordanian problem would otherwise be in point).

21. Richter (*Bearbeitung* [n. 5], 23–26, 56–58) assigns 3:7–11 *alone* to an Rdt₂ between H(M+) and H(Dtr) (the author of 2:11–19, and so on). His formal analysis shows it to be closest to 2:11–19, however, and the real reason for differentiating the authors of the two is the chronological problem (Joshua's generation is dead in 2:10), which is resolved if Qenaz, not Othniel, is Caleb's brother in 1:13 (as the marriage suggests). In any event, 2:10 could not logically have been attached to an M+ with Othniel if the contradiction was perceived as real.

22. See especially Richter, *TUR* (n. 2), 37–42; Richter, *Bearbeitung* (n. 5), where all of 10:6–16 is excised (13–23, 55, 58–60). Samson could stem from the H(Dtr) stratum, or 15:20 could have come in with 2:11–19 (it was more appropriate than the rest formula). Note that Othniel, Jephthah, and Samson, the three M+ figures who "judged Israel" (3:10; 12:7; 15:20) are all invested with "Yhwh's spirit" (3:10; 11:29; 15:14). Is this evidence that Gideon once stood in M − (6:34), or simply the reason that 3:10 was stitched together in the way it now stands?

23. H. Weippert, "Die 'deuteronomistischen' Beurteilungen der Könige von Israel und Juda und das Problem der Redaktion der Königsbücher," *Bib* 53 (1972): 301–39; *idem*, "Die Ätiologie des Nordreiches und seines Königshauses (I Reg. 11, 29–40)," *ZAW* 95 (1983): 344–75. Note that the rest motif, so prominent in M+, is vestigial in Kings (2 Sam. 7:1; 1 Kings 5:16f.): B. Halpern, "Sacred History and Ideology," in R. E. Friedman, ed., *The Creation of Sacred Literature* (Berkeley: University of California, 1981), 35–54. See further Chapter 5. The first exponent of this position was J. J. Stähelin, *Kritische Untersuchungen über den Pentateuch, die Bücher Josua, Richter, Samuels und der Könige* (Berlin: Reimer, 1843), 137–40.

24. On some of the texts in question, see M. Weinfeld, *Deuteronomy and the Deuteronomic School* (Oxford: Clarendon, 1972), 332, 366. On the theme, see chapters 7, 9.

25. Judges 1:34f. also converts into a consolation for failure, unworthy of remark, what Joshua 19:47 treats as a Danite success. Inability to conquer is pleaded only for Judah in 1:19G (from Joshua 17:18, unless one attributes the text in 1:19 to a glossator); Judah then does not figure in the M+ accounts of oppression and liberation. On Judges 1 as a document, see my *Emergence of Israel in Canaan* (SBLMS 29; Chico, CA: Scholars, 1983), 179–82.

26. See the review in Gooding, "Composition," (n. 9) 70*f., to which should be added Richter, *Bearbeitung* (n. 5), 35–40; R. D. Nelson, *The Double Redaction of the Deuteronomistic History* (JSOTSup 18; Sheffield, U.K.: JSOT, 1981), 45–53; M. Weippert, "Fragen des israelitischen Geschichtsbewusstseins," *VT* 23 (1973): 415–42, especially 432f.

Contrast (with bibliography) J. A. Soggin, *Judges* (OTL; Philadelphia: Westminster, 1981), 41–43.

27. E.g., Noth, *US* (n. 1), 9, n. 2; K. Budde, *Das Buch der Richter* (Freiburg, W. Germany: Mohr, 1897), 10. G attempts to clear the problem up in 1:18 at the expense of creating redundancy in v. 19. For the distinction drawn here, see M. Weinfeld, "The Period of the Conquest and of the Judges as Seen by the Earlier and the Later Sources," *VT* 17 (1967): 93–113. Weinfeld assigns the peripheral and interstitial peoples to different sources.

28. See S. Talmon, "The Presentation of Synchroneity and Simultaneity in Biblical Narrative," *SH* 27 (1978): 9–26; Chapter 3 on this function of the epanalepsis.

29. See J. H. Tigay, "The Stylistic Criterion of Source Criticism," in J. H. Tigay, ed., *Empirical Models for Biblical Criticism* (Philadelphia: University of Pennsylvania, 1985), 161–72. On Joshua 23–24, the first is a call to assembly, the latter a speech in assembly; a parallel is to be found in 1 Samuel 7:3–4, 5ff.

30. See Soggin, *Judges* (n. 26), 43, with bibliography, for such a construction of 2:6–3:6.

31. For the case of Exodus 32, see, e.g., F. M. Cross, *Canaanite Myth and Hebrew Epic* (Cambridge: Harvard University, 1973), 73–75, 198–200.

32. Contrast D. F. Murray, "Narrative Structure and Technique in the Deborah–Baraq Story," in J. A. Emerton, ed., *Studies in the Historical Books of the Old Testament* (Leiden, Netherlands: Brill, 1979), 179, n. 45: "The tightness of structure and compression so characteristic of Hebrew narrative dispensed with a detailed exposition of such peripheral questions." This is his argument for excising Judges 4:17b as a secondary explanation of Jael's relations with Sisera. But the explanatory urge, which may be called a critical faculty, if not at home in Israelite romance, lies precisely at the heart of the historiographic tradition.

CHAPTER 7

Dr. Faustus or Mr. Hyde (?): The Problem of Solomon ben-David

The man to whom all was clear as the sun, / He reviled the day of his own birth, / And saw that all was vain.

B. BRECHT

Judges 1–3 has been rich ground in the hunt to isolate E(Dtr)x or E(Dtr)n in segments of the history not directly relevant to the Babylonian exile. More important still is the conditional dynastic covenant with David. This covenant appears only in the account of Solomon's reign. Before assessing the linkage that Cross in particular has forged between E(Dtr)x and the conditional covenant, it is worthwhile to observe the antiquarian construction of the account.

THE SIGNIFICANCE OF SOLOMON

Under Solomon, Israel's fortunes reach their zenith. It has, as never before, rest,[1] unrivaled plenty, and prestige. Yet Solomon sews the seeds of schism (1 Kings 11): from this point forward the factors develop that play themselves out in Israel's destruction (2 Kings 17) and Josiah's reform (2 Kings 22f.). Solomon is the fulcrum of Israel's history in the land.

Three issues are involved. First, Solomon builds the temple. H(Dtr) henceforth measures Judah's loyalty to Yhwh by their use of the *bāmôt*, the rural "high places," until Josiah makes an end of them once and for all.

Second, Solomon's accession fulfills Yhwh's promise that David's dynasty will endure. The promise is concretized in the form of the temple (2 Sam. 7): in Israel, as in neighboring states, a temple's completion stood surety for divine dynastic sanction.[2]

Finally, Solomon's own infidelity occasions the division of the kingdom (1 Kings 12). From this springs Jeroboam's idolatrous cult

(12:26–33; 13), the "sin" that precipitates Israel's eventual destruction.

This reign thus embodies an extraordinary array of doctrine. The curtailing of David's covenant, the preconditions for centralization, and the "sin of Jeroboam" all start here. Cross identifies just these issues as the themes of Kings;[3] they are of pressing import to H(Dtr).

Here, if anywhere, the historian must elaborate thematic concerns. H(Dtr) does not disappoint the expectation. Noth produces abundant evidence of his activity; Cross, Veijola, and Dietrich discover contributions from each rung of their redactorial ladders.[4] At the same time, scholars trace much of the text to pre-Dtr sources, often citing the Book of the Acts of Solomon mentioned in 1 Kings 11:41. Unfortunately, the reference is enigmatic, and what the source supplied cannot be determined.[5]

This circumstance complicates the task of inspecting the work. The account in Kings 1–11 (12) is composite: no single source runs through it, as in Samuel or the Pentateuch. The historian has created movement through a skillful deployment of sources and a studied application of themes.

THE ACCOUNT OF SOLOMON'S REIGN

SOLOMON ON THE SCENE: 1 KINGS 1–2

1 Kings 1–2 has, since the past century, been tagged as part of a source, the Succession Narrative (2 Sam. 9–20). Still, signs of H(Dtr)'s editing are present: Noth found them in 2:2–4, 10–12, 27b.[6]

Other verbiage here echoes 2 Samuel 7: the "establishment" (*kwn*) of Solomon's regime (2:12, 24//23, 45) answers to the prophecy of 2 Samuel 7:13, 16—except in relation to Solomon, the verb *kwn*, "establish," does not occur in Kings. And the concern to expunge Joab's blood guilt (2:5f., 28–34) stretches back to the assassination of Abner (2 Samuel 3:27–37). It reflects a view of David's troubles more ancient than that laid out in 2 Samuel 12:9f., where the cause is Uriah's murder. In outline, however, 1 Kings 1–2 is an indispensable conclusion to that historical tract, devoid of Deuteronomistic language, which serves as the major source for David's reign.

This source, as T. Ishida has shown, is uniformly pro-Solomonic— it may even have created a coup of Adonijah by exaggeration.[7] It stresses Solomon's prudence: Adonijah is a second Absalom (especially 1:5f.); Solomon, though, does not thrust himself forward. His election is divine (1:11–14, 27) and paternal (1:13, 30). He is the object, not the instigator, of intrigue. His first action is to spare Adonijah (1:52f.). Solomon is the first grown character in biblical narrative who is introduced altogether offstage. The text has all the expectant quality of a story of miraculous birth.

Solomon is passive even in carnage. This posture brings rest to David's house at last. Thus Adonijah invites his own demise (and further comparison to Absalom—2 Samuel 16:22) by soliciting rights to David's concubine (2:13–25). Joab, "who took the part of Adonijah, though he did not Absalom's" (2:28), dictates his own death even in the sanctuary of Yhwh's tent. Bidden to emerge, Joab stymies his executioner, "No, I will die here" (2:28–30); "Do as he says," says the king, and Joab dies on the spot (2:31–34). Similarly, Solomon does not murder David's enemy Shimei (2:8f.). Instead he circumscribes Shimei's movements; the Benjaminite violates the restriction and brings on his own death (2:26–44). Solomon nowhere initiates a cycle of violence and guilt. He requites, balances, like Yhwh, whose agent his is.

How much of this stylized portrait comes from H(Dtr)? The materials are not typical of what follows; they link only loosely to the themes of Kings. Most of the text may have been inherited, as most scholars claim. But it is skillfully resculpted to fit with the rest of the reign, as we shall see.

SOLOMON'S CONSOLIDATION: 1 KINGS 3

The second movement of the account, the king's inaugural sacrifice at the "great 'high place' " at Gibeon, stems from a similar source. H(Dtr) hedges: "Solomon loved Yhwh, following the statutes of David, his father"; and recourse to the bāmôt was normal, "because the house for Yhwh's name had not been built until those days" (3:3f.).

Whatever its provenience,[8] this pericope confirms Solomon's prudence and justice: in an incubation Solomon unselfishly requests "an understanding heart, to judge your people, to discern between good and evil." Yhwh bestows "a wise, insightful heart," and wealth and honor too (3:5–14).

This augurs well. Like 1 Kings 2:2–4, 3:14 conditions Solomon's fate on his behavior—in 2:2–4 the reward is the continuation of his dynasty, in 3:14 the length of his reign. All the indications (and, explicitly, 3:3a) are that he will meet the test. And it turns out that he reigns for forty years.

Solomon next displays Yhwh's gifts. He solves the puzzle of the whores who each claim the same baby (3:14–28), a problem of a sort that consistently confounded David (2 Sam. 16:1–4; 19:18, 25–31). Flatterers sometimes compared David's discernment to that of "an angel of god" (2 Sam. 14:17; 19:28; cf. 1 Sam. 29:9; Zech. 12:8; also Gen. 3:5, 22). Solomon *demonstrates* that "the wisdom of god was in him to perform justice" (3:28). This captivating exhibition may stem from the storytelling tradition. Its juxtaposition with the Gibeon incubation masterfully advances the development of Solomon's character.

SOLOMON'S ORGANIZATION: 1 KINGS 4:1–5:14

H(Dtr) could not draw the third movement from an integrated narrative source. 1 Kings 4:1–5:8 instead catalogues Solomon's administration, in parallel with 9:10–10:29. The list has undergone disruption in transmission that, in this instance, is unusually severe.[9] One therefore cannot stand too firmly on the relative order of the individual notices.

In the collection is an old list of governors (4:7–19). The provinces cross tribal lines, and most of the appointees can be tied to the court. The list therefore has a context in royal efforts to wrench political control from the lineage structures, a policy that led to the Solomonic schism.[10] G. E. Wright found a different indication of its antiquity: the omission of the first names of several governors at the start of the list suggested to him a document whose upper right-hand margin had deteriorated.[11].

The district list (and 4:1–6) exemplifies Solomon's organization. This channeled the wealth of an empire to the court; 5:2f., 7f. underscore the orderly functioning of the machine. Solomon ruled the land to the Euphrates, in plenty, peace, and security (5:4, 5). He thereby secured the welfare of Israel (5:1; G 2:46b).

H(Dtr) links Solomon's peace and organization to his wisdom: he closes this movement off with a paean to the king's "wisdom and very great insight and breadth of intellect" and his forays into natural philosophy (5:9–14). This view of Solomon was probably traditional.[12] Even the hammering at the point in every movement may come from an earlier version of the reign. In any event, the staccato notices of 4:1–5:14 were originally assembled from very different types of documents and, moreover, documents different from those preserved in 1 Kings 1–2; 3. In no case does there appear to be extensive composition by the historian himself.

The paragraph on the proverbs trenches on the central movement, on the building of the temple. Hiram initiates a correspondence (5:15). In it Solomon sounds the chords that the historian has already developed.

David, Solomon writes, could not build the temple, because he had no respite from war. Solomon has rest, and must build the temple to secure the succession (2 Sam. 7; 1 Kings 5:16–19). Hiram responds, "Blessed this day is Yhwh, who gave David a wise son to rule that numerous nation" (5:21). Solomon's wisdom, remarked on in an allusion to the Gibeon incubation (3:9), is linked to rest, to the temple, and to the life of the dynasty.

The narrator is even more explicit than Hiram. In 5:26, between summaries of the arrangements with Hiram (5:20, 22–25) and of domestic measures, he remarks that Yhwh had bestowed the wisdom he had promised. Peaceful relations with Hiram follow from the gift, and lead in turn to the construction. Solomon's wisdom is now turned on Yhwh's needs.

Sources are in evidence. 1 Kings 5:27–32 describes Solomon's corvee, starting with 30,000 men leveed from "all Israel" to work the Lebanon. This dovetails with 1 Kings 11:28; 12:4, 18, where Israelite corvee labor is at issue. But 9:15–22 (OG 10:22a–c) denies that Israelites were draft-ed. One or both claims may antedate H(Dtr).[13]

Chronicles omits the 30,000 men of 5:27f. and identifies the 150,000 of 5:29f. as non-Israelites (2 Chron. 2:1, 16f.). This is harmonization. Chronicles likewise concludes from the transactions with Hiram, 2 Sam-uel 7, 24, and 1 Kings 7:51 that David planned the temple project. It retrojects Israel's mobilization to David's time (1 Chron. 22–27, where 27:16ff//1 Kings 4:7–19). And, portraying Solomon's coronation with-out digressing to deal with Adonijah, Chronicles patterns the old king's speeches, which instruct and advert to the dynastic covenant (1 Chron. 22:11–13; 28:6–9; the private charge in 22:5ff.), on the source in Kings (1 Kings 2:1ff.; private designation in 1:17, 27). The themes are the same; the treatment is faithful, but derivative.[14].

How H(Dtr) approached the tension over corvee is a matter for specu-lation. He may have linked the Israelite corvee in 5:27 specifically to the temple: the building of a temple sometimes entailed tax remission; the levee in 9:15–23, conversely, is for fortification. Still, 1 Kings 11:28 re-fers to Israelite corvee after the temple was complete. 1 Kings 9:20–23 denies not just this possibility, but even that described (as "corvee") in 5:27f.[15] H(Dtr) thus appears to have incorporated or tolerated sources occasioning tension in his treatment. Even the thematically pregnant story of Solomon is not homogeneous in its implications.

SOLOMON AND THE TEMPLE: 1 KINGS 6:1–9:9

Written sources also furnished the description of the temple and pal-ace that is the fourth movement (1 Kings 6f.//2 Chron. 3f.). Van Seters rebels against longstanding consensus on this point, claiming that only exiles would write a description of the temple. But the palace (7:1–12) is hardly described out of piety. Rather, the text fits the mold of other Near Eastern building reports closely.[16] Further, as Wellhausen saw, the order of the text is based on the geography of the palace-temple com-plex (especially 7:13).[17] This is hardly an exile's concern: in Chronicles, a post–exilic work, the temple is of such interest that the palace is forgot-ten (2 Chron. 3f.).

Further, there is a discrepancy in the height of the temple pillars' cap-itals. The building report lists it as 5 or 4 cubits (7:16, 19, the latter a scribal error); 2 Kings 25:17, however, which describes Babylonian loot-ing, records a height of 3 cubits. Whatever the explanation, it is not like-ly that the exilic author of 2 Kings 25:17 wrote 1 Kings 6–7.

There are other indications of sources. 1 Kings 8:4 records the instal-lation of the ark with its old sacra; yet Solomon manufactures items that duplicate some of this paraphernalia (as 7:48). Possibly, 8:4 is a gloss, un-der the influence of P (and 2 Chron. 1:4–6 with 1 Kings 3:15; 2 Chron. 5:5).[18] But 1 Kings 6:1, 37f.; 8:2 also employ the old Canaanite month names, and the old word, *yerah*, for "month" (absent in 6:1), side by side with the later usage—ḥōdeš ("month") and number. The combination of systems bespeaks the use of sources (also 2 Chron. 3:3 for such a combination). This material probably derives from antique records, whether monumental or administrative.[19]

The length of this segment mirrors a concern with the building: only in Solomon's case are the weight and dimensions of a king's donations to the temple recorded; building specifications are also rarely furnished. Much of this data is included out of sheer natural interest. Nevertheless, it is linked, from start to finish, with the themes of dynasty and rest. Thus even after these appear to be secured (1 Kings 4f.), Yhwh reiterates that the promise to David hinges on fidelity; so does Yhwh's presence in the temple (6:11–13). This text confers divine approval on the temple—something otherwise lacking after 2 Samuel 7:13—in terms corresponding to those of 9:6–9 (Fig. 10). It thus updates the conditional formulations of 2:2–4; 3:14. But the text is absent from OG and Chronicles.[20]

1 Kings 6:11–13 conforms to the sentiment expressed after the building finishes: 8:1–11 depicts Yhwh's installation in his new abode. Speeches by Solomon follow. The integrity of this material is often questioned—it is speech, after all, and therefore prone to fabrication; and there is no trace of an underlying source (see the sections in this chapter entitled "1 Kings 8: H(Dtr) or E(Dtr)x?" and "1 Kings 8: The 'Conditional' Covenant and 2 Samuel 7"). But it, too, refers to the Davidic covenant and the election of Jerusalem (8:15–21, 24–26). The same themes recur in a revelation to Solomon in 9:3–9, after the speeches of dedication. As in Judges, therefore, it is the framework *around* the action—5:15–27; 6:11–13; 8:1–9:9—which gives prominence to the historian's concerns.

SOLOMON'S GLORY: 1 KINGS 9:10–10:29

The narrative now recurs to Solomon's wealth, as in 1 Kings 4f. Dealings with Hiram occupy 9:10–28, with a digression into Solomon's domestic activity (9:15–25, elsewhere in OG). Some of this information must derive from sources—the sale of the Cabul to Hiram, for example, and the chronology of Solomon's building activities outside Jerusalem.[21]

1 Kings 10, the visit of the queen of Sheba (vv. 1–13), again links wisdom with Yhwh's favor and the fate of the dynasty (10:8f.). Here, Solomon assumes mature dignity—no longer as the trader who bested Hiram (9:12f.), but as the magnanimous monarch of a grand empire of universal repute (10:3f). The remainder of the chapter, about Solomon's income (vv. 14–17), throne (18–20), and wealth and commerce (vv. 21–29), underscores the point.

Again (see the sections in this chapter entitled "Solomon's Organization: 1 Kings 4:1–5:14" and Solomon and the Temple: 1 Kings 6:1–9:9), the details originate in sources. The report that Solomon manufactured ceremonial gold shields (10:16f.) prepares the reader only to learn that Rehoboam lost them to Shishak and furnished replacements from bronze (1 Kings 14:25–28). Shishak's booty raid is plentifully attested. The foregoing notice about Solomon is therefore probably antique. This applies, if less forcefully, to other indications of his wealth.[22]

SOLOMON'S SIN: 1 KINGS 11

From 1 Kings 1, then, through 1 Kings 10, the historian homogenizes inherited materials on his personal palette: Solomon is the passive, prudent king, whose first real act is the construction of the temple. The struggle for the succession, the incubation at Gibeon, the dissection of the harlots' claims, all establish what the narrator says directly: Solomon was, from the first, pious and insightful; he won Yhwh's favor and, with it, dynastic continuity, rest, prosperity, and the chance to build the temple. Hiram, in 1 Kings 5, and, after the temple construction, the queen of Sheba in 1 Kings 10, expressly acknowledge that Israel is blessed to enjoy Solomon's offices

> And Solomon grew greater than all the kings of the earth as to wealth and wisdom. All the earth sought after Solomon to hear his wisdom, which God emplaced in his heart. And each one brought his tribute. (1 Kings 10:23–25)

There is a progression in 1 Kings 1–10: 1) Solomon is exhibited as the perfect instrument for Yhwh to fulfill a promise to David (1:11–14, 48); 2) he acquires wisdom, for domestic repute and temple building; 3) he organizes to build the temple, and wins repute abroad; 4) he builds the temple; and 5) he wins universal prestige. Solomon wears his life long the tangible badges of divine esteem. In each of these first five movements, the themes of David's dynasty, the building of the temple, peace, and prosperity occur. The reversal comes in the sixth and seventh movements. All is transformed: 6) Solomon sins; and 7) Yhwh deprives Solomon's son of Israel (12:15). The arrangement of the movements is susceptible to the presentation of Figure 8.

The turning point is 1 Kings 11. In his dotage Solomon succumbs to the influence of his foreign harem, "from the nations of which Yhwh had said to the Israelites, 'Do not go among them . . . for they will certainly pervert your heart after their gods'" (11:1–3). The king builds bāmôt to Chemosh and Milcom (?) "and did the same for all his [one thousand] alien wives, who burnt incense and sacrificed to their gods" (11:4–8).

Solomon's apostasy precipitates the wrath of Yhwh, who resolves to "rend" the kingdom from him (11:11)—not in his lifetime, "for the sake of David" (11:12), and not all the kingdom "for the sake of David, my servant, and for the sake of Jerusalem which I have elected" (11:13): one tribe will remain. This explains the division of the kingdom, the final

FIGURE 8: THE SHAPE OF THE SOLOMON ACCOUNT

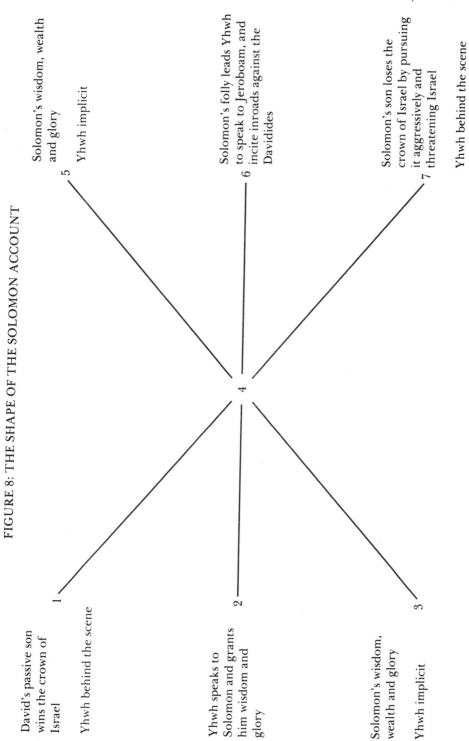

David's passive son
wins the crown of
Israel

Yhwh behind the scene

Yhwh speaks to
Solomon and grants
him wisdom and
glory

Solomon's wisdom,
wealth and glory

Yhwh implicit

Solomon's wisdom, wealth
and glory

Yhwh implicit

Solomon's folly leads Yhwh
to speak to Jeroboam, and
incite inroads against the
Davidides

Solomon's son loses the
crown of Israel by pursuing
it aggressively and
threatening Israel

Yhwh behind the scene

movement of the reign. The cause of the schism is thus identical to that of oppression in Judges 1–3: intermarriage invites apostasy, apostasy incurs wrath and catastrophe.

The sixth movement, in sum, invokes a system of causation elsewhere used by H(Dtr). It develops a portrait of a decisive event, as thematically central as that in Judges 1–3. Here, particularly, one expects the historian to stoke the engine of his imagination to advance his ideological goals.

Even so, much of the material is inherited. Ahijah the Shilonite inspires Jeroboam's coup just after the temple dedication—Solomon's sale of the tribe of Asher was probably the immediate cause of the uprising.[23] The date is at odds with the impression one gets from 11:4 that Solomon deviated from piety only in "the time of [his] old age." There is no inescapable conflict, and the historian obscures the coup's date by eliminating any reference to a particular year. But dating the coup late in the reign would have eliminated some tension.

The same pericope supplies the name of Jeroboam's mother (v. 26), a datum missing for every other ruler of the northern kingdom: H(Dtr) furnishes this detail only for Judahite kings. The claim that Jeroboam commanded the corvee of the central hills (v. 28) has the timbre of verisimilitude. It has long been recognized that underlying the report is an Ephraimite source, probably legitimating Jeroboam's career.[24]

The historian has added to this skeleton of "facts" the flesh of living discourse, including a prophecy to Jeroboam that sounds familiar themes: Jeroboam gets ten tribes, the Davidides one, "for the sake of David . . . and Jerusalem" (11:31f.).[25] Solomon's senile apostasy cancels out much of David's fidelity. But the kingdom will remain intact during Solomon's lifetime—another element that does not square with a coup in Solomon's 25th year. Judah is thereafter reserved as a Davidic fief (vv. 33–36). Jeroboam is offered the same terms as Solomon: if he is faithful to Yhwh, his house will be secure (11:37f.).[26] Here the biography of Solomon ends (11:41–43).

A last element deserves note. Two episodes intervene between Yhwh's condemnation of Solomon (11:1–13) and Ahijah's prophecy to Jeroboam (vv. 26ff.). Revolts in Edom (11:14–22) and Damascus (vv. 23–25) show that Yhwh punished Solomon during his lifetime. But the chronology again occasions difficulties: 11:21f. set the Edomite uprising at Solomon's *accession*, long before his dotage (11:4). And 11:25 states that Rezin, the filibusterer in Damascus, was "an adversary to Israel all the days of Solomon."[27] Did Solomon's punishment antedate his provocation?

The material has inspired the claim that the regnal account is organized by subject rather than chronology.[28] But the foregoing review indicates that the historian had the process of development very much in view; and the account furnishes dates, especially for non–military events, with a frequency unparalleled in DtrH (see Fig. 15). Chronology is on H(Dtr)'s mind.

This applies to the Edomite revolt. Hadad's return to Edom is *not* dated—only his request for leave from the pharaonic court; but foreign nationals were held as counters in negotiation in Egypt, as at other Near Eastern courts. Literally, 1 Kings 11:14–22 trace Hadad's hatred back to David's day. The account, intentionally vague, makes no insinuation of unrest until much later. The same is true of the report about Rezin (11:23–25).

Solomon could not have become an apostate until some time had passed after the building of the temple; the troubles in the empire are evidence of Solomon's sin (cf. 2 Sam. 7:14f.). The developmental interpretation of Solomon's reign, dictated (see the following section) by other commitments, skewed the treatment of this data. The historian, in effect, preserves the early etiology of the troubles Rezin and Hadad instigated. Simultaneously, the episodes are framed by a chronological sequence that is a considered construction: the real chronology is obscured, muting the collision with the apostasy in Solomon's dotage. Jeroboam's coup is not dated to a year, but roughly, to an era (11:26f.). Hadad and Rezin cannot be said to have acted at the start of Solomon's reign, but only to have had the motive then to do so. Yet the chronological indicators are not willfully suppressed—they are redirected, reinterpreted. The wonder is that any trace of them remains at all.

Even in reversing the older view of Solomon as the archetype of a successful monarch, the historian in 1 Kings 11 does not violate his sources. Instead, he reinterprets them.[29] The sources are a mold into which the historian injects his concerns.

The sequence, too, was foregone: after the accession the sacrifice at Gibeon implied a date before the temple project; Near Eastern temple-building paradigms often start from a revelation. The paradigm also commended attention to the mobilization for construction (1 Kings 4f.). And the temple dedication and occupation fit the paradigm and the theme of centralized worship. Finally, Solomon's fabled prosperity and repute followed from his public works (9:10–10:28). Only afterward could the account of his tribulations (11–12) be introduced. The organization is thematic, but the thematic progression reflects a chronological reconstruction. The algebra of antiquarianism thus confines the historian in the articulation of his themes, in much the same measure as it does a van Seters or a Noth. This point will have implications for the history of composition.

1 KINGS 11 AND THE THEMES OF DtrH

The blocks of Solomon's reign are quarried from archives. But the stones are bossed with pronouncements on David's dynasty, apostasy, the *bāmôt*, and the temple. These issues, of moment for H(Dtr), may have been developed in an earlier (Hezekian?) history or inscription. How does one link to H(Dtr) the themes that he himself developed? The key text is 1 Kings 11: the text is H(Dtr)'s creation; its themes ripple out across the whole presentation.

SOLOMON'S HIGH PLACES AND JOSIAH'S REFORM

It is important to understand in detail the intellectual process that made 1 Kings 11 a linchpin in the history. 1 Kings 11 legitimates the division of the Israelite kingdom. The contrast is to Chronicles: there Solomon never sins; Rehoboam causes the schism (2 Chron. 13:7ff.), though a trace of DtrH's treatment lingers (2 Chron. 10:15//1 Kings 12:15). Chronicles views the northern secession as illegimate, therefore, and omits the history of the north. Thus a strategy that acquitted Solomon was possible even after Kings was written. Why did Kings adopt the opposite approach?

The key to understanding 1 Kings 11 lies in a notice about Josiah, who

> defiled the high places that faced Jerusalem (*hab-bāmôt ʾašer ʿal pᵉnê yᵉrûsā-layim*), that were on the south of the mount of the Mashhit, that Solomon, king of Israel, built to Ashtoret, the abomination (*šiqqûṣ*) of the Sidonians and to Chemosh, the abomination of Moab, and to Milcom, the odiousness of the Ammonites. He shattered the cult–pillars and filled their stands with human bones. (2 Kings 23:13f.)

1 Kings 11 parrots this passage: the gods of 2 Kings 23:13 are all (11:5–7) objects of Solomon's devotion; only here does Kings use the noun *šiqqûṣ*, or "abomination". Moreover, 1 Kings 11:3 locates the *bāmôt* "on the mount which faces Jerusalem" (*bā–hār ʾašer ʿal pᵉnê yᵉ rûsᵃlayim*). 1 Kings 11 and 2 Kings 23 are thus mutually referential. Conversely, 2 Samuel 15:32 probably refers to the same locus without censure and in different words.

Josiah and H(Dtr) stigmatize Solomon's *bāmôt* as alien. These *bāmôt*, however, had survived in sight of the temple even Hezekiah's reforms. Their identification with foreign cults reflects therefore a new and fanatical xenophobia, which infused state policy only under Josiah.[30]

1 Kings 11 shares Josiah's evaluation of the *bāmôt*. It lends to 2 Kings 23:13f. a heightened significance: Josiah expunges the causes of the schism. Josiah next destroys Jeroboam's sanctuary at Bethel, fulfilling the prophecy of 1 Kings 13, and again healing the schism (23:15–20). This issues in a united Passover, the like of which was unknown "since the days of the 'Judges' " (23:21–23). 1 Kings 11, like 1 Kings 13 (Chap. 10), thus leans forward across the centuries. It is the work of H(Dtr), and another mark of his Josianic affiliations.[31] That the system of causality in Kings 11 duplicates that of Judges 1–3 (see the section in this chapter

entitled "Solomon's Sin: 1 Kings 11") is therefore no coincidence: H(Dtr) wrote both.

H(Dtr) regarded Solomon's lapse as the exaggeration of a proclivity remarked early in his reign. 1 Kings 3:2f. implies that it was in the way of piety that Solomon vented his devotion at high places before the temple was built. It was at a "great *bāmâ*" that Solomon received his first epiphany (3:4–15).[32] 1 Kings 11, by contrast, identifies the *bāmôt* as foreign.

If the *bāmôt* were foreign, as Josiah's party thought, Solomon stood convicted as an apostate. Here, suddenly, is the cause of the schism; and Josiah's reform should lead to a Davidic restoration in the north (1 Kings 11:39?). As in Judges, however, the historian must answer one more question: where did Solomon find his other gods? How did the noble architect of Israel's temple and empire fall into such error?

As in Judges, the historian answers, fraternization is to blame. Solomon married at least two aliens—a pharaoh's daughter (1 Kings 7:8; 9:16, 24) and Rehoboam's Ammonite mother (14:21). Whether the tradition about the size of his harem antedates Josiah's time is moot (it could be deduced from his apostasy). But H(Dtr) linked foreign gods to foreign wives, and the *bāmôt* implied that Solomon had wives from specific nations.

Logically, Solomon could not have been an apostate before reaping the rewards that a reverential tradition accorded him; he sinned only late, his age acting on him as ignorance of Yhwh did on Joshua's successors. The mechanics of H(Dtr)'s presentation reflect this circumstance: in H(Dtr)'s materials about Hadad, Rezin, and Jeroboam, the dates are obscured, the contradictions tempered, the chain of causation, from wives to *bāmôt*, carefully and chronologically secured.

1 KINGS 11 AND THE DYNASTIC COVENANT

1 Kings makes of Josiah's reform a remedy for the division of the kingdom. Still, it establishes the causes of the schism by historical reasoning (Solomon's *bāmôt*) and the presentation of evidence (Hadad, Rezin, Jeroboam). What changes would transform it into history? None. Dialogue is supplied, even revelation, but, as in Judges, Yhwh's intentions are deduced from the events (the schism, Josiah's policy toward *bāmôt*). H(Dtr)'s marginal characterization of Solomon also follows from the historical process. 1 Kings 11 argues Josiah's case: the high places toppled David's kingship over Israel. But the argument is couched in historical terms, in conformity with the rules of the antiquarian enterprise.

1 Kings 11 also expresses H(Dtr)'s views on David's dynastic covenant, allegedly a central issue for E(Dtr)x/n. If E(Dtr)x invented it, the conditional dynastic covenant is an exilic artifice to explain the exile —the end of David's dynasty. Or was the conditional covenant invoked by H(Dtr) to explain events described in the Josianic history?

Yhwh ordains the schism because Solomon worshipped other gods. Yhwh had appeared to Solomon twice (3:5; 9:2; not 6:11–13). He had "enjoined Solomon on this very matter, not to go after other gods" (11:9f.). The enjoinder is found in 9:6 ("if you go and serve other gods"). Here Solomon's apostasy precipitates the schism (11:11, presumably referring to 9:4f.), not the exile, although the latter is the threat in 9:7–9.[33] 1 Kings 9:6 must have entered the text before 11:9f. And 11:9 refers to 9:2ff. as a whole.

Ahijah reiterates this background to Jeroboam. Solomon *and Israel* have abandoned Davidic fidelity (11:33 with 3:3; 2:2–4; Fig. 9). The language of 9:4–9 again appears in unison: 11:33 even speaks of apostates in the plural, although Solomon alone is guilty, just as 9:6 shifts to the plural to discuss apostasy after 9:4f. addresses Solomon alone.[34] 1 Kings 11 understands the loss of Israel as a punishment for Solomon's infidelity, a warning against which had been issued in 9:4–9.

The qualification of Yhwh's punishment also echoes themes developed in 1 Kings 1–10. Yhwh spares Solomon the ignominy of dethronement, and reserves one tribe to his heirs, "for the sake of David . . . and Jerusalem" (11:13, 32, 34, 36; only v. 34 omits Jerusalem). Judah, thus, is a cup of consolation for the Davidides deprived of the north.

The citations of David's election in these passages recall Solomon's speech in 8:16 (read with 2 Chron. 6:5f. and G). which quotes 2 Samuel 7:

> From the day when I brought Israel out from Egypt I have not chosen a city from among all the tribes of Israel to build a temple for my name to be there, nor have I chosen a man to be *nāgîd* [Yhwh's king designate] over Israel. But [now] I have chosen Jerusalem for my name to be there, and I have chosen David to be over my people, Israel.

The source is 2 Samuel 7:8b–11. Solomon next observes:

> Yhwh fulfilled the oracle he spoke and I arose after David, my father, and I sat on the throne of Israel as Yhwh said, and I built the temple for the name of Yhwh, God of Israel. And I provided there a place for the ark. (1 Kings 8:20f.)

The reference to the temple construction as the fulfillment of Yhwh's promise alludes unmistakably to 2 Samuel 7 as well. In other words, 1 Kings 11 invokes 2 Samuel 7 for the preservation of the fief, and the conditional covenant (at least in 9:2–9) for the loss of the northern tribes.

The theology is clear; covenant violation leads to the loss of Israel, but David's and Jerusalem's election persists (11:13, 32–36). This must be the reference in 11:38: Jeroboam can earn a secure dynasty, as David did, by fidelity to Yhwh. His dynasty depends on his behavior; but he can, to a certain extent, make it proof against total dissolution.

Overall, H(Dtr)'s perspective can be outlined as follows:

1. The causes of the schism were those that led to oppression in the period of the judges: intermarriage, catalyzed (by forgetting) into apostasy.

2. Yhwh first promised David a united Israel (as 1 Kings 8:20); but Israel was stripped from the Davidides as a punishment for Solomon's infidelity (11:11f., 31–34, 37). That is, dynasty over the kingdom originally vouchsafed was conditional. The conditional formulations of the dynastic grant thus culminate in 1 Kings 11, and are tied (9:4–6 in 11:9–13, 31ff.) to the schism (see figures 9, and 10 and the next section).

3. David's and Zion's election was maintained in the face of infidelity. "For the sake of David"—from Rehoboam to Hezekiah (1 Kings 15:4; 2 Kings 8:19; cf. 19:34; 20:6)—Yhwh bears Solomon's sins, and those of his successors; Yhwh preserves a tribe of the original kingdom, "so that David, my servant, should have a fief forever before me in Jerusalem, the city which I have chosen for myself, to put my name there" (11:36). That is, David's dynasty is not rescinded, but reduced to a token kingdom around Jerusalem.

4. These views are complementary: by infidelity, Solomon forfeited the kingship over the ten tribes of Israel; but David's earlier fidelity entitled his descendants to a fief, a single tribe, forever. These doctrines apply an antiquarian logic to the Solomonic schism: Solomon caused the schism, but his dynasty persisted in a restricted domain (Fig. 10). Although 1 Kings 9:7 raises the specter of dispossession for the people, nothing indicates that any of these texts addresses the Babylonian exile. The hand of H(Dtr) is in evidence.

THE DYNASTIC COVENANT: E(DTR)X OR H(DTR)?

No scholar yet detects E(Dtr)x in 1 Kings 11, a text whose ambition is limited to explaining the schism. 1 Kings 11 is antiquarian, if partisan, and it would be incautious to discover in it a reference to the exile. But Cross and others identify E(Dtr)x in formulations, similar to those of 1 Kings 11, earlier in Solomon's reign. Have these no antiquarian valence? Are they moles, so to speak, implanted against an event four centuries later?

THE CONDITIONAL DYNASTIC COVENANT—THE TROUBLE WITH E(DTR)X

Cross begins by identifying the unconditional covenant of 2 Samuel 7 with H(Dtr). 1 Kings 2:2–4; 8:15–26; 9:3–9 all cite 2 Samuel 7 or a similar promise to David. 3:6; 5:18–21 (cf. 1:48) refer to Yhwh's promise to enthrone David's son. And 3:14; 6:11–13 mention demands that Solomon must meet in order to succeed as king. But these passages are conditional: each makes Solomon's behavior (and his line's) the determinant of the dynasty's fate. Here Cross sees an insuperable conflict with the unconditional grant of H(Dtr); he excises conditional elements and consigns them to E(Dtr)x.[35]

Cross hypothesizes that E(Dtr)x, writing in exile, deduced from the ostensible end of the dynasty that the dynastic covenant with David was not, as 2 Samuel 7 suggested, unconditional, but, in fact, contingent on royal fidelity to Yhwh. This solution occasions four problems:

1. E(Dtr)x also authors 2 Kings 25:27–30, verses that cling to the Davidides' legitimacy and offer hope of a restoration:[36] Yhwh had *not* stripped his loyalty from the line (2 Sam. 7:13–16; Ps. 89:29–38; Jer. 33:14–26). E(Dtr)x never actually rejects David's dynasty: he speaks only of removing Judah and destroying Jerusalem. So E(Dtr)x appears, like the returnees from Persian Babylon, to adhere to the doctrine of *unconditional* dynastic grant. Why, if the exile was compatible with David's perpetual election in 2 Samuel 7, did E(Dtr)x create a conditional covenant that suggested the dynasty was disqualified? Or, if the dynasty was disqualified, why did E(Dtr)x find hope for it in the exile? Moreover, as noted in the section of Chapter 5 entitled "Twin Redaction Based on Historical Evidence," Josiah's reform (and Deut. 17:20) presupposed conditionality: no party interested in socializing such a doctrine in the exile has been identified.

2. If E(Dtr)x hatches the conditional covenant in order to allow for the exile, he should avoid reference to 2 Samuel 7 when diagnosing the exile's etiology. He does not: 2 Kings 21:8 (after 21:7 refers to 2 Samuel 7 and 1 Kings 9:3) mixes the sentiments of 1 Kings 9:6f. (also Deut. 28) with those of 2 Samuel 7:10. There is no unmistakable reference to the conditions imposed on Solomon. Conversely, 1 Kings 11:10, 33 and (to Jeroboam, with comparison to David's arrangement) 38 (read OG) all cite the conditional covenant directly in an explanation for the Solomonic schism that no scholar assigns to E(Dtr)x (see Fig. 9). The conditional dynastic covenant is evoked primarily by the schism, not the exile (see the section in this chapter entitled "1 Kings 11 and the Dynastic Covenant" and the section that follows this one).

3. E(Dtr)x failed to revise 2 Samuel 7. Did it elude his observation? Was it not in his text? Was it too sacred to alter? The first possibility presumes that E(Dtr)x was myopic or indolent. The second is untrue: 2 Samuel 7 is repeatedly cited in 1 Kings 1–11 (see the section in this chapter entitled "1 Kings 11 and the Dynastic Covenant" and the three sections that follow this one). The third is trebly contraindicated: a) if E(Dtr)x had no qualms about altering a revelation to Solomon (9:1–9), the revelatory character of 2 Samuel 7 should not have stilled his pen; b) 2 Samuel 7 precedes E(Dtr)x's insertions, and thus programs one's reading of the insertions: so conditionality should have

been introduced earlier; and c) E(Dtr)x need only have adopted the strategy of 1 Samuel 2:27–36 and rejected an eternal covenant to avoid all contradiction; yet he did not.

4. Most important, all the conditional formulations come in Solomon's regnal account. Why did E(Dtr)x confine his pronouncements on this subject—his only insertions between Deuteronomy (on a maximalist reading, 1 Samuel) and Manasseh—to Solomon's reign? If the conditional covenant relates directly to the schism, the answer is, It comes up in connection with Solomon, because Solomon triggers its sanctions; it does not come up thereafter, because Solomon has voided it.

A review of the conditional covenant is in order. On the point two issues turn: Is this covenant the product of antiquarian speculation colored by Josianic commitments, or is it an effort to reconcile the exile with a tradition of unconditional Davidic covenant? And did E(Dtr)x write about the exile so remotely in such remote contexts, or do these materials stem from H(Dtr)?

THE CONDITIONAL DYNASTIC COVENANT—DYNASTY OVER ISRAEL?

Solomon's regnal account adverts to the dynastic grant regularly, in its every narrative movement (see the section in this chapter entitled "The Account of Solomon's Reign"). The issue comes to a head in the sixth and seventh movements, 1 Kings 11 and 12. 1 Kings 11 invokes the violation of the conditions and, in 11:10, specifically refers to one of the conditional formulations, to account for the division of the kingdom; 11:33 and 11:38 both seem to take the texts of 9:4; 2:3; 8:25b (and 3:14) as models. In other words, the conditional formulations are integral here; their assignment to E(Dtr)x is correspondingly problematic.

The three major conditional formulations (2:2–4; 8:25; 9:4f.) are relatively homogeneous (for the Hebrew, see Figure 9):

> 2:3: Observe the charge of Yhwh your god, to go in his ways, to observe his statutes and commands and judgments and stipulations, as is written in the Torah of Moses.

> 2:4: If your sons observe their way, to go before me in truth, with all their heart and with all their soul . . .

> 8:25: If your sons observe their way, to go before me, as you went before me . . .

> 9:4: If you [David's son] go before me, as David your father went, in perfection of heart and uprightness, to do according to all that I command you, and observe my statutes and judgments . . .

Similar is 3:14, which states conditions for longevity, not dynasty:

> 3:14: If you [David's son] go in my way, to observe my statutes and commands, as David your father went . . .

and

FIGURE 9: THE CONDITIONS OF THE COVENANT IN 1 KINGS 1–11

	hlkw[1]	bdrky	l'śwt hyśr b'yny	whqty	wmšpṭy[2]	kdwd 'byw
11:33 l'						
2:3 wšmrt 't mšmrt yhwh 'lhyk	llkt	bdrkyw	lšmr	hqtyw mṣwtyw	wmšpṭyw w'dwtyw	kktwb btwrt mšh[3]
2:4 'm yšmrw bnyk 't	llkt	drkm	b'mt bkl lbbm wbkl npšm			
9:4 'm	tlk	lpny	btm lbb wbyšr / l'śwt kkl 'šr ṣwytyk[4]	hqy	wmšpṭy tšmr	k'šr hlk dwd 'byk
8:25 'm yšmrw bnyk 't	llkt	drkm				k'šr hlkt (dwd) lpny
3:14 w'm	tlk	bdrky	lšmr	hqy wmšwty		k'šr hlk dwyd 'byk
6:12 'm	tlk	bhm[5]		bhqty w't mšpty t'śh wšmrt / 't kl mṣwty		
11:38 'm	whlkt	bdrky	w'śyt hyśr b'yny lšmr tśmr[6]	hqwty wmšwty		k'šr 'śh dwd 'bdy

Notes

1. OG singular is *lectio facilior.*
2. OG omits this segment.
3. The shorter Greek texts bring the verse still closer to 11:33.
4. OG *śwytyhw.*
5. OG omits this entire verse.
6. OG *tśmr?*

6:12: If you [David's son] go in my statutes and do my judgments . . .

11:33: They did not go in my way, to do the upright in my sight, and my statutes and judgments, like David his father.

11:38: If you obey all that I command and go in my ways, and do the upright in my sight, to observe my statutes and commands as David my servant did . . .

1 Kings 11 quotes the conditions imposed on the dynastic covenant earlier. It applies the conditions to the schism, and to a new deal with Jeroboam that puts him on an equal footing with the young David (11:38).

The dynastic *promise* is even more homogeneous. If Solomon complies, Yhwh will fulfill "the oracle he spoke of [David] saying, [. . .] 'There will not fail [David] a man upon the throne of Israel' " (2:4; 8:25; 9:5). All three passages refer to the "throne"; all three refer to kingship over "Israel"; all three refer to a conditional dynastic promise to David (compare "throne of Israel" in 2 Kings 10:30; 15:12).

In these respects, 2:2–4; 8:25; 9:4f. differ from the fief formula—"for the sake of David . . . and . . . Jerusalem." This never mentions a throne, Israel, or an earlier oath to David. It justifies instead perpetual Davidic rule over a fief[37] in Jerusalem and Judah.

Cross identifies H(Dtr)'s fief formula as unconditional: E(Dtr)x's conditional covenant contradicts it. But 1 Kings 11 embraces both traditions. Solomon's line loses the kingship over Israel, and gets the fief as consolation (see the section in this chapter entitled "1 Kings 11 and the Dynastic Covenant"). So the fief formula comes into play only when the conditional covenant has been abrogated: a formulation that Cross identifies as unconditional is, in fact, a corollary of the conditional covenant. Both are linked directly to the schism.

This is why 1 Kings 11:34 contrasts Solomon with a true dynast—because his heirs will not inherit all Israel, he is a *nāśî*, a tribal officer, without dynastic expectations.[38] This is also why H(Dtr) is at pains to observe that Yhwh fulfilled his promise to enthrone one of David's offspring over (all) Israel (see the section in this chapter entitled "The Account of Solomon's Reign"): Solomon failed to win dynasty over all Israel. And this is why the fief formula and the conditional dynastic covenant conflict (Israel, throne, earlier promise): the fief, as R. E. Friedman first showed (n. 39), is a replacement for Israel when the conditional covenant is revoked (see Fig. 11).

How, on Cross's reading, did E(Dtr)x read 2 Samuel 7? He can only have understood Davidic kingship over Judah to have fulfilled the unconditional terms of the grant: otherwise there would have been no need to account for the supposed end of the dynasty in the exile. Yet the conditional dynastic covenant in 1 Kings 2:2–4; 8:25f.; 9:4–9 addresses

FIGURE 10: THE LOGIC OF THE DAVIDIC DYNASTIC COVENANTS

Text	Fact/Condition	Consequence
2 Samuel		
7	A David was good	> 1 heir gets "throne" (over ??): v. 12
		> 2 heir builds temple: v. 13
		> 3 heir/David gets dynasty (over ??): vv. 13, 16
		> 4 heir/dynasty liable to chastisement: v. 14
1 Kings		
2:4	A Omitted, because David is in the act of enthroning Solomon in Israel	
	B If heirs good	> 3 subsequent heirs get dynasty over Israel
3:14	B′ If Solomon is good	> 5 Solomon gets longevity (cf. KAI 4, 6, 7 etc.)
6:12–13	B′ If Solomon is good	> 6 Yhwh will dwell amid Israel (and fulfill his promise to David [2 Sam. 7]) (= [1–4′])
8:18–25	A David was good	> 1 heir got throne over Israel
		> 2 heir built temple
	B If heirs good	> 3 subsequent heirs get dynasty over Israel
9:4–5	B′ If Solomon is good	> 3 subsequent heirs get dynasty over Israel
9:6–9	C If Israel evil	> 6 Yhwh will dismiss them from his presence (cf. 6:12f.) (= 4′ · ˜ [1–3])
1 Kings 11		
11, 33	B″ Solomon was evil	> 4 heirs forfeit dynasty over Israel
13, 32, 34–35	(A David was good)	> 1 Solomon retains Israel in his lifetime
		> 3′ Solomon's heirs retain fief

dynasty specifically over Israel; it never speaks of dynasty alone or of dynasty over Judah.

If E(Dtr)x introduced the conditional covenant to explain the exile, why did he not limit it to Judah? As it stands, 1 Kings 11–12 describes how, under the conditional grant, Solomon lost his kingship over Israel. Placing the conditional covenant only in Solomon's reign turns out to have been the worst possible strategy: after the schism it would be unambiguous; in David's reign it might have several valences. Placed under Solomon it affects the schism alone; thereafter it is replaced by the consolation prize, the fief formula. If E(Dtr)x wrote the conditional covenant, he wrote it ineffectively. The conditional formulations, with their unconditional corollaries, in fact make most sense as the work of H(Dtr).

This conclusion meets the evidence (see the sections in this chapter entitled "1 Kings 11 and the Themes of DtrH" and "The Dynastic Covenant: E(Dtr)x or H(Dtr)?"). The distribution of the conditional passages, the relationship of the conditional covenant to the fief, the references to Israel and to the throne as a metonym for kingship over Israel, the integrity of the conditional covenant with 1 Kings 11, the reference to the conditional covenant of 1 Kings 9:4–6 in 1 Kings 11:9f., 33, and the repeated adversion in 1 Kings 1–10 to Yhwh's promise to enthrone David's son over all Israel (with an implication that the rest is to be determined)—all these pose no problems if H(Dtr) penned the conditional covenant formulations. The inconsistencies of E(Dtr)x—not retouching 2 Samuel 7, insisting on the dynasty's legitimacy in the exile, and so on—evaporate. The conditional covenant belongs to H(Dtr).

Similar reasoning has led two of its proponents to amend Cross's analysis. R. E. Friedman and R. D. Nelson argue that 2:2–4; 8:25; 9:4f. conditionalize not David's dynasty, but David's dynasty over Israel.[39] Both relate the conditional covenant to Solomon's violation of it in 1 Kings 11, and the schism. 1 Kings 11 thus takes these passages to set out the conditions for continued Davidic ascendance over all Israel. Solomon fails the test, and the unconditional fief formula mitigates the punishment. None of this material addresses the exile.

J. D. Levenson defends the assignment of 2:2–4; 8:25; 9:4f. to E(Dtr)x. Levenson holds that these passages allude to a previous but unattested promise to David—no revelation to David says that if his sons are faithful, "there will not fail (you) a man on the throne of Israel." So, continues Levenson, to connect these texts to kingship over the north, one must hypothesize the suppression of the original oracle promising conditional dynasty over that realm. But why would such a text be suppressed? Only to defend the view that the northern secession was illegitimate—the opposite intention Friedman and Nelson impute to H(Dtr).[40]

Levenson's riposte does not reckon with the relationship between the conditional and unconditional dynastic covenants (over all Israel and over the fief) in 1 Kings 1–10 and, especially, 1 Kings 11. It, in effect, attempts to explain away the distribution of terms such that Israel and throne occur only in connection with the conditional formulations (Fig. 11). But his argument is valuable for spotlighting two related issues.

First, Yhwh never says to David, "There will not fail you a man on the throne of Israel." But Levenson does not explain why E(Dtr)x, a redactor, is more likely than H(Dtr) to have cited an unattested oracle. Again, the question is why the author of 2:2–4; 8:25; 9:4f., whether E(Dtr)x or H(Dtr), did not revise 2 Samuel 7. Editor or historian, thus, the problem is the same, and the argument does not tell on Cross's behalf against Friedman and Nelson.

Second, 1 Kings 2:2–4; 8:25; 9:4f. refer to kingship not only over the north, as Levenson takes it, but over a united Israel.[41] Again, 1 Kings 11:31 speaks of "rending" the kingdom from Solomon (v. 33; the section in this chapter entitled "The Conditional Dynastic Covenant—the Trouble with E(Dtr)x"; Fig. 9). 1 Kings 11:13, 34f., however, reserve Judah as a fief (11:36) forever. The kingdom is "rent" because Yhwh is loyal to David in the face of Solomon's infidelity: the rending, acted out on cloth (11:30–32), tears north from south; thus Solomon lost dynasty over all Israel, and part of the forfeit was restored. No oracle about the northern kingdom alone was suppressed.

H(Dtr) applies these doctrines to the Solomonic schism in 1 Kings 11, a text traced to him on other grounds (see the section in this chapter entitled "Solomon's High Places and Josiah's Reform). Levenson argues that "the Davidic courtiers who authored . . . the *unconditional* covenant of 2 Samuel 7" would not legitimate Israel's secession: H(Dtr) "approves of no northern king at all."[42] But at the vortex of H(Dtr)'s indignation is the "sin of Jeroboam." The secession is Yhwh's work. H(Dtr) reports the divine election of Jeroboam and of subsequent northern kings. He assails northern kings for what they do once in power; he does not assail their right to come to power. The same perspective suffuses the sermon on the fall of Israel in 2 Kings 17, a *locus classicus* of H(Dtr)'s theology: Yhwh rent the kingdom from David's house, but Jeroboam led Israel astray; despite repeated warnings, Israel persisted in the "sin of Jeroboam" (especially 17:21–23). The secession is not numbered among Israel's sins; it was Yhwh's doing.

H(Dtr)'s criticism of individual monarchs no more impugns the legitimacy of the northern kingdom than it does the institution of monarchy—an institution commended even in the last four verses in Kings. The opposite posture is attested—in Hosea (as 8:4) and Chronicles (as 2 Chron. 13:4–20)—but not in DtrH. Levenson's assertion that, for H(Dtr), Israel's independence was illegitimate, is sweeping: 1 Kings 11; 12:15 (and much of 12); 14, and, among other things, the elections of Baasha and of Jehu must all be secondary; much of 2 Kings 17 must go as well. Here, and in the case of 1 Kings 11–12, there are good grounds for rejecting the epicycle.

Levenson—and Cross—predicate that H(Dtr)'s (freely composed?) unconditional grant (2 Samuel 7) contradicts the conditional dynastic covenant of 1 Kings 1–11. What, in fact, is the relationship?

The most economical explanation for the citations of an earlier dynastic oracle in 2:2–4; 8:25; 9:4f. is that the author of those passages thought David had received one. Otherwise, he could have placed such an oracle in Nathan's mouth, if nowhere else, in 1 Kings 1. This approach led Rost and Noth to read 2:2–4; 8:25; 9:4f. as the historian's interpretation of 2 Samuel 7 *in light of the division of the kingdom.*[43] That the fief formula, a corollary of the conditional covenant, cites 2 Samuel 7 (see the section in this chapter entitled "1 Kings 11 and the Dynastic Covenant") confirms that some such relationship must exist.

It is likely that H(Dtr) had sources, even a version of 2 Samuel 7 (and 1 Kings 12:19//2 Chron. 10:19) that claimed that Yhwh had promised David a perpetual dynasty over Israel. No doubt this was a common view at the court; it would have been promoted in periods of friction (Ahaz', for example; also Jer. 33:17–26), and muzzled in times of cooperation (Jehoshaphat, for example, or Uzziah). Denizens of the north, and political realists in Judah, would have denied the doctrine. So the disparity between theological theory and reality did not surface first in the exile: it arose with the Solomonic schism, in time to challenge H(Dtr).

H(Dtr) took the schism to be legitimate. To harmonize the dissonance between the unconditional dynastic grant and the schism therefore involved interpreting the unconditional grant as one of dynasty in the abstract, not dynasty over a particular territory. This is the expedient of 1 Kings 11. It is reflected in three other texts—2 Samuel 7, Psalm 89, and Psalm 132.

Psalm 132 is clearest. Yhwh has told David that a son will succeed him, and "if your sons observe my covenant . . . their sons, too, for always, will sit upon your throne" (11f.) The language is that of the conditional formulations (see the section in this chapter entitled "The Conditional Dynastic Covenant—the Trouble with E(Dtr)x" and Fig. 9). And, like 1 Kings 1–10, Psalm 132 associates the promise with the election of Jerusalem. It also separates the throne—in the conditional formulation—from the Davidic fief, in an unencumbered promise (v. 17, the only oracular reference to a fief). The psalm may imply that David's son did earn his own promise of perpetual dynasty.[44] Otherwise, it is identical in structure to Kings.

Psalm 89 and 2 Samuel 7 do not encumber the dynastic promise. But they are imprecise (as is Psalm 132) as to what territory the promise governs. To be sure, Psalm 89:19 applies to Yhwh Isaiah's epithet, "Holy One of Israel." But nowhere does the psalm vouchsafe kingship over Israel as a whole. 2 Samuel 7 is even more delicate: before David, no one from Israel was elected to build a temple (7:5–7); David himself is Yhwh's king over Israel (7:8). But the name *Israel* next vanishes: David's

FIGURE 11: DYNASTY IN DTRH

King	Text	King Over	Dynasty Unconditional Over	Dynasty Conditional Over	Comment
David	2 Sam 7	Israel	unspecified	heirs' kingdom (7:14)	7:16 *n'mn bytk*, as 11:38; 7:13 cites throne of heir, in only text to guarantee it
	1 Kings 2:4	Israel	———	Israel	throne
	8:25	Israel	———	Israel	throne
	9:4f.	Israel	———	Israel	throne

KINGSHIP OVER NORTH IS FORFEIT

King	Text	King Over	Dynasty Unconditional Over	Dynasty Conditional Over	Comment
Solomon	11:11	Israel	———	Israel	kingdom
	11:31, 33	Israel	———	Israel	kingdom (31)
	11:13	Israel	(fief), part of kingdom	———	some of kingdom
	11:34f.	Israel	fief (Judah)	———	some of kingdom
Rehoboam /Abijah	15:4f.	Judah /fief	fief	———	———
Jeroboam	11:37f.	Israel /north	unspecified, if good	Israel, implied	*byt n'mn*, like David, if J is good

1. Note: The fief formula is invoked when the Davidides are deprived of the territory of Israel (as 1 Kings 11; 15:4), and where the dynasty is interrupted (2 Kings 8:8, before the interregnum under Athalyah), i.e., when the Davidides lose their fief.

2. Note: The change from texts with conditional formulations about dynasty over Israel to texts with unconditional formulations about dynasty over a fief or a limited part of Israel begins with 1 Kings 11, when the schism is in immediate view.

3. Note: Like Ezekiel, E(Dtr)x has Yhwh reject Jerusalem and the temple, but not David's line (2 Kings 21:12–14; 23:27; 24:20). So dynasty in Israel is reduced to dynasty in Judah, after which dynasty in Judah is reduced to dynasty in theory.

son will sit on his throne (v. 12); David's and his heir's kingdom will be firmly fixed forever (vv. 13, 16). Dynasty is guaranteed, but not over all Israel: kingship in a nutshell, in a fief, will fulfill the terms of the promise.

This reading of 2 Samuel 7 is idiosyncratic. More idiosyncratic still is the failure of that chapter to stipulate a territory. The other two dynastic guarantees in Kings do so (1 Kings 11:37f. [OG]; 2 Kings 10:30). Even Chronicles, which reproduces 2 Samuel 7 (1 Chron. 17), stipulates the dynasty's domain when reprising Nathan's grant (as 1 Chron. 22:10; 2 Chron. 13:5).[45] It is a rule that Near Eastern promises of dynasty identify the state or territory, just as the land grant, a transaction to which the unconditional dynastic grant is often likened, stipulates what land is being granted.[46] The silence of 2 Samuel 7 is peculiar enough to demand explanation—and H(Dtr)'s treatment of the schism is distinctive enough to furnish it: dynasty is inalienable, dynasty over all Israel provisional. When the provisions are violated, a minimal territory remains (see figs. 10, 11).

This approach reproduces—by harmonization—not necessarily the original logic of 2 Samuel 7, but that of the author of 1 Kings 2:2–4; 8:25; 9:4f. in interpreting 2 Samuel 7; it even suggests that the author of the texts in Kings reshaped 2 Samuel 7. All these features must stem from H(Dtr): E(Dtr)x, on Cross's hypothesis, did not traffic in the antiquarian issue of the schism.

This solution presumes that 2 Samuel 7 was present in H(Dtr)'s work, as texts in 1 Kings 1–11 testify. Jeroboam is promised a "secure house" (*byt n'mn*), like David (11:38): the reference can only be to 2 Samuel 7:16. 1 Kings 2:12 (and 2:45) states that Solomon's "kingship was very firmly fixed," fulfilling 2 Samuel 7:13, 16, 26. In 1 Kings 3:6, Solomon mentions that Yhwh made good his oath to enthrone David's son: the throne here, as in 2:2–4; 8:25; 9:4f., is a metonym for kingship over all Israel; the promise to install David's son occurs in 2 Samuel 7:12f. Again, David could not build a temple, says 1 Kings 5:16–19, because he was busy with conquests. Only in 2 Samuel 7 does David contemplate building a temple; what follows in 2 Samuel 8 is precisely a list of his wars. And 1 Kings 5:19 closes with a direct citation of 2 Samuel 7:13a. Here, too, the throne (of all Israel) plays a role, linking the text to 2:2–4, 8:25; 9:4f. Moving on from 3:6, which cites 2 Samuel 7:12, the historian proceeds to the element (2 Sam. 7:13) of building a temple (cf. also 1 Kings 6:11–13, reconciling the theory of 2 Samuel 7:10 with the facts of history).

H(Dtr) reconciled 2 Samuel 7 with the schism by interpreting that event as a territorial sanction against a perpetual dynasty. The dynastic charter is irrevocable; conditions attach to the extent of the kingdom. This much, of course, is clear from 2 Samuel 7:14. "The rod of men" in that verse —however one takes 1 Kings 2:2–4; 8:25; 9:4f.—is, on H(Dtr)'s view, the agency that repossessed the north.

1 KINGS 8: H(DTR) OR E(DTR)X?

The text that brings 2 Samuel 7 into closest contact with the conditional dynastic covenant is 1 Kings 8, Solomon's speech at the temple dedication. With a divine response in 9:2–9, this is the other text in 1 Kings where scholars detect E(Dtr)x: if this verdict is not sustained, E(Dtr)x redacted neither 2 Samuel nor 1 Kings; Chap. 5 and Chap. 8 indicate that he left Judges and 1 Samuel unrevised as well. Even were parts of 1 Kings 8 exilic, thus, it would be dangerous to assign them to E(Dtr)x, an author unrepresented in a wide context, instead of to glossation (of the sort, for example, that produced parts of the prose of Jeremiah). The case for a systemic exilic redaction weakens dramatically once the conditional covenant is referred to H(Dtr).

The consensus has it that 8:44–53 is exilic; opinions vary as to the rest. But Levenson has shown that the structure of Solomon's speech defies textual surgery. The logic of his argument embraces vv. 22–53.[47]

Levenson concludes that E(Dtr)x wrote 8:22–53. Here 8:46–50 expresses the hope that Yhwh will move the captors to mercy when Israelites captive abroad implore forgiveness. "For they are the people", v. 51 reminds Yhwh, "that you brought out from Egypt." Levenson's argument is this: a pre–exilic author might invoke exile as a draconian sanction; but what would possess him to depict forgiveness as a return from an exile?[48]

There have been arguments for a pre–exilic dating:[49] first, because it advises prayer toward a temple, the text presumes that the temple stands; Levenson replies that even after its destruction, northerners made pilgrimage to the site (Jer. 41:5). The issue is thorny: if the speech promotes prayer toward a temple in ruins, the author should mention the fact, if only to forestall objections from theologians who, like Ezekiel, held that Yhwh had, in fact, *abandoned* the temple. To what despair must this party have been moved by the speech, had they no tokens of Yhwh's presence in Babylon. With what ridicule must they have used fellow exiles who telegraphed petitions across a continent, when the Holy One was in their very midst.

The other argument that 8:44–53 is pre–exilic is that it could refer to Israel's exile to Assyria in 722 B.C.E., not Judah's exile to Babylon in 586 B.C.E. Levenson appeals to Wellhausen: the Israelites rejected this temple. The retort is deflated by a text Levenson cites—the pilgrimage of 80 northerners to the temple, in mourning, in Jeremiah 41:5. 1 Kings 8 could address Israelites in exile, or even exiles settled by the kings of Assyria in Israel.

Both Hezekiah and Josiah reasserted Davidic sovereignty in the north.[50] The earliest hope for Israel's return from exile is in fact, conjoined with an oracle about David's dynasty (Isa. 11:1–16); Hosea 3:5, redactional or not, is similar. Judah survived Israel, a powerful argu-

ment for Israelites abroad—and those who supplanted them at home—
to advert to the Jerusalem temple. After 586 B.C.E., the text would have
been less compelling.

But does 8:46 refer to a return from a general exile? The structure of
1 Kings 8 is as follows:[51]

1. Rubric, vv. 28–30: HEAR THE PRAYER OF SOLOMON DAY
OR NIGHT . . .

2. Paragraph, vv. 31–32: When a man sins against his neighbor, and
[the neighbor] takes an oath, so as to bring
him to a trial of the oath, and comes and takes
the oath before your altar . . .

3. Paragraph, vv. 33–34: When your people, Israel, *are smitten before a
foe,* because they sinned against you, but re-
turn to you . . .

4. Paragraph, vv. 35–36: When *the heavens are stopped up, and there is no
rain,* because they sinned against you, but
they pray toward this place . . .

Summary of paragraphs 2–4:

5. Subparagraph, *Should there be famine in the land, should
vv. 37–40 there be pestilence, should there be crop blight or
rust, locusts or caterpillars, should an enemy be-
siege him in one of his gates—whatever affliction,
whatever illness*—ANY PRAYER, ANY PE-
TITION THAT ANY MAN IN ALL
YOUR PEOPLE, ISRAEL, HAS, WHO
KNOW EACH THE AFFLICTION OF HIS
HEART . . .

6. Subsubparagraph, THE FOREIGNER, too, who is not from
vv. 41–43 your people, and comes from a far-off land
for your Name's sake . . .

New paragraph:

7. Paragraph, vv. 44–45: When your people goes out to war against its
foe on a campaign on which you send them,
and they pray to you . . .

8. Subparagraph, When they sin against you—for there is no
vv. 46–50 man who does not sin—and you grow wroth
against them and *deliver them over before the foe,
and their captors take them captive to the land of
the foe, far or near,* and they take this to heart
in the land where they are held captive and
repent . . .

9. Rubric, vv.51–53:
HEAR THE PRAYER OF SOLOMON AND OF ISRAEL WHENEVER THEY CALL UPON YOU . . .

All the petitions are subordinated to rubrics 1 and 9. Further, paragraphs 3 and 4 are subsumed under petition 5, which generalizes from specific to all possible divine punishments. Petition 6 then extends the chance for remission of distress to all petitioners, even if not Israelite. Petition 7 begins a new unit, where foreign supplication is not effective: it offers Israel the favor of Yhwh when fighting abroad. Numbers 3 and 5 protect it in wars at home; but 6 offers the same protection to foreigners, and must be modified for cases where Israel is the enemy they are fighting.

But subparagraph 8 is a special case of paragraph 7. Without the eighth petition, paragraph 7 is the only provision concerning Israel that deals with no Israelite sin. Even the subject in petition 8 must be identified by reference to paragraph 7: it begins "When they sin," where "they" can only be the "people" on campaign of the preceding verse—whose possible "sin" has not yet been mentioned. The situation resembles that in petition 4, whose subject is that of 3, "your people, Israel" (v. 33). 1 Kings 8:46–50 (petition 8) continues the formulation of v. 45 (petition 7).

1 Kings 8:46–50 deals only with Israelites captured while campaigning abroad. It is v. 33 (petition 3) that envisions the eviction of the local population by invaders. Verse 34 speaks of "restoration to the land," a remedy applicable on a wholesale basis. This is the paragraph to which the exiles would look; yet *it* demands physical access to the temple—it assumes Jerusalem has not fallen. Conversely, the talk in vv. 46–50 is of leniency, which can be meted out individually; it does not assume physical access to the temple. The verbiage there describes capture at war (*šābûm šôbēhem*, v. 46), not a displacement or deportation of the local population. That the fate and rights of captured expeditionaries claimed attention in the ancient Near East is sufficiently attested by several law codes.[52] Captivity was a possibility against which one had to provide.

If E(Dtr)x introduced 8:46–50 after v. 45, he was anything but lucid. He did not add words to the effect, "even should the temple be in ruins" or "even should Jerusalem be razed," to forestall objections that Zion's election was voided. He wrote a text (or inside a text) in which Solomon's prayer was preeminent—Solomon, who flunked the text of the conditional covenant—and in which the links between the temple and the (rejected?) dynasty are indissoluble (see the following section). He failed to refer to exile: he expected readers to understand that his talk of war abroad and prisoners of war were literary expedients; in this unanachronistic guise, he meant to describe an invasion of Israel and the exile of the entire population. The argument to an exilic date is weak even if one allows that 8:46–50 speak of exile. When one weighs it down further with the defects of a hypothesis that the exilic author was writing so elliptically, so ineffectively, it collapses altogether.

1 KINGS 8: THE CONDITIONAL COVENANT AND 2 SAMUEL 7

Solomon's speech in 8:22–53 follows a speech, in 8:15–21, that summarizes 2 Samuel 7. The juxtaposition of 2 Samuel 7 with formulations of the conditional covenant reveals their unity in H(Dtr)'s thought. It perplexes the Cross–Levenson scenario: E(Dtr)x should have muted the contradictions he was creating by keeping clear of 2 Samuel 7.

1 Kings 8:15–21 (quoted in this chapter's section entitled "1 Kings 11 and Dynastic Covenant") runs as follows: Yhwh had said that he had elected neither town nor citizen from the exodus until David (vv. 15f.); the source is 2 Samuel 7:6–8, 11. The same source informs 1 Kings 8:17–19: David had intended to build a temple; delighted, Yhwh responded, "You will not build the temple, but your son, who issues from your loins, he will build the temple for my name"—the very words come from 2 Samuel 7:5, 12f. Solomon sums up (8:20f.). Yhwh fulfilled his oracle: Solomon succeeded David and built the temple, installing the ark (cf. 2 Sam. 7:6; especially Ps. 132:2–8).

This is only half a citation. What about the dynastic oracle of 2 Samuel 7? The continuation—the other part of the citation—comes in 8:24–26. Solomon repeats that Yhwh has so far kept his word. He goes on (8:25):

> And now, Yhwh, god of Israel, abide, for your servant, David, my father [cf. Ps. 132:1], by what you said to him, saying, "There will not fail you a man, before me [cf. 2 Sam. 7:29], sitting on the throne of Israel, provided only that your sons take care for their way, going before me as you have gone before me."

He asks that this promise be fulfilled. (8:26).

Solomon cites 2 Samuel 7 until he comes to the dynastic promise. Then what he cites is a promise in which dynasty over Israel is conditional. The speech affirms that David earned an heir over all Israel; the dynasty hinges on the heir, just as in Psalm 132. Yet the citation of 2 Samuel 7 in 15–21 is incomplete without 24–26; and 24–26 is placed so as to be read as the continuation of the citation. The implication is that the historian in 8:24–26 interprets or redirects the dynastic promise of 2 Samuel 7.

1 Kings 8:15–26 is a conceptual unit, linking the conditional covenant to 2 Samuel 7. In 9:2–9 Yhwh grants Solomon's requests: the response again combines the two covenant traditions. Yhwh accepts the temple for his name, eyes, and heart (cf. especially 8:27, 29; 2 Chronicles 7:12ff. supplement to make the reference clear). He then reiterates the promise to David in an unusual conditional form: if Solomon is faithful, as David

was (v. 4), "I will establish the throne of your kingdom over Israel forever" (*whqmty 't ks' mmlktk 'l ysr'l l'lm*) (v. 5). This is an abridgement of 2 Samuel 7:12f. (*whqymty 't zr'k . . . wknnty 't ks' mmlktw 'd 'wlm*); the abridgment reflects the nuance that Solomon is not unconditionally guaranteed a successor over a united Israel, as David was (so 8:15–26 on 2 Sam. 7:12f.). Still, 2 Sam. 7:12f. is cited as the original conditional covenant— "there will not fail [David] a man on the throne of Israel" (9:5). 1 Kings 2:2–4; 8:25; and 9:4f. here—as in 8:15–26—come together with 2 Samuel 7. They are related to dynasty over all Israel.

1 Kings 9:6–9 articulates threats for the first time since 2 Samuel 7:14. This text is assigned to E(Dtr)x even by those who maintain the pre–exilic origin of 9:4f. (and 2:2–4; 8:25), although Friedman articulates important reservations about the constraints of the antiquarian format.[53] The chief literary connections are to pre–exilic segments of Jeremiah.[54] More important, 1 Kings 11:9f. cites this passage, and this passage only, as a warning connected with the division of the kingdom (see the section in this chapter entitled "1 Kings 11 and the Dynastic Covenant"). Because 1 Kings 11 sets 9:4f. (and 2:2–4; 8:25) in the same frame of reference, an attempt to connect 9:6–9 primarily with the exile is inadvisable.

The consequences of apostasy in 9:6–9 include the loss of the land. The warning echoes Deuteronomy 28:37; 29:24f., as well as Jeremiah. Possibly H(Dtr) had Israel's exile to Assyria in mind. Exile was, in any event, an established curse in the pre–exilic era:[55] Josiah may have used it to goad the nation on to a holy zeal. Against the linkage with 1 Kings 11:9f., 33, and with 8:15–26 and 2 Samuel 7, the threat of exile is pale evidence for exilic authorship.

If the conditional covenant stems from H(Dtr), no serious difficulty obtrudes: all the elements enumerated to this point have a straightforward explanation. H(Dtr) justified Josiah's policy toward *bāmôt* in general, and toward Solomon's *bāmôt* in particular, by tracing the devastating consequences of their use. Solomon was made responsible for the schism. Even were there problems with this reconstruction, it would have the advantages of most of Noth's hypotheses: the antiquarian impulse, hand in glove with the political, might have dictated the inclusion of some sources virtually verbatim.

The alternative—assigning the conditional formulations to E(Dtr)x —stumbles at every point. H(Dtr) did not include 9:1–9, thus, or provide any real closure with 2 Samuel 7: he never announced that Yhwh had fulfilled his vow to secure David's ongoing dynasty. E(Dtr)x did not edit 2 Samuel 7 to suppress the name of the territory promised in perpetuity—he conditionalized the covenant to disqualify the dynasty altogether. The distribution of the conditional formulations is inept. The wording of 1 Kings 8:46–50 camouflages the author's meaning; the linkage of the conditional covenant of 1 Kings 8:25 and 9:4–5 to 2 Samuel 7 heightens, if anything, the alleged contradiction between them: why did

E(Dtr)x not revise 2 Samuel 7? Levenson claims that in insisting on observance of the Deuteronomic law, the author of 2:2–4; 8:25; 9:4–9 "is more Deuteronomic" than H(Dtr).[56] This is improbable historically: E(Dtr)x clung doggedly to a dynasty over nothing, when Pandora had loosed disaster and forlorn hope was all that remained (2 Kings 25:27–30); Josiah, hopes in full blossom, was spurred on by expectations of imminent cataclysm (2 Kings 22:11, 16f.). To discover a doctrine of invulnerable dynasty at Josiah's court is, again, to trivialize the reform.

Cross began by setting a promise of inalienable dynasty in 2 Samuel 7 against what seemed to be the end of the dynasty. Conditional dynastic promises seem to harmonize the antithesis. But Cross did not ask how 2 Samuel 7 was read before the exile. What did the irrevocable dynasty govern? The natural answer was *Israel*; if so, dissonance was already created by the schism. Cross brought the doctrines of conditional and unconditional covenants into opposition in the abstract. But the conditional formulations are carefully contextualized in Solomon's reign, again in the division of the kingdom. The conditional formulations explicitly treat dynasty over Israel, the unconditional dynasty in the abstract, or (the fief) over Judah alone (Fig. 11). There is no substantive contradiction.

In these passages, thus, H(Dtr) vents a political program in the context of an antiquarian problem—the relation of 2 Samuel 7 to the schism. He detaches the unconditional promise of dynasty (2 Sam. 7:15f.) from the guarantee of kingship over Israel as a whole (7:12f.?). In 1 Kings 2:2–4; 8:25; 9:4f.; 11:11, 33, H(Dtr) reformulates 2 Samuel 7 to clarify that it is the throne over all Israel that is subject to "the rod of men" (2 Sam. 7:14). Because only 2 Samuel 7:14 allows for the view that Yhwh ordained the schism, and because H(Dtr) explains the schism as the result of covenant infidelity, H(Dtr)'s reading was logical. Its logic was, in fact, historical (see the section in this chapter entitled "1 Kings 11 and the Dynastic Covenant").

In this light one must hypothesize either that E(Dtr)x rewrote the entire history (as Peckham; equals H[Dtr]x), or that he made no insertions in 1 Kings. Even verses scattered here and there which may seem to stem from an exilic milieu are not evidence of a single–minded, exilic retouching of the narrative. Such a hypothesis creates difficulties without alleviating the tension between the covenants of 1 Kings 1–11 and 2 Samuel 7. Indeed, with no unmistakable trace of E(Dtr)x between Deuteronomy or Joshua and 2 Kings 21, all appearances are against it.[57]

The conditional covenant never refers to the exile; it serves the account of the schism. To ransack it for insinuations of the dynasty's end is to operate on it in a way that readers, generally, cannot have been expected to do. E(Dtr)x was capable of explaining the exile directly—he did so in the account of Manasseh's reign (2 Kings 21:2–16; 22:16–20; 24:2–4). Anagogic exegesis of texts about Solomon—like such exegesis of texts in Judges—supposes that the author made unreasonable demands on the analytical skills of his audience. Otherwise, it implies that the redactor was too dense to revise the text he was contradicting, and perfectly happy to contradict a source he evidently revered, all in the service of an oblique and incomplete etiology of the exile. The enterprise of E(Dtr)x, his work as an index of his intentions, must make good, sound sense. The proposals so far advanced about E(Dtr)x's work in 1 Kings are superficially appealing; as Friedman, among others, has recognized, they would be more redoubtable were they grounded in a hypothesis of an intelligent and sentient author writing effectively and in good faith.[58]

THE ACCOUNT OF SOLOMON'S REIGN

If the redactor's work should exhibit sensitivity and consistency of thought and method, this is no less true of the historian's work with his sources. The character of the Solomon account has been reviewed (see the sections in this chapter entitled "The Account of Solomon's Reign" especially "Solomon's Organization: 1 Kings 4:1–5:14" and "Solomon's High Places and Josiah's Reform"). H(Dtr)'s treatment artfully welds narrative to administrative sources, and each to the historian's own composition. Inherited materials are linked with limited thematic frameworks, and the sources strung together to create a picture of steady growth, steady maturation, followed by sudden senility and disaster. Solomon, so great and wise, is undone by a character flaw.

The text describes developments in and flowing from Solomon's regime. Thus, H(Dtr)'s views on the dynastic covenant progress with each movement of the text, and culminate in chap. 11. In this sense, and in its logic, the narrative is consciously antiquarian. As in Judges, political concerns color the selection of topics. Even here the governing principle is that the present state of affairs is explained by causes in the past, which must be dealt with in their proper frame of reference.

H(Dtr)'s contemporary interest focuses on 1 Kings 11–12. These chapters explain the origin of the official bāmôt in Jerusalem and Bethel-/Dan. Like Judges (and Deuteronomy), they blame the introduction of the bāmôt into the regime on foreign influence. The rest of Kings then documents the persistence of the shrines (see the section in Chapter 9 entitled "DtrH: A Cultic Interpretation of History"): from Solomon to Josiah, the Davidides whom Kings assesses positively are, Hezekiah excepted (2 Kings 18:3), endorsed with the reservation that the bāmôt remained (1 Kings 3:2f.; 15:14; 22:44; 2 Kings 12:4; 14:4; 15:4, 35). Explicitly in the cases of Rehoboam and Ahaz (1 Kings 14:22; 2 Kings 16:4), and implicitly in others (1 Kings 15:3; 2 Kings 8:18, 27; 21:3, 20), the kings H(Dtr) judges negatively actively patronized these shrines. The north, too, is accused of such activity (1 Kings 12:32; 13:2, 32; 2

Kings 17:29, 32), but without remission, and in a form aggravated by the sin of Jeroboam.

The problem ends with the only narrative (not regnal evaluation) about *bāmôt* in Judah: Josiah eradicates the *bāmôt* (2 Kings 23:5, 8–20); afterward they are not mentioned. Judges 1–3 and 1 Kings 1–11 therefore furnish the etiology of a condition rectified by Josiah. The condition originates in the distant past; in both cases the past is reconstructed according to the dictates of the evidence (oppressions, the schism).

H(Dtr)'s treatment answers the question that a traditionalist, reading Deuteronomy in the late 7th Century, should have posed (cf. Jer. 44): if the *bāmôt* and their associated minor deities are not Israelite, how is it that Israelites have patronized them, and kings such as Solomon built them, since time immemorial? The answer is a history. It is history summoned to serve the historian's politics; like Macaulay's, it is history nonetheless. And it is not arbitrary history—it could not be arbitrary and still answer its purpose.

In the introduction to Judges and in 1 Kings 1–11, H(Dtr) recreates Israel's antiquities from sources—sometimes liberally construed—and from principles of causality. His object is to persuade the reader, to fortify the partisan, by argument instead of ukase. His logic is therefore antiquarian: it is the past *as past*, as a source, not an analogue of the present, that has relevance. This is why the historian writes about history— about Solomon or the era of the judges. What is the difference between H(Dtr)'s reportage and other historical narratives? Consistently, the evidence indicates that H(Dtr) wrote to recover the events (or we would not have 1 Kings 1–2; 3:16ff.; 4:1–5:14; 9:10–25), even when his selection and reconstruction were tinted by contemporary developments.

Notes to Chapter 7

1. See 5:17f.; 9:20, on which cf. Judges 1:28–35 and G^AB on v. 29; Joshua 16:10; 17:13; 9:26.
2. See B. Halpern, *The Constitution of the Monarchy in Israel* (HSM 25; Chico, CA: Scholars, 1981), 19–31, with implications for Jeroboam's cultic policy.
3. F. M. Cross, *Canaanite Myth and Hebrew Epic* (Cambridge: Harvard University, 1973), 275–89.
4. Cross, *Canaanite Myth* (n. 3), 275–89; T. Veijola, *Die ewige Dynastie* (Helsinki: Suomalainen Tiedeakatemia, 1975); M. Noth, *Überlieferungsgeschichtliche Studien* (Halle, E. Germany: Niemeyer, 1943), 66–72 (hereafter *US*); W. O. Dietrich, *Prophetie und Geschichte* (FRLANT 104; Göttingen: Vandenhoeck & Ruprecht, 1972), 15–20 and *passim*, especially 72, n. 35.
5. See, e.g., J. Wellhausen, in F. Bleek, *Einleitung in das Alte Testament* (4th ed.; Berlin: Reimer, 1878), 240; Noth, *US* (n. 4), 66f., n. 3; J. Liver, "The Book of the Acts of Solomon," *Bib* 48 (1967): 75–101 (as 1 Kings 11).
6. Noth, *US* (n. 4), 64–66; Wellhausen, in Bleek, *Einleitung* (n. 5), 225f. On the age of the Court History, see L. Rost, *Die Überlieferung von der Thronnachfolge Davids* (BWANT 3/6; Stuttgart: Kohlhammer, 1926). J. Van Seters (*In Search of History* [New Haven: Yale University, 1983]) takes it as exilic because it disparages David, which H(Dtr) would not have countenanced.
7. T. Ishida, "Adonijah, the Son of Haggith and his Supporters: An Inquiry into Problems of History and Historiography in 1 Kings 1–2," in R. E. Friedman and H. G. M. Williamson, eds., *The Future of Biblical Studies* (Semeia Supplements; Decatur: Scholars, 1987), 165–87. Cf. F. Langlamet, "Pour ou contre Salomon? Le rédaction pro-salomonienne de I Rois I–II," *RB* 83 (1976): 321–79, 481–528. The considerations here complement Ishida's, especially on the defensive character of Solomon's intrigue (1:12). See further, H. Tadmor, "Autobiographical Apology in the Royal Assyrian Literature," in H. Tadmor and M. Weinfeld, eds., *History, Historiography and Interpretation: Studies in Biblical and Cuneiform Literatures* (Jerusalem: Magnes, 1983), 36–57.
8. See Noth, *US* (n. 4), 67f. On 1 Kings 3 as an Egyptian *Königsnovelle*, see van Seters, *In Search* (n. 6), 162–64.
9. So OG puts MT 4:20–5:1 in 2:46a, b: MT divides the list of Solomon's districts from what they supply. Likewise, OG locates MT 5:5f. in 2:46g,i: MT is probably from 10:26 (equals 2 Chron. 9:25), explaining the horses of 5:8. Cf. the movement of MT 9:15–25 in OG, again on logical grounds. Chronological concerns are prominent. See Wellhausen, in Bleek, *Einleitung* (n. 5), 231f.; D. W. Gooding, *Relics of Ancient Exegesis: A Study of the Miscellanies in 3 Reigns 2* (SOTSMS 4; Cambridge: Cambridge University, 1976), especially on 2:46a–1.
10. See T. N. D. Mettinger, *Solomonic State Officials* (Lund, Sweden: Gleerup, 1970), 121f.; B. Halpern, "Sectionalism and the Schism," *JBL* 93 (1974): 519–32.
11. G. E. Wright, "The Provinces of Solomon," *EI* 8 (1967): 58*–68*.
12. Proverbs 25:1. See R. B. Y. Scott, "Solomon and the Beginnings of Wisdom in Israel," in M. Noth and D. Winton Thomas, eds., *Wisdom in Israel* (SVT 3; Leiden, Netherlands: Brill, 1955), 262–79; M. Weinfeld, *Deuteronomy and the Deuteronomic School* (Oxford: Clarendon, 1972), 161f.
13. Noth (*US* [n. 4], 68f.) takes 9:15ff. as the source. But the number of overseers varies. Wellhausen (in Bleek, *Einleitung* [n. 5], 237) thought 5:27 (10,000 men) contradicted 5:29 (150,000); but different activities are in point. The tradition in 1 Kings 5:24, 32 inspired 2 Samuel 5:11; what the direction of *textual* dependence was is more difficult to say.

14. In 1 Chronicles 23:1; 28:1ff., David crowns Solomon before the army, as 1 Kings 1:10, 38ff. Cf. further 1 Kings 2:2; 3:7 with 1 Chronicles 22:5; 29:1; David's blessing with 1 Kings 1:48 (1 Chron. 29:10–19); the festival of coronation (1 Chron. 29:20–25) with 1 Kings 1:40; the subscription of the officials, army, and king's sons (1 Chron. 29:24) with 1 Kings 1:47 (plus 49). For the themes, see S. Japhet, *The Ideology of the Book of Chronicles and its Place in Biblical Thought* (Jerusalem: Bialik, 1977), 401–10.

15. On the exchange, and for what follows, see V. Hurowitz, "Temple Building in the Bible in Light of Mesopotamian and North-West Semitic Writings" (dss. Hebrew University; Jerusalem, 1983), 158–218. Further, 9:20–23 stands in tension with 5:27f. in speaking of Israel's inability, not (willful) failure, to displace Canaan's aborigines. The tradition (Chapter 6) antedates H(Dtr) and may even have characterized the first recension of Judges 1.

16. Van Seters, *In Search* (n. 6), 309f. (cf. D. W. Gooding, "An Impossible Shrine," *VT* 15 [1965]: 405–20). His parallel to TB Middot is not to the point; against his claim that we have no parallel descriptions of temples from the ancient Near East, cf. building descriptions cited in Chapter 3; especially Hurowitz, "Temple Building" (n. 15), 223ff., with documentation for descriptions stretching back to Tiglath-Pileser I.

17. Wellhausen, in Bleek, *Einleitung* (n. 5), 231f. Cf. Noth, *US* (n. 4), 66f. n. 3.

18. Is Hur introduced into Bezalel's genealogy in 2 Chronicles 1:5 by association with Solomon's Cellini, Huram, in 1 Kings 7:13ff.; 2 Chronicles 2:12f.? The catalogue of 1 Kings 7:40–50 parallels the earlier description of his work, as in Chronicles. The vocabulary is different in the catalogue.

19. See Hurowitz, "Temple Building" (n. 15); on the month names, Wellhausen, in Bleek, *Einleitung* 232; on other vocabulary, C. Rabin, "The Emergence of Classical Hebrew," in A. Malamat, ed., *The Age of the Monarchies: Culture and Society* (WHJP 1/5B; Jerusalem: Massada, 1979), 71–78, especially 71, 73 n. 12.

20. 1 Kings 6:11 is late for bestowing approval, but is affixed to the description of the adyton, which Yhwh must occupy. This does not militate for OG.

21. On Solomon's fortresses, see W. G. Dever, "Monumental Architecture in Ancient Israel in the Period of the United Monarchy," in T. Ishida, ed., *Studies in the Period of David and Solomon and Other Essays* (Tokyo: Yamakawa-Shuppansha, 1982), 269–306.

22. See A. R. Millard, "Solomon's Gold," forthcoming. The motif of Solomon's reputation is also the stuff of temple-building inscriptions.

23. Solomon promotes Jeroboam during the building of the Millo (11:27f.), which 9:15 dates to his twenty-fifth year. See my "Sectionalism" (n. 10).

24. See A. Šanda, *Die Bücher der Könige übersetzt und erklärt* (Exegetisches Handbuch zum Alten Testament 9/1: Münster: Aschendorff, 1911), XXX, 347; latterly, H. Weippert, "Die Ätiologie des Nordreiches und seines Königshauses" (I Reg. 11$_{29–40}$)," *ZAW* 95 (1983): 344–75. On G's account in 12:24a–z, see recently J. C. Trebolle Barrera, *Salomón y Jeroboán. Historia de la recension y redaction de I Reyes 2–12, 14* (Bibliotheca Salmanticensis. Dissertationes 3; Salamanca: Universita Pontificale, 1980). The survival of Jeroboam's mother's name is particularly suggestive in light of Tadmor, "Autobiographical Apology" (n. 7).

25. Ahijah's coat is rent into twelve pieces (equals twelve tribes, 11:30), of which Jeroboam gets ten (Israel) and Rehoboam one (Judah). The discrepancy (ten plus one does not equal twelve) has fueled a series of redactional hypotheses, for which see Weippert, "Ätiologie" (n. 24), 357ff. (Weippert has an original ten tribes for Jeroboam *minus* one for Rehoboam.) Benjamin is not reckoned to Rehoboam by rights in 12:20f. One need not bring the components of the contradiction into relationship with one another, however, because Judah and Israel are similarly contrasted (ten plus one) in 2 Samuel 19:44. The numbers reflect traditional conceptions of Israel (10 tribes) and Judah (one tribe), and of the united kingdom (12 tribes).

26. 1 Kings 11:39, "I will oppress David's seed for the sake of this, but not for always," is absent, along with the last clause in v. 38, from OG. It may prophesy political reunion under Hezekiah or Josiah (cf. the section in this chapter entitled "The Dynastic Covenant: E(Dtr)x or H(Dtr)?"). If late (as OG suggests), the verse is probably a messianic gloss.

27. Rezin's action is coordinated with a Davidic campaign (11:24; cf. vv. 15–17). G treats Rezin ahead of Hadad (11:14) and reads "Edom" for "Aram" in v. 25, which may refer to Hadad only. Confusion arose from the resemblance between Aram (ʾrm) and Edom (ʾdm), and between Hadad and Hadadezer (v. 23).

28. Wellhausen, in Bleek, *Einleitung* (n. 5), 239f.; Šanda, *Könige* (n. 24), 326f.; Noth, *US* (n. 4), 66f. n. 3.

29. This sort of dual chronology is attested in the inscriptions of Esarhaddon (Babylon texts) and Nabonidus (on the Sin temple in Harran), and in Ezra 1–6. On Chronicles, and on Chronicles in what follows, see my "Sacred History and Ideology—Chronicles' Thematic Structure," in R. E. Friedman, ed., *The Creation of Sacred Literature* (Berkeley: University of California, 1981), 35–54. On the temple building typology, see Hurowitz, "Temple Building" (n. 15).

30. See B. Halpern, " 'Brisker Pipes than Poetry': The Development of Israelite Monotheism," in J. A. Neusner, B. Levine, and M. Haran, eds., *Judaic Perspectives on Ancient Israel* (Philadelphia: Fortress, 1987), 77–115.

31. On 1 Kings 13 as the work of Josiah's historian, see W. E. Lemke, "The Way of Obedience: 1 Kings 13 and the Structure of the Deuteronomistic History," in F. M. Cross, W. E. Lemke, and P. D. Miller, eds., *Magnalia Dei / The Mighty Acts of God* (Fs. G. E. Wright; Garden City, NY: Doubleday, 1976), 301–26.

32. Verse 15, "And behold, it was a dream," absent from Chronicles, may qualify the revelation. Still, H(Dtr) takes it seriously in 11:9 and chapters 3ff.

33. The verbiage in 9:7–9 is Jeremianic: v. 7 *lmšl wlšnynh* is paralleled only in Deuteronomy 28:37; Jeremiah 24:9; v. 8 "whistle (*wšrq*)" in Jeremiah 19:8; 25:9; 49:17; 50:13 in similar contexts, and the question there in Deuteronomy 29:24f.; Jeremiah 22:8f.; v. 9, "to take hold of other gods" only in Jeremiah 8:5. Verse 6, "Go and worship other gods and prostrate yourselves to them" has close parallels only in the work of H(Dtr) and, arguably, Jeremiah: Joshua 23:16, "Go and worship other gods and prostrate yourselves to them" (with loss of land as in 1 Kings 9:7); Deuteronomy 17:3, "has gone and worshipped other gods and prostrated himself to them"; 1 Kings 16:13, "went and worshipped the Baal and prostrated himself to him" (cf. also 22:53f.; 2 Kings 21:21); Deuteronomy 13:7, 14, "Go and worship other gods"; 8:19, "Go after other gods and worship them and prostrate yourself to them"; 28:14, "to go after other gods and worship them"; 13:3, "Go after other gods . . . and worship them"; Judges 2:19, "to go after other gods to worship them and prostrate themselves to them"; Jeremiah 13:10, "went after other gods to worship them and prostrate themselves to them"; 25:6, "Go after other gods to worship them and prostrate yourselves to them"; Deuteronomy 29:17, "to go to worship the gods of those nations"; Jeremiah 44:3, "to go, to burn incense, to worship other gods"; Jeremiah 11:10, "They went after other gods to worship them"; 35:15, "Go after other gods to worship them." Several texts have "go, worship!": with other gods, 1 Samuel 26:19; with Yhwh, Exodus 5:18; 10:8, 11, 24; 12:31; Ezekiel 20:39. 1 Kings 9:9; 2 Kings 17:35; 21:3; Jeremiah 22:9 "prostrate oneself . . . and worship" invert the usual "worship . . . and prostrate oneself." On 9:6–9 and 6:11–13, see the section in Chapter 7 entitled "Solomon and the Temple: 1 Kings 6:1–9:9," and Figure 10.

34. OG and Syr. read singular in 11:33; but plural is *lectio difficilior*. Weippert ("Ätiologie" [n. 24], 372–74) takes the plural to imply glossation, dislocated from v. 31, but neglects the linkage to 9:4–9. Cf. R. E. Friedman, *The Exile and Biblical Narrative* (HSM 22; Chico, CA: Scholars, 1981) 13 on the shift in number.

35. Cross, *Canaanite Myth* (n. 3), 275–89, excising 2:4; 6:11–13; 8:25b (and 46–53); 9:4–9. These are the only texts in 1 Kings he assigns to E(Dtr)x. Other analyses are similar: see the section in Chapter 5 entitled "Twin Redaction Based on Historical Evidence."

36. See on the text latterly, J. D. Levenson, "The Last Four Verses in Kings," *JBL* 103 (1984): 353–61, with bibliography. Levenson, too, sees the text as assuming Jehoiachin's and the line's legitimacy, if only implicitly.

37. See Figure 11. On *nir* equals "fief," see P. D. Hanson, "The Song of Heshbon and David's Nir," *HTR* 61 (1968): 297–320 (and Rashi to 1 Kings 11:36).

38. For MT *nśy' 'ṣtnw*, OG reads *ṣtn 'ṣtnhw* (cf. 11:14, 23, 25) as chastisement. The continuation favors MT; the scribal lapse was audial.

39. Friedman, *Exile* (n. 34), 12; R. D. Nelson, *The Double Redaction of the Deuteronomistic History* (Sheffield, U.K.: JSOT, 1981), 99–105.

40. Levenson, "Last Four Verses," (n. 36), especially 355, n. 10. See also Nelson, *Double Redaction* (n. 39), 102.

41. In *Constitution* (n. 2), 36–40, I was insufficiently clear, and did not propose, as Levenson understood, to take "Israel" in those passages as "the northern kingdom," but as all Israel. Friedman (*Exile* [n. 34], 12–13) takes the opposite view.

42. Levenson, "Last Four Verses" (n. 36), 355, n. 10. Contrast H. Reviv, "History and Historiography During the Time of the Division of the Kingdom: Toward an Understanding of the Term *'Edah* in 1 Kings 12:20," *Zion* 50 (1985): 59–63.

43. Rost, *Thronnachfolge* (n. 6), 89ff.; Noth, *US* (n. 4), 66, 70. Noth hints at implications for the exile, but links the passages to the schism.

44. In Chronicles Solomon earns such a right, but is deprived of it by northern renegades: Halpern, "Chronicles' Thematic Structure" (n. 29).

45. Chronicles' position, perhaps from a pre-exilic source, is that *if* Solomon was obedient, Yhwh vouchsafed eternal Davidic (and Solomonic) dynasty over all Israel. See preceding n.

46. On the land grant and dynastic grant, see Cross, *Canaanite Myth* (n. 3), 241–64; M. Weinfeld, "The Covenant of Grant in the Old Testament and in the Ancient Near East," *JAOS* 90 (1970): 184–203; J. D. Levenson, "The Davidic Covenant and its Modern Interpreters," *CBQ* 41 (1979): 205–19, with further bibliography. For dynastic guarantees, see, e.g., *ANET* 204a; D. J. Wiseman, *The Alalakh Tablets* (London: British Institute of Archaeology at Ankara, 1953), 6; D. J. McCarthy, *Treaty and Covenant* (AnBib 21; Rome: P.B.I., 1963), App. 3, 4; *KAI* 222 B:21–25; J. Friedrich, *Staatsverträge des Hatti Reiches* (MVAG 31/1, 1926; 34/1, 1930), 3.7–22; 6.1ff.; E. F. Weidner, *Politische Dokumente aus Kleinasien* (BoSt 8; Leipzig: Hinrichs, 1923), 86:15f.; 94:49–54 (with "his land," defined later in the treaty); 118:40f.; 128:20–130:33.

47. J. D. Levenson, "From Temple to Synagogue: 1 Kings 8," in B. Halpern and J. D. Levenson, eds., *Traditions in Transformation* (Fs. F. M. Cross; Winona Lake: Eisenbrauns, 1981), 143–66, especially 148–57.

48. Levenson, "From Temple" (n. 47), 157f. More accurately, in "Last Four Verses" (n. 36), 360, he speaks of "mercy for the exiles," which he refers to Jehoiachin in 2 Kings 25:27–30. He also observes that Solomon is silent about sacrifice: that reflects, not an exilic interest in a nonsacrificial cult, but a concern with the petitions that accompany sacrifice; Solomon demonstrates how to make petitions effective by a sacrifice in 8:62–64. To charter a nonsacrificial cult, E(Dtr)x should have removed the sacrifice. Every Israelite knew what the business of the temple was, especially in Josiah's day; and, lest a few forget, the author of 8:22, 31 places Solomon at the altar.

49. Levenson, "From Temple" (n. 47), 157f.; Levenson, "Last Four Verses" (n. 36), 360.

50. 2 Chronicles 30f.; 1 Kings 23:13–23 (see the section in Chapter 7 entitled "Solomon's High Places and Josiah's Reform" and Chapter 9). The name of Hezekiah's heir, Manasseh, also echoes that of the northern tribe. If 2 Chronicles 30:6–9 is not from H(Dtr)hez, note that Chronicles addresses it to a population that never returns from exile; yet it has effect in 30:11.

51. For the text, see Levenson, "From Temple" (n. 47), 150f. Sections I and IX are summarized, the others quoted; subjects and sins are underlined, punishments italicized.

52. Eshnunna 29; Hammurabi 27–33; Middle Assyrian 36, 45. Note that even the loss of a few sections would bring vv. 33f. into play.

53. Nelson (*Double Redaction* [n. 39], 73–76) cites the change of person in 9:6 (not solved by a hypothesis of redaction or glossation, it probably takes up from "Israel" at the end of 9:5, much like 11:33 after 11:32), and argues that dependence on Deuteronomy 29:24f. implies a date after H(Dtr). But his argument applies equally to Jeremiah 22:8f., which is pre-exilic. And he effectively shows that Deuteronomy 29:24f. could stem from H(Dtr) himself. Cf. Friedman, *Exile* (n. 34), 12f. with the point that E(Dtr)x

must *speak* of Israel's exile when he means to refer to Judah's.

54. See n. 33. On v. 9a, see n. 53 (to Deut. 29:24f.).
55. See D. R. Hillers, *Treaty-Curses and the Old Testament Prophets* (Rome: P.B.I., 1964), 33f.
56. Levenson, "Last Four Verses" (n. 36), 355.
57. For reasoning that suggests the likelihood of E(Dtr)x's activity in Deuteronomy, see R. E. Friedman, "From Egypt to Egypt: Dtr¹ and Dtr²," in Halpern and Levenson, eds., *Traditions in Transformation* (n. 47), 167–92.
58. Friedman, ibid. 185–92. See also his "Sacred History and Theology: The Redaction of Torah," in Friedman, ed., *The Creation of Sacred Literature* (n. 29), 25–34.

CHAPTER 8

The Way of a Snake on a Rock?
The Historian and the Sources

Look how we can, or sad or merrily, interpretation will misquote our
looks.

HENRY IV

CONTEXTUALIZING THE PROBLEM

The argument of the past two chapters is twofold:

First, texts in DtrH have their historical topics as their *primary* objects
of reference. If a Josianic historian (H[Dtr]) wrote the bulk of the corpus, then it is inappropriate to impute antiquarian text to the exilic redactor. E(Dtr)x was attempting to salvage a treasure, a cultural legacy in
papyrus, from a historical maelstrom. He accounted for the exile in light
of his source, and an economical view of his enterprise dictates a mini-
malist view of his editorial work:[1] E(Dtr)x's chief sphere of activity is the
end (and perhaps the start) of the history.

Second, chapters 6–7 illustrate the relationship between antiquarian
and contemporary concerns in H(Dtr)'s work. Some of this work justifies
Josiah's policies. But Josianic standards are not forced on the material.
We do not read of intermarriage with Canaanites under Manasseh or of
Ahaz building *bāmôt* (cf. 2 Kings 16:4ff.). The Josianic program is car-
ried through only where the evidence invites it.

Here, Noth's basic intuition—shared by Y. Kaufmann[2]—is confirmed: H(Dtr) had antiquarian interests and a sense for the past as past;
the evidence narrowed the latitude and scope for ideology. Contemporary interests guided H(Dtr)'s interpretations, but did not determine
them a priori.

Part 1 fortifies this conclusion: H(Dtr)'s treatments are a harmony of
historical logic and sources. In larger blocks he developed more momen-
tous themes by wedding selection to editorialization. Thus Solomon's
grandeur emerges from records the like of which appear nowhere else in
the history. This reign is a zenith: wealth pertains to it programmatical-

ly; says the text, "This is what it is to attain glory." By contrast, H(Dtr) makes nothing of Ahab's "house of ivory, and all the towns that he built" (1 Kings 22:39). But sources, judiciously applied, dictate the lines of the portrait. A certain raw curiosity affects the process of selection (Chapter 9).

Texts that test these principles are examined in Part 3. The principles themselves have been defended in concert with a disadvantageous thesis: that H(Dtr) wrote at Josiah's court; and that E(Dtr)x updated in the exile. Cross's view is appealing precisely because it suggests a nonantiquarian motive for DtrH's most dramatic themes. But were DtrH of a piece, from the exile, even the treatment of the Solomonic schism in relation to Josiah's program would be antiquarian.

In this light the present chapter examines 1 Samuel 8–12 to show: 1) that inconsistency in DtrH is best explained by conflicting sources; 2) that the hypothesis of exilic redaction in historical narrative has unacceptable epicycles (this is the other antiquarian report in which such redaction is sometimes detected); and 3) that H(Dtr) (or a source) used antiquarian logic on conflicting sources—as they were found in 1 Samuel and, sporadically, in the rest of the corpus.

PRELIMINARY REMARKS: CONTRADICTIONS IN DtrH

These points restate Noth's insight that H(Dtr) was a historian. They revolve around the issue of discrepancy: too often this is treated as summary evidence of redaction.

An example is Judges 1, sometimes assigned to E(Dtr)n/x (see the Chapter 6 section entitled "The Logic of Judges 1–3"). Scholars contrast its piecemeal conquest to Joshua's united conquest. So Josh. 10:40f. claims that Joshua depopulated the hills of Judah and "smote" the entire south. Compare Judges 1:1–20—Judah settled the highlands, but dominated without supplanting the lowlands populations (especially vv. 18f.).

The conflict between Judges 1 and Joshua 10–12 lies at a remove from the surface of the presentation: tradition had it that Israel had ousted the Amorites—the Amorites were giants (Amos 2:9), and giants were nowhere to be seen. But Canaanite demes survived (e.g., as Josh. 9; 13:13). The disparity was a given, and the historian introduced a distinction between conquest and supplanting in order to mute it. Both Joshua and Judges 1 reflect it.[3]

Consistently, *capture* links to Israel, lowlands, and narratives, *supplanting* to highlands, Judah, and notes that Canaanites remained. Those who ascribe Judges 1 to E(Dtr)x should claim that E(Dtr)x revised the whole terminology. But here the editor becomes an author reworking sources: why is the insertion of Judges 1 *ex hypothesi* so awkward? The hypothesis is narrowly local, its implications complex and contradictory. This is the case with every activist view of E(Dtr)x in the early history.

The hypothesis that E(Dtr)x wrote Judges 1 no more heals disharmony than the hypothesis that H(Dtr) was working with refractory sources. Did E(Dtr)x introduce gratuitous cacophony into half-canonized history? Or did H(Dtr), who bore the burden of constructing it, echo a clash of traditions? If the dissonance occasioned by Judges 1 is substantial, not produced by misprision, then it should not come from E(Dtr)x: E(Dtr)x in this part of the corpus is, at best, a glossator.[4] If the contradictions are insubstantial, there is no cause to suspect a second hand. Either way, invoking E(Dtr)x is needless.

The author(s) of DtrH should be envisioned as avoiding or muting disharmony, not as excelling in it. E(Dtr)x should be sought not in incoherent redaction jangling against the strains of DtrH, but in coherent thinking expressed *in unison* with the inherited corpus.[5] He and H(Dtr) were alive to contradictions, to what they wrote, and to the text they transmitted. Wherever possible, therefore, problems must be explained as conflicts from the sources. To isolate a disparity without inquiring how its author resolved it is to find half a contradiction—the sound of one hand clapping. 1 Samuel 8–12 provides a serviceable test case for these principles.

1 SAMUEL 8–12 IN CONTEXT: TWO SOURCES STITCHED TOGETHER

1 Samuel 8–12 breaks down into five scenes (see Fig. 12):

1) *9:1–10:16:* Saul ben-Kish, hunting some lost asses, turns to a seer, Samuel. Samuel instructs him to leave off the hunt; he names Saul *nāgîd* (Yhwh's designee for the throne), to rescue Israel from Philistia. After receiving signs, he is to proceed to Gibeah of Elohim, and to reduce a "Philistine garrison" (10:2–7).[6] Afterward he is to wait seven days for Samuel at Gilgal (10:8). The signs come to pass (10:9–12).

Here Samuel is an obscure local seer. The story is about Saul—and it is Saul who is introduced by patronym and tribal affiliation, and described as towering, at the outset (9:1f.). Saul is called out against *Philistia.*[7] Finally, the episode leads to 1 Samuel 13, where the reduction of the Philistine garrison at Gibeah heralds liberation (13:2); Saul also waits seven days for Samuel at Gilgal (13:7b–15). Yet 10:13–16 close by ignoring Samuel's instructions in 10:1ff.: Saul goes home instead of carrying them out. It has long been recognized that 9:1–10:12 originate in distant antiquity.[8] Unless Saul goes home to assemble an army against Gibeah (13:2)—which is unlikely in light of 10:16—10:13–16 break the original continuity with chapters 13f.

2) Before the tale of the asses comes *1 Samuel 8.* Samuel is aged and his sons are unworthy to succeed him; so Israel demands of him a monarch. The shift to monarchy is a public crisis. It is not, as in 1 Samuel 9:1ff., remarked in passing. Yhwh disapproves of the change, though he is will-

ing to accept it (8:7–9). Here, too, Samuel is no obscure seer. He rules Israel—and needs a successor. He convenes and conducts the assembly of the tribes.

3) *10:17–27:* Samuel reconvenes the assembly (10:17), dismissed in 8:22. After citing history against the constitutional change, as in 8:7f. (10:18f.), Samuel selects a king by lot. Saul is again introduced by tribe and patronym (10:20f.), and again described as towering (10:23); these elements duplicate 9:1f. Too, Saul is not waiting for Samuel at Gilgal, as 10:1–12 demands: 10:17–27 disrupts the flow of 9:1–10:16, and resumes that of Chapter 8. It warrants remark that Saul is not yet entrenched in power. Some of the (arms-bearing) citizenry (*ha-ḥayil*) squire him home to Gibeah. Others scoff at his lordship (10:26f.).

4) *11:* Nahash of Ammon has driven the whole population of Gilead into the town of Jabesh. A month later (so the original 10:27c),[9] he invests this last outpost. The Gileadites send messenger to all Israel, including Gibeah of Saul; there "all the people raised their voice and wept" (11:4). Saul summons the muster and relieves Jabesh. His partisans offer to kill those who had scoffed at his prowess, though Saul refuses (11:12f.; cf. 14:45; 2 Sam. 19:19–24). So all proceed to Gilgal to "renew the kingship" there (11:14f.).

Scholars often detach 1 Samuel 11 from 10:17–27. The arguments are as follows: a) against 10:26 (*ha-ḥayil*), Saul has no army at Gibeah in 1 Samuel 11, but summons the msuter (11:7); b) the Gileadite messengers canvass all Israel (11:3f.), and must know nothing of Saul's kingship; and c) 1 Samuel 11 portrays the monarchy favorably, and 8; 10:17–27 take a dim view of it.[10]

These arguments are misleading. a) There *are* people with Saul in Gibeah, probably the *ḥayil* of 10:26. The usage "The people . . . wept" (11:4) forbids the assumption that the "people of Gibeah" only are the actors: some qualification ("of Gibeah") would be expected (cf. 11:1, 3, 5, 8–10; "people" [11:4f., 7, 11f., 14f.] is general). Saul summons the muster (11:7f.) to field a national, not makeshift, militia (10:26). b) Messengers are sent throughout Israel because Saul's position is not entrenched (10:27). Indeed, Ammon's depradations antedate his election (n. 9; so 12:12). c) Chapter 8 and 10:17–27 are not antimonarchic. Kingship was approved, if reluctantly, by Yhwh; Yhwh himself elected this king (cf. Deut. 17:14f.). That the electee of 10:17ff. shines in Chapter 11 is no evidence of literary disjunction. Nor does his success endorse the kingship—only Yhwh's choice of kings.

The case for severing 1 Samuel 11 from 10:17–27 is deficient. Conversely, the two are linked: Saul's home is the same (10:25; 11:4). Samuel plays the same role—he conducts assemblies. The scoffers of 10:26 reappear only in 11:12f.: the need to renew the kingship in 11:14f. arises from there having been scoffers in the first place. The renewal implies a previous constitution of the monarchy, of which nothing is said either in

9:1–10:16 or in Chapter 8 (still no king). These elements of 1 Samuel 11 make sense only after 10:17–27.

Finally, the Israelite mythos of leadership dictated that Yhwh's designee should prove himself, ideally in battle, before being confirmed. Chapter 11 provides such proof between the inauguration of Saul's kingship in 10:17–27 and its renewal in 11:14–12:25.[11] 1 Samuel 11 thus follows 10:17–27 literarily, logically, and thematically. There is no basis for Wellhausen's claim that the redactor linked the chapters late (10:26f.; 11:14f.).

5) *12:* The finale is the renewal of the kingship. Again, the shift to kingship is a crisis. Again, Samuel leads the assembly, and must resign to make way for a king (12:3–5). And again, he reviews the past to disparage the shift to kingship. These connections to 8; 10:17–27; 11 are straightforward. So is the renewal: Samuel subordinates the kingship to the terms of Israel's covenant with Yhwh.

In all, there are two accounts of Saul's rise. The first is 9:1–10:12: the Philistines, not the constitution, are the crisis, and chapters 13f. detail how Saul dealt with them. Conversely, 8; 10:17–27; 11; 12 center on the constitutional shift, attaching it to a threat from Ammon. This strand resumes in 1 Samuel 15, with Saul's campaign against the Amaleqites: chapter 13 contains a narrative of Saul's rejection from the kingship (vv. 7b–15a); 15:10ff. has a parallel. Scholars have argued that the rejection accounts are both secondary.[12] Even were this so, the double rejection reflects the combination of two sources—the texts could be secondary within each source; it is improbable that a single author would have felt the need to repeat himself on the subject.

To combine 1 Samuel 9:1–10:12; (13f.) and 8; 10:17–27; 11; 12 (13:1; 15), the historian found it necessary to introduce 10:13–16. Anointed to liberate Israel, Saul returns home and keeps incongruously quiet. This was, in fact, logical. In 10:1–8, Samuel tells Saul to meet him in Gilgal seven days hence. But the events of 10:17–27; 11; 12 derail the schedule; they also divide the reduction of the Philistine garrison at Gibeah (13:2f.)—the first consequence of Saul's election—from the events that were to signal him to act. Somehow the compiler had to uncouple 10:1–12 from 13:2.

Probably the historian took 10:8 as Josephus did (*Ant.* 6.57, 100): Samuel means to tell Saul to wait at Gilgal later on. But Samuel joins Saul at Gilgal already in 11:12–12:25; an assembly and a battle have already intervened; yet the seven-day wait begins only in 13:7b–15. This was intolerable if Samuel had told Saul to reduce the Philistine garrison and proceed directly to Gilgal: it followed that Samuel had said no such thing. 1 Samuel 10:14–16 therefore reinterprets 10:7, "Do what comes to hand" (n. 6): it meant that Saul was off duty (so *Ant.* 6.57). Samuel had not instructed Saul to reduce a garrison, but to be about his business until called: harmonizing, Josephus recreates the thought of the redactor (cf. also MT 10:27c, "[Saul] remained silent" [kmḥrš], for, "About a month later" [OG *km ḥdš]).

Simplicity on the whole commends this view: from the two sources the combination followed. The request for monarchy (Chapter 8) had to open the segment: afterward Saul acts as king; and the people could not demand a monarchy once they had a monarch. The private designation of Saul (9:1–10:12) had to come next: the private designation could not follow the public one; but it was conceivable that a personal announcement antedated the official installation. Later, kings of the north (as Jeroboam ben-Nebat, Jehu) would claim to have received such private oracles. Nor was it illogical that Saul's career, like David's (1 Sam. 16:1–13 before 2 Sam. 5:1–3), should follow this pattern.

Next, of necessity, came 10:17–27; 11; 12. Chapters 13f. could not precede them, because in this narrative Saul operates publicly as king. Chapters 13f. thus *presumed* the public designation of 10:17–27. Nor could chapters 13f. be inserted between 10:17–27 and the Ammonite war in Chapter 11: the texts about the scoffers in 10:26 and 11:12f. could not be prised apart; they had to be spared just after Saul first proved his fitness to be king. Only by dismantling Chapter 11, thus, could the compiler have placed it after the war of chapters 13f. Samuel's speech in Chapter 12 was the culmination of the kingdom's inauguration. Again, this had to precede Chapter 13, in which Saul acts as unquestioned ruler. Finally, Saul is first rejected in Chapter 13. The covenant ceremony confirming him in office could not be placed after that text, which again meant that Chapter 12 (and 11:14f.) had to precede it.

In short, if these sources underlie 1 Samuel 8–12—9:1–10:13 and 8; 10:17–27; 11; 12—the work of combining them reflects a logical interest in their order, integrity, and sense. The current arrangement of chapters 8–15 is the only one that could have emerged from such raw materials. The contrast is to standard analyses of these chapters, examples of which are reviewed in the succeeding section. The argument will be close, and demands consultation with a text.

ALTERNATIVE ANALYSES OF 1 SAMUEL 8–12: WANTON REDACTION?

BUDDE

The classic source division is that of Karl Budde: 9:1–10:16; 11; 13f. versus 8; 10:17–27; 12. Even if Chapter 11 could have divided 10:1–8 from 13:2ff., the compiler must have supplied the scoffers that link 10:17–27 to 11 (10:26f.; 11:12–14). But why are similar links across the sources lacking elsewhere? The sources could have stood almost as they were: with 11:1–11 already interposed between 9:1–10:16 and 13:2ff., the order, 8; 9:1–10:16; 10:17–25; 12; 11:1–11; 13f. would have erased all further dissonance—and the need to add 10:26f.; 11:12–15 (see Fig. 12).

Budde has the historian gratuitously reworking Chapter 11 and inventing the scoffers.[13] This is not a conscious reconstruction—quite the reverse. But consider the historical implications for the redactor's mentality: he would have chosen to treat the sources idiosyncratically, without concern for their accuracy. The reconstruction may be correct; it is not probable.[14]

WELLHAUSEN

Budde meant to defend the source hypothesis against Wellhausen's view. The principal difference was, Wellhausen viewed 8; 10:17–27; 12 as a post-Deuteronomistic addition to the source in 9:1–10:16; 11:1–11; 13:2–14:52.

Wellhausen's late source was derivative (he cites 10:23//9:2). Mizpeh in 8; 10:17–27; 12 figured the center of government after the fall of the Judaean monarchy, and the "antimonarchic" strain expressed exilic disillusionment; too, the "law of the kingship" (10:25) referred to Deuteronomy 17:14–20, which implied a late date. But the role of Mizpeh has no thematic resonance—it is restricted to 10:17–27—and one can find the exile in it only obliquely. Connections to Deuteronomy 17:14–20 imply a late date only if Deuteronomy is of a piece and Josianic.[15] And antimonarchic sentiment is not all late: Wellhausen cites the parallel of Hosea's criticisms of monarchy after the fall of the north, a century before H(Dtr); recent studies indicate that the antagonism to the monarchy memorialized in 8; 10:17–27; 12 reflects historical reality.[16] Finally, Wellhausen cited Deuteronomistic language in 1 Samuel 12 to show that the text was late. This is not plainly present, and the text may stem from H(M+/M−) (equals H[Dtr]hez?).[17]

NOTH

Noth took Wellhausen's part against Budde, but added a refinement: 9:1–10:16 came from a source, and 8; 10:17–27; 12 were composed by H(Dtr), not later. Noth shunned his usual explanation for discrepancies—conflicting sources—because of continuity between 8; 10:17–27; 12 and Chapter 7. In 7, Samuel defeats the Philistines. Noth took this report to deny Saul's achievements (as chapters 13f.). This logic works for a source in 8; 10:17–27; 11; 12; 15: here Saul confronts not the Philistines (defeated by Samuel in Chapter 7), but the Ammonites and Amaleqites. But Chapter 7 nowhere claims that Samuel *subjected* Philistia, precluding renewed inroads—there is no contradiction of 1 Samuel 13f.

What most betrayed the hand of H(Dtr) in 1 Samuel 7 is the tradition that Samuel judged Israel (vv. 15–17; cf. v. 6). Samuel executes both the military and the juridical role of the judge—a combination Noth correctly attributed to H(Dtr). Because Samuel plays the national leader in Chapter 7 as in 8; 10:17–27; 12, and because 7:6, like 10:17, reports an assembly at Mizpeh, 7 was linked to 8; 10:17–27; 12 as H(Dtr)'s creation.

The evidence for H(Dtr)'s composition in Chapter 7 runs deeper than Noth discerned. An aside in 7:14 states, "There was peace between Israel and the Amorites." The notice echoes the prologue to Judges—proscribed elements survived the conquest. It must stem from the same author (H[Dtr]; especially 1:35). And 1 Samuel 7:16f. situates Samuel at Bethel, Gilgal, Mizpeh, and Ramah. Ramah, Samuel's home, is drawn from 8:4 (cf. 1:19; 2:11). At Gilgal (11:12–12:25; 13:7b–15) and Mizpeh (7; 10:17–27), he convenes assemblies. Bethel is a pilgrimage site in 10:3—the text may have been read to imply Samuel's activity there. In all, the notices in 7:15–17 punctuate the transition from Samuel's active career to his introducing the monarchy; they thus derive from the author who chronicled Israel's passage into statehood. Phrases from M+ ("were subdued"—7:13) in the preceding narrative suggested to Noth that H(Dtr) had composed the chapter as a whole.

Noth felt no need to excise (7;) 8; 10:17–27; 12 as secondary. H(Dtr) meant to condemn the monarchy, even if this meant contradicting his sources. Even here, H(Dtr) based himself in part on sources, of which Noth, following Eissfeldt, found traces in 10:21bα–27a.[18] This solitary refinement amended the substance of Wellhausen's view less than its form: Noth, like Wellhausen, maintained the exilic origin of 8; 10:17–27; 12; only, Noth dated DtrH to the exile, and Wellhausen thought exilic materials were secondary.

EISSFELDT

Eissfeldt struck back for Budde: he dismissed the idea that here alone H(Dtr) contradicted his sources. 1 Samuel 7; 8; 10:17–27; 12 were a "narrative sequence self-enclosed and wholly comprehensible as such," with no signs of H(Dtr) (n. 17). The only problem was that the shift to monarchy is blamed on fear of Ammon in 12:12, and in 8:5 on Samuel's sons' shiftlessness. Eissfeldt struck 12:12a, setting 8:1–5 in an earlier source, against Noth's view that it was H(Dtr)'s handiwork.[19] The expedient is not indicated: the elders cite the sons' corruption in 8:5; but the narrator avoids identifying this as a real motive—much as Samuel and Yhwh abominate kingship theologically, but fight it (8:7–18) in economic terms. There is no contradiction with 12:12, which tallies with 4QSamᵃ and Josephus (see the section in this chapter entitled "1 Samuel 8–12 in Context: Two Sources Stitched Together" and n. 9).

VEIJOLA

To acquit H(Dtr) of contradicting his sources without adopting Budde's and Eissfeldt's source hypothesis, T. Veijola returns to Well-

FIGURE 12: PROPOSALS ON THE COMPOSITION OF 1 SAMUEL 8–12

1: Stähelin/Halpern	2: Budde	4: Noth	5: Veijola	6: van Seters
I 8 Israel request king of leader Samuel, cite sons' actions All Israel / King = rejection of Yhwh / National history / No enemy named	*I 8* A 9:1–10:16 *II 10:17–25* (R-a 10:26f.) B 11:1–11 (R-b 11:12–15) *III 12* C 13–14	H-a 8 *I 9:1–10:16* H-b 10:17–27 *II 11:1–11* H-c 11:12–15 H-d 12 *III 13–14*	*I 8:1-5* (E-a 8:6–22) *II 8:22b* *III 9:1–10:16* R-a 10:17 (E-b 10:18–19a) R-b 10:19b–27 *IV 11:1–11* R-c 11:12–14 (E-c 11:15) (E-d 12) *V 13–14*	H-a 8 *I 9:1–8, 10–14, 18f., 22–27a;* *10:2–6, 9–13* H-b 9:9, 15–17, 20f., 27b; 10:1, 7f., 14–16 H-c 10:17–27 *II 11:1–11* H-d 11:12–15 H-e 12 *III 13–14 (+/−)* H-f 13:7b–15a H-g 15
A 9:1–10:13 Seer Samuel designates Saul to wait at Gilgal Saul, must re-duce Gibeah (H: 10:13–16) Kingship no issue / Private, local / Enemy: Philistines / Saul at home)				
II 10:17–27 Leader Samuel selects Saul by lot; some follow him All Israel / King = rejection of Yhwh / National history / Scoffers / Saul home at Gibeah				

A superior path for the Redactor would be:

I 8 A 9:1–10:16 *II 10:17–25* *III 12* B 11:1–11 C 13–14	H-a 8 *I 9:1–10:16* *II 11:1–11* H-b 10:17–25 H-c 12 *III 13–14*	*I 8:1–5* (E-a 8:6–22) *II 8:22b* *III 9:1–10:16* *IV 11:1–11* (E-b 12 [adjusted]) *V 13–14*	*I 9:1–8, 10–14, 18f., 22–27a;* *10:2–6, 9–13* *II 11:1–11* H-a 8 H-b 10:17–25 H-c 12 *III 13–14 (+/−)* H-d 15

or

H-a 8
   I 9:1-8, 10-14, 18, 22-27a;
     10:2-6, 9-13
H-b 10:17-25
H-c 12
   III 13-14 (+/-)
   II 11:1-11
H-d 15

Key: Underlined and italicized segments represent sources
H = H(Dtr)
R = Late redactor in Veijola's reconstruction
E = E(Dtr)n in Veijola's reconstruction
Parentheses indicate retouching hand in #1, 2, 5
Stähelin/Halpern scenario presumes minor H(Dtr) recasting of sources as perhaps in 8:8, 12:11

III 11
Saul rescues Jabesh, leader Samuel renews kingdom

IV 12
Leader Samuel retires, confirms kingship

V 15
Saul defeats Amaleq

Saul at Gibeah, with warriors
Scoffers spared
All Israel
Enemy: Ammon
Gilgal w/o 7-day wait (≠ A)

All Israel
King = rejection of Yhwh
National history
Enemy: Ammon
B 13:2-14:52

Saul waits at Gilgal
Enemy: Philistines
Israel = 600 men
Saul rejected

Saul takes Gibeah, routs Philistines

Saul rejected //B
Israel = 210,000 men

hausen's model. Veijola puts 8; 10:17–27; 12 to the scalpel, based on the texts' attitude toward monarchy. This has, of course, been the procedure of choice since J. J. Stähelin proposed the analysis defended here.[20] In it, Veijola shines. Antimonarchic sentiment is excavated verse by verse (as 10:18f. [equals E(Dtr)x/n] detached from 10:17, 20–27). Exilic polyps on DtrH include 8:6–22a; 12. But 8:1–5, 22b are the flesh of H(Dtr).

Now the tension between 12:12 and 8:1–5 is redactorial. Where Noth read 8:1–5 to imply that the demand for monarchy was precipitate, Veijola counters, justly, that only 12:12 makes that point: 8:1–5 *justifies* the demand for different organs of leadership. Conversely, 12:6–12 deprecates monarchic rule—Yhwh, not kings, provided succor in the past. We may go further: 12:12 exposes the justification of 8:1–5 as a blind.

By tying 12:12 to a late stratum, and 8:1–5 to its source, Veijola rationalizes some disorder in Noth's view. But the cost is upheaval elsewhere. Thus 11:1–11 is the work of H(Dtr)—in the old, promonarchic cast. So 10:17, 19b–27; 11:12–14 reflect "a relatively late stage of the tradition-history": they link H(Dtr)'s 11:1–11 with the antimonarchic (equals E[Dtr]n) material in 8; 10:18f.; 12; and they derange the narrative sequence, not least by bringing Saul and Samuel together in Gilgal before they keep, in 13:7–15, an earlier appointment to meet there (10:8).[21] What possessed a "relatively late" tradent to disrupt the sequence from 10:1–8 to 13:7b–15 with a long, problematic insertion?

Similarly, did H(Dtr) make kingship the fruit of human initiative (8:1–5, 22b)? The people in H(Dtr) also demand the reconnaissance of Canaan (Deut. 1:21–23, against Num. 13:1ff.). Moses' agreement is a cardinal error (Deut. 1:37). Where is the similar discussion one expects with 1 Samuel 8:1–5, 22b? Veijola sunders it away (vv. 6–22a).

Veijola subpoenas extensive lexical evidence. Some of the verbiage coheres with particular thematic contexts; this is not to gainsay all of it. Still, his main criterion is a treacherous touchstone—H. J. Boecker has observed that antimonarchic materials in Samuel are more subtle than most critics admit; Yhwh, after all, agrees to the monarchy, and even selects the first kings.[22] And the upshot is that kingship alters no ground rules: Yhwh will chastise infidelity alone. Veijola must take Wellhausen's line that the debate about kingship in 8; 10:17–27; 12 was current in the historian's time. Yet it could equally reconstruct a *historical* debate: to portray antimonarchic sentiment in the past is not to impeach the kingship in the present. Veijola makes the converse assumption the core of his argument.

Veijola recurs to Noth's scheme (accretion) where Deuteronomistic language characterizes one component of a contradiction. H(Dtr) would not contradict sources—it must be a redactor. The present treatment has stressed that this is a hypothesis to be invoked only where unavoidable. Reviewing one last analysis of 1 Samuel 8–12 will help to clarify the point.

VAN SETERS

In another variation on Wellhausen, van Seters finds Deuteronomistic usage in 8; 10:17–27; 12:[23] in 10:18 the appeal to sacred history is diagnostic; it echoes H(Dtr) in Judges 6:8f. (the exodus and oppressors).[24] But appeals to the exodus are common among the prophets and psalms (e.g., Amos 3:1), which is to say, in the cult. The term *oppressors* reflects the influence of Exodus 3:9, which refers to the Egyptians; in Judges it refers to Egyptians and to the supplanted Amorites; in 1 Samuel 10:18 it refers to the oppressors of Judges (as 12:6–12; cf. Amos 6:14; Isa. 19:20; Ps. 106:42). The treachery of vocabulary as a clue to authorship is here in evidence. At any rate, links within 8; 10:17–27; 12 then lead van Seters to ascribe it whole to H(Dtr).

Van Seters admits that H(Dtr) had sources in 9:1–10:13; 11; (13f.). He claims, however, that these originally had no bearing on how Saul became king—H(Dtr) added to 9:1–10:13 and to Chapter 11 all the material linking them to the monarchy. Why? The editor found these tales in

> fixed written form and felt under some constraint to retain them as they were. Only by supplementation did he seek to reinterpret them, . . . even at the expense of creating obvious tensions and absurdities.[25]

Van Seters, thus, concurs with Wellhausen, Noth, and Veijola that 8; 10:17–27; 12 are late compositions interspersed among inherited materials.

Van Seters flaunts the defects of this approach: H(Dtr) arbitrarily associated two reports in "fixed written form" with Saul's rise to the throne. He tied one source (9:1–10:13) to chapters 13f. by adding Saul's appointment with Samuel at Gilgal (10:8) and an account of their meeting (13:7–15). Then he put Chapter 11, which disrupts this schedule, and another meeting at Gilgal (11:12–12:25) in between. Finally, he confected 8; 10:17–27; 12, and strewed his confection carelessly among the fixed traditions it contradicts.

So H(Dtr) altered his inherited traditions. Then he concocted an account that contradicted his amendments. Then he put them together in a way that made of both a chronological and historical hash. This does not trouble van Seters—who, incidentally, attributes to H(Dtr) both elements of the doublet in 1 Samuel 24 and 26 (Chapter 3); van Seters wants to defend Noth's theory of DtrH's unity. Even leaving aside the fact that the analysis proposed here repairs the literary damage the view of van Seters inflicts, his conception of the redactor's mentality is improbable and cavalier.

Van Seter's view is only marginally more problematic than Wellhausen's, Noth's, or Veijola's. In each, H(Dtr) included promonarchic texts he set out to eclipse; in each, 8; 10:17–27; 12 and 11:12–15 disrupt and contradict the older sources. Why did H(Dtr) invent accounts that created tension with sources he elected to include? Either the materials Noth attributed to H(Dtr) were secondary—the problem remains why they were inserted—or they stemmed from a source the historian felt called upon to integrate into his narrative, for which no better place could be found. This is the position that has been argued here; it makes for a neater reconstruction than that of Wellhausen. It boasts the advantage that it does not hypothesize a historian who meant to condemn the monarchy, but did so in such a way as to obfuscate his meaning. It generates a picture of a historian who worked logically and sincerely at a historical enterprise.

A CRITIQUE OF THE WANTON REDACTOR

Wellhausen, Noth, Veijola, and van Seters suggest that H(Dtr) or E(Dtr)n conspired against the sources he preserved. But such subversion would be out of character, to judge from the historiography elsewhere. Noth's argument was that the historian did not contradict the sources he included, because he wrote history, with antiquarian concerns, and included these sources. If this is circular, the arguments to redaction are nothing more than 180-degree arcs: they ignore the workings of the historian's mind. They dissect the logic of the presentation. But to look at the literature historically means engaging the logic of the reconstruction, not that of the presentation. Every case in which this has been done indicates that H(Dtr) was driven, by evidence and logic, to the conclusions he presents.

None of these scholars explains the form the late concoctions take (see Fig. 12). Why was Chapter 11 inserted between 9:1–10:12 and 13:2ff.? If originally it had no connection with Saul's enthronement or with 10:17–27; 12, why was it not set *after* Chapter 14? Noth could respond that Chapter 11 precedes Chapter 13 because 13:7–15 already relate Saul's rejection. This option is closed to Wellhausen and van Seters: for them, H(Dtr) *also* added the rejection in 13:7–15.[26] Were this so, H(Dtr) should have contented himself with the rejection in Chapter 15 and placed 11:1–11 after Chapter 14. Further, the rejection (13:7–15) notwithstanding, Chapter 11 could have been added to Saul's military achievements in 14:46–52. Even Noth's view thus supposes that H(Dtr) created an awkward sequence in the face of a better choice.

Again, if a redactor wrote 8; 10:17–27; 12 to condemn kingship, he badly muddied his message. Where it stands, Chapter 11 vindicates Yhwh's chosen king; after 1 Samuel 8, 9:1–10:12 have similar implications. Even Chapter 12 does not deny the king divine sanction. Rather, it articulates a principle H(Dtr) believed to have operated throughout Israel's history: righteousness, kings or no, will earn prosperity; evil kings or an evil people rate the scourge. Again, the guiding impulse is apparently antiquarian. The qualifications eviscerate any antimonarchic statement E(Dtr)x or H(Dtr) makes. It was wicked to have demanded a king. But Yhwh met the demand, and kings who earn Yhwh's approval can guarantee the welfare of the nation. This stance is not antimonarchic; a redactor who meant it as such can only have been thinking fuzzily.

The historian could have avoided tangling the timetable of 9:1–10:12; 13:2–14:46 (seven days) by attacking kingship only in Chapter 8 (and after Chapter 14). Why did he concoct a public designation of Saul in 10:17–27? After inventing Chapter 8 he could have left 9:1–10:12; 13:2–14:52 to describe Saul's installation. The redactor's logic in the scenarios of Wellhausen, Noth, Veijola, and van Seters is not just whimsical—it is downright deficient.

Finally, there is an early reference to 8; 10:17–27; 12. Hosea 13:10f. states that Israel, not Yhwh, chose the path of monarchy. There is no hint of such a view in 1 Samuel 9:1–10:12; this text suggests that kingship was lowered from heaven. Its pattern is typical—Saul is chosen in time of need (9:1–10:12), and then defeats the enemy (chapters 13f.) and assumes imperium (14:47, 48–52).[27] The same sequence infuses 10:17–12:25. But only in 8; 10:17–27; 11; 12, in all the literature of the region, does it transpire that the people themselves created the kingship. This is less likely late polemic than it is an old tradition or a reconstruction. Hosea (eighth century) cites it verbatim (Hos. 13:10; 1 Sam. 8:6), and indicates that the request displeased the deity (13:11; cf. 1 Sam. 8:7; 12:17).[28] And the tradition on which Hosea drew was known to his audience–he alludes to it; he does not expound it. It probably existed in much the same form a century before H(Dtr). Indeed, Deuteronomy 17:14f. presupposes it as a point of common reference in Israelite history.

Taking 1 Samuel 8–15 as a synthesis of two parallel sources—one in 8; 10:17–27; 11; 12; 15, the other in 9:1–10:12; 13:2–14:52—heals all the defects of the alternative proposals. It is economical: 10:13–16 represents the redactor's only effort to anneal discrepancies in the presentation. Signs of parallel sources abound right through to 2 Samuel 1.[29] Most important, the text's assembly reflects a sincere effort to reconstruct the history. It is this property that distinguishes the solution not just as possible, but as historically legitimate.

SOME CONCLUSIONS ON REDACTION

H(DTR) IN THE PRESENTATION: A NEEDLE IN THE HAYSTACK?

Every authorial analysis expresses suppositions about the author's aims and prowess. Examining them enhances our control over the literary and historical data.

If it overlooks this point, redaction criticism is identical to modern literary study. Thus, much like van Seters, one scholar advocates "*literary* (compositional–aesthetic) explanations for what appears to us as redundant, digressive, proleptic, or analeptic in a document—all in the interest of asking about a single author with complex vision."[30] Literarily, this is the only prescription. But unless used as a form of harmonization, to get at the single (i.e., last) author's reasoning, it ignores the properties of the historian as historian, of the presentation as a vehicle of a reconstruction. The author is not a human being fitting strategies to problems, but a self-appointed cataleptic, an accident of the theory.

Such theories are patronizing: the editor was lackadaisical and created contradictions (E[Dtr]x in Judges or van Seters' H[Dtr] in Samuel); and he was historically incompetent, apathetic about accuracy. How can we know this is improbable? First, a community preserved the text as one immune to facile impeachment. Second, chapters 3–8 show that an antiquarian component shapes the historian's reconstruction. Third, the assumption that DtrH is history, not romance, stems from DtrH itself. And the assumption produces hypotheses that are no more complex—if anything, simpler—than those of orthodox analysis. To presume that the historians were indifferent to dissonance is nonsense—no Near Eastern historiography exhibits a tin ear for self-contradiction. To posit one in Israel to shore up visions of literary prehistory is an extreme recourse (see also Part 3).

This is not to say that the study of editing is inappropriate. It is not, and has yielded tangible value, as in Richter's work on Judges. But the procedure is linear. Structural or incongruous passages furnish a dictionary of diagnostic vocabulary (Deuteronomistic language) for ascribing other passages to the same hand. The technique isolates a homogeneous corpus: it is geared to do so, on a formal basis. But the process prohibits control—one cannot check the results—except for the historical correlatives, the implications for the redactor's intention and intellect. When it evades this issue, literary study resembles a crooked shell game, in which the barker never has to produce the pea.

The sample of diagnostic vocabulary is always skewed. Thus, H(Dtr) is identified by his interest in cult centralization. But the language is distributed in Kings, and pertains to themes such as disobedience. Only a component of H(Dtr)'s opus exhibits this vocabulary. Judges 4, too, is the work of H(M+) (Chapter 4). Usage offers no support: Judges 4 relates specific events, and M+ is a framework; their vocabulary and ideology are skewed. The speech of Moses in Deuteronomy 1–3, universally attributed to H(Dtr), rephrases its sources,[31] but is virtually devoid of Deuteronomistic language. The language is missing because the text relates only indirectly to the themes of the history. Content determines diction.

This principle applies to the diagnostic terms. So the phrase *ʾelōhîm ʾaḥerîm*, "other gods" (thirty-eight times in DtrH, eighteen times in Jeremiah, four times elsewhere, sg. in Exodus 34:14), appears in monitions (twenty-three times) and thematic overviews (eleven times; exceptions in direct discourse, 1 Samuel 26:19; 2 Kings 5:17), but figures in running narrative only in 1 Kings 11:4 (cf. 9:6–9; close is 1 Kings 14:9, direct discourse). H(Dtr) invokes the term only where content demands; he also draws upon synonymous expressions.[32] Thus the significance of the words *ʾelōhîm ʾaḥērîm* can be expressed only statistically, against the number of times H(Dtr) might have, but did not, use them, in comparison with other authors.[33] The statistics are valid only *after* one distinguishes H(Dtr)'s use of the phrase from usage that he inherited from a source (Deut. 13–18 [five times]; 1 Sam. 26:19; 2 Kings 5:17?).

After all, sources condition diction (as Judges 4–5). The ancients were notorious copycats, as the tale of Ahaz' Syrian altar illustrates (2 Kings 16:10–18; or the Phoenician template of Solomon's temple); the proclivity extended to text. Thus H(Dtr)'s invective ("He did evil," and so on) was as traditional (cf. M+) as Bolshevik language (revisionist, imperialist, and so on). For *ʾelōhîm ʾaḥērîm*, the source is openly cited: the first commandment (Exodus 20:3//23:13; 34:14) proscribes "other gods"; Deuteronomy 5:7 reproduces it, in the first mention of "other gods" in DtrH.[34] H(Dtr) harps on the phrase to say "Apostasy violates the first rule." But the phrase was in H(Dtr)'s sources (and Hosea 3:1). And H(Dtr) did not level it through where the presentation did not require it.

There is no Deuteronomistic language. There are only Deuteronomistic themes, each traveling with its own lexical luggage. Nor did H(Dtr) have a monopoly on the themes. A tradition in Jerusalem, based in the reforms of the eighth to seventh centuries B.C.E., nurtured them before H(Dtr). Thus the chief drawback to lexical work is that sources condition diction.

Yet other features of style are even less reliable. Even the series of sermons that marks moments of transition in DtrH is inconsistent. Until 2 Kings 17, all the addresses are placed in the mouths of major actors—Moses (Deuteronomy), Joshua (23f.), Samuel (1 Samuel 12), Yhwh-/Nathan (and David, 2 Samuel 7), and Solomon (1 Kings 8). The sermon in 2 Kings 17 is in narrative voice. Centralization language is absent from Joshua, Judges, and Samuel—even 2 Samuel 7. Yet the "chosen place," against 1 Kings 3:2, could have existed before Solomon—Psalm 78:59f.; Jeremiah 7:12 and Joshua 17ff.; 1 Samuel 2:22; 4–6 all place it first at Shiloh. Where is the condemnation of *bāmôt* that pertains to this theme?[35] Why is the theme not developed between Deuteronomy and 1 Kings? Are the sources at fault (2 Sam. 7:6; cf. Chapter 6)?

Style does not consistently indicate what was invented. Even Deuteronomistic texts can recast older tales (Deut. 1–3): Judges 1–3 and M+ typify this process (Chapter 6; also Chapter 3). Thus it is difficult to isolate the historian's contributions—verbal and substantive—from inherited information. Scholars try to do so, with occasional success (mostly in finding intact documents inside the larger historical work).[36] Certainty, however, rarely attends their exertions.

FINDING THE HAYSTACK: H(DTR) IN THE RECONSTRUCTION

Unfortunately, only when we *can* isolate the sources is it possible to assess H(Dtr)'s work. The sections in this chapter entitled "1 Samuel 8–12 in Context: Two Sources Stitched Together" and "A Critique of the Wanton Redactor" and chapters 6–7 illustrate that, in his attempt to represent the past, H(Dtr) sometimes reproduced sources verbatim. These results converge with the implications of source criticism in the Pentateuch: there twists in the plot arose from a redactor's (R) efforts to intertwine inherited narratives.

An example is Genesis 37, with twin versions of Joseph's sale. In one (J), Jacob's sons, bent on murder, yield when Judah suggests that they sell Joseph to some passing Ishmaelites. In the other source (E), Reuben convinces the brothers to cast Joseph into a cistern. Reuben means to return; but in the interim, Midianite itinerants carry Joseph off.

R_{JE}'s conflation accords equal weight to each source (see Fig. 13). Reuben maneuvers Joseph into the pit (E) and Judah persuades the brothers to sell him to the Ishmaelites (J), but the Midianites meanwhile spirit him away (E), and sell him to the Ishmaelites (J). R_{JEP} preserved both sources intact. In his account ideology took a back seat to harmonization.

Friedman argues that this motive governs all source combination in the Pentateuch.[37] This is likely. For some years I have asked students to take singly the sources found, say, in Genesis 6–9, and, keeping each source's internal sequence intact, to recombine them. Invariably the alternatives are either less logical than R's account or so intricate as to atomize the sources. The point is that R tried to preserve the flow of the received materials, while avoiding contradictions; he took the sources as complementary reflections on the events.

One sees the same impulse in R's use of old lyric—Deuteronomy 33 presages the conquest because its blessings (except for Reuben and Levi) relate to tribal lands; the end of the song concerns the taking of the land. Genesis 49 stands in for Jacob's benediction, because it blesses the tribes (the "children of Israel") as personified in eponyms. R uses other old poems in a similar way (see especially Num. 21). As in the cases examined in chapters 3–8, the historian exploits sources: antiquarian concern infuses the process. The method did not preclude the introduction of fable. It does caution us against the assumption that R made such importation a linchpin of his compositional technique. It is thus fundamentally wrong to assume that every passage can be taken purely to purvey ideology.

The source-critical hypothesis explains doublets and contradictions—the telltale smudges of (incomplete) harmonization—without intimating that R was unlettered or insincere. The contrast is to literary analyses that do not reckon with R's antiquarian interest. These assume that the author was free to say what he wanted in any way he wanted to say it: he

FIGURE 13: CONFLATION IN THE SALE OF JOSEPH
(GENESIS 37)

J	Conflate Account	E
1 Brothers decide to kill Joseph 19–20, 23	J1; E1 Brothers decide to kill Joseph	1 Brothers decide to kill Joseph 18
2 ————	E2 Reuben persuades them to cast Joseph into pit and they do	2 Reuben persuades them to throw Joseph into pit, and they do [21]–22, 24
3 ————	E3 Brothers go eat	3 Brothers go to eat 25aα
4 Ishmaelites appear 25aβ–b	J4 Ishmaelites appear	4 ————
5 Judah persuades brothers to sell Joseph 26–27	J5 Judah persuades brothers to sell Joseph	5 ————
6 ————	E6 Midianites steal Joseph from pit	6 Meanwhile, Midianites sneak by and steal Joseph from pit 28a
7 They (brothers) sell Joseph to Ishmaelites 28b	J7 They (Midianites) sell Joseph to Ishmaelites	7 ————
8 ————	E8 Reuben returns to find Joseph missing	8 Reuben returns to pit, Joseph gone 29–30
9 Ishmaelites sell Joseph in Egypt 39:1	E9; J9 Midianites sell Joseph to Egypt; Ishmaelites take him there	9 Midianites sell Joseph into Egyptian bondage 36

wrote doublets and created contradictions—he stuttered and stammered—*by choice*. This may be true of prophets. It does not apply to conscientious students of history: the author's and the author's contemporaries' knowledge of the events limit the literary product. This is why the source analysis of the Pentateuch enjoys such a striking longevity. R has, like Noth's H(Dtr), a consistent working logic. Given the sources, in Genesis or 1 Samuel, what must one change in R's work to convert it from romance to history? The case is rather that if one much alters the order of combination, the work changes from history to fancy, from research to romance.

Analysts of DtrH differ not only over what text comes from what redactor, but over how many redactors furrowed the text. They range from Veijola's cascade of contrary theologians and Noth's lone H(Dtr) with countless glossators to the complex counterfeiter of van Seters. The only perfect strategy would be to generate all possible histories of redaction, and take the implications for H(Dtr)'s purpose and lucidity for a yardstick of relative probability. Chapter 2 has shown how the exaltation of (pseudomathematical) proof led to solipsism in historiographic analysis. A reversion to probability as a standard of argument offers hope for improvement; and, in the absence of doublets, the historian's purpose is the only potential object of scrutiny with which the results of literary work can be compared.[38]

THE HISTORIAN AS HISTORIAN: AN AGENDA

The position advanced here is not that Israelite historians prized history as an academic pursuit. Rather, history had meaning for the present—as an etiology, an explanation of causality, a spur to policy. The Israelite historian, like his modern colleagues, came at the sources with all manner of commitments. Nevertheless, this historian, exemplified by H(Dtr) and by some of his sources (as M+/M−), employed a logic of reconstruction to which the term *theology* attaches in no greater measure than it does to our own scientific rationalism. Too, as chapters 3–4 suggest and Chapter 9 confirms, this historian introduced from sources data he might have finessed, data irrelevant or inimical to his thematic concerns. His interest in events, politics aside, reflects a genuine historical curiosity.

Orthodox analyses incidentally impugn the sincerity of the historian's interest in the past, and assume that, if at all operative, this was abased before some higher homiletic purpose. This view arises from purely literary analysis. It insists that the practice of history in *any* sense during the seventh and sixth centuries B.C.E. (or earlier) is a rank anachronism.[39]

On the surface this sounds plausible. But it takes a naive view, equating history with the modern textbook. The question smolders only in the afterglow of source criticism. After all, thematic links to contemporary issues imply that the past was not spun whole: reconstructed fact could be brought to harness in the framework of interpretation. Assyrian scribes, when producing annals, adapt sources to their immediate ends. Where the shape of a prism demands, they abridge or even telescope. They vary the phraseology, for aesthetic or semantic reasons. Yet they do not seem to veil the meaning of the sources, or the facts about the events they are relating.[40] Artful representation plays its part in this tradition too.[41] It is more obvious at the level of composition than at that of redaction; overall, loyalty to the sources remains the rule.

Indeed, one lesson that classical historiography teaches is that historians, like prophets, thought it their duty first and foremost to correct their colleagues and forebears (so Polybius 31.22). This makes it all the less inviting to accuse the Israelite historian of outright invention or of perverting sources. Nor does the use of sources in DtrH (as chapters 3–8) suggest, on the whole, a penchant for fabrication.

The question posed here has been, What drove the historian to *this* reconstruction, not some other? Those who affirm the fanciful character of the historiography must reckon not just with this discussion, but also with the question, Why do the historian's concoctions take the form they take? Why are all alternative inventions eschewed? One must account for additions, for redaction, in their specific forms, against all alternatives. The ancient authors were logical (or no analysis holds): if they had no other aim than to win political converts, their inventions should produce the most effective propaganda. Scholarship that claims this is so, but fails to demonstrate the fact, slights the ancient author; in it inclement conjecture drives out reasoned reconstruction as the specie of historical discussion.

To study Israel's historiography we must work like the builders of the Siloam tunnel—from the literary and historical ends at once—in the hope that, by conscientious planning and careful execution, the approaches will coincide. Where the two do not meet, or where one works from one end only, tortuous and solipsistic analysis results. It remains now, in Part 3, to examine the properties of DtrH as a whole, in the light of all the foregoing. The limitations of the history, and the extent of its forays into the field of romance, must be examined.

Notes to Chapter 8

1. As R. E. Friedman, *The Exile and Biblical Narrative* (Chico, CA: Scholars, 1981), especially 22.

2. Y. Kaufmann, *History of the Israelite Faith* (Jerusalem: Kiryath-Sepher, 1937–56), 2/1.357ff. Kaufmann envisions a library of histories, bound and collected, to which H(Dtr) added only the books of Kings: H(Dtr)'s theme, centralization, arises only when the temple is built. This submission dismisses from consideration the antiquarian dimension of DtrH. Cf. M. Haran, "Biblical Issues from the Problems of the Composition of the Books of Kings and of the Books of the Former Prophets," *Tarbiz* 37 (1967): 1–14.

3. In Judges 1 and Joshua 11f., two problems arise: 1) Joshua 11:16–20 has Joshua "take" the land. Judges 1 lists exceptions. Judges 1 may link Joshua 11:16–20 to towns defeated in 11:1–9. (The recapitulation of 10:40ff. in 11:21f. implies that 11:16–20 does not include the southern hills.) Further, 11:16–20 speaks of "taking" territory, even towns (those of vv. 1–15), but not of "supplanting" the aborigines. Judges 1 denies only "supplanting." Likewise, the "taking" of Joshua 11:23 (after 11:22!) leads to an allotment for "supplanting" (13ff.). 2) Joshua 12 (< Josh 11:10–15) lists as depopulated three towns (Taanach, Megiddo, Dor) not "supplanted" according to Judges 1. Like Joshua, Judges 1 assumes that the tribes settled severally (supplanted) land which Joshua "took." Joshua 11f. says that Joshua denuded northern forts, not whole regions. H(Dtr) must have distinguished this from recolonization or the destruction of "environs": in Judges 1, only v. 27, with Taanach, Dor, and Megiddo, mentions "environs." It resolves (illusory) conflict with Joshua 12 by stressing that the Canaanites of the *region* (*'ereṣ*) were not supplanted.

4. Similarly, Friedman, *Exile* (n. 1), 22.

5. Even Chronicles departs from Kings mainly to actualize its reconstruction. On Solomon's designation see Chapter 7. In Asa's case, Chronicles deduces centralization (2 Chron. 14:1–4) from Asa's reform (1 Kings 15:12–14) and DtrH's endorsement (1 Kings 15:11).

6. "Do what comes to hand" is an expression that denotes violent action commissioned by Yhwh: see my *Constitution of the Monarchy in Israel* (Chico, CA: Scholars, 1981), 155f. This is why the Philistine garrison is mentioned.

7. See W. Richter, *Die sogenannten vorprophetischen Berufungsberichte* (Göttingen: Vandenhoeck & Ruprecht, 1970).

8. See already J. G. Eichhorn, *Einleitung ins Alte Testament* (3 vols.; Leipzig, E. Germany: Weidmanns Erben und Reich, 1780–83), 568. For recent attempts to carve out the inherited portions of the "ass tale," cf. T.N.D. Mettinger, *King and Messiah* (Lund, Sweden: Gleerup, 1976), 64–79; F. Crüsemann, *Der Widerstand gegen das Königtum* (WMANT 49; Neukirchen-Vluyn: W. Germany: Neukirchener, 1978), 57ff.

9. On the text of 10:27c–11:1, see F. M. Cross, "The Ammonite Oppression of the Tribes of Gad and Reuben: Missing Verses from 1 Samuel 11 Found in 4QSamuel[a]," in H. Tadmor and M. Weinfeld, eds., *History, Historiography and Interpretation* (Jerusalem: Magnes, 1983), 148–58.

10. See J. Wellhausen, in F. Bleek, *Einleitung in das Alte Testament* (4th ed.; Berlin: Reimer, 1878), 210f.; K. Budde, *Die Bücher Richter und Samuel* (Giessen: J. Ricker, 1890), 172–75.

11. On the myth of leadership in connection with 1 Samuel 11, see my *Constitution* (n. 6), 111–23, 138–46, 154ff.

12. On 1 Samuel 13:7b–15a, see already Wellhausen, in Bleek, *Einleitung* (n. 10), 215. On 15:10ff., see especially A. Weiser, "I Samuel 15," *ZAW* 54 (1936): 1–28.

13. R did not rework Chapter 11 to conform with the myth of leadership in Israel: the combination of the sources somewhat obscures the pattern.
14. See Budde, *Bücher Richter und Samuel* (n. 10), 172–247; O. Eissfeldt, *Die Komposition der Samuelbücher* (Leipzig, E. Germany: Hinrichs, 1931), 7–10; *idem*, *The Old Testament: An Introduction* (New York: Harper & Row, 1965), 272, for 8; 10:17–27; 12 as the reduction of a pre-Dtr source; latterly, J. M. Miller, "Saul's Rise to Power: Some Observations Concerning 1 Sam. 9.1–10.16; 10.26–11.15 and 13.2–14.46," *CBQ* 35 (1974): 157–74.
15. See my *Constitution* (n. 6), 223–35 on 1 Samuel 8–12 and Deuteronomy 17; on Deuteronomy, latterly my "Centralization Formulae in Deuteronomy," *VT* 28 (1978): 21–38, both with bibliography.
16. See, among others, Crüsemann, *Widerstand* (n. 8).
17. See Wellhausen, in Bleek, *Einleitung* (n. 10), 213. On the absence of "Deuteronomistic language" in the passage, see the painstaking refutation of Budde (*Bücher Richter und Samuel* [n. 10], 182–85), with which no scholar has adequately reckoned. For the extension of Wellhausen's position (11 is a third source), see I. Hylander, *Der literarische Samuel-Saul-Komplex (I. Sam. 1–15) traditionsgeschichtlich untersucht* (Uppsala, Sweden: Almqvist & Wiksell; Leipzig, E. Germany: O. Harrassowitz, 1932), 125–32, 155-60.
18. Noth, *Überlieferungsgeschichtliche Studien* (Halle, E. Germany: Niemeyer, 1943), 54–60, 99f.; Eissfeldt, *Komposition* (n. 14), 7–10. Eissfeldt divides 10:21b–27a from 10:17–21a (Noth, 10:17–21a equals H[Dtr]): 1) vv. 21ff. have an oracle, vv. 17ff. the lot; and 2) vv. 21ff. treat Saul favorably, where 10:17–19 condemn monarchy. But Saul is not the monarchy, and the position on monarchy here is complex, as we shall see. And the oracle in vv. 21ff. is used to *find* Saul, not to select him; for the latter, the lot, a binary system, is apt.
19. O. Eissfeldt, *Geschichtsschreibung im Alten Testament: Ein kritischer Bericht über die neueste Literatur dazu* (Berlin: Evangelische, 1948).
20. See J. J. Stähelin, *Untersuchungen über den Pentateuch, die Bücher Joshua, Richter, Samuelis und Könige* (Berlin: Reimer, 1843), 112–18.
21. T. Veijola, *Das Königtum in der Beurteilung der deuteronomistischen Historiographie: Eine redaktionsgeschichtliche Untersuchung* (Annales Academiae Scientarum Fennicae B/198; Helsinki: Suomalainen Tiedeakatemia, 1977). R. Smend (*Die Entstehung des Alten Testaments* [Stuttgart: Kohlhammer, 1978], 118f.) also posits that the pristine text blamed Samuel's sons for the change to monarchy; E(Dtr)n then introduced the threat from Ammon to blame the people. This seems a drastic method for accomplishing this end.
22. H. J. Boecker, *Die Beurteilung der Anfänge des Königtums in den deuteronomistischen Abschnitten des I. Samuelbuches. Ein Beitrag zum Problem des "Deuteronomistischen Geschichtswerkes"* (WMANT 31; Neukirchen-Vluyn: Neukirchener, 1969), 89f., among others.
23. Against Budde, n. 17; B. C. Birch, *The Rise of the Israelite Monarchy: The Growth and Development of I Samuel 7–15* (SBLDS 27; Missoula: Scholars, 1976), 45f., especially on 1 Samuel 10:17–19.
24. J. van Seters, *In Search of History* (New Haven: Yale University, 1983), 253, and n. 15.
25. Van Seters, *In Search* (n. 24), 258.
26. Wellhausen (Bleek, *Einleitung* [n. 10], 211–15) has a promonarchic 11:1–11 added into the antimonarchic material, and tied to a renewal in Gilgal; and he imputes 10:8; 13:7–15 (on cryptic grounds) to H(Dtr) as well; so van Seters, *In Search* (n. 24), 256f. So (10:7; 13:2 to the contrary) 11:1–11 belong between 10:7 and 13:2. Why, then, did H(Dtr) create the timetable for one meeting in Gilgal (10:8; 13:7ff.) but interpose a different meeting in Gilgal (11:12–12:25)? Cf. B. Peckham, "The Deuteronomistic History of Saul and David," *ZAW* 97 (1985): 194–96, where similar argument applies.
27. 1 Samuel 13:1, an accession formula, follows from Chapter 12, and is not part of the source in 9:1–10:12; 13:2–14:52. Absent from OG, it caps the confirmation of Saul's rise (10:17–12:25) in MT. On the pattern, see n. 11. D. Edelmann ("Saul's Rescue of Jabesh-Gilead [1 Sam. 11:1–11]: Sorting Story from History," *ZAW* 96 [1984]: 195–209) locates the pattern in a unified reading of chapters 9–11. But the doublet elections, rejections, and introductions of Saul, as well as others inside

(10:10–13//19:19–24) and outside (24//26; also, e.g., 19:1–7//20) these narratives indicate the presence of two sources here.

28. Hosea 13:10 also refers to kings and royal officials as "judges," in line with 1 Samuel 8:6. "Judges" here does not denote premonarchic leaders: Hosea stresses that the "judges" conjured by the Israelites themselves had failed.

29. See my *Constitution* (n. 6), 149–74. This voids an otherwise telling objection to the source hypothesis (van Seters, *in Search* [n. 24], 253; cf. Peckham, "Deuteronomistic" [n. 26], 191).

30. B. O. Long, review of R. D. Nelson, *The Double Redaction of the Deuteronomistic History*, *JBL* 102 (1983): 455f.

31. Deuteronomy 1–3 revises Numbers 13f.; 20f. chiefly on two counts. 1) the people, not Yhwh, inaugurate the reconnaissance of Canaan (1:22f.); and 2) the march through Transjordan includes a) movement through Edomite and Moabite territory (2:1–13; cf. Num. 20:14–21:15); b) an injunction against confronting non-Amorites; and c) the inclusion of Ammon, omitted in Numbers (2:14–23, but cf. v. 29). Deuteronomy systematizes the geography and theory of "supplanting" Amorites, and interprets the detour around Edom and Moab in Numbers 20:14–21:15 as avoidance of mountain terrain. The prettification of the tradition lends credibility to the idea that Deuteronomy depends on JE.

32. Especially *ʾelōhê han-nēkār*, "alien gods", twinned with *ʾelōhîm ʾaḥērîm* in Judges 10:16; this always relates to purification from apostasy. It occurs elsewhere in Genesis 35:2, 4; Joshua 24:23 (cf. 24:2, 16); 1 Samuel 7:3; 2 Chronicles 33:15 (cf. 14:2); without the article in Joshua 24:20; Deuteronomy 32:12; Jeremiah 5:19 (cf. 8:19); adjectival in Malachi 2:11; Psalm 81:10; Daniel 11:39. Other accusations name gods or types of gods, or use polemical terms about them, or cite icons or luminaries.

33. See further, W. J. Martin, *Stylistic Criteria and the Analysis of the Pentateuch* (London: Tyndale, 1955), 9f., 12–15. Accusations of apostasy (as distinct from idolatry) are, in fact, rare before the Josianic era.

34. LXX reads "other gods" for MT "gods" in Deuteronomy 4:28, and could be original (by homoioteleuton). J. D. Levenson ("Who Inserted the Book of the Torah?" *HTR* 68 [1975]: 3–33) and R. E. Friedman (*The Exile and Biblical Narrative* [Chico: Scholars, 1981], 16–18), among others, impute the text to E(Dtr)x (with 28:36f., 63–68, the other texts with "other gods" of "wood and stone"—but cf. Jeremiah 1:16; 25:6; especially 16:9–18). This would take the passage out of the realm of H(Dtr). But OG "other" may be supplied by scribal reflex on the model presented by E. Tov, "The Literary History of Jeremiah," in J. H. Tigay, ed., *Empirical Models for Biblical Criticism* (Philadelphia: University of Pennsylvania, 1985), 233. Most of the subsequent occurrences echo Deuteronomy 5:9.

35. Similarly, Y. Kaufmann, *History of Israelite Religion* (n. 2), 357–60. His distinction between foreign and domestic "high places" is, however, invalid.

36. See, e.g., Budde, *Bücher Richter und Samuel* (n. 10), 273–76 on older hypotheses about the Court History; H. H. Rowley, *The Growth of the Old Testament* (St. Albans: Gainsborough, 1950), 37–42, 68f., 71–76. See further Chapter 9.

37. R. E. Friedman, "Sacred History and Theology: The Redaction of Torah," R. E. Friedman, ed., *The Creation of Sacred Literature* (Berkeley: University of California, 1978), 25–34.

38. Ideally, grammars of each permutation of each hypothecated redaction or source would eliminate *impossible* scenarios. They might contribute to a hierarchy of probabilities among those that remain.

39. This view is elaborated especially by van Seters (*In Search* [n. 24]), who, however, argues mainly that there is no *comprehensive* national history before DtrH. See also Part 3.

40. See, e.g., P. Hulin, "The Inscriptions on the Carved Throne-Base of Shalmaneser III," *Iraq* 25 (1963): 48–69, especially 58–60; L. D. Levine, "The Second Campaign of Sennacherib," *JNES* 32 (1973): 312–17; N. Naʾaman, "Two Notes on the Monolith Inscription of Shalmaneser III from Kurkh," *TA* 3 (1976): 89–106; M. Cogan, "Ashurbanipal Prism F: Notes on Scribal Techniques and Editorial Procedures," *JCS* 29

(1977): 97–107; M. Cogan and H. Tadmor, "Gyges and Ashurbanipal. A Study in Literary Transmission," *Or* 46 (1977): 65–85; *idem*, "Ashurbanipal's Conquest of Babylon: The First Official Report—Prism K," *Or* 50 (1981): 229–40.

41. See H. Tadmor, "Sennacherib's Campaign to Judah: Historical and Historiographic Considerations," *Zion* 50 (1985): 65–80.

Part 3

Conclusions: Bible and Babel;
The Languages of History in Israel

CHAPTER 9

The Grammar of History in DtrH

No book, least of all a text-book, offers a short cut to the historical truth.
The truth is not grey, it is black and white in patches.

—G. M. TREVELYAN,

H (Dtr)'s history is sometimes wrong. Like others, it is much imbued by party passion and personal philosophy. Yet zealous conviction welcomes the test of evidence. However much he might twist contradictory detail, or press refractory fact into uneasy ideological service, H(Dtr) relied upon a fair representation of the past to prove his point.

Against these propositions, Noth's detractors (for they are Noth's propositions) insist that H(Dtr) wrote no history in any sense that we might mean by the term. Israel's historians were not scholars, but novelists, like the Augustan poets, devoid of interest in or even a sense of historical truth.

Chapters 9–10 assess this question globally. Focusing on 1–2 Kings, Chapter 9 considers the impact of sources on DtrH, and its notion of history, as a whole. Chapter 10 tackles the ahistorical elements, the apparent romance, Chapter 11 reverts to the character of the historian.

THE SOURCES OF DtrH

CONCRETE EVIDENCE OF SOURCES

Much of the time H(Dtr) recorded literal fact. His reports of Jerusalem's plundering (as 1 Kings 14:25f.; 2 Kings 12:18f.; 14:13f.; cf. 25) are as historical as any ancient writing. Nor are these cases extraordinary. External texts afford control over the history, chiefly during the Divided Monarchy, the time for which H(Dtr) had most ample documentation. Almost uniformly, biblical claims are corroborated.

About Israel, Omride dominion in Transjordan until Mesha's revolt, Ahab's importance in an era when the Assyrian tide was staunched, and even the contemporary might of Hazael's Damascus are documented.[1] Assyrian sources date the accession of Jehu,[2] Joash's kingship,[3] Menachem's tribute (2 Kings 15:19), the overthrow of Pekah and installation of Hosea,[4], and even the fall of Samaria.[5]

About Judah, Assyrian texts document Uzziah's power,[6] Ahaz' subjection to Tiglath-Pileser III,[7], Hezekiah's transactions with Sennacherib,[8] and even the siege of Lachish.[9] Babylonian records corroborate claims about Necho (2 Kings 23:29) and Jehoiachin's exile (2 Kings 25:27–30).[10] Shishak memorialized his campaign against Rehoboam.[11] And seals and seal impressions preserve the names of several kings, and of an official, Shaphan, prominent under Josiah.[12]

This list, by no means comprehensive,[13] is balanced by occasional inaccuracy. Chronological displacement appears to be common. Thus 2 Kings 19:9 probably makes Tirhaqah a king a decade too early. And 2 Kings 19:36f. suffixes Sennacherib's murder to his 701 B.C.E. campaign: Sennacherib died in 681 B.C.E. This text may mean that Sennacherib later was punished (cf. 2 Kings 19:21–24). Even if Kings misdates the murder, it nevertheless preserves the name of one assassin.[14]

Inaccuracy need not be apologetic—Tirhaqah's name adds little. Even where he distorts, as one might infer in 2 Kings 19:36f. (also in n. 1; Chapter 7, on 1 Kings 11), H(Dtr) takes data seriously: the distortion is not schematic. This variety (see the section entitled "Myopia and Selection in DtrH" in this chapter, and the Chapter 10 section entitled "Nonhistorical Language in DtrH: The Unhistorical") reflects a hodgepodge fund of sources. The evidence starts with external corroboration, and in texts such as Judges 1–3; 4. But what sources can be hypothesized for the monarchic era?

LIMITED AND OCCASIONAL SOURCES

H(Dtr)'s library housed folktales (Chapter 3), and topographic and physical data (chapters 3, 4). Some written sources are undisputed: Judges 5 (Chapter 4), lists of Solomon's (1 Kings 4) and David's officers (2 Sam. 20:23–26; 21:15–22; 23:8– 39) and conquests (2 Sam. 8). 2 Samuel, the parallel narratives in 1 Samuel 8– 31, and the (oral?) Elijah and Elisha cycles probably typify H(Dtr)'s longer sources. 2 Samuel itself employs poetic sources,[15] perhaps inspiring the tableau in 1 Samuel 16:14–23; other old songs figure in Judges 4–5; Joshua 10:12–14; 1 Kings 8:12f. (see OG [at 8:53]). H(Dtr) also had access at least to Deuteronomy (so 2 Kings 14:6, Deut. 24:16).

Sanctuaries displayed texts as well. Plaster is inscribed at shrines at Deir Alla (probably at Kuntillet Ajrud) and in Deuteronomy 27:2ff.; Joshua 8:32 (a source for Elisha?). Secular inscriptions did exist (KAI 189; > 2 Kings 20:20?). And invaders scattered calling cards throughout the country.[16] H(Dtr) may have enjoyed access to foreign annals. Those of Tyre duplicate Kings in form and content (e.g., see Josephus, *Ap.* 1.116–25). That 1 Kings 15:19, alone, calls Tiglath-Pileser III Pul(u) hints at the use of a foreign record (cf. ANET 272).

Another unofficial source may have been burial inscriptions. Excavated examples lack color.[17] But Absalom's stela (2 Sam. 18:18) probably had a vita. Normally, carving tombs was a filial duty (see Isa. 22:15f.; 2 Chron. 16:14): Absalom erects his "because I have no son to call out my name." Because Absalom had sons (2 Sam. 14:27), and his offspring were not proscribed (1 Kings 15:2, a populist agnatic marriage), 2 Samuel 18:18 may be a deduction from first-person narrative on the tomb. Such a memorial might exaggerate; if wildly overblown, it would invite public ridicule (cf. KAI 215; M—?)

Official public texts probably included building inscriptions. The king's omission from the Siloam tunnel slab commends caution. But Mesha's stone, recording military achievements, is such an inscription, and one expects that similar texts decorated shrines and, possibly, donations. Saul and David also erected victory stelae;[18] none is mentioned thereafter.

Scholars have collected oblique evidence that H(Dtr) used such texts.[19] It warrants remark that the form of the Kilamuwa inscription (KAI 26) would have been apt for Ahaz, Asa, Jehu, and several others. Conversely, if Hezekiah's scribes framed the events of 701 B.C.E. in language like that of the Zakkur stela (KAI 202), attributing survival to the god, the confusion between 2 Kings 18:13–16 and 2 Kings 18:17–19:37 would be explained. Overall, there is reason to believe that H(Dtr) made use of monumental texts (so 1 Kings 11:7?).

COMPILED SOURCES: A TEMPLE CHRONICLE

It has been claimed that H(Dtr) had a "temple chronicle."[20] Kings tabulates donations to and outlay from the temple (Fig. 14). But Babylonian chronicles[21] also join cultic reports to political.

A high proportion of events H(Dtr) dates concern the temple (Fig. 15); yet some depredations on the temple are undated. Hazael's (2 Kings 12:18f.) raid is placed vaguely after Joash's twenty-third year (12:7). Amaziah's despoiling is undated (14:13f.). The inconsistency intimates diverse sources of data.

In fact, 13:12 places Amaziah's encounter with Joash (14:13f. in Amaziah's account) among "the chronicles of the kings of Israel." Elsewhere, except in folklore about the Omrides, DtrH treats relations between Judah and Israel in Judahite regnal accounts; 2 Kings 13:12 is the only note (as opposed to narrative) in an Israelite regnal account that mentions specific interactions between Judah and Israel (see Fig. 16; cf. especially 2 Kings 15:29; 16:5–9). The episode compliments Joash and denigrates Amaziah (a "good" king, 14:3); no other Davidid, still less a "good" one, is likened unfavorably to a reigning Israelite. Finally, the incident leads not to Amaziah's, but to a repetition of Joash's death formulae (14:15f.), as though the formulae rode in on the coattails of the narrative.[22] Similarly, in the regnal account of Ahazyah of Judah, 2 Kings 8:28f. derives

FIGURE 14: TEMPLE NOTICES IN KINGS

	Income	*Outlay*
1 Kings		
1.6:21f., 28, 32, 35	gold plating	(see nos. 9, 10, 12, 13, 15, 20, 27)
2.7:15–22	bronze pillars	(see no. 28)
3.7:23–37	bronze sea, oxen, laver stands	(see nos. 17, 28)
4.7:38f.	bronze lavers	(see no. 28)
5.7:40	implements (gold, etc.)	(see no. 27)
6.7:48–50	gold altar, table, lamps, and implements	(see no. 27)
7.7:51	gold, silver of David	(see nos. 9, 10)
8.10:16f.	gold shields, ≠ temple (ṣnh, mgnym)	(see no. 9)
9.14:26	(see no. 7, 8)	treasuries, shields (mgny); cf. 2 Kings 11:10, šlṭym
10.15:18	(see no. 7)	*silver*, gold, remaining in treasuries
2 Kings		
11.12:5–17	money for repairs, not treasures (cf. no. 23)	(see no. 12)
12.12:18f.	(see no. 11!, 9–10)	dedications of Joash, Jehoshaphat, Jehoram, Ahazyah; gold in treasuries.
13.14:14	(see no. 11)	gold, *silver*, and vessels in treasuries
[14.15:35	the upper gate]	
15.16:8		gold, *silver* in treasuries
16.16:10–15	large bronze altar	(see no. 29)
17.16:17	(see nos. 3, 28!)	12 bronze oxen, laver bases
[18.16:18		??]
[19.18:4		??]
20.18:14–16	(reference to unnoted sources)	30 gold, 300 silver talents; nave door metal, pillars donated by Hezekiah
21.20:13, 17		(see no. 27)
22.21:5, 7	altars, statue	(see nos. 24, 26)
23.22:3–7	money for repair (cf. no. 11)	

	Income	Outlay
24.23:4, 6	(see no. 22)	Baal/Asherah vessels; statue
25.23:11		horses/chariots of sun
26.23:12	(see no. 22)	Manasseh's, others' altars (roof
		of Ahaz' ('aliyyâ)
27.24:13	(see nos. 5, 6, 21, 12, 13)	treasuries and Solomonic gold
		vessels in nave
28.25:13,		
16f.	(see nos. 3, 17)	bronze pillars, laver bases, sea
		($\neq$ 2 Kings 16:17 on temple
		contents or their dimensions)
29.25:14f.	(see no. 5)	bronze, silver, gold implements
		($\neq$ 1 Kings 7:40, 49f.)

Imposts not involving temple: 2 Kings 15:19f.; 23:33–35.

Nontemple dedications: 1 Kings 11:7f. + 2 Kings 23:13; further, Nehushtan (2 Kings 18:4); high places generally.

Note treatment of vessels, distinct from treasuries; assessment against Jehoiakim (2 Kings 23:33–35), small compared to Sennacherib's, necessitates special levy, despite Josiah's reform

from 9:14–16 in Jehu's northern coup. The Amaziah–Joash confrontation comes from an Israelite record book.

That H(Dtr) had several sources on the temple is no surprise. Kings cites three literary sources: the "book of the transactions of (*spr dbry*) Solomon" (1 Kings 11:42); and, respectively, the "book of the 'chronicles' (*spr dbry hymym*, lit., "transactions of the term[s]") of the kings of Judah" and that "of the 'chronicles' of the kings of Israel." If these texts conformed even remotely to the model of other royal literature, temple-related construction fell well within their purview (so 2 Kings 12:5–12; 15:35; 16:10–18; 21:3–8; 22:3–7). Indeed, citations of the royal chronicles regularly refer to construction. Again, no temple chronicle need be hypothesized.

This view is the more appealing when contrasted with the idea of van Seters that the description of the temple, for example, was concocted during the exile. E(Dtr)x diverges from H(Dtr)'s records (see the section in Chapter 7 entitled "Solomon and the Temple: 1 Kings 6:1–9:9; further, 1 Kings 7:27–37 and 2 Kings 25:16 against 2 Kings 16:17; but cf. 1 Kings 10:16f.; 14:26f.; 2 Kings 11:10). An exile would have taken the temple description from 2 Kings 25; the dissonance is more natural if the author of 2 Kings 25 used a contemporary source, whose claims he did not coordinate with earlier reports in DtrH. H(Dtr) had no "temple chronicle," but he did have sources about the temple.

FIGURE 15: DATED EVENTS IN KINGS, OTHER THAN JUDAH–ISRAEL REGNAL SYNCHRONISMS (AND ASSASSINATIONS /COUPS DATING TO LAST YEAR OF A KING)

Defeats	Defeats with Imposts	Building	Other	Incidental Dating
		1 Kings		
			2:39: Shimei's death	
		6:1 temple 6:37: temple 6:38: temple completed 7:1 palace		ca. 970–930 B.C.E.
			9:10: Cabul barter	
	14:25 Shishak			
		2 Kings		
1:1; 3:5 Mesha revolt				
		12:7: temple repair		12:18: Hazael (approx.)
17:5f.; 18:9f. Fall of Samaria				
	18:13: Sennacherib			722–701 B.C.E.
			20:1, 6: Hezekiah cured 20:12: Babylonian embassy	
		22:3 Josianic repair (and book)		622 B.C.E.
			23:22: reform and Passover	
	24:12: 597 Exile			597–560 B.C.E.
25:1: Second Babylonian siege 25:2: flight of Zedeqiah	25:8: Babylonian destruction		25:25: murder of Gedaliah 25:27: elevation of Jehoiachin	

Undated:

Deeds of Tiglath-Pileser III: 2 Kings 15:19f., 29; 16:7f.
Hazael at Jerusalem: 2 Kings 12:18f.
Joash of Israel at Jerusalem: 2 Kings 14:14
Aramean incursions into Israel
Asa's payment to Ben–Hadad: 1 Kings 15:18

CHRONICLES OF THE KINGS OF JUDAH/ISRAEL

H(Dtr)'s source citations, which have Near Eastern parallels,[23] are borne out in cases such as those of Joash and Amaziah. H(Dtr) visibly interweaves Judahite and Israelite sources elsewhere: Edom, still a province (2 Sam. 8:14), had no king through Jehoshaphat's time (1 Kings 22:48); Edom revolted against Jehoshaphat's son, Jehoram (2 Kings 8:20–22). These are nodes in a running thread: Amaziah reconquered part of Edom (14:7); Uzziah constructed Eilat (14:22); Eilat was lost in the Syro-Ephraimite war (16:6).[24] Yet between 1 Kings 22:48 (no king in Edom) and 2 Kings 8:20–22 (revolt under Jehoram), H(Dtr) interposes 2 Kings 3, in which an Edomite *vassal king* accompanies Jehoshaphat and an Israelite ally to war. The notices concerning Judahite kings hang together; the narrative about the Israelite king stands out.

A similar pattern relates to Aramea. As he anoints Hazael, Elisha bewails the havoc Hazael will wreak on Israel (2 Kings 8:7–15). Israelite regnal accounts tell of Hazael's depredations (2 Kings 9:14–16 [> 8:28f.]; 10:32f.), and a mitigation of the scourge (13:3–5, 22–25; 14:25–27). Yet Elisha is silent about Hazael's foray against Judah, in Joash's reign (2 Kings 12:18f). And the Israelite-Aramean axis of 2 Kings 15:37; 16:5–10 (Judahite reigns) does not fit the Israelite pattern at all (after 14:25–27). Here the Israelite notices hang together; the Judahite accounts are separate.

Other details confirm that Kings has at least two literary sources.[25] The accuracy of H(Dtr)'s data about invasions alone (see the section in this chapter entitled "Concrete Evidence of Sources") precludes total reliance on monuments—which in neighboring states report defeats, if at all, only when they are overcome, and which do not furnish dates. Van Seters maintains that the chronicles were culled from such monuments; but the same considerations invalidate this conjecture.[26]

Van Seters' intuition is, however, right. H(Dtr) cites the chronicles for a narrow range of data—in the main, apart from coups (1 Kings 14:19; 16:20; 2 Kings 15:15), to supply details of a career, or to corroborate claims of successful campaigns[27] or impressive building (1 Kings 15:23; 22:39; 2 Kings 20:20). Such achievements are the cornerstone of Mesopotamian royal records (annals, building texts, boundary stones). Western exemplars lack the periodization of the Assyrian; but the Mesha stone and some Aramean texts incarnate the genre. Even the theme of Solomon's wisdom could have entered the chronicles (1 Kings 11:41) from an inscription (cf. *KAI* 24; 214). Only one source citation mentions a king's virtue or sin (Manasseh, 2 Kings 21:17), and even this may have been concrete (the building of a shrine?). The chronicles exhibit close contact with lapidary literature, which may be their model.

Still, other sources were available, to H(Dtr) and to the chroniclers. Judahite accession formulae name queen mothers. Possibly royal tombs

FIGURE 16: JUDAHITE–ISRAELITE RELATIONS IN KINGS

A. Narrative

1. Not inside regnal accounts
   1 Kings 12:1–24   After Rehoboam named Solomon's successor (11:43)

2. Shared between two regnal accounts
   2 Kings 8:28f.; 9:25f.   In Ahazyah of Judah (8:25–9:27) and Jehoram of Israel (3:1 [OG 1:18a]–9:26, transitional to Jehu

3. Israel
   1 Kings 13:2   Jeroboam (12:25–14:20), but to predict 2 Kings 23:15–20

   1 Kings 22   Ahab (16:29–22:40); death account; possible counterparts in 22:45; 2 Kings 8:28f.

   2 Kings 3   Jehoram (3:1[OG 1:18a]–9:26); Mesha revolt; possible counterpart in 1 Kings 22:45

4. Judah
   1 Kings 15:16–22   Asa (15:9–24); possible counterpart under obelisk in 15:32 (no reign)

   2 Kings 14:8–14   Amaziah (14:1–22); counterpart in 13:12
   2 Kings 16:5–9   Ahaz (16:1–20); no counterpart
   2 Kings 23:15–20   Josiah (22:1–23:30); no counterpart; cf. 1 Kings 13:2

B. Notices

1. Israel
   1 Kings 15:32   Between Baasha and Nadab; under obelisk (<15:16)

   2 Kings 13:12   Joash (13:1-13/25); counterpart in 14:6–14
   2 Kings 14:28   Jeroboam II (14:23–29); cryptic

2. Judah
   1 Kings 14:30   Rehoboam (14:21–31); no counterpart
   1 Kings 15:6   Abijah (15:1–8); under obelisk (< 14:30); no counterpart

   1 Kings 15:7   Abijah (15:1–8); no counterpart
   1 Kings 15:16   Asa (15:9–24); counterpart (?) in 15:32 (< 15:16) under obelisk

   1 Kings 22:45   Jehoshaphat (22:41–50); counterpart in 22:1–36; 2 Kings 3

   1 Kings 22:47   Jehoshaphat (22:41–50); no counterpart
   2 Kings 8:18   Jehoram (8:16-24); no counterpart
   2 Kings 8:27(f.?)   Ahazyah (8:25–9:28); cf. 8:18
   2 Kings 14:15   Amaziah (14:1–22); = 13:12; purely about Israel
   2 Kings 14:17   Amaziah (14:1–22); follows from 14:15, 23 (= counterpart?)

   2 Kings 18:9–12   Hezekiah (18:1–20:21); counterpart in 17:3–6; purely about Israel

divulged the names; the queen mother formulary changes when royal burial does. But there may have been a list of queen mothers:[28] the formulae also stipulate the king's age at accession, a detail no monument supplies, and no collection of stones would supply systematically.

Likewise, the synchronisms between Judah's and Israel's kings come from a source. S. R. Bin-Nun demurred: differences in the Judahite and Israelite formulae mean H(Dtr) joined separate king lists.[29] But the synchronisms belie this thesis: they do not match either backward from the fall of Samaria or forward from Solomon; had H(Dtr) calculated them, with coregencies—the numbers demand some—he would have been more explicit (as 2 Kings 15:5). H(Dtr) inherited the synchronisms, which are too precise, but singularly unschematic, to have been constructed late. Unlike the source citations, they suppose more data than H(Dtr) preserves. Underlying DtrH, thus, are two chronicles, both with king lists, and a synchronistic king list.

One other feature implies literary, not monumental, sources—the supplementary notes on Judah's monarchs. Typically, these come not in the body of the regnal account, but after the source citation and before the naming of the successor. The Israelite cases, 1 Kings 16:7; 2 Kings 15:12, are both extraordinary—they refer to prophecies, and come after the notice of succession—and are left out of account here.

Supplementary notes are generally not the stuff of royal monuments: Asa "grew ill in his legs" (1 Kings 15:23); Joash and Amaziah were assassinated (2 Kings 12:21f.; 14:19–22); Josiah was killed (2 Kings 23:29f.); Rehoboam and Abijah fought incessantly with Jeroboam (1 Kings 14:30; 15:7); Ahaz' war actually began under Jotham (2 Kings 15:37); Jehoshaphat's commercial fleet failed (1 Kings 22:48–50).[30] The source may be the Judahite chronicles: supplementary notes follow the source citation; like the chronicles, supplementary notes revolve exclusively about the monarch. Too, Mesopotamian chronicles often contain such data, unflattering to royal principals. But the chronicles did not get this material from public inscriptions.

H(Dtr) enjoyed access, direct or through the chronicles (= Dtr[hez]?), to various nonmonumental records. This reveals itself, too, in the form of Kings. Kings sounds a virtuoso medley: foreign relations, cultic affairs, building projects (1 Kings 9:15–19; 12:25; 15:17, 22f.; 16:24, 34, 39; 2 Kings 14:22); two king lists with regnal lengths and synchronisms (some with Aram and Tyre). It identifies capitals, and evaluates reigns by religious standards; it locates burials and, for Judah, supplies age at accession and the queen mother's name. Most of these features are duplicated in one or another piece of Mesopotamian historiography. But no piece synthesizes so many factors (Fig. 17). The suggestion is that H(Dtr) had varied, and still reliable, sources.

Kings also makes liberal use of direct discourse. In Mesopotamia this occurs mainly in poetic history and the like,[31] never in annals, and in one chronicle only (ABC 22). Too, DtrH's admixture of prophetic/miracle tales is without parallel in serious Mesopotamian historiography. The same holds for DtrH's scope: Mesopotamian chronicles do not affix pre-monarchic history to monarchic, or treat the origins of monarchy. DtrH is, in comparative terms, a portmanteau, folding popular lore into the framework of monarchic historical records. Like Mesopotamian king lists, it is comprehensive; like Mesopotamian chronicles, it is synthetic, not annalistic. It has no year-by-year summary, like some Mesopotamian chronicles, yet maintains chronological continuity. DtrH is a singular, sophisticated aggregation. Everything suggests that H(Dtr) racked his resources, eclectically.

Most scholars concede that H(Dtr) had a rich fund of materials, and argue about what he added to it. But the sources held H(Dtr) in check (see chapters 2–6)—whether for antiquarian reasons or for fear of falsification. No doubt the further one strays from the political records of the Judahite monarchy, the more personal and miraculous DtrH becomes. Still, where records were probably extant—in notices touching the nation and its monarchs—the history is largely responsible, if inevitably interpretative. DtrH bases itself, if partly on historical imagination, heavily on antiquarian research.

FIGURE 17: FORMAL FEATURES OF KINGS SHARED WITH MESOPOTAMIAN HISTORIOGRAPHY OTHER THAN ROYAL INSCRIPTIONS

Feature	1–7	14	15	16	17	18	19	20	21	22	23	24
Kinglist:	x					x		[OTHER?]				
Synchronisms (+ SynchKL):	1	x							x			x
Reigns evaluated:							x			?		
Regnal length Tyrian annals (BKL A, B; AKL):	x					x				?		
Kings' deaths (chronicle fragments + Tyrian Annals):	x	x				x		x	x	x		
Royal burials:						x						
Foreign affairs:	Nearly all chronicles; all annals											
Defeat by foreigners:	x		x	x	x		x	x		x		x
Cult affairs (chronicle fragments + Tyrian Annals):	x	x	x	x	x					x		x

Feature	1–7	14	15	16	17	18	19	20	21	22	23	24
Myth, miracle (chronicle fragments):					x	x	x					
Updating (AKL):	x											
Divine Speech (chronicle fragments):							x					
Human speech:										x		
Punishment not military:								x				
Prehistory (AKL):							x					

Annotations to Figure 17

Complete king list:	All king lists; ABC 1–7; 18
Regnal synchronisms:	Synchronistic King list (not by year); ABC 21 (ditto), by reign of Assyrian king, with one exception; by reign of Babylonian king in ABC 1; 14 (Esarhaddon); 24 r. 2–7
good/bad reigns evaluated:	ABC 19:44, 48, 52–52b, and marks of divine causality in punishment throughout; but not identical with Kings in that the regnal evaluation is not stylized, and evil deeds are simply presented as they stand (Weidner; Grayson and Lambert, JCS 18 [1964] 7–30 tie this to the Akkadian prophecies); 22.iv.9f.?
Regnal lengths:	Tyrian Annals: Josephus, *Ant.* 8.144, 147; *Contra Apionem* 1.116ff.;ABC 1—Babylonian and relevant Elamite (i:39; ii:34; iii:8, 26, 31f.; iv: 12) Assyrian (i:25f., Tiglath-Pileser III; iii: 35f., Sennacherib; iv:32, Esarhaddon, all controlling Babylon); ABC 5:9; 18; 22:7f. (Assyrian control of Babylon)
Notice of kings' deaths:	ABC 1.i:11; 5:10 (not regular) = Babylonian. 1.1:24, 29; iii:34f.; iv:30f.; 3:44 (?) = Babylonian series reports of deaths of Assyrian kings; 1.1:38; iii:8, 14, 25, 30f.; iv:11 = deaths and succession in Elam
Deaths reported mainly of foes as signs of divine wrath:	Assyrian = 14:16 (Elamite); 14:28f. (Esarhaddon); 18.i:2f. (violent death, Dynastic Chronicle, and implied obviously in burial notices); 21.i:11', 15' (violent death); iii:8(?), 26 (all deaths of Babylonian kings reported in the Assyrian Synchronistic History); 22.i:10, 14(?); iv:11, 19 (deaths of

Feature	1–7 14 15 16 17 18 19 20 21 22 23 24
	enemies in Chronicle P). 20:30, 34 as punishment (CEK): 186:25f.(?); 189:8 Tyrian Annals: Josephus, *Ant.* 8. 144, 147; *Contra Apionem* 1.116ff.
Royal burials:	ABC 18 (Dynastic Chronicle)
Foreign affairs:	Nearly all chronicles; all annals
Defeat by foreigners:	ABC 1.i:3–5, 19–23; ii:25–30, 45–iii:6; iii:22–24; 2:7, 23f.; 3:17f., 37, 66–68; 4:16–18; 7.iii:12–20(?); 15:6, 19; 16:9–15 (= Babylonian); 17.iii:7f.; 19:52–56; 20.A:18–22 (last two both internal revolt), B:8–12, r. 11–14; 22.i:9–14; iv:1–10, 14–22 (Chronicle P); 24:10f.
Temple affairs:	ABC 1.ii:41; iii:1, 28f.; iv:9f., 17f., 34–36; 7 (Nabonidus); 14:21f., 31–37 (Esarhaddon; 15:4f., 22 (Shamash-shuma-ukin); 16 (Akitu); 17 (Religious); 22.iv:5f., 13f. (Chronicle P); 24:11–14, 15-r. 1(?), r. 14; 190:1–10(?); Tyrian annals
Earliest history:	ABC 18 (antedeluvian); = AKL
Myth, miracle:	ABC 18.i:17f. (flood); 19 (Weidner); 20:18–23 (Sargon I's sin and affliction with revolt and with insomnia—CEK); 190:8–10(?)
Updating of text:	Babylonian Chronicle Series (ABC 1–7) through Cyrus, copying continuing in reign of Darius
Divine speech:	ABC 19 (Weidner); 190:5(?)
Direct discourse:	ABC 22.ii:9ff.; iii:8–19 (but, unlike Kings, all with reference to foreign affairs)
Punishment not by foreign powers:	ABC 20:23 (Sargon's affliction with insomnia)
Regnal accounts starting with cultic policy:	
Premonarchic times:	
Omens not in kings:	ABC 17; 24

(Note further: form of Kings regnal accounts: he did X; queen mother's name [death noted in ABC 7.ii:13–15; cf. death of king's wife in 1.iv:22; 7.iii:23f.]; age at accession; punishment of whole nation for sin, rather than king alone; admission of king's guilt by scribe of country of document's origin)

THE LIMITATIONS OF THE HISTORY

STYLIZING HISTORY

DtrH is sometimes schematic, even in such diverse verbal contexts as regnal evaluation formulae and assassination accounts. But some of this material derives from stylized sources; some reflects H(Dtr)'s systematization of acquired data (the name of the queen mother or the sequence on Israel and Aram). Stylization does not, as one may think, imply concoction.

Nor do H(Dtr)'s schemes overpower the evidence. Kings lists officers and the weight of donations for Solomon, but never thereafter. Some events are dated, parallels are not (Fig. 15). Building is reported where apposite. After Solomon's works (1 Kings 9:10ff.; 11:26ff.), projects outside the capital rarely rate description: Jeroboam's (12:25) for securing independence; Asa's (15:22[f.]) against Baasha (and vice versa); Omri's (16:24) in his capital; Ahab's (16:34; cf. 22:39), fulfilling a prophecy and betokening power; and Uzziah's (2 Kings 14:22) at Eilat. Historical interests, not grand themes, made this data germane (for the rest, see the chronicles). In detail, DtrH is not schematic. Libnah revolts against Jehoram (2 Kings 8:22): no other king, however evil, suffers the indignity of a town's secession. Jehoahaz of Israel entreats Yhwh (2 Kings 13:4), without his prayer being quoted: only here does Yhwh spare the northern kingdom on royal request. Causation, not effect, is manipulated. Sennacherib dies at home, not outside Jerusalem. H(Dtr) reports events each in its individuality. His unevenness answers variety in the events. It reflects a patchwork of sources.

Stylization means that H(Dtr) saw a pattern in events. His culture furnished various tropes for assimilating the data (Chapter 1). Assyrian annals, too, achieve raptures of stylization; no one doubts the "facts" (enemy, tolls extorted, foes "who got away"), liberally analyzed, are correct. Indeed, Assyrian scribes jettison formulary when the data bridle at it; the patterns help to fix proportions, to pad out the figure of the king; but they are tailored to the events—not to conscious invention.

DtrH by nature demanded stylization: it is integrated, structured. Kings is organized by reign: H(Dtr), who qualifies the equation of nationhood with statehood (1 Sam. 8:5f.), sees monarchy, like those prophets who thought life without kings tantamount to exile, as the nation's life's breath.[32] Without kings, "each man did what was right in his own eyes" (Judg. 17:6; 21:25)—a recipe for disaster (18:1; 19:1) or vagrancy (Deut. 12:8f.). Later, E(Dtr)x discerns glimmerings of restoration in the ragtag figure of a hostage king (2 Kings 25:27–30). DtrH positively wheezes with royalism.

Kings situates events between accession and death formulae (but see n. 22). Athaliah (2 Kings 11) makes a sort of prelude to the reign of Joash

(12:1ff.). And a civil war between Omri and Tibni (1 Kings 16:21f.) occurs after Zimri's and before Omri's account. 2 Kings 17:7–41, the sermon on the fall of Israel, is the only other substantial text certainly outside the compass of the formulae.[33] The exceptions are all appropriate.

This scheme leaves H(Dtr) leeway only inside regnal accounts. Solomon's has been examined in Chapter 5. Kings from Rehoboam to Ahaz, however, are addressed in brief (13.3 verses per king, excluding Ahaziah). H(Dtr) sticks chiefly to the temple and war.

In such perfunctory reviews, one expects straightforward correlation: bad kings will suffer, good kings prosper. But the correspondence is not patent (Fig. 18). Jehu's dynasty excites Yhwh's mercy (2 Kings 13:4f., 22–25; 14:25–27), perhaps to reward Jehu (2 Kings 10:30; 15:12). Judah's rulers fall into four categories: good kings who removed the _bāmôt_, good kings who did not, wicked kings, and wicked kings who patronized or built _bāmôt_. Those in the last category, Amon excepted, suffer no real sanctions; the others fare variously. Good kings are assassinated (Joash, Amaziah) or fall ill (Uzziah, Asa; also Hezekiah; cf. only Ahazyah); like evil kings (Rehoboam, Abijah, Jehoram, Ahaz), they are beset by war (Asa, Joash, Amaziah, Jotham). Hosea, the Israelite exile, is, perversely, better than his forebears (2 Kings 17:2). The reportage does not line up mechanically with H(Dtr)'s algebra of royal sin.

Only autopsy can show whether H(Dtr) concocted which king fell prey to assassins, which to disease. That he did not apply these tonics schematically suggests, however, that H(Dtr) had sources. H(Dtr) judges Judahite kings (Israel's are condemned) on several variables. But the events of individual reigns are not the ideological focus of the history: in isolated cases H(Dtr)'s ideology is elastic enough to accommodate the loosest correlation of cause and effect. At issue is the fate of the nation as a whole.

DtrH: A CULTIC INTERPRETATION OF HISTORY

Examination of a thematic linchpin—Israel's apostasy—will help to expose all these issues. H(Dtr), like Deuteronomy,[34] traces it to the Amorites, a view enunciated programmatically in Exodus 23:23f.; 34:11–16; Numbers 33:50–56. The chief danger to Israel is the snare of Canaan's gods.

The theme unfurls in Joshua 24:13–27. Israel "puts away" the gods to which it was exposed in Mesopotamia (24:2, 14), Egypt (24:14), and Canaan (24:15)—any pollution must (cf. Hosea, Ezekiel) postdate the conquest, which establishes that cultic practices reviled by H(Dtr) are not ancestral, but alien (indeed, Amorite). The text may provide an alternative to Genesis 35:1–4 as the cult myth of an annual ritual. In both, the verb for disposing of foreign gods is _hāsēr_ (root _swr_), "to cause to depart." This verb, used in similar ceremonies in Judges 10:16; 1 Samuel

FIGURE 18: VIRTUE–FATE CORRELATIONS IN KINGS

I. GOOD KINGS

King	Sins	Punishments	Rewards
David	Murdered Uriah	Absalom revolt	Natural death Dynasty
Solomon 3:3a, loved Yhwh, David's statutes	People used *bāmôt* (no temple: 3:2) He used *bāmôt* (3:3b) *Bāmôt*, apostasy (11:4–10) Heart not like Da- vid's (11:4, 6)	——— ——— Revolts Schism	Natural death Son keeps crown
	Rehoboam, Abijah		
Asa 15:11, = David 15:14b; cf. 3:3a; 11:4–6	*Bāmôt* did not depart	Constant war (15:16)? Sick when old (15:23)	Natural death? Defeated Baasha?
Jehoshaphat 22:43, = Asa	*Bāmôt* did not de- part; people used (22:49) Allied with Israel?	Lost fleet?	Natural death
	Jehoram, Ahaziah (Athaliah)		
Joash 12:3; cf. 14:3 ≠ David	*Bāmôt* did not de- part; people used (12:4)	Hazael enthralls? Assassinated?	?
Amaziah 14:3, = Joash	*Bāmôt* did not de- part; people used (14:4)	Defeated by Joash? Assassinated?	Conquered Edom Outlived Joash (14:17)?
Uzziah 15:3, = Amaziah	*Bāmôt* did not de- part; people used (15:4)	Leper (15:5)?	Natural death Restored Eilat (14:22)

King	Sins	Punishments	Rewards
Jotham 15:34, = Uzziah	*Bāmôt* did not depart; people used (15:35)	Rezin and Pekah attacked (15:37)?	Natural death
	Ahaz		
Hezekiah 18:3, = <u>David</u> Caused *bā-môt* to depart (18:4a, 6)		Sennacherib enthralls (18:13–14)? Deathly ill (20:1–3)? Children will be captives (20:17f.)	Yhwh with him (18:7) Conquers (18:8) Weathers Sennacherib Healed (20:4–11) Peace in his time Natural death
	Manasseh, Amon		
Josiah 22:2, = <u>David</u> 23:8, 13, defiled Judah's *bāmôt*; 23:15f., tore down Bethel *bāmâ* and defiled altar; 23:19, caused other *bāmôt* to depart, like Bethel's		Died in battle (E[Dtr]x)	

II. WICKED KINGS

King	Sins	Punishments	Rewards
Rehoboam 14:22–24	(OG, He and) Judah did worse than fathers; Built *bāmôt* and pillars "on every high hill" (cf. Ahaz)	Shishak enthralls (14:25f.) Constant war (14:30)?	Jerusalem still elected (14:21) Natural death

King	Sins	Punishments	Rewards
Abijah 15:3	Followed sins of *Rehoboam,* and heart not whole (cf. 11:4, 6; 3:3a; 15:14b; 22:43)	War with Jeroboam (15:7)?	Jerusalem still elected for <u>David's</u> sake (15:4) Natural death

Asa, Jehoshaphat

King	Sins	Punishments	Rewards
Jehoram 8:18	Followed paths of kings of Israel as did house of Ahab and did evil in Yhwh's sight	Edom revolts "to this day" (8:20–22) Libnah revolts (8:22)	Jerusalem still elected for David's sake (8:19; cf. Abijah) Natural death
Ahaziah 8:27	Followed path of house of Ahab and did evil in Yhwh's sight, like house of Ahab (cf. *Jehoram*)	Assassinated (9:27)	

Joash, Amaziah, Uzziah, Jotham

King	Sins	Punishments	Rewards
Ahaz 16:2–4	Not upright, like <u>David</u>; followed path of kings of Israel (= *Jehoram, Ahaziah,* 2 Kings 17), sacrificed son like <u>supplantees</u>; sacrificed and burnt incense "on *bāmôt* and on the hills" (= *Rehoboam*)	War with Rezin and vassalship to Assyria (16:6–9)	Assyria defeats Rezin (16:9) Natural death

Hezekiah

King	Sins	Punishments	Rewards
Manasseh 21:22ff.	Did evil in Yhwh's sight like <u>supplantees</u> (= *Ahaz*) Rebuilt *bāmôt* Built altars to Baal and Host Made Asherah like Ahab; put altars in	Exile to come later (cf. *Hezekiah* in 2 Kgs 20:17ff.)	Natural death

King	Sins	Punishments	Rewards
	temple; sacrificed son (=*Ahaz*; <u>supplantees</u>); had mantics; did evil in Yhwh's sight; put Asherah-icon in temple; led astray to do evil worse than <u>supplantees</u>, Amorites Spilled endless innocent blood; led Israel to do evil in Yhwh's sight		
	Josiah		
Jehoahaz 23:32	Did evil in Yhwh's sight, like his fathers (can't be father)	Imprisoned; deposed; impost (23:33f.)	
Jehoiakim 23:37	Did evil in Yhwh's sight, like his fathers (can't be father)	In thrall to Babylon (24:1) Plundered (24:2–4)	Natural death
Jehiachin 24:9	Did evil in Yhwh's sight, like his father	Siege; exile (24:10–16)	
Zedeqiah	Did evil in Yhwh's sight like *Jehoiakim* (= brother, not nephew-predecessor)	Fall of Jerusalem; sons killed, and he blinded; imprisoned; exiled (25:7)	

7:3f., is connected in Kings to the *bāmôt*: they did not "depart" (*sārû*); Hezekiah "removed" them (*hēsîr*; cf. Fig. 18). H(Dtr) treats the *bāmôt*, thus, in language he uses of foreign gods.

Early on, gods, not *bāmôt*, give cause for concern. Per Joshua 23:4–16 (Num. 33:50–56; Deut. 29:15–28), Amorite influence infects the cult (Judg. 3:7; 6:7–10; 8:33f.), and produces a cycle of oppressions (Chapter 6).

H(Dtr) breaks the cycle twice. In Judges 10:11–16, the Israelites divest themselves of foreign gods (*swr*), in a period of orderly succession (10:1–5; 12:7–12)—when the cycle is not apropos (Chapter 6; Judg. 1:1; 2:10, 19). There follows regression (13:1), but no talk of alien deities: idolatry (18:30f.) and immorality (and 1 Sam. 2:12ff., 22, but 2:25), but not apostasy.

Still, a second divestiture (*hāsēr*) occurs where orderly succession is instituted permanently, in 1 Samuel 7:3f. Subsequent texts tar kingship as apostasy (8:8; 12:9–21); they do not suggest alien worship. *Bāmôt* are used (1 Sam. 9:12–14, 19–26; 10:5, 13), icons maintained (19:13, 16), and necromancers consulted (28:6f.). David's state embraces Amorites (1 Sam. 7:14; 2 Sam. 21:2; 24:6f.; 1 Kings 9:20f.). But the Amorite gods are gone to ground.

Under Saul and David, the *bāmôt* remain (1 Sam. 9f.; 2 Sam. 15:24, 32; 1 Kings 3:4), but as outlets of Yahwistic devotion (1 Kings 3:2f.; Chapter 7). Only when Solomon builds *bāmôt for strange gods* (1 Kings 11:7f.; 2 Kings 23:13; cf. 2 Sam. 15:32) are sanctions triggered (1 Kings 11:9ff.; 12).

At this point H(Dtr) enunciates his cultic themes. Jeroboam builds *bāmôt* for "other gods" (his "calves"), and consecrates a non- Levitic clergy (12:28–31; 13:33; 14:9). His "sin" (12:30) ends in exile (13:34; 14:15f.; 2 Kings 17:22f.): accession formulae document its regular royal renewal.[35]

The course of infidelity runs smooth. Omri "did worse" (1 Kings 16:25), Ahab worse still (v. 30), pursuing "baals" (18:18), with paraphernalia (16:31–33), "pursuing *gillûlîm*" (a scatological term for gods or icons) like "the Amorites whom Yhwh supplanted" (21:25f.). After Ahaziah (22:53f.), affairs improve: Jehoram removes (*swr*) Ahab's "pillar of the baal" (2 Kings 3:2); Jehu abolishes the Baal cult (10:15–28). So where kings up to Ahaziah "pursued" "Jeroboam's sin," those from Jehoram forward "did not depart" (*swr*) from it. Still, the sin survives.

When 2 Kings 17:7–23 outlines the causes of the Assyrian exile, then, it evokes Ahab[36] and Jeroboam,[37] respectively. Israel copied supplanted peoples, the Amorites (17:8, 11). They served other gods and patronized *bāmôt* (17:7–12), succumbing to the seduction of surrounding peoples (17:15)—Jeroboam's idols and Ahab's Baal and Asherah number among the examples.

Yet Amorite influence is indirect. Jeroboam concocts his gods (2 Kings 17:9); Ahab gets his from Tyre. In the monarchy, Amorites are mainly a point of comparison: Israel behaves like the supplanted peoples (as Genesis 15:16, the "sin of the Amorites"; cf. Deuteronomy 2). Unfazed by Samaria's fate, new transplants (2 Kings 17:24–41), too, choose gods, consecrate priests and high places, and observe customs graphically correlated to exile (17:33). The idea is Josianic (Chapter 10): apostasy is a communicable, not a hereditary, disease.

Judah's history is more mottled. After Solomon, there were *bāmôt*, and pillars, "asherim," and male prostitutes, like "the nations Yhwh supplanted" (1 Kings 14:22–24). "Alien gods" are quiescent; after 1 Samuel 7:3f., the paraphernalia are the only vestiges of Amorite immorality.

Asa next rids (*swr*) Judah of "all the *gillûlîm* [paraphernalia] his fathers made," prostitutes included (1 Kings 15:12). His son finishes the job (22:47). The *bāmôt* do not "depart" (*swr*: 15:14; 22:44), but this blemishes, rather than obscures, the good Asa and Jehoshaphat did. Wicked kings must go further: so Jehoram (2 Kings 8:18) and Ahazyah (2 Kings 8:27), like Omrides, outfit a Baal temple (2 Kings 11:18). But Jehoiada's coup (11) extinguishes the apostasy, and retires the seesaw: a string of good kings follows, under whom the bāmôt alone "did not depart" (swr: 12:4; 14:4; 15:4, 35).

The next wicked Davidid, a century later, is Ahaz, who prosecutes "the path of the kings of Israel," of the supplanted peoples (2 Kings 16:3f.). He, like Rehoboam (in G), patronizes bāmôt and acts like the Amorites. He is not convicted of alien worship—but neither is Ahazyah or Jehoram. Were it not for the shrine in 2 Kings 11:18, and Solomon's shrines, one would suspect that the issue was alien iconography, not gods. After all, the survival of the bāmôt themselves barely qualifies the endorsement of good kings: remove the paraphernalia, and the bāmôt are Yahwistic.

Hezekiah's regnal account vents this view. It begins, "He removed (hēsîr) the bāmôt" (2 Kings 18:4). He purges paraphernalia (pillars, the "asherah"), even the "snake that Moses had made." Hezekiah obliterates both Amorite-like heteropraxis and the Amorite legacy of the high places. An Assyrian testifies: advising surrender, Rab-Shakeh reasons, "If you say to me, 'We trust in Yhwh, our God,' is it not he whose bāmôt and altars Hezekiah has removed, saying . . . 'Bow before this altar, in Jerusalem'?" (18:22). Solomon's bāmôt survive (cf. 18:4, 22). But the rural bāmôt are tagged—by a foreigner, but by one making a powerful case—as Yhwh's. The nuance is, good kings could tolerate bāmôt; and no text after 2 Kings 11 refers to alien gods. Icons, tokens of Amorite-like, false, subordinate gods, these debauched Judah. On H(Dtr)'s presentation, the bāmôt, otherwise innocuous, are dangerous only because they are potential hotbeds of syncretism (see what follows concerning Manasseh and Josiah).

But one last twist remains. Manasseh "rebuilt the bāmôt" Hezekiah had destroyed. He did "as Ahab . . . had done," like "the nations whom Yhwh supplanted" (2 Kings 21:2–7), and even "misled Israel into doing worse than the nations whom Yhwh eradicated from before the Israelites" (21:9, 11). He raised "altars to all the host of heaven," the first Davidid since Solomon to build shrines to other gods; but his gods are subordinate gods (as 1 Kings 22:19–22).

Some of the rhetoric comes from E(Dtr)x, who blames Manasseh for the exile (21:10–16; 22:17[?]; 23:26f.; 24:3f., 20), and even poses Manasseh's sin against Jeroboam's (21:11, 16f.; 24:3).[38] Josiah wipes the reaction out: alien gods, bāmôt, every stain vanishes in an ashen wake. Even Solomon's shrines succumb (2 Kings 23:12–14). Judah is freed of Amorite taint.

Josiah is most radical in Samaria (2 Kings 17:29–41). He "tore down the altar" in Bethel, "and burned" it (23:15) and all Israelite bāmôt, with their priests (23:19f.). This removed the last source of pollution, the Assyrian successors (2 Kings 17:32) to Jeroboam's illicit priesthoods (1 Kings 12:31; 13:33f.). He is gentler toward Judah's priesthoods: he "cashiers"[39] those serving "the baal," the "host of heaven" (23:5), and concentrates the others in the temple (23:8f.): the insinuation is that these are Yhwh's rural priests.

In this account the verb "remove" (*swr*) is used late, only of northern shrines outside Bethel (23:19). First, Josiah "defiled" (23:8, 13) Judah's *bāmôt*, and "burned" Jeroboam's (23:15; cf. 23:7, 8, 12). The divergence from the formulary, "the *bāmôt* did not depart" (cf. 2 Kings 18:4) may reflect reliance earlier in the history on a Hezekian document.

After Josiah the *bāmôt* evaporate; from Josiah to the exile comes H(Dtr)'s longest series (four) of "evil" Davidides. Yet, unlike other "evil" kings, none is accused either of building *bāmôt* or of alien cult practices. E(Dtr)x could have cried regression, like Ezekiel (8:7ff.) and Jeremiah (44:2–25). But by tracing the exile to Manasseh, E(Dtr)x deprived these reigns of all suspense: Josiah *could not* reverse Yhwh's judgment, and his reform, so pregnant with fervid hope, was utterly trivial. That Kings still makes so much of Josiah is an argument against Noth's unitary composition.[40] Conversely, E(Dtr)x's regnal accounts are insipid: for him, nothing turned on any issue after Manasseh.

H(Dtr)'s history is more unified: its themes converge in Josiah's reign. Josiah eradicated Amorite-like practice, purged priesthoods. He repaired the errors of the generations, breaking the cult to the bridle of Yhwh's will. Apostasy on the *bāmôt*, with possession of the land, are the themes that unify DtrH. DtrH resembles nothing so much as a cultic interpretation of political history (cf. ABC 17, 19, 21). Josiah is its logical culmination.

To present an interpretation of history demands stylization, no less of H(Dtr) than of Charles Beard. Principles must be applied over and over, correlations, however rough, dramatized. Nevertheless, "good" and "bad" kings are treated indifferently (see the section in this chapter entitled "Stylizing History" and Fig. 18). More, the *bāmôt* are not stigmatized blindly as centers of alien worship; they are Yahwistic shrines sometimes debauched. H(Dtr)'s fanaticism is sensitive to the data.

Schematic though it is, the cultic interpretation synthesizes rather than supplants the evidence. Baals can only have been introduced after Joshua, but appeared in the premonarchic era (Judg. 6:25–32; 9:4 > 8:33; and icons in 8:27; 17f.). Thereafter the first evidence of alien worship comes from Solomon's *bāmôt*; the course of Judges and Samuel is the result. In Judah Solomon built shrines in Jerusalem. But Asa's purge, which did not remove them, implied Rehoboam's and Abijah's depravity. Hezekiah rectified depravity, as did Josiah—heightened by Ahaz and Manasseh. In the north Ahab must have introduced the Baal, whence, with Athalyah, it came to Judah. Jehu arose—and alien gods thereafter disappeared. Throughout, however, the idols of Bethel remained. H(Dtr) never loses sight of the fact that the archetypal sin is apostasy—intermarrying with Amorites, patronizing the *bāmôt*, are forbidden against this evil only. The distinction between the Law and its intent accounts for ambivalence toward the high places, for the juxtaposition of good kings with *bāmôt*, for the Rab-Shakeh's distortions, and for Josiah's gentle handling of Judah's rural clergy.

H(Dtr)'s interpretation is heavily tempered by doctrine. But why did he not simply impose his doctrine regularly on the history—tarring as apostate every king who suffered defeat or assassination, making a reformer of those monarchs with long reigns? Rather, causation is logical. Jehu wipes out the Omrides; his dynasty endures: linking these facts was sensible (2 Kings 10:35f., against Hosea 1:4). Jeroboam I had no dynasty—the calves were to blame. H(Dtr) fabricates, perhaps, Jehoahaz' appeal to Yhwh (13:4) or Yhwh's logic in not eradicating Israel (14:27)—causation, not national transaction. He stylizes only within the confines of what his research determined. He provides a defensible evaluation of the events.

MYOPIA AND SELECTION IN DtrH

H(Dtr) selects topics to treat, causes to expose, from a Josianic standpoint. Predictably, we hear little of domestic politics and nearly nothing of economics. Even the import of developments in foreign relations, an arena of interest to H(Dtr), is lost or deliberately ignored.

DtrH is not a global history. It omits major political developments. We hear nothing of Shishak outside Jerusalem (cf. 2 Chron. 12:4), though he landscaped the country from Eilat to the Jezreel; of Omri's domination of Moab (KAI 181:4f.); of Ahab's role in the battle of Qarqar; of Uzziah's actions against Tiglath-Pileser III; of Assyria's invading Egypt; of that earthshaking event, the fall of Nineveh. N. Sarna is surely right to attribute the omissions to the historian's purpose.[41] Only in 2 Kings 24:7 (= E[Dtr]x; arguably, 2 Kings 8:7–15) does DtrH provide data on third parties. Such information is irrelevant to the correlation of cultic and political history.

Even when H(Dtr) chronicles movement in Israelite domestic policy, he shies away from rounded analysis. The threat from Shishak probably entailed the loss of Syria (1 Kings 11:23f.), the pawning of the tribe of Asher (1 Kings 9:11), a burdensome corvee, and, eventually, the Solomonic schism.[42] H(Dtr) acknowledges the role of the corvee, but Shishak (11:40) takes a back seat to Solomon's apostasy. Solomon's marriage to an Egyptian princess is reported, but not the diplomatic implications. The compacts concretized in the giving of Jezebel, or in the person of Athaliah, remain implicit only.

Foreign relations with political ramifications (as 1 Kings 15:17ff.) are reported only incidentally. So Jehu dissolved Omride ties to Judah (1

Kings 22), a patch in the quiltwork of alliances that stymied Shalmaneser at Qarqar. Jehu joined hands with Assyria[43] to enter into contest with Damascus. Kings documents the shift with notices of conflict with Aram (10:32f.; 13:3–5, 22–25; 14:25–27), but never mentions Assyria. Nor does it explain the next reversal: with Assyria the more potent threat, Israel again made common cause with Damascus. This connection lies latent in 2 Kings 15:19f., 29, 37, about Tiglath-Pileser's advent and Pekah's Aramean alliance. Further, Pekah usurped the crown against a party (15:25) that had revived discarded anti-Aramean policies (15:10, 13–16). And Hosea, Pekah's assassin (15:30), mounted the throne at the connivance of Tiglath-Pileser.[44] None of the background appears.

Even in regard to the temple, H(Dtr)'s history is a reflection in a pool: its surface reflects events in two dimensions; it never plumbs human causes. So Solomon built the temple, among other things, to aggrandize central authority and to insulate it against charges of godlessness. The temple, Yhwh's dynastic imprimatur, lent luster to the capital; it strengthened Solomon in domestic and diplomatic dealings. H(Dtr) hides these motives behind the facade of piety. Yet H(Dtr) was no ingenue in cathedral politics: Jeroboam built his shrines, we hear, to steal the traffic from Solomon's (1 Kings 12:25–33). Even this sketch is unfinished: Jeroboam, unlike Solomon, put up two shrines, at the extremities of the state, not in his own back yard, to pacify concerns about big government and sectional interests. Further, as it had done for Solomon, the building of temples articulated Jeroboam's sovereignty. H(Dtr) explores only the elements of Jeroboam's reasoning that affect the Jerusalem temple.

H(Dtr) metes out the same treatment to Hezekiah's and Josiah's reforms, reducing a welter of concrete motives to that of piety. Hezekiah's efforts went hand in hand with his foreign alliances, his appeals to Samaria, his conquests in Philistia, and his policy in rural Judah. Incidental notes reflect the reorganization, and the source citation (2 Kings 20:20) mentions some fortification. Josiah's policies were similar, and H(Dtr) must have been conversant with them. The history reflects no such familiarity.

In no case does H(Dtr) give the least hint that any king pursued an integrated political program. Policy is sequestered from its aims. Of no king, therefore, does DtrH furnish a three-dimensional portrait.

Three explanations are possible: that the sources did not furnish such information (which, although true, only displaces the difficulty); that H(Dtr)'s thematic interests made such analysis redundant; or that such analysis was not the business of a historian. Of these, the first affects what information is given, more than how it is analyzed. The treatment of Shishak's expedition (see the section in this chapter entitled "Stylizing History") means that H(Dtr) had access to different types of sources for Judah than for Israel. Thus, of twenty-one events that Kings dates, only two relate to Israel (2 Kings 1:1 = 3:5; 17:5f. = 18:9f.), the second of which, Samaria's fall, would not have figured in the annals of Israelite kings (see Fig. 15). Still, the sources are not altogether to blame. H(Dtr) does relate that Hezekiah revolted, and touches on the politics of the schism (1 Kings 11–12); his sources analyzed the arguments, and the convictions behind them, for and against the adoption of kingship (Chapter 8). Moreover, H(Dtr)'s sources (even a version of Shalmaneser's annals) must have cited Ahab's role at Qarqar, and Israel's leagues with and against Assyria.

DtrH's thematic focus also will not explain all the lacunae. The battle of Qarqar might be too far afield; but the links between revolt and reform, between Assyrian pressure and foreign alliances, between the building of a temple and government, were not. Some of these connections are hinted at (1 Kings 11–12; 15:18–20; 2 Kings 16:6–9; 18:4–8). Again, H(Dtr)'s thematic focus explains his selection, not the vicissitudes of his analysis.

Indeed, H(Dtr) tends to transmit information even at the expense of his themes. He does not supply a judge in the story of Dan's migration (Judg. 17f.). Good kings and bad are indifferently punished or rewarded (see the section in this chapter entitled "Stylizing History"). H(Dtr) even suffers contradiction—and, in 1 Samuel, interweaves two contradictory sources. His method is to develop his themes around the materials, as the book of Judges, Solomon's regnal account (see chapters 4 and 5, and the section in this chapter entitled "DtrH: A Cultic Interpretation of History"), and the detailed coverage of the conquest and the tribal territories illustrate. Nor is the text a closed set, a self-referential world. 2 Kings 20:11 speaks of shadow on the "steps" (ma'$a$lôt) of Ahaz; 2 Kings 23:12 mentions altars on the roof of Ahaz' "upper story" ('$a$liyyâ). Ahaz is never damned for building the structure.

Here DtrH raises a set of problems alien to Mesopotamian historiography. There sources are sharply subordinated to narrow interests: the texts are to the point, leaving little doubt about their theories of causation (as ABC 16, 17, 19, 21). In DtrH the sources tend to take over the narrative, so that their concerns cross the grain of the historian's. For example, M. Haran has argued that the Elijah cycle came to H(Dtr) already formed: the story of the sacrifice on Carmel (1 Kings 18) does not censure a rural sacrifice.[45] H(Dtr) had grounds not to censure Elijah—Yhwh vindicated his action, which refuted the claims of the Baal. But Haran is right: this is not a tradition H(Dtr) concocted. Inconsistency in the text stems from sources, from a reverence toward them that transcends H(Dtr)'s central themes.

Three factors, then, limit DtrH: its sources, often spotty, and subject also to the succeeding restrictions; its thematic focus; and the Israelite idea of history, which discouraged coherent political analysis. The aversion to complex political analysis is not peculiar to DtrH. Assyrian and

Babylonian texts, for example, present events as isolated accessions to the record of a king proceeding from one discrete objective to the next. No Near Eastern historiography conceives of policy as grand strategy; no writer before Herodotus depicts a series of maneuvers as a directed effort to achieve specific goals.

If anything, H(Dtr) evinces greater sophistication than most Near Eastern scribes. Naturally, Merodach-Baladan II portrays his tax reform and land reform as a pious restoration of a *status quo ante* disrupted by Assyria. But Assyria's kings do not discuss his policies as Machiavellian measures to "steal the heart of the men" of Babylonia. Sennacherib, too, does not link the western revolt he put down in 701 B.C.E. to Merodach-Baladan's incitement. Again, Nabonidus' scribes understandably sequester his cultic reforms from his struggle with the Medes. Even his move to Tema evokes no strategic explanation. But no later text relates the cultic upheaval to fear of Cyrus, or interprets the change of capital in political terms.

Few Near Eastern sources expose the political aims of any royal program—just why a king builds a temple or chastises a vassal. Piety motivates devotional activity and provocation mililtary activity. Two texts from Yaudi stand out: Bar-Rakib explains that siege compelled his father, Panamuwa, to call upon the aid of Tiglath-Pileser III (KAI 215:2–10); and Kilamuwa (KAI 24:5–8) justifies hiring an earlier Assyrian king against his own enemies. Both texts explain a decision to accept vassalhood. Two of the rare analyses of motivation in Kings sound the same theme: Asa (roughly contemporary with Kilamuwa) bribes Ben-Hadad to divert Baasha's concentrations from the border (1 Kings 15:17–22); and Ahaz (contemporary with Panamuwa) bribes Tiglath-Pileser to rescue Judah from an Aramean-Israelite coalition (2 Kings 16:5–9).

Cogan and Tadmor argue that, to damn Ahaz, H(Dtr) added the term bribe, and Ahaz' declaration of submission (2 Kings 16:7f.) to a written source.[46] Asa, however, also sends a bribe (Kilamuwa says, "hired"), inducing Ben-Hadad to abrogate a treaty with Israel; here there is no question of derisive treatment. H(Dtr)'s criticism would have been more devastating had he diminished Ahaz' incentive. As things stand, Asa is moved by a blockade, Ahaz by territorial loss and a present threat to the capital (16:5f.). The parallel to the Yaudi inscriptions suggests that voluntary vassalage, like usurpation,[47] evoked reasoned apology.

Such insights are exceptional in DtrH (Jeroboam's cult reform furnishes another instance). No Mesopotamian king makes a similar confession, although foreign kings are sometimes described as appealing to third parties (as OIP 2.31:78– 81). But it is striking that Kings records two cases of "hiring" foreign kings, and that this is the only topos in West Semitic inscriptions in which salvation from military threats is not ascribed entirely to the gods. Probably H(Dtr) or his source (H[Dtr]hez, which may or may not be the same as the Judahite chronicles) drew the data—and with it, the political analysis—from lapidary remains.

H(Dtr), like other Near Eastern historians, frames incidents in isolation, not interlock. He does not exert himself to plumb the hopes and fears embodied in policy. It does not follow, however, that he was naive. In 1 Kings 11–12 DtrH distinguishes mundane causation from divine interference (cf. 1 Samuel 8 and 12 and Chapter 8): the north seceded over taxation and corvee; the real cause, says H(Dtr), was Solomon's senile apostasy. Yhwh determined the outcome, but other considerations moved the human actors. This is typical. The omission of Assyria's role in the history of Israel's relations with Aram indicates to what extent H(Dtr) took history as the expression of Yhwh's will. Yhwh punishes infidelity, yet concern for their own welfare drives Israel to behave as they do.

In short, events respond to a complementary causation. Behind each incident stands Yhwh, the ultimate cause. Yhwh did not lure Jeroboam or other kings into the snare of the calf cult. But his failing called down on Israel the sufferings of two centuries, ending in exile. Yhwh sometimes instigates individual action (2 Sam. 17:14; 1 Kings 12:13–15). Behind events of broader consequence, his influence is all but assumed.

This does not imply that human agents consciously execute Yhwh's will. Rehoboam (1 Kings 12:13–15) unwittingly acts the drama whose denouement sunders his kingdom. Baasha, Zimri, and other Israelite usurpers fulfill divine curses on their predecessors; except in Jehu's case, we may assume that their zeal is excited by a tincture of personal ambition. It is the coincidence of velleity and opportunity that Yhwh wreaks, so that it is Yhwh who sends Rezin against Jotham (2 Kings 15:37), Yhwh who engineers Hazael's rise (and Hazael, like Macbeth, helps himself [contrast ANET 280]) and the ebb and flow of Aramean power (2 Kings 8:13, 14, 28; 10:33; 13:4f., 23–25; 14:25ff.).

This principle operates throughout the history. The Danites take Laish militarily (Judg. 18:7ff.); Yhwh is the one who gives it to them (18:10). God drives a wedge between Abimelek and Shechem (Judg. 9:23); it is Gual who incites the revolt (9:26–29). Revolts by Hadad and Rezin (1 Kings 11:14, 23) are Yhwh's response to Solomon's sin. Divine manipulation is manifest in the fulfillment of prophecies, and the gap between human volition and divine instigation is apparent in military defeat. History is a stage on which the god works out his authorial intentions; so few events defy analysis as products both of divine and of human motivation. The language of divine causation, correspondingly, does not exclude political causation: "Yhwh subdued PN" implies that Israel had to fight a battle, just as the claim that "Clive conquered India" does not preclude the presence of troops and the relevance of other factors. There are exceptions—when the sun stands still or its shadow recedes across the face of Ahaz' steps.

Most artful are the variations on this theme in the Court History, largely inherited by H(Dtr). Solomon succeeds by a putsch; but Yhwh placed him on the throne (1 Kings 1:48; 2:15, 24 and so on). Abiathar is banished (1 Kings 2:27) for supporting Adonijah, but also for the sin of Eli's sons (1 Sam. 2:27–36). Joab is killed for his identical political affiliations, but also in retribution for his earlier murders (1 Kings 2:32–34).

2 Samuel worries the issue more explicitly. Ishbaal's killers announce that Yhwh executed Ishbaal on David's behalf (4:8). David disagrees, killing the killers; yet the assassins were not really mistaken (5:1–3). Again, Shimei sees David's dethronement as a requital for spilled Saulide blood (16:8); the reader knows Uriah is being avenged (12:7–12). And although David frets that Yhwh has incited Shimei to curse him and avoids retaliation (16:10–12), the narrator makes it clear that Shimei is not immune from retaliation (1 Kings 2:44). Discovering divine intent is treacherous business.

More involuted is Absalom's revolt. After David's adultery, Yhwh condemns him to domestic unrest and ordains that a rebel will publicly bed his wives (2 Sam. 12:7–12). Absalom, for personal reasons, revolts. Back in Jerusalem, he consults Ahitophel, who divines that, for political reasons, Absalom must bed David's wives (16:20–22). Lest the reader miss the link to Yhwh's curse, the narrator adds at just this juncture, "The advice of Ahitophel which he counselled in those days was as though one had inquired of the word of God" (16:23). Similarly, in order to revolt, Absalom begs leave to go to Hebron "to serve Yhwh" (15:7f.). Absalom's deceit is the author's truth: the revolt is in Yhwh's cause. Hushai's remark, that Yhwh had elected Absalom (16:18), is likewise unconsciously accurate (cf. Genesis 44:16, with the same irony). Divine and human intention converge from different directions. Climbing the Mount of Olives to flee, David asks Yhwh to confound Ahitophel's counsel (15:31); as he comes "to the peak, where one prostrates oneself to God," he encounters Hushai (v. 32), and commissions him to outwit Ahitophel (vv. 32–37). Has Yhwh answered David's plea by supplying Hushai, or has David taken matters into his own hands? Hushai succeeds, but the narrator gives the credit to Yhwh: Yhwh confounds Ahitophel's advice in order to punish Absalom (17:14). Causation is dual, complementary.

This explains why H(Dtr) does not, as a rule, plumb political motivation. Events have overt causes that modern readers recognize as historical. Behind them, however, is Yhwh. Human interests are the agencies of his activity, manipulated in reaction to Israelites' behavior.

H(Dtr) sometimes detects causes that offend rationalist sensibilities. The line to Absalom's insurrection from David's adultery is, after all, a bit gnarled. But philosophy governs any selection of events and causes. The reader, as Thucydides already states (1.22), must isolate ideological elements and weigh the judgments that sustain them. H(Dtr)'s commitments in no way precluded preserving information about human causation. Precisely because he conceived of divine intervention as transcending human agencies, as converging with them in effect, but not intention, he enjoyed the utmost latitude in the interpretation of recorded events. H(Dtr) did not need to fabricate facts: nothing in his historical philosophy discouraged antiquarian research.

This is why even the history of Israelite apostasy conforms to the evidence (see the section in this chapter entitled "DtrH: A Cultic Interpretation of History"), why divine punishment is distributed so unschematically in Kings (see the section in this chapter entitled "Stylizing History"): metahistorical commitments programmed H(Dtr) to select from his records, but not to falsify misfortune for Ahaz or Manasseh. Instead of confecting events, H(Dtr) could, and did, interpret human events as the result of divine intent: war was a trial for Asa, but a form of discipline for Ahaz. Human history was a key to unlock—by a logical analysis (see the sections mentioned earlier in this paragraph)—a deeper, truer causality, where human behavior touched on divine.

H(Dtr) takes a partisan view, in the company of Gibbon, Macaulay, Mommsen, Syme, and any outstanding historian. He uses paradigmatic, or ideological, sources, and substantive sources; and, of the latter, some are physical, some antiquarian, and some, such as votives, not antiquarian but celebratory. His work is sometimes inaccurate—what historical work is not? He selects his data, taps only some of his resources (the chronicles), and his choices are, in part, ideologically conditioned. He sits squarely in the mainstream of narrative history, from Herodotus to the present (Chapter 1).

Israelite historiography differs from modern chiefly in its doctrines of causation, its sense of what the ultimate object of study should be. These evolve even today. The political history of the eighteenth century engendered the legal and philological history of the nineteenth century, and the latter the social history, the "scientific" history, of our time. Still, the process of applying to the evidence for vindication of the analysis remains much the same.

H(Dtr), in sum, committed himself first to the data disclosed by his research, a commitment that sometimes (Chapter 4) led him to reify metaphor or telescope years. The events for which he had to account thus remain the same, whether coupled to economic or to theological engines of explanation. Indeed, H(Dtr) sincerely believed that the high places and the baals were the causes of Israel's misfortunes; his interest in accurately recalling those misfortunes was sharp. H(Dtr) and his sources believed in their theses, and adduced events as historical evidence in their behalf.

What, after all, did H(Dtr) write? Not *the* history of Israel, not a sociological, economic, and climatic history of all events in Israel's past. His history services Israelite concerns: it offers up salient political events in the temple of the first principle. He wrote *a* history of Israel, a cultic interpretation of it. The product is still a history, just as it is when a social historian studies Boston or Philadelphia.

The secret of historical method—that one must put the sources to proof—was no mystery in antiquity. Thucydides and Hecateus were conscious of it; the urge, found in Hesiod's *Theogony*, to find the literal truth probably presupposes the same principle. Whether H(Dtr) employed the method is moot. But that he attempted sincerely to analyze the past insofar as he could know it, to learn from the past as he could grasp it, should be clear. H(Dtr) saw a pattern in the transactions of Yhwh with Israel, a pattern more profound than the ones Mesopotamians refined from portents (Deut. 4:19). Because *all* human history, in his view, manifested and certified divine intent, every aspect of history was a field for collecting data. This is a start in the development of the genre of history, of antiquarian research, as we know it.

Notes to Chapter 9

1. For Moab, *KAI* 181:4–8; for Qarqar, *ANET* 278f. (Monolith II 90ff.), with Hadadezer, not Ben-Hadad; for Hazael, E. Michel, "Die Assur-Texte Salmanassars III. (858–824)," *WdO* 1/2 (1947): 57–58:I 25–II 6, e.g. Mesha's (*KAI* 181:5) claim to have revolted after "half the days of his [Omri's] son," not at Ahab's death, may imply displacement by H(Dtr)'s sources, or antedating by Mesha, or the difference between revolt and victory (2 Kings 1:1; 3:4ff.; cf. also 2 Chron. 20).

2. See my "Yau(a), Son of Omri, Yet Again," *BASOR* 264 (1986): 81–85, with bibliography.

3. See S. Page, "A Stela of Adad-Nirari III and Nergal- Ereš from Tell al Rimah," *Iraq* 30 (1968): 142:8. Assyrian kings claim Israel as a vassal; Israel probably thought they were allies against Aram. Cf. n. 1.

4. 2 Kings 15:29f.; *ANET* 283f., on Transjordan (also 1 Chron. 5:6ff.).

5. 2 Kings 17:3–6; 18:9f. (*ABC* 73:28; cf. *ANET* 284f.) recollect after a century of Sargonides that Shalmaneser (V) was the Assyrian king. Cf. C. J. Gadd, "Inscribed Prisms of Sargon II from Nimrud," *Iraq* 16 (1954): 193–201, especially 179–182.

6. On Uzziah, H. Tadmor, "Azriau of Yaudi," *SH* 8 (1961): 232–71, adjusted based on N. Na'aman, "Sennacherib's 'Letter to God' on his Campaign to Judah," *BASOR* 214 (1974): 25–39.

7. 2 Kings 16:5–10; see *ANET* 282; H. W. F. Saggs, "Nimrud Letters 1952—Part II. Relations with the West," *Iraq* 17 (1955): 126–60, especially 134.

8. 2 Kings 18:13– 16, 17–19:37; D. D. Luckenbill, *The Annals of Sennacherib* (OIP 2; Chicago: University of Chicago, 1924), 34:41–49; 60:56–58. Sennacherib claims to have extracted thirty talents of gold and eight hundred of silver (2 Kings 18:14, thirty of gold and three hundred of silver). Though the discrepancy is large, the biblical version has the order of magnitude right. Cf. variation in tribute tabulation under Adad-Nirari III: S. Page, "Stela of Adad-Nirari III" (n. 3).

9. 2 Kings 18:14, 17; 19:8; Luckenbill, *Annals* (n. 8), 156. Lachish III is Sennacherib's stratum: no other shows signs of his siege ramp or campaign.

10. For Necho, *ABC* 128:44 and 98f.; Streck, *Asb.* 3.713; for Jehoiachin, E. F. Weidner, "Jojachin, König von Juda, in babylonischen Keilschrifttexten," *Mélanges syriens offerts à Monsieur René Dussaud* (Paris: P. Geuthner, 1939), 2.923–35. On Chronicles: Cyrus takes Babylon (2 Chron. 36:22f.), and Manasseh serves Assyria (2 Chron. 33:11): *ANET* 291, 294. On Manasseh's shackling, cf. D. J. Wiseman, "An Esarhaddon Cylinder from Nimrud," *Iraq* 14 (1952): 54–60, and *ABC* 125:7f., where notables "on the wadi of Egypt" suffer a similar fate; further, M. Elat, "The Political Status of the Kingdom of Judah Within the Assyrian Empire in the 7th Century B.C.E.," *Lachish V*, ed. Y. Aharoni, et al. (Tel Aviv: Tel Aviv University, 1975), 61–70 (66–69), citing Asshurbanipal's treatment of Necho; R. Frankena, "The Vassal Treaties of Esarhaddon and the Dating of Deuteronomy," *OTS* 14 (1965): 122–54, especially 150f. (if the reference is the crown prince's installation in 672). The mention of Babylon in Chronicles is the sticking point; Friedman (orally) links it to 2 Kings 20:18.

11. See *ANET* 242f.; R. S. Lamon and G. M. Shipton, *Megiddo* I (OIP 42; Chicago: University of Chicago, 1939), 60f.

12. Figures known from seals or bullae include Shaphan's son, Gemaryahu (Jer. 36:10f.), Jezebel, Jeroboam II, Manasseh ("son of the king"), Hezekiah, Baruch ben-Neriah, and others. See Y. Shiloh, "A Hoard of Hebrew Bullae from the City of David," *EI* 18 (1985): 73–88, no. 2; the hoard probably contains the names of other known contemporaries. Further, R. Hestrin and M. Dayagi, *Inscribed Seals* (Jerusalem: Israel Museum, 1979); C. C. Torrey, "A Hebrew Seal from the Reign of Ahaz," *BASOR* 79 (1940):

27f.; D. Diringer, *Le iscrizioni antico-ebraiche palestinesi* (Florence: F. le Monnier, 1934), XXI 2, 4. The title, and perhaps the tomb, of the vizier, Shebna (Isa. 22:15, with the tomb up high) have been found: see *KAI* 191 (Shebanyahu?). The fragility of such identifications has, however, been illustrated by D. Ussishkin, "Royal Judean Storage Jars and Private Seal Impressions," *BASOR* 223 (1976): 1–13; *idem* "The Destruction of Lachish by Sennacherib and the Dating of the Royal Judean Storage Jars," *Tel-Aviv* 4 (1977): 28–60, showing that sealings formerly related to Jehoiachin stem from the eighth century.

13. I omit as not specific archaeological corroboration, as of the "Solomonic" gates at Gezer, Megiddo, and Hazor, of Shishak's or Tiglath-Pileser's campaigns, both with textual correspondence, and so on. I have also omitted later texts, and data such as the names of various rulers of surrounding states (such as Hiram, Bar-Hadad, Rezin).

14. S. Parpola, "The Murder of Sennacherib," in *Death in Mesopotamia* (*Mesopotamia* 8 [1980]; CRRA 26), 171–82. For a lower dating of the campaign, cf. W. H. Shea, "Sennacherib's Second Palestinian Campaign," *JBL* 104 (1985): 401–18. On Tirhaqah in 2 Kings 19:9, compare the confusion over which king of Tyre Tiglath-Pileser III subjected: M. Weippert, "Menachem von Israel und seine Zeitgenossen in einer Steleninschrift des assyrischen Königs Tiglathpileser III. aus dem Iran," *ZDPV* 89 (1973): 26–53; M. Cogan, "Tyre and Tiglath-Pileser III," *JSC* 25 (1973): 96–99.

15. As 2 Samuel 1:17–27; 3:33f.; 23:1–5; cf. 1 Samuel 18:7f.; 21:12–14; 29:3–5, a ditty exploited in parallel sources (denying or affirming David's Philistine affiliations), both preserved by H(Dtr) (or H[1 Sam]): H(Dtr)'s sources, too, have sources (and, further, 1 Sam. 2:1–10; 2 Sam. 22). For poetic sources for the dynastic charter (2 Sam. 7), see my *Constitution of the Monarchy in Israel* (Chico: Scholars, 1981), 47–49. See further in Chapter 8, n. 36.

16. Deir Alla in J. A. Hoftijzer and G. van der Kooij, *Aramaic Texts from Deir ʿAlla* (Documenta et Monumenta Orientis Antiqui 19; Leiden, Netherlands: Brill, 1976); Kuntillet Ajrud, communication from Z. Meshel. Stelae include those of Shishak at Megiddo and Shalmaneser III at Baʿli Raʾasi, others in the Lebanon and in Philistia (one of Sargon's at Ashdod). Others are to be expected in Samaria and Transjordan.

17. E.g., *KAI* 191; W. Dever's cruder "Iron Age Epigraphic Material from the Area of Khirbet el-Kom," *HUCA* 40/41 (1969/70): 139–204; *KAI* 225, among others.

18. 1 Samuel 15:12; 2 Samuel 8:3 (= 1 Chronicles 18:3), if these are reliable. On *yad*, "monument," see M. Elat, "History and Historiography in the Story of the Lives of Samuel and Saul," *Shnaton* 3 (1979): 8–28 [Heb.], especially 22–24.

19. So J. A. Montgomery ("Archival Data in the Book of Kings," *JBL* 53 [1934]: 46–52) holds that the word order of 1 Kings 15:22, and *hwʾ* or *w* plus perfect (original *wʾnk* plus perfect: 2 Kings 18:4; 14:7, 14 and 23:8, 10, 12) are lapidary, "then, at that time" annalistic; regnal formulae come from king lists. Cf. S. Mowinckel, "Die vorderasiatischen Königs- und Fürsteninschriften: Eine stilistische Studie," *EUCHARISTERION. Studien zur Religion und Literatur des Alten und Neuen Testaments Hermann Gunkel zum 60. Geburtstage, den 23. Mai 1922 dargebracht von seinen Schülern und Freunden*, ed. H. Schmidt (FRLANT NF 19/1; Göttingen: Vandenhoeck & Ruprecht, 1923), 278–322, especially 283–300 ("then," and so on); M. Liverani, "L'histoire de Joas," *VT* 24 (1974): 438–53. G. Levi della Vida argues ("The Shiloah Inscription Reconsidered," in *In Memoriam Paul Kahle*, ed. M. Black and G. Fohrer [BZAW 103; Berlin: Töpelmann, 1968], 162–66) that the Siloam slab is a chronicle extract, based on the usage "*zh hdbr*"; also Z. Talshir, "The Detailing Formula *wzh (h)dbr*," *Tarbiz* 51 (1981): 23–35, citing 1 Kings 9:15–22; 11:6–28. But note the question "What was *had-dābār*?" (2 Sam. 1:4; cf. 2 Sam. 14:20, and, again with battle, 1 Sam. 4:16). See BDB *dābār* IV, especially 3 (and Deut. 19:4). On the verbiage of 1 Kings 11:26f., cf. also *EA* 59:32f. On Arad #88 as a copy from a monument, see A. R. Millard, "Epigraphic Notes, Aramaic and Hebrew," *PEQ* 110 (1978): 23–26, especially 26; D. Pardee, "Letters from Tel Arad," *UF* 10 (1978): 289–336, especially 290, n. 3. There *is* evidence of copying from sources in Assyria—see Chapter 8, n. 41. A key indication is a switch from first to third person.

20. E.g., J. Gray, *I & II Kings* (2nd ed.; OTL; Philadelphia: Westminster, 1975), 13f.

21. *ABC* 7, 16, 17, 19, 20.

22. 2 Kings 14:17 follows from 14:16. But Joash (MT) is the only Israelite king with regular formulae between whose accession (13:10f.) and source notices (13:12f.) no data is provided. OG has the death in 13:25, perhaps to efface the irregularity (as Jehoram of Israel in 2 Kings 1:18a, to embrace 2 Kings 2); but on OG Jehoshaphat in 1 Kings 16:28a– h, see J. D. Shenkel, *Chronology and Recensional Development in the Greek Text of Kings* (HSM 1; Cambridge: Harvard University, 1968). Are 14:15f. the original death formulae?

23. Grayson questions indirect citations in the Gutian legend of Naram Sin (to a stela) and the Synchronistic History (*ABC*, 52f.). But see A. R. Millard, *JAOS* 100 (1980): 366f.; H. Tadmor, "Observations on Assyrian Historiography," *Ancient Near Eastern Studies in Memory of J. J. Finkelstein* (Memoir 19; New Haven: Connecticut Academy of Arts and Sciences, 1977), 209–13; Z. Zevit, "Deuteronomistic Historiography in 1 Kings 12–2 Kings 17 and the Reinvestiture of the Israelian Cult," *JSOT* 32 (1985): 57–73, especially 58f.

24. See M. Cogan and H. Tadmor, "Ahaz and Tiglath-Pileser in the Book of Kings: Historiographic Considerations," *EI* 14 (1978): 55–61: the Edom texts are Josianic. 2 Kings 8:22; 14:7; 16:6 use the expression "to this day." 1 Kings 22:48 is reversed in 8:20–22; 2 Kings 14:22 is reversed in 16:6, so "to this day" (four other times after Solomon) is attached wherever possible. Note that the Edomite vassal in 2 Kings 3 is anachronistic even if the Judahite king was originally Jehoram; on the latter issue, see A. R. Green, "Regnal Formulas in the Hebrew and Greek Texts of the Books of Kings," *JNES* 42 (1983): 167– 80; cf. J. M. Miller, "The Elisha Cycle and the Accounts of the Omride Wars," *JBL* 85 (1966): 276–88.

25. So Shishak's campaign affects Judah, but not Israel (it could have been chalked up to Jeroboam); the Syro-Ephraimite war figures in Judahite, not Israelite, accounts; see further the continuation in this section. There are also sources within the Israelite and Judahite accounts: so Jehoram removes Ahab's Baal pillar (2 Kings 3:2), yet Jehu destroys it (10:26, with versions); 2 Kings 18:5 describes Hezekiah, 23:25 Josiah, as unequaled among the kings of Judah.

26. See J. van Seters, *In Search of History* (New Haven: Yale University, 1983), 298, 301, 357.

27. 1 Kings 15:23 (Asa); 16:5 (Baasha), 27 (Omri); 22:46 (Jehoshaphat); 2 Kings 10:34 (Jehu); 13:8 (Jehoahaz), 12 (Joash of Israel); 14:15 (Joash again), 28 (Jeroboam II); 20:20 (Hezekiah). Only 1 Kings 14:19 mentions indecisive warfare (22:46, "and that he fought" is late).

28. This is a strong formal position, as Adonijah's supplication (1 Kings 2:13–17, 19), Asa's aggrandizement, and Athaliah's coup show. Asa fired the old queen mother (1 Kings 15:2, 10, 13; 2 Chronicles 13:2 does not equal 11:18–22; 15:16), identified as his own mother because she, like Athaliah, survived her son. Through Hezekiah's, except for Jehoram's and Ahaz' (predeceasing the succession?), mothers' praenomens are qualified by either patronym or place of origin. Manasseh's has only the praenomen, all thereafter patronym and place of origin. And Chronicles omits the queen mother from Manasseh forward. Starting with Manasseh, the old royal tombs are out of use. Thus, H(Dtr)hez (or the chronicler if this was not H(Dtr)hez) could have used the tombs, and E(Dtr)x updated the list in a different style (also in 2 Chron. 13:2), from memory. There is no change in the formulary for age at accession, evidently from a different source. Also linked to Hezekiah are incidental notes, "he did X" (*hw'* plus perfect plus *'et* plus object), from Amaziah to Hezekiah (2 Kings 14:7, 22, 25; 15:35; 18:4, 8): only that for Jeroboam II (14:25) is integral to a regnal summary. The form (cf. n. 19), normal for a list (as 2 Sam. 23:8–21), and distribution suggest a common source of limited scope, perhaps the chronicles (cf. *ABC* 1.i.29–30).

29. Bin-Nun "Formulas form the Royal Records of Israel and of Judah," *VT* 18 (1968): 414–32 (Van Seters [*In Search* (n. 26), 297f.] arbitrarily concludes the chronicles were late expansions of late king lists). But the Judahite formulae are inverted (regnal length at the start, not end, of a clause) because the length of reign is preceded by age at accession, and followed by the queen mother's name (contra Bin-Nun [p. 421], one

or the other is always present). Extra information skews the formulary, and is itself the evidence for separate king lists. Note the form *whymym* ʾ*sr mlk RN* ῾*l yŝr* ʾ*l N šnh* in 1 Kings 2:11 (David, capitals appended, after the burial notice); 11:42 (equals 1 Chron. 29:27, Solomon, capital after his name, before the death, burial notice); 14:20a (Jeroboam, neither capital nor "over Israel," before death, burial notice); 2 Kings 10:36 (Jehu, capital appended, after burial notice), for kings whose regnal accounts do not naturally begin with accession formulae. On the synchronisms (postdating, and so on), see E. R. Thiele, "An Additional Chronological Note on 'Yaw, Son of "Omri," ' " *BASOR* 222 (1976): 19–23, with bibliography.

30. Other notices occur in (1 Kings 16:24, Omri and Samaria) or before (2 Kings 14:22, Uzziah and Eilat; 15:16, Menachem destroying Tiphsah) accession formulae, but away from the source-citation. The line between them and so-called annalistic reports (as 1 Kings 16:34) is perhaps too fine to draw.

31. See W. G. Lambert, "The Sultantepe Tablets VIII: Shalmaneser in Ararat," *AnSt* 11 (1961): 143–58; J. Goodnick and V. Hurowitz, "LKA 63: A Heroic Poem in Celebration of Tiglath-Pileser I's Musru-Qumanu Campaign," in *Assur* forthcoming, with full treatment of the texts concerned; the forthcoming edition by P. Machinist of the Tukulti-Ninurta Epic (*Studia Pohl*); A. K. Grayson, *Babylonian Historical-Literary Texts* (Toronto: University of Toronto, 1975), with an enumeration on 7f. (also *ABC*, 2–3, 57).

32. See, e.g., 1 Samuel 28:16–19 plus 31; 2 Samuel 7f.; 12:10f.; 24; 1 Kings 3:3 plus 4:20 (MT); 11.6ff. plus 12; 14:15f. plus 2 Kings 17, and so on; cf. Hosea 3:4; 10:3–7; 13:10f.; especially 8:10, all despite 8:4; 9:9; 10:9; Amos 1:15; 5:26, despite the pun in 7:13.

33. On 2 Kings 2 (Elisha succeeding Elijah); 13:14–25 (Elisha's death), see n. 22. Joram's account enfolds those of Jehoram and Ahazyah of Judah (2 Kings 8:16–24, 25; 9), in order to accommodate Jehu's coup. And Zedeqiah's reign is compassed by Jehoiachin's (2 Kings 24:18); they share the Babylonian destruction (25:8–26). A note in 2 Kings 24:7 (with 23:29f., 33–35; 24:2) occurs between Jehoiakim and Jehoiachin. 2 Kings 14:22 is placed between Amaziah and Uzziah.

34. Deuteronomy 6:14; 7:1–6, 16, 20–26; 18:9–14; 20:17f.; 31:16–20; especially 12:2–4, where the issue is Canaanite gods, a prescription governing subsequent, less definite texts (as 12:29–31; 13:2–4, 7–9, 13–16; 32:16–22).

35. 1 Kings 15:26, 34; 16:25f., 30f.; 22:53; 2 Kings 3:2f.; 10:31; 13:2, 11; 14:24; 16:9, 18, 24, 28. Exceptions are Elah (1 Kings 16:8f., with the sin in 16:13) and Shallum (2 Kings 15:13). Zimri's notice comes outside the accession formula (1 Kings 16:19), Zechariah's in it (2 Kings 16:9). All are short-lived. There is no notice for Hosea (2 Kings 17:2). Against Zevit, "Historiography" (n. 23), 65, Tibni is never king.

36. 2 Kings 17:10—"pillars" (2 Kings 3:2; 10:26f.) and asherim (1 Kings 16:33?), 12— *gillûlîm* (only 1 Kings 21:26 in the north), 16—an Asherah (1 Kings 16:33) and the baal (1 Kings 16:31f., and so on), 17—"selling themselves to do evil" (1 Kings 21:25).

37. 2 Kings 17:9 ("high places"), 11 (burning incense, in the north only 1 Kings 13.1f.), 16 (calves), 21f. (Jeroboam named), 23 (1 Kings 13:34; 14:15f. is fulfilled). In 17:7–23 the first two parts (7–12, 13–17) cite various violations, and the last returns specifically to Jeroboam.

38. Jeroboam and Manasseh are the kings par excellence to whom the term *sin* applies. It is used otherwise of Baasha (1 Kings 16:2, 13, with Elah) and Ahab (1 Kings 21:22), who are also accused of "leading Israel/Judah to sin," at least in direct discourse. Two royal sins in Samuel (1 Sam. 15:23, 25; 2 Sam. 12:13) have a different reference.

39. On the term, see S. Talmon, "The New Hebrew Letter from the Seventh Century B.C.E. in Historical Perspective," in *King, Cult and Calendar in Ancient Israel* (Jerusalem: Magnes, 1986), 82.

40. C. Begg ("2 Kings 20:12–19 as an Element of the Deuteronomistic History," *CBQ* 48 [1986]: 27–38) and C. Levin ("Joschija im deuteronomistischen Geschichtswerk," *ZAW* 96 [1984]: 351–71) consciously attribute the trivialization of the reform and the crescendo under Josiah to an exilic compositor. See especially, Lohfink, "Die Bundesurkunde des Königs Josias," *Bib* 44 (1963): 261–88.

41. "The Biblical Sources for the History of the Monarchy," in A. Malamat, ed., *The Age of*

the Monarchies: Political History (WHJP 4/1; Jerusalem: Massada, 1979), 3–21, especially 10–13. For another list of lacunae in DtrH, see H. Weippert, "Fragen des israelitischen Geschichtsbewusstseins," *VT* 23 (1973): 415–42, especially 436f.; further, see the section in this chapter entitled "Stylizing History" and n. 25.

42. See my "Sectionalism and the Schism," *JBL* 93 (1974): 519–32.

43. See H. C. Rawlinson, *Cuneiform Inscriptions of Western Asia: A Selection from the Miscellaneous Inscriptions of Assyria III* (London: R. E. Bowler, 1870), 5:6, 25f.; A. H. Layard, *Inscriptions in the Cuneiform Character from Assyrian Monuments discovered by A. H. Layard, D.C.L.* (London: Harrison and Sons, 1851), 98:2; E. Michel, "Die Assur-Texte Salmanassars III. (858–824). 6. Fortsetzung," *WdO* 2 (1954): 38.4:11; J. V. Kinnier-Wilson, "The Kurbail Statue of Shalmaneser III," *Iraq* 24 (1962): 94:29.

44. See P. Rost, *Die Keilschrifttexte Tiglat-Pilesers III. I* (Leipzig, E. Germany: E. Pfeiffer, 1893), 80:17f. Menachem ben-Gadi may not have been hostile to Rezin's anti-Assyrian coalition from the outset, despite this evidence.

45. M. Haran, "Biblical Topics," *Tarbiz* 37 (1967): 4f..

46. M. Cogan and H. Tadmor, "Ahaz and Tiglath-Pileser in the Book of Kings: Historiographic Considerations," *EI* 14 (1978): 55–61.

47. See H. Tadmor, "Autobiographical Apology in the Royal Assyrian Literature," in H. Tadmor and M. Weinfeld, eds., *History, Historiography and Interpretation* (Jerusalem: Magnes, 1983); cf. Mowinckel, "Königsinschriften" (n. 19), on Jehu; Liverani, "L'histoire" (n. 19), on Joash; T. Ishida, "Adonijah, the Son of Haggith, and his Supporters," in R. E. Friedman and H. G. M. Williamson, eds., *The Future of Biblical Studies* (Semeia Supplements; Decatur, GA: Scholars, 1987), 165–187 on 1 Kings 1–2.

CHAPTER 10

A Mythed Metaphor?
Miracle in Israelite
Historiography

There was ... no historian since the beginning of things who did not
profess that his sole aim was to present to his readers untainted and
unpainted truth. But the axiom was loosely understood and interpreted,
and the notion of truth was elastic. ... It would be a most fruitful
investigation to trace from the earliest age the history of public opinion in
regard to the meaning of falsehood and the obligation of veracity.

—J. B. BURY

NON-HISTORICAL LANGUAGE IN DtrH: THE UNHISTORICAL

The thesis of an antiquarian component in H(Dtr)'s work is not self-
evident. DtrH from the outset confounds it with miracles, with validated
vaticinations (1 Kings 13:2; 2 Kings 10:30), with regular divine revelation. Unmistakable exaggeration and contradictions[1] riddle our reports.
And there is actualization—Ehud speaks, Ahab pouts, Solomon de-
claims: does this not suggest the fictional (i.e., romantic) character of
DtrH?[2]

Most of this does not imply an abdication of antiquarian principles.
Contradictions have traditionally been imputed to the use of diverse
sources, or to a compulsion to reverse a source's claims. They are, in
fact, evidence of an antiquarian impulse. The sources were not all reliable. Displacement was common: the slaying of Goliath wanders from
Elhanan ben-Dodo to David (2 Sam. 21:19–21; 1 Sam. 17). 1 Samuel 24,
26 probably attribute to David the exploits of his heroes in 2 Samuel
23:17 (Chapter 3); the process was oral.[3] But the attempt to work with
such sources in no way implies falsification.

Even telescoping, a variety of exaggeration (as Sennacherib's death),
can come from sources: Joshua's massive conquest followed from promises in Genesis and Exodus, and from kerygmatic presentations of

Yhwh's "righteous acts." But H(Dtr)'s aim is not pure celebration: the Gibeonite treaty, in force in Saul's day (2 Sam. 21:1–14), belonged to the era because an old source (Josh. 10:12f.) located Joshua's climactic battle in the vicinity of Gibeon. Antiquarian interest mottled theological interest as much as the reverse.

H(Dtr)'s harmonizations, too, conform to historical logic (Chapter 8). Hagiographic tendencies are held in check. For example, one source claimed that David did not, after all, work for the Philistines (1 Sam. 21:11–16). Another (27:1ff.) confessed the asssociation, providing David with an alibi only for the battle of Gilboa (1 Sam. 30). H(Dtr) did not elect the first, more congenial, tradition. He placed the claims in a chronological sequence, according credence to both.

No doubt H(Dtr) is sometimes tendentious. This is most readily apparent in the recasting of Pentateuchal traditions (e.g., Chapter 8, n. 31). It shows up, too, in the selection: murders committed by David (Uriah), Ahab (Naboth), and Manasseh (unnamed—E[Dtr]x) are singled out among all the murders done by all the kings. Strictly speaking, as with omissions in Chronicles (David's civil war, Uriah, Adonijah), such data do not appear because they are not germane. What matters, say, in Josiah's reign is the history of his reform, not his other acts. Too, other ancient historians— such as Thucydides, in his antiquities—schematize quite as markedly. We may allow the point without prejudice to the historical character of the text.

Generally, H(Dtr)'s partisan distortion is minor, because the central events, whatever their causes, were given. If H(Dtr) believed, or hoped to persuade others, that baals and bāmôt caused misfortune, his interest lay in recalling real misfortunes. This is why the history of baal worship (see the section in Chapter 9 entitled "DtrH: A Cultic Interpretation of History") so sticks to the evidence, why the treatment of good and wicked kings is uneven. Our historian, and some of the authors whose work he used, believed that the evidence sustained their historical theses. Metahistory is the point of the history: it demands persuasive research.

In all this there is evidence for inaccuracy, for judgment with which a modern historian will differ. There is also evidence for conscientious research. Again, the sources for premonarchic times were not all that H(Dtr) (or we) could desire. Here, then, the historian enjoyed ample freedom. Yet he riddles his text with doublets and inconsistencies. All this is better explained on the hypothesis that H(Dtr) wrestled with his sources than it is on the hypothesis that he composed sheer fantasy in an inconsistent fashion. No Israelite narrator evinces an aesthetic predilection for self-contradiction. Had H(Dtr) concocted the history, he would have gone to the trouble of keeping it consistent.

What about the fact that God is a major player in DtrH? This element isolates us from H(Dtr)'s culture, from his "universe of suppositions." It calls into question, as we shall see, the antiquarian character of the history. How far has theology interfered with H(Dtr)'s history?

The problem does not arise when causation is complementary, as in interpretation not intended to be taken for witnessable event—the catch phrase "Yhwh raised up a savior" standing in for the processes by which a Baraq or a Jephthah might rise to command (see the section in Chapter 9 entitled "The Limitations of the History"). All other ancient Near Eastern literatures impute victory, for example, to gods, without denying that human agents took care of the mechanics. In DtrH Yhwh overthrows Sisera, but Israel fields the army, and its size and the quality of its disposition influence the outcome. Even Leopold von Ranke, the patron saint of positivist history, saw history as *der Gang Gottes in der Welt*, "the way of God in the world."[4] That this is the historian's metahistorical interpretation, rather than factual recitation, is a conclusion as available to ancient reflection as to modern. Where Yhwh intervenes through natural agencies, DtrH can and should be read as any other historiography is.

H(Dtr) expresses his theology, usually, in his portrayal of large periods, as in the frameworks of the book of Judges, or in epochal speeches, like those of Joshua 23–24 or 1 Kings 8. Here ultimate causes are laid bare, analysis is programmatic. These texts resemble the actualization, say, inside the Ehud story. Theological language and actualization are both metaphoric, nonliteral means to convey data or dramatize lines of interpretation.[5]

Examples are numerous. Ahab's pout over Naboth's negotiating posture represents—as much, or as little, to the ancient reader as to the modern—the historian's interpretation: Jezebel was in control, Ahab merely petulant. The episode takes place behind closed boudoir doors: all of it is concocted or, as we should prefer to understand it, reconstructed; the presentation is the reconstruction in action, all the proportions skillfully rendered to communicate reality as H(Dtr) sees it. In the telling, these metaphors undergo modal metamorphosis—insensitive hearers take them for literal reportage. But this is not necesssarily the teller's intention (Chapter 11).

That Thucydides applies this principle to speeches (1.22) is well known; these serve for characterization and for clarifying issues. The reader must understand the metaphoric character of the language. It is not marked off formally from all the other language in the history, which is why Thucydides makes a point of it in his preface. The only way to decipher it, therefore, is to decipher the teller's meaning, rather than the literal meanings of the teller's words.

Readers of this ilk are few. But to read history well, one must be more than a philologian or literary critic, one must be a psychologist. Historians, the ancients more so, do not always mean exactly what they write, in the sense that a molecular biologist sometimes does. Narrative history involves telling a tale—it demands fiction. It is an error to think that this makes the history romance (Chapter 1). Ask the historian— ask Thucydides—which elements are factual, which metaphoric or fanciful, and if he is a good historian, he will be able to tell you.

When H(Dtr) writes of "Israel" in Judges (Chapter 6, n. 20), when he writes that "half" of Israel supported Tibni and "half" Omri, when he writes that Joshua warned Israel against fraternization, he means the words no more literally than these: "Menachem smote Tiphsah . . . and cleft open all her pregnant women" (2 Kings 15:16). Menachem's army, perhaps, breached Tiphsah, and committed atrocities there. Why does the reader surmount the metaphor in this case, but trip over it in others? The problem is tricky. But how did H(Dtr) understand his own actualizations of events? Did he believe, in short, that Sisera had said, "I thirst?"

The language of revelation and actualization does not itself imply the ahistorical character of DtrH. It can be taken as metaphor. Some historians in antiquity are skeptical about the claims of the gods, yet relate them nonetheless. Thucydides is the prize example (especially 5.26). Polybius even describes an occasion on which Scipio attributes a tactic he has hatched to an incubation, in a variation of psychological warfare (10.11), to raise morale. Conversely, Xenophon and Livy endlessly tell stories involving the gods, very much like H(Dtr). This does not prejudice the antiquarian character of their work. In this arena we are not so far from good modern narrative history: a Parkman, or Macaulay, or Gibbon, or Carlyle fairly brim with actualization and other metaphoric art. These elements are part of the strategy of presentation (Chapter 1). The reader need only be skilled enough to recognize them, and they will cause no misapprehension.

THE PROBLEM OF MIRACLE

MIRACLE AND THE SOURCES

Of all the nonliteral language in DtrH, the type that most beclouds the history's antiquarian properties is the language of miracle. Miracle heightens the questions, To what extent did H(Dtr) distinguish what might really have happened and what assuredly did not? To what extent did H(Dtr) consciously insert falsehoods into his narrative in the hope that his readership, like Scipio's soldiery, would think it literally true? In applying these questions to miracle reports, one calls the author's sincerity legitimately into question. Did he believe that Joshua made the sun stand still? Did he hope that *we* would believe it?

Again, the problem does not arise in connection with divine activity through natural media—such as speech, oracles, omens, judgments (Yhwh "was angry"), and dual causation. The latter reflects habits of language and of historical interpretation: Yhwh determined events and expressed his reasons and purposes. The slaughtering angel in Sennacherib's camp, the role of Yhwh in the death of Bathsheba's first child:

these are editorializations in a religious mode of thought, of phrase, that do not exclude complementary causation. They are the language of religious and political conviction.

It is, therefore, the event that is not accomplished by natural means—the supernatural, the miraculous—that tests the limits of H(Dtr)'s antiquarianism. The phenomenon is not monolithic. When Xenophon rehearses the miraculous, the likely explanation is that the miracles come from sources, and this is also often true in DtrH. H(Dtr)'s references to the ten plagues belong to this category; no doubt there are examples in the Elijah-Elisha materials. In this respect the storytelling tradition and the cult converge—both furnish unhistorical data H(Dtr) incorporated in good faith.

Some of these sources may originally have been metaphoric. An example is the case of Joshua 10:12–13, where H(Dtr) misunderstands an old ditty about a favorable omen as a narrative about the sun stopped in its course.[6] Again, modal metamorphosis is in point—H(Dtr) treated such reified metaphor on the same plane with his other historical sources. This sort of explanation for a tradition occasionally appears in the scholarly journals.[7] The phenomenon is probably more common than we hypothesize.

This approach acquits H(Dtr) of jejune concoction. It places him in a class with Xenophon (and so on), taking over from the storytelling tradition the embellishment that arises from a generic indifference to reality. In Greece the reaction to this sort of historiography comes early (as Thucydides 1.9–11): Hecateus, Thucydides, even Hesiod, tax themselves to tell the "truth," to sort out the fanciful tales to which the Greeks give credence. It is their view that Greek poetry and myth have undergone modal metamorphosis; they have been canonized as literal truth (cf. Augustine on *The Iliad*), and must now be reinterpreted critically to get at the events.

This sort of modal metamorphosis is perhaps clearest in the reification of kinship language. Jephthah, for example, becomes Gilead's son by a harlot because he was landless, and the Gileadites were his "brothers" (Judg. 11:1–3). P may have made Aaron Moses' biological brother because he is his brother Levite in J (Exod: 4:14).[8] One critic plausibly suggests that J had originally no name for Moses' father-in-law (htn, Exod. 2:16, 21): E had Jethro as Moses' htn (3:1; 4:18; 18); another passage had Hobab as his htn (Num. 10:29 and Judg. 4:11, cf. G, Jethro in 1:16). Because two figures were identified as the htn, the term must mean "brother-in-law," not "father-in-law" (as Judg. 19:4, 7, 9), and the redactor therefore supplied the name Reuel as that of the father-in-law in Exodus 2:18 (< Num. 10:29). Genealogical relationships are of great moment in Israelite society—they are the essence of identity, and one must straighten them out in order to put each actor in his place. This is why the tendency to literalize this type of metaphor is so pronounced.

Not dissimilar is the fundamentalist's treatment of theological or meta-historical shorthand, where the language of divine causation is taken to exclude human causation ("Yhwh subdued Moab," "raised up a judge," "diverted the kingship to David").

Where H(Dtr) takes over materials from the storytelling tradition, he misprizes the whole nature of the source. The Elijah-Elisha cycle, thus, is not first-hand reportage. It cooks the bill of indictment about Naboth, just as it accuses Jezebel of doing. It defends Jehu's coup—and Elisha collaborates with Jehu's successor. The cycle is Nimshide, and H(Dtr) parrots its partisan vitriol, even to the extent of portraying Ahab as a weakling. The folklore is accorded equal weight, thus, with the chronicles. It is the probable source of fictionalization in such romances as 1 Kings 17–19; 20.[9] H(Dtr), like Xenophon, Aeschines, and Livy, approaches it uncritically.

THE DISTRIBUTION OF THE MIRACULOUS

The distribution of miracles in DtrH is uneven enough to confirm that most do come from sources. Infranatural divine action occurs with a certain regularity. Divine speech is perhaps less concentrated in 2 Kings (especially chapters 2–18; 23–25) than in other narrative segments of the history. The language of divine causation of human events, more evenly distributed, is markedly less frequent after Solomon's reign than before (Fig. 19). Still, no section of the corpus is devoid of explicit divine activity; the implicit assumption is that Yhwh is active throughout.

The situation with miracle—with divine action that overthrows rather than levers nature—is different. True, the category is fuzzy at the edges. A sudden thunderstorm, given as a sign (1 Sam. 12:18; 1 Kings 18:1, 41–45), lions serving as moral pedagogues (1 Kings 13:24; 20:36; 2 Kings 17:25; cf. 2 Kings 2:24, bears), a hailstorm at the impeccable moment (Josh. 10:10ff.), are things intrinsically mundane, whose providence coincidence authenticates. And, if in a thunderstorm, does Yhwh not speak through conquest, through Solomon's wisdom (1 Kings 5:9, 28), as plainly as through a resurrection (17:21f.)? Still, making allowance for the fact that H(Dtr) detects Yhwh's hand as tangibly in a drought as in the sun's standing still, a brief review is in order.

In Joshua three texts yield unmistakable evidence of Yhwh's manipulation: the currents of the Jordan cease, so that Israel can cross on dry land (3:14–17; 4:10–14); Jericho's walls inexplicably collapse (6:20); and the sun reins in, midcourse, to extend the Amorites' rout (with the hailstorm, 10:11–14). Each event marks a climax in the narrative.

In Judges miracles are less public and less central. Sudden fire consumes Gideon's sacrifice (6:21); in a more subdued, more public instance, he directs Yhwh how to distribute dew (6:36–40). An angel disappears (13:19f.); and Yhwh produces water for Samson in the desert (15:19). In contrast to Joshua, the episodes of divine salvation which compose the bulk of the book are remarkably clear of any but mundane political action.

The ark narrative in 1 Samuel 4–6; 2 Samuel 6 reports that Yhwh knocked down Dagon's statue (5:3–4), that the ark occasioned plague (5:6, 9; 6:19), and that Yhwh struck down a man who touched the ark (2 Sam. 6:7)—the last two remarkable only by dint of coincidence. Otherwise, 1–2 Samuel trade only indirectly in the supernatural. This is not so astounding in a work that emphasizes dual causation, the manipulation of human agencies (see the section in Chapter 9 entitled "Myopia and Selection in DtrH"). Only in the angelic plague of 2 Samuel 24:15–17, 25, ending with the acquisition of the temple precinct, does Yhwh act supernaturally.

Even this episode portrays Yhwh as employing natural means to do his work. Only revelation certifies the divine cause of the events. It is fitting, thus, that 2 Samuel 24 forms a preface to Solomon's reign. Yhwh treats Solomon to two epiphanies (1 Kings 3:5; 9:2). Arguably, the smoke at the temple's dedication is meant to be unnatural as well (8:10f.). Still, however profound the awe that suffuses these encounters between the human and the divine, however graphic 8:10f. may be (it plays on the incense and fire-altar in the nave), none affects the progress of events. These are the last direct epiphanies to Israel's leaders.

Worthy of contrast is the account in 1 Kings 13. Here Jeroboam's arm withers and is restored; the altar at Bethel cracks on cue; a lion kills a refractory prophet, then stands harmlessly with a donkey by the corpse (13:4–6, 24, 28). From this point, most of the miracles in Kings, numbering from twenty to thirty, relate to Elijah and Elisha (Fig. 19). Afterward there is one resurrection (2 Kings 13:21), but of a man hurled into Elisha's grave.

Elsewhere in 2 Kings, only a sign to Hezekiah—the recession of the shadow across Ahaz' steps (20:9–11)[10]—genuinely overflows the banks of nature. Lions prey upon the heathens Assyria transplants into Samaria (17:25)—again, it is coincidence that suggests divine manipulation. H(Dtr) portrays the plague in Sennacherib's camp as a miracle (2 Kings 19:35), as he or his source (a Hezekian dedication?) must have seen it. That something untoward did befall the beleaguerers—whether at Jerusalem or in the Philistine plain—is to be inferred from the fact that Hezekiah, alone among vassals besieged, forwarded his tribute to Assyria, rather than paying up on the spot.[11] Thus the text interprets a military catastrophe, possibly plague (common enough in camps—as late as 1870, when their Prussian opponents adopted and they rejected inoculation, the French army lost twenty thousand soldiers to smallpox). It reports unnatural causes, not unnatural events.

Except touching Hezekiah, there are no miracles in the regnal accounts of kings of Judah. From Rehoboam's time on, all pertain to Israel, or are related inside Israelite regnal accounts. The situation in Kings thus tallies with the uneven use of miracle throughout DtrH—with a heavy dose of public, climactic miracle in Joshua and the Elijah–Elisha cycles, and with sporadic, mostly minor, miracles in Judges and Samuel (in the latter, in cult-connected narrative). That no miracles occur in Josiah's reign is striking—and no miraculous (as distinct from divinely instigated) punishments result from the apostasy H(Dtr) reconstructs in Judges or in Kings.

The distribution suggests that most of the miracles stem from sources. The Elisha cycle provides confirmation. In 2 Kings 8:4f. an Israelite king invites Gehazi, Elisha's former aide, to regale him with tales of the prophet. This text situates the Elijah and Elisha cycles in their natural context, in a storytelling context, among northern kings. Ultimately, it insinuates, these tales come from eyewitnesses.[12] This is as much a deduction as it is a transmitted datum, more the reconstruction of a tradent than a recollection. Still, the text stands in for a source citation.

Here is an important clue to the provenience of miracles in DtrH. They come in their heaviest concentration (Elisha) when they come from oral sources. Misprision of lyric accounts for some—the sun's daylong sojourn at its zenith. But by and large they come from popular entertainments, from word of mouth. Significantly, no text in Kings even remotely proximate to a citation of the chronicles so much as hints at unnatural events or unnatural causes in a king's career. All this speaks for the thesis that H(Dtr) inherited most of the miracle stories; in good antiquarian style, perhaps, like Xenophon, a touch naively, he noted them down, dramatized and all.

It must be conceded that in dramatizing "true" causes—in introducing divine speech or divine causation—H(Dtr) decorates his history with the tokens of Yhwh's vigor. Such elements distinguish themselves by their content and their style from information H(Dtr) gleans from official sources (as the dated notices in Kings, Fig. 15). They are recognizable as conventions, promoting the author's vision of the historical drama. But they do not consciously distort the course of human political interaction. They enable H(Dtr) to manipulate cause and meaning without fabricating their result.

The stories H(Dtr) inherited about Elijah and Elisha were of a different genre, much closer to that of the early Christian gospel. Here mundane political history is not the heart of the matter. And in this genre, miracle—manipulated event—functions much like the language of divine causation in historiography. Like divine speech and divine causation, miracle is a form of editorialization. It certifies the author's views; it helps the reader identify characters and postures on which the deity smiles.

MIRACLE AND H(Dtr): 1 KINGS 13

If H(Dtr) invented miracles, his intention may be the same. It is unlikely that he concocted Hezekiah's plague (see the preceding section), or the story of the death of Jeroboam's son (1 Kings 14 [OG 12:24g–n]; cf. 2 Sam. 12:14–18). The latter account creates difficulty: its remark that "all Israel mourned" the child (14:18) confutes the prophecy in 14:7–14 that all in Jeroboam's house would go unentombed. The prophecy is a standard composition for northern kings (cf. 16:2–4; 21:[17]21–24) before the Nimshides. Its use in the story of the boy's demise necessitates the qualification that the lad would be exempted, "because in him among the house of Jeroboam is something good found" (14:13). This sort of wrinkle, and the fact that the story must find good in a condemned child, even though the themes of the history demand only the eradication of Jeroboam's house, suggests that a source has furnished the detail to H(Dtr)'s imagination.

H(Dtr) impressed a plainer thumbprint on 1 Kings 13, where the Bethel altar cracks to herald Josiah's destruction of the shrine. This account transforms the story of Josiah's reform from a workaday record of royal programs to a numinous, long-awaited depiction of Yhwh's Israelite, the future king, the savior of Judah and Israel. For this reason and because, for the purposes of this discussion, it is most disadvantageous to do so and thus poses a more formidable challenge to the thesis of this study, I propose to trace it to H(Dtr)'s own intelligence, not to an intact folktale into which Josiah's name was conveniently plugged.[13]

The author of this story, we may assume, knew it to be literally untrue. How, then, did he mean it—literally, as theological language, as metaphor expressing the dimension of Josiah's measures? Why did he render revelation into romance, instead of stating baldly, as in 13:33f., that Yhwh proposed to destroy Bethel and exile Israel, or that Yhwh sent a (nameless) prophet to denounce Jeroboam's deviations? Why did H(Dtr) create an elaborate structure, showcasing multiple tiers of revelation and obedience? Why did he refrain from inserting the prophecy into Ahijah's mouth in 1 Kings 14, or into Shemaiah's in 12:22–24?[14] H(Dtr) could have made the same point, perhaps with the same effect, in other ways. The question, thus, is not why he invented miracles in 1 Kings 13. The question is why he invented *this* story, and not some other. We have earlier examined the logic of reconstruction (chapters 3–8). How much more extended is the logic of concoction?

The thematic relations are transparent. Jeroboam's cult caused Israel's obliteration. Josiah removed the stigmata of the cult from Israel, in prospect paving the way for reunification under David's escutcheon. But Josiah could not destroy the calves—they had already been carried off; nor was he active as far north as Dan, having been restricted by Assyrian or allied control of the Jezreel to the central hills (2 Kings 23:19, 29). Unlike 1 Kings 12:28–30 and the polemic of Exodus 32 (which attacks Jeroboam's calves by condemning Aaron's),[15] Chapter 13 accordingly addresses neither Dan nor the calves. For similar reasons, 2 Kings 17 cites the calves almost incidentally in the catalogue of the northern kingdom's sins (2 Kings 17:16).

Further, if the cracking of the altar (1 Kings 13:3, 5) foreshadows Josiah's demolition of the high place (2 Kings 23:15), it is also an earnest (*môpēt*) of other events. Twin notices frame 1 Kings 13: Jeroboam ordained "priests . . . who were not Levites," "*bāmôt*-priests," in Bethel (12:31–33; 13:32–34). The prediction for which the altar's collapse stands in pledge (13:2) is that, on the altar, Josiah will burn these illegitimate priests.

1 Kings 13 spotlights Josiah's eradication of non-Levitic priests. 1 Kings 13:34 identifies them as the essence of Jeroboam's sin, toppling his dynasty and the nation. 1 Kings 13:32 (OG 12:31) links the priests to a network of high places (14:9, "other gods *and* 'molten images,' " suggests alien worship). These accusations may derive from the description of Bethel as a *bêt bāmôt*, "house of 'high places,' " a term liable to be construed as a singular or as a plural (12:31; v. 32 suggests singular); they reflect an urge to trace the cultic system Josiah uprooted to a single figure. In any case, 2 Kings 17:9–12 mentions the high places, not the priests, as a cause of the exile. But this is because the illegitimate priesthoods survive the exile: the chapter is at some rhetorical pains to establish the continuity between the pre-exilic establishment, with its multiple shrines and syncretistic proclivities, and the priesthoods of Samaria in the wake of Assyria's deportations (17:25–41). Josiah thus remedies a problem even Yhwh's exile left behind.

These verbal contortions validate the efficacy of Josiah's policy. In Judah, Josiah "brought the priests of the 'high places' " to Jerusalem, defiling *bāmôt* into the bargain. At Bethel, however, Josiah tore down the altar, and burned on it the bones of those interred in the precinct's hillside (2 Kings 23:15f.); elsewhere in Samaria he did the same, sacrificing "upon the altars all the priests of the 'high places' who were there" (23:19f.; cf. the section in Chapter 9 entitled "DtrH: A Cultic Interpretation of History"). These *bāmôt* are attributed to Israel's kings in general, not just Jeroboam. But the principle is clear. Jeroboam's heterogeneous, heterodox priestly caste nettled Yhwh; Josiah plugged the breach.

1 Kings 13 justifies Josiah's policy toward northern priests. 2 Kings 17 then links the time of Jeroboam and that of Josiah. The importance of this step is difficult to exaggerate: the calves gone, the population gone, were there no continuity in the cult, Josiah would be powerless to undo what Solomon and Jeroboam had together accomplished; he would be powerless to rehabilitate Israel into the Davidic fold. That he did so is central to the historian's argument (Chapter 7). 1 Kings 13, thus, is H(Dtr)'s vehicle for obscuring the discontinuity caused by exile, thrusting cultic continuity into the foreground, and articulating the moral import of Josiah's zeal.

All this constitutes a motive for packaging the message graphically. It does not explain why 1 Kings 13 emerged. Here another factor was primary. According to 2 Kings 23:16–18, there was in the Bethel cemetery the tomb of a "man of God," perhaps with a distinctive "marker," which, alone, Josiah's henchmen were ordered not to defile. The reason—the man of God had predicted Josiah's purge.[16] Eschew the explanation that a local tradition had it that the occupant of this grave anticipated Josiah's arrival: this would already account for much of 1 Kings 13. But the account insists that Josiah spared a single tomb. There was bound to have been a reason for this unexampled clemency; it is an explanation that H(Dtr) offers.

The tomb would have been spared only if a tradition, or the hope of fostering one, suggested that it contained a prophet, probably a Judahite, who inveighed against the Bethel cult. One such Judahite, Amos, *had* prophesied in Bethel, against Jeroboam II, the destruction of the sanctuary (7:9–17); his visions end with the apparition of Yhwh poised, at the altar, to sweep the underworld for those cringing from retribution (9:1ff., for which cf. Isa. 28:15–22; Job 14:13–19). Here we have all the elements of the prophecy in 1 Kings 13: 1) a Judahite prophet, forbidden to eat in Bethel (Amos 7:12), foretold, 2) the shrine's desecration, 3) focused on the altar, and 4) the ransacking of the surrounding tombs[17] 5) to Jeroboam (I or II). It is no less striking that H(Dtr) insistently calls the Judahite in 1 Kings 13 "the man of God," never "the prophet."[18] Amos, in the same episode, vigorously denies being a "prophet" (7:14), i.e., a trained professional.

Possibly, therefore, oral tradition imposed Amos' likeness upon a burial at Bethel. The tradition focused on the gravestone (2 Kings 23:16). H(Dtr) then took over a story Josiah's raiders had heard, and developed it. In favor of such an analysis is the fact that H(Dtr) neither names the man of God nor drags in some other, known figure (cf. 2 Chron. 12:15). Had he concocted the account, we might expect slightly more attention to this detail.

The other scenario stipulates that H(Dtr) was responsible for much more. As already noted, one object of 1 Kings 13 is to justify Josiah's drastic measures toward northern priesthoods.[19] H(Dtr), then, could have seized on a burial Josiah left undisturbed: it became the grave of a holy man who had, on the model of Amos, expressed Yhwh's will when the altar was first consecrated.

Either scenario would have left H(Dtr) with the kernel of 1 Kings 13. The elaboration bears all the marks of Josianic propaganda, yet all the marks of reason. His concoction here is as logical as his reconstruction elsewhere—his literary purpose supplying the place of evidence (as Judg. 1–3; 4). Specifically, H(Dtr) had to account for one problem: how was the inspired Judahite interred in Bethel, away from the familial care of his own home?

To protect the man of God against charges of depravity—leveled against no "true" prophet in DtrH—H(Dtr) wanted the Judahite to sin through no fault of his own. Apostasy, adultery, were out of the question. H(Dtr) had to circumscribe the Judahite's mission, and lead the Judahite to believe that the restrictions had been lifted. That the prophet should be enjoined against "returning on the way you came" was sufficiently resonant (e.g., Deut. 17:16; Amos 9:7 and 1:5; and "turn right or left") to fill the bill. An enjoinder against supping in Bethel, too, was lifted from Amos 7:12.

The man of God interprets the instruction to mean that he must return home by a route he did not take to Bethel (13:10). He recognizes, too, that it precludes his return to Bethel (13:17). Only a (false) prophecy validated by a claim of divine commission persuades him that his orders are superseded (13:19), with disastrous results (13:20–24). The Judahite does not see that abandoning his orders is also "going back" on his mission.

The mechanics of the narrative follow duly. Jeroboam—for the sake of narrative economy—invites the man of God to sup: H(Dtr) can now explain the restrictions on the Judahite (13:7–9)—not to eat there, not to double back. And Jeroboam's invitation appears to be the temptation the man of God must withstand, disarming him against future tests. Now why would Jeroboam invite a hostile prophet to dinner (cf. Amos 7:12f.)? The prophet must have interceded on the king's behalf—to heal a wound inflicted on the prophet's behalf. The logic behind 1 Kings 13 is that of the possible, not of the necessary—that of what might, not must, have been.

The elderly prophet of Bethel persuades the Judahite man of God to return, to eat, to violate his commission (13:19). The lion who kills the Judahite stands by the corpse (v. 24), not eating it, so that the prophet in Bethel will hear, and arrange the burial (13:25–30). The elderly prophet must be, in some measure, good to care for the corpse (13:20); though the narrator furnishes no motive for his countermanding the Judahite (13:18), the elderly prophet sees in the Judahite's fate proof of his inspiration, and foresees that his own bones will be safe from Josiah only in repose next to those of the man of God (13:31f.). He therefore provides the necessary burial.

1 Kings 13 thus meets the requirements of Josianic apologetic and of a logic premised on that apologetic. The text is not literal history-writing; it does not record developments that one might find in royal records; and it is not antiquarian, but elaborative— it details what might, not what must, have been. The elaboration legitimates Josiah's advent in the north.

In this sense, 1 Kings 13 is all editorialization, and recognizable as such. Its idiom is not that of divine revelation—"Yhwh charged Josiah, 'Go desecrate the tombs of Bethel!'" It employs the topos of prediction certified by fulfillment (as 1 Kings 14:7–14; 15:27–30)[20] and by miracle (as 2 Kings 20:9–11, fulfillment assumed). H(Dtr)'s insertion of prophecies need occasion no confusion about literal accuracy—they are speeches, editorialization. But miracle is different: readers may take the report literally; it may have been H(Dtr)'s hope that they *would* do so.[21] Here, however, H(Dtr)'s primary objective was to use available materials (the altar, the tomb) to anchor the ideological focus of his history. His principles generated the facts, rather than being collated with them. The "truth" of the particulars was secondary to the other "truth" being conveyed.

The miracle in 1 Kings 13 is a vein of expression through which courses the life's blood of historical judgment—in this case, on Jeroboam and Josiah. H(Dtr) could have written, "Yhwh resolved to destroy Jeroboam's priests, by the hand of Josiah, a Davidid." But the narrative in 1 Kings 13 (or 1 Kings 14, and so on) differs from editorialization, and from direct revelation (as Judg. 2:1–5), in the vividness with which it makes its point. It is editorialization actualized—actualization cobbled together by the historian (or, elsewhere, the storyteller). That no such miracle attends the account of Josiah's reign is probably more a function of fear that contemporaries would ridicule the claim than of H(Dtr)'s lack of desire to outfit that king with evidence of Yhwh's imprimatur. Here we have indications of prevarication—assuming always that local informants did not—as I think likely—mediate a refracted recollection of Amos to Josiah's henchmen at Bethel.

H(Dtr) is, however, a nervous liar, intensely conscious that nonliteral language played him and his audience false. Where he claims that Yhwh manipulated phenomena unnaturally, H(Dtr) cites sources (Josh. 10:10f., the Book of the Jashar) or concrete evidence (as the altar in Joshua 22). The phrase, "It is still there to this day," for example, occurs more or less in this form about thirty-nine times in the history. Among other things, it indicates that Yhwh's edicts were[22] or were not[23] fulfilled, and illustrates the consequences of failure to fulfill them.[24] A plurality of occurrences, however, certifies extraordinary or miraculous claims, accounts in which the supernatural figures prominently.[25] The distribution indicates a certain defensiveness about claims that Yhwh has mixed into human events.

This is one indication among several (see chapter 11) that H(Dtr) recognized a distinction between miracle and complementary causation through natural agencies. He may have understood that miracles in his sources were metaphorical; or he may have been naive. The ancients, like us, were uneven in their response to miracle stories. H(Dtr) at first blush seems an ingenue. He may, in fact, have been ambivalent.

The vast majority of miracles in DtrH were probably inherited from the folklore. Others were deduced by a misapprehension of metaphoric sources. H(Dtr) may have invented prophecies (as Josh. 6:26; Judg.

2:1–5; 1 Sam. 2:27–36; 1 Kings 11:11–13; 13:2; 14:7–16; 16:1–4; 21:20–24, 29; 2 Kings 10:30). But instances in which he confected miracles seem to have been few. In these cases we impugn the historian's sincerity. We should take care to temper our judgment. The miracles of 1 Kings 13 do not affect the course of national history, but color instead our interpretation of later events. They are thus not related as objects of scrutiny and knowledge in their own right; the contrast is to the event at the Reed Sea in P, or the heavenly phenomena of Joshua 10:10–14, and so on. The historian, in other words, can have meant them as a species of commentary; sensitive readers, too, can have taken them as such. Miracle, in this sense, helps us to hone our convictions. It teaches us no new beliefs, or we should reject it, but reinforces the prejudices we bring to the text. It offers, like all romance, an imitation, not a duplicate, of reality, a spur to reflection, to association, but not to historical judgment.

A more adversarial view deserves testing: H(Dtr) meant, when he wrote 1 Kings 13, to perpetrate lies on his readers. In that case—as opposed to cases of miracles the historian found in his sources—we may convict H(Dtr) for a cheat. But this is a tactic it will not do to overuse. 1 Kings 13 is an isolated instance: there may be others, but not in great numbers; and if they resemble 1 Kings 13, they will not have affected the course of H(Dtr)'s narrative. The historian may be presumed, thus, to prevaricate, in defense of his liege, Josiah. But nothing entitles or entices us to suppose that he was pathological about it.

FIGURE 19: THE LANGUAGE OF DIVINE ACTION IN DTRH

Keys: * = angelic speech; & = divine speech mediated by a prophet
% = sign for future; " = direct discourse (in theological language)
Y. = Yhwh

Speech = divine speech, through various media
Language = theological language, epiphanies, divine causation
Midway = natural events rendered providential by coincidence
Miracle = unnatural events

Speech	Language	Midway	Miracle
Joshua			
1:1–9			
	2:10f., 24 [Y. melts Canaanite hearts]		
3:7			
			3:14–17; 4:10–14 [Jordan crossed on dry land]
4:1–3, 15f.			
	4:4 [Y. magnifies Joshua]		

Speech	Language	Midway	Miracle
5:2, 9			
*5:14f.			
6:1–5			
			6:20 [Jericho walls fall]
	7:1 [Y. angry]		
		7:16–18 [Achan found out in lot]	
8:1f.			
10:8			
	10:10 [Y. discomfits]		
		10:11 [hail kills Amorites]	
			10:13f. [sun stands still]
	10:42 [Y. makes it lightning war]		
11:6			
	11:8 [Y. discomfits]		
	11:20 [Y. made Amorites fight and die]		
13:1–7?			
	19:50 [Y. gave town to Joshua]		
20:1–6			
	21:43–45 [Y. gave rest]		
	"23:4 [Y. fought for Israel]		
Judges			
1:2			
*2:1–3			
	2:14 [Y. angry]		
	2:14–16 [Y. sold Israel, raised judges]		
2:20–22			
	2:23 [Y. left testers]		
	3:7–10 [M+ cycle and spirit of Y.]		
	3:12–15 [M+ cycle]		
	4:1–3 [M+ cycle]		
	4:15 [Y. discomfits]		
	4:23 [cycle end]		
*5:23			
	5:20? [stars fight]		
	6:1ff. [M+ cycle]		
&6:8–10			
*6:12			
6:14, 16, 18			
*6:20			
			%6:21 [fire consumes Gideon's sacrifice]

Speech	Language	Midway	Miracle
6:23			
6:25f.			
	6:34 [spirit on Gideon]		
			%6:36–40 [dew on/off fleece]
7:2–4, 5, 7			
7:9–11			
			%7:13f. [Midianite dream overheard]
	"7:15 [Y. has wrought it]		
	"8:3, 7 [Y. gave victory]		
	9:23 [Y. foments revolt]		
	9:57 [Y. requites Abimelek]		
	10:6–16 [M+ cycle]		
10:11–14			
	11:28 [spirit on Jephthah]		
	11:32 [Y. gave victory]		
	13:1 [M+ cycle starts]		
	%"13:2–5 [angel predicts Samson]		
*13:3–5, 11, 13f., 16, 18			
	%"13:9–18 [angel predicts Samson]		
			%13:19f. [angel disappears]
	14:6 [spirit on Samson]		
	"15:18 [Y. gave "me" victory]		
			15:19 [Y. produces water in desert]
	"18:10 [Y. gave "you" Laish]		
&20:18, 23, 28 [oracles]			
	20:35 [Y. smites Benjamin]		
1 Samuel			
	1:19f. [Y. impregnates Hana]		
	2:21 [Hana's other children]		
	2:22–25 [Y. hardens Eli's sons' heart]		
&2:27–36			
3:4, 6, 8, 10			
3:11–14			
	"4:3, 7, 8 [Y. has smitten "us"]		
			5:3f. [Dagon's statue falls]
		5:6, 9, 11–12 [plagues]	
		6:9, 12 [ark route dovetails with plagues]	
		6:19 [plague for looking]	
	7:10, "12 [Y. defeats Philistines]		

Speech	Language	Midway	Miracle
8:8–9, 22			
9:12, 15f.			
		9:16f. [Saul comes to Samuel]	
&10:1–8			
			%10:9f. [Saul gets signs]
&10:18f.			
		10:18f. [Saul in lot]	
10:22 [oracle]			
	11:6 [spirit on Saul]		
	11:7 [awe musters Israel]		
	"11:13 [Y. gave victory]		
			%12:18 [thunderstorm]
			%14:8–12 [sign to Jonathan]
	14:15, 20 [Y. panics Philistines]		
14:16, 19 (G)			
	14:23 [Y. saved Israel]		
		14:36–43 [Jonathan in lot]	
&15:2f.			
&15:10f., 22f., 28f. [lines between Y. and Samuel blur here]			
16:1, 2f., 7, 12			
	16:13 [spirit on David]		
	16:14 [evil spirit on Saul]		
	"17:37 [Y. saved "me"]		
	"17:46f. [Y. will kill Goliath]		
	18:10–12 [Y. saves David from evil spirit]		
	18:12, 14, 28 [Y. with David]		
	"19:5 [Y. killed Philistines]		
	19:9f. [evil spirit incites Saul]		
		19:20–24 [Saul and others seized to prophesy]	
&22:5			
23:2, 4, 11f. [oracle]			
	23:14 [Y. loyal to David]		
	"24:4, 18 [Y. delivers Saul to David]		
	"25:26, 32, 34 (30) [Y. saved David]		
	25:38 [Y. smote Nabal]		
	26:8,"8, 12, "23 [Y. delivered Saul to David]		
	"&28:16–19 [Y. hates Saul]		
30:8 [oracle]			
	"30:23 [Y. gave "us" spoils]		
2 Samuel			
2:1 [oracle]			
	"3:9f., 18 [Y. chose David]		

Speech	Language	Midway	Miracle
	"4:8 [Y. killed Ishbaal]		
	"4:9 [Y. saved "me"]		
	"5:2 [Y. elected David]		
	5:10 [Y. with David]		
	5:12 [Y. with David]		
5:19, 23f. [oracle]			
	5:20 [Y. kills Philistines]		
	6:7 [Y. angry]		
		6:7 [Y. kills Uzza]	
	6:11 [Y. blesses Obed-Edom]		
	"6:21 [Y. chose me]		
	7:21 [Y. gave rest]		
7:5–16			
	8:6, 14 [Y. succored David]		
	"10:12 [may Y. save "us"]		
	11:27 [Y. angry] >		
&12:1–4, 7–12			
		12:15 [Y. smites infant]	
	12:24 [Y. loved Solomon] >		
&12:25			
	? <=	13–15 [events leading to Absalom revolt manipulated to fulfill 12:7–12]	
	"15:25f. [If Y. likes "me"]		
	15:31–37 [David asks Y.'s help, solicits Hushai's]		
	"16:8 [Y. has repaid blood]		
	"16:10–17 [Y. incited Shimei]		
	"16:18 [Y. elected Absalom]		
	? <=	16:20–23 [Absalom, on Ahitophel's godlike counsel, beds concubines, = 12:7–12]	
	?<=	17:1–18 [David survives, = 12;13; 15:25f., 31; 16:10–12]	
	?<=	17:14 [Y. punished Absalom]	
	"18:19 [Y. acquitted David]		
	"18:28 [Y. acquitted David]		
	"18:30 [Y. acquitted David]		
	21:1 [famine]		
21:1 [oracle]			
		21:14 [Y. appeased, famine lifts]	
	22:1 [Y. saved David]		
	22:5–21 [lyric]		
23:3–4			
	23:5 [covenant with David]		
	23:10 [Y. saved]		

Speech	Language	Midway	Miracle

	23:12 [Y. saved]		
	24:1 [Y. incited David]		
&24:11–13			
	? <=	24:15f. [plague on and off]	
	24:17 [David sees angel]		
			? 24:17
&24:18 (+ 19)			
		24:25 [Y. placated, plague lifts]	

1 Kings

	"1:37 [May Y. do to Solomon]		
	"1:47 [May Y. do to Solomon]		
	"1:48 [Y. enthroned Solomon]		
	"2:4 [let Y. keep faith]		
	"2:15 [Y. chose Solomon]		
	"2:24 [Y. chose "me"]		
	2:27 [Solomon fulfills 1 Sam. 2:27ff.]		
	"2:32–34 [Yhwh executes Joab]		
	"2:44 [Yhwh traps Shimei]		
	3:5 [Solomon sees Yhwh]		
3:5			
	"3:6 [Y. enthroned "me"]		
3:11–14			
	3:28 [Solomon's wisdom divine]		
	5:9 [Y. gave Solomon wisdom]		
	"5:17–19 [Y. gave rest, etc.]		
	"5:21 [Y. gave David heir]		
	"5:28 [Y. gave Solomon wisdom]		
6:11–13?			
		8:10f. [Smoke in temple]	
	"8:15–24 [Y. fulfilled 2 Sam. 7]		
	"8:56 [Y. gave rest]		
	9:2 [Y. appears to Solomon]		
9:3–9			
	"10:9 [Y. enthroned Solomon]		
11:11–13			
	11:14, 23 [Y. raised thorns]		
&11:31–39			
	12:15 [Y. incited Rehoboam]		
&12:23f.			
&13:2f.			
			13:4f. [Jeroboam's arm withers, altar cracks]
			13:6 [arm healed]

Speech	Language	Midway	Miracle
&13:21f.			
		13:24 [lion kills prophet]	
			13:28 [lion stands with donkey]
14:5			
&14:7–16			
		14:17f. [infant dies per vv. 7ff.]	
	15:4f. [Y. left fief]		
	15:28 [Baasha acts per 14:7ff.]		
&16:1–4			
	16:11–13 [Zimri acts per 16:1–4]		
		17:1 [Elijah proclaims drought]	
17:2–4			
		17:6 [ravens feed Elijah] => ?	
17:8f.			
			17:12–16 [endless food supply]
&17:14			
			17:21f. [resurrection]
18:1			
			18:38 [fire takes Elijah's sacrifice]
		18:41–45 [Y. ends drought, per 18:1]	
	? <=	18:45 [Elijah outruns Ahab's chariot to Jezreel]	
*19:5, 7			
19:9, 11, 13, 15–18			
&20:13, 14			
	20:16–21 [victory per 20:13f.] => ?		
&20:22			
	20:26 [invasion per 20:22]		
&20:28			
		20:30 [wall kills Arameans]	
&20:35-37			
		20:36 [lion kills per 20:36]	
&20:39f., 42			
21:17–19			
&21:20–24/26			
21:28f.			
&22:6?			
&22:15, 17, 19–23, 25, 28			
	22:34f. [king dies per 22:17, 19–23]		
	22:38 [dogs lick Ahab's blood per 21:24]		

Speech	Language	Midway	Miracle
2 Kings *1:3f.			
			1:10, 12 [fire consumes Ahaziah's soldiers]
*1:15 &1:16			
	1:17 [Ahaziah dies per 1:3f.]		
			2:8 [Elijah divides Jordan] 2:11f. [Elijah's assumption seen] 2:14 [Elisha divides Jordan] 2:21f. [Elisha heals waters]
		2:24 [Bears rip up children]	
	3:15 [Y.'s hand on Elisha]		
&3:16–20			
		3:22f. [water misleads Moab]	
			4:3–7 [Elisha generates oil]
		4:17 [aged woman has son per 4:16]	
	"4:27 [Y. "hid" illness from "me"]		
			4:33–35 [resurrection] 4:41 [Elisha detoxifies stew] 4:43f. [Elisha feeds multitude]
&4:43			
	5:1 [Y. saved Aram]		
			5:14 [Elisha cures Naaman] 5:26f. [Elisha transfers leprosy to Gehazi] 6:5f. [Elisha raises axehead]
	6:8–10 [Elisha warns of Aram] => ?		
			6:14-20 [Elisha blinds Aram]
	6:17 [Y. opens aide's eyes] 6:32 [Elisha foresees arrest]		

Speech	Language	Midway	Miracle
&7:1			
	7:6f. [Y. spooked Aram's army]		
	7:16–20 [food cheap per 7:2]		
&8:10, 13			
	8:15 [Hazael king per 8:13]		
	8:28 [Hazael terrorizes Transjordan per 8:12]		
&9:3, 6–10, 12			
	9:25f. [Jehoram killed per 1 Kings 21:21–26]		
	9:33–37 [Jezebel dies per 1 Kings 21:21–26]		
	10:10f., 17 [Jehu kills Omrides per 1 Kings 21:21–26]		
	10:25–27 [Jehu kills Baalists, per 1 Kings 19:15–18]		
10:30			
	10:33 [Hazael attacks per 8:12]		
	13:3 [Y. angry] >		
	13:3 [Aramean oppression]		
	13:4f. [Y. forgives > saves]		
	13:17–19 [Elisha promises victory]		
			13:21 [resurrection]
	13:23–25 [Y. pities > saves]		
14:6 [< Deut]			
	14:25ff. [Y. pities > restores]		
	15:5 [Y. smote Azaryah with leprosy]		
	15:12 [Jehu's 4th generation succeeds per 10:30f.]		
	15:37 [Y. sent Rezin against Jotham]		
	17:7–23 [Y. exiled Israel for sin]		
17:12 [< Deut]			
		17:25 [lions kill Assyrian transplants until priest arrives]	
	18:7f. [Y. with Hezekiah]		
	18:12 [Y. exiled Israel]		
18:25 [per Rabshakeh]			
&19:21–34			
		19:35 [plague in Assyrian camp]	
	19:37 [Sennacherib murdered]		
&20:1			
20:5f.			
	(Hezekiah vouchsafed life)		
			%20:10f. [shade recedes]
&20:16–18			
21:4 [quotation]			
21:7f. [< 1 Kings 9:3; 2 Sam 7:10]			
&21:10–15			
	"22:13 [Y. angry with "us"]		

Speech	Language	Midway	Miracle

&22:15–20

 23:15–18 [Josiah acts per 1 Kings 13:2-5]
 23:26 [Y. angry >]

23:27

 24:2–4 [Y. sends plunderers per 21:10–15; 21:16]
 24:13–16 [exile per 20:17f.]
 24:19f. [Y. incited Zedeqiah to evil]
 25 [exile, per 21:10–15; 22:15-17; 23:26f.]

Annotations:

1. The categories blur one into the other, and the distribution is not meant as a rigid one (though it does, to my mind, reflect gradations in the use of the language). The object of the exercise, however, is to expose the overall pattern of divine activity in DtrH.

2. Note the clusters: of miracle, particularly in the Elisha material, of divine speech, mediated or direct, between Elisha and Josiah, and so on. "Midway" instances can occur without divine speech, and the language of divine causation, of complementary causation, predominates in Judges, for example, and Samuel. Compare the even distribution of the genres in Joshua with their fitful intermixture elsewhere.

Notes to Chapter 10

1. As the constituents of Solomon's press (Chapter 7), or Joshua 11:21f.; Judges 1:20 on the Anaqim.
2. B. O. Long, "Historical Narrative and the Fictionalizing Imagination," *VT* 35 (1985): 405–16.
3. In a literary example, OG to 1 Kings 12:24aff. shifts Ahijah's oracle to Jeroboam (1 Kings 11:26–40) onto Shemaiah: Ahijah condemned Jeroboam (1 Kings 14); Shemaiah deterred Rehoboam from attacking him (12:22–24). OG, which adds numerous details (as the name of Jeroboam's wife), also removes the oracle to the time after Solomon's death: in MT Ahijah prophesies in Solomon's twenty-fifth year, and Jeroboam must wait sixteen years for the oracle to be fulfilled.
4. A lucid exposition of Ranke's theology of history is C. A. Beard's "That Noble Dream," *American Historical Review* 41 (1935): 74–87.
5. Similarly, Long, "Historical Narrative" (n. 2).
6. J. S. Holladay, "The Day(s) the *Moon* Stood Still," *JBL* 87 (1968): 166–78.
7. See latterly, Z. Zevit, "Archaeological and Literary Stratigraphy in Joshua 7–8," *BASOR* 251 (1983): 23–35; *idem*, "The Problem of Ai," *BAR* 11 (1985): 58–69, with the story derived from the abandoned Iron I ruins with collapsed EB fortifications, and reinterpreted theologically.
8. See B. Halpern, "The Resourceful Israelite Historian," *HTR* 76 (1983): 398f., with further cases and bibliography; for the next case, cf. B. W. Bacon, "JE in the Middle Books of the Pentateuch: Analysis of Ex. i.–vii.," *JBL* 10 (1891): 107–30, especially 111f.
9. See Long, "Historical Narrative" (n. 2).
10. For the structure see Y. Yadin, "The Steps of Ahaz," *EI* 5 (1958): 91–96.
11. Among others, see J. J. M. Roberts, "Isaiah 33: An Isaianic Elaboration of the Zion Tradition," in C. L. Meyers, M. O'Connor, eds., *The Word of the Lord Shall Go Forth* (Fs. D. N. Freedman; Winona Lake: Eisenbrauns, 1983), 15–25, especially 20. The effort of Roberts to show from Isaiah 18:13–17ff. that Sennacherib reneged on an earlier agreement is forced.
12. Cf. A. Lemaire, "Vers L'histoire de la Rédaction des Livres des Rois," *ZAW* 98 (1986): 232, n. 52, who identifies the king in 2 Kings 8:4 (against the chronology of Kings) as a Nimshide. This is probably correct.
13. See on 1 Kings 13, W. E. Lemke, "The Way of Obedience," in F. M. Cross, P. D. Miller, and W. E. Lemke, eds., *Magnalia Dei: The Saving Acts of God. Essays in Memory of G. Ernest Wright* (Garden City, N.Y.: Doubleday, 1976), 301–26. Lemke shows that the chapter is integral to the history, and reviews efforts to discern an old folktale behind the text.
14. This would have helped streamline the Jeroboam saga, along the lines of the recension in OG. See J. C. Trebolle Barrera, *Salomón y Jeroboán. Historia de la recension y redaction de I Reyes 2–12, 14* (Bibliotheca Salmanticensis, Dissertationes, 3; Salamanca: Universitas pontificalis, 1980) for a discussion of the text and its evolution.
15. See F. M. Cross, *Canaanite Myth and Hebrew Epic* (Cambridge: Harvard University, 1973), 195–215; J. Wellhausen, in F. Bleek, *Einleitung in das alte Testament* (4th ed.; Berlin: Reimer, 1878), 561f.; further references in Deuteronomy 9:16, 21; Hosea 8:5f.; 10:5, 11; 13:2, Psalm 106:19; Nehemiah 9:18; especially 2 Kings 10:29 and 2 Chronicles 11:15; 13:8.
16. Read OG(G_L) in 23:16, "He defiled it according to Yhwh's word, which the man of God called out when Jeroboam stood at the altar on the festival. And Josiah

turned and lifted his eyes to the grave of the man of God who called these words," much of which is lost to MT by homoioteleuton.

17. For the related implications of Isaiah 28:15ff. (and, by extension, Amos 9:2), see B. Halpern, " "The Excremental Vision': The Doomed Priests of Doom in Isaiah 28," *HAR* 10 (1986): 109–21.

18. 1 Kings 13:1, 4, 5, 6 *bis*, 7, 8, 11, 12, 14 *bis*, 21, 26, 29, 31. Only v. 18 violates the rule ("I, too, am a prophet like you"). Verse 23, "the prophet who induced him to return," refers to the Samarian prophet (cf. vv. 20, 25). Nor is this solely a ploy to distinguish the Samarian "prophet" from the Judahite "man of God." The same aim could be accomplished by the formulation of vv. 20, 23, 25, or by that of v. 26 ("the old prophet") or by stipulating place of origin ("the prophet from Samaria/Judah"). The imprint of Amos was first detected by Wellhausen (Bleek, *Einleitung* [n. 15], 244), but not systematically examined.

19. For a parallel to the scenario, see A. L. Oppenheim, "The City of Assur in 714 B.C.," *JNES* 19 (1960): 133–47.

20. On this renowned feature of Deuteronomistic historiography, see N. Wyatt, "The Old Testament Historiography of the Exilic Period," *Studia Theologica* 33 (1979): 45–67, especially 56–62. For close parallels, see A. K. Grayson, *Babylonian Historical–Literary Texts* (Toronto Semitic Texts and Studies 3; Toronto: University of Toronto, 1975), 13–39.

21. J. Gray (*I & II Kings* [2nd ed.; Philadelphia: Westminster, 1975], 320ff.) and M. Noth (*1. Könige* [BKAT 9/1; Neukirchen: Neukirchener, 1968], 295) take v. 5 as the reification of a v. 3 (Gray) originally directed toward the distant future.

22. Joshua 5:9; 7:26 *bis*; 8:28, 29; 10:27; 14:14; Judges 1:26; 6:24; 10:4 (= Deuteronomy 3:14); 1 Kings 9:21; 2 Kings 10:27.

23. Joshua 9:26; 13:13; 15:63; 16:10; Judges 1:21, all on Amorites' survival.

24. 2 Kings 16:6; 17:23, 34, 41. Otherwise, Judges 18:12; 1 Samuel 27:6; 30:25; 2 Samuel 4:3; 18:18; 1 Kings 9:13; 10:12; Edom in 2 Kings 8:22; 14:7; 16:6.

25. Joshua 4:9; 5:9; 6:25; 7:26 *bis*; 8:28, 29; 10:27; Judges 6:24; 15:19; 1 Samuel 5:5; 6:18; 2 Samuel 6:8; 1 Kings 8:8; 12:19 (fulfilling Ahijah's prophecy); 2 Kings 2:22. The cases in Samuel (with miracle) all come inside the "ark narrative."

CHAPTER 11

The Israelite Historian:
Lyrical or Logical?

We know all about the habits of the ant, we know all about the habits of
the bee, but we know nothing at all about the habits of the oyster. It seems
almost certain that we have been choosing the wrong time for studying
the oyster.

—PUDD'NHEAD WILSON'S CALENDAR

A POET AND NOT A HISTORIAN

One tactic scholars adopt to deny the historiographic character of the
Former Prophets has been to reject the distinction made in the preceding chapter (see the section in Chapter 10 entitled "Miracle and H(Dtr):
1 Kings 13") between accounts of miracle and more quotidian reports.
The Israelites, thus, confused the two: they took metaphorical, theological language as literally as they did mundane descriptions of royal administration. They had no notion that the truths communicated in a text
such as Genesis 1 or Genesis 2–3 concerned the nature of Yhwh and the
cosmos, rather than how they came into being, but the truths communicated in Judges 4 concerned the concrete mechanics of a triumph over
the Canaanite hosts.

The import of this view is plain. Israelites were incapable of understanding text as a response to specific concerns. They were generically
unequipped to interpret figurative language. Further, when they wrote
about events in the past, they used figure or myth, with no concept of
authentic history, no capacity to reproduce the past as past. They were,
in Levy-Bruhlian terms, logical primitives who could not make the distinction between events to which language might refer and the language
and imagination which made reference to those events.

Such assertions tend to focus on the Pentateuch. They spill over onto
DtrH, in the main, when their authors work themselves up to generalization. Some are relatively benign. F. M. Cross, for example, states that
Israelites (scil., in the Pentateuch) did not distinguish myth from history—lacking the categories, they meant to write neither.[1] A whole school

of scholarship of late tears the label *history* from biblical historiography, and substitutes that of *story* or *prose fiction*— based on the presence of romance and, naively, of fiction in the presentation (cf. Chapter 1).[2] The argument is that historians, concerned with event, would not trouble themselves to shape narrative(!).[3]

Much the same is the view from anthropology. J. R. Goody and I. Watt report that Thucydides first introduced the cloisson into a chiaroscuro of myth and history, "a distinction to which little attention is paid in non-literate society." Oral transmission, runs the argument, obliterates those perspectives on the past which it has recast or discarded; non-literate communities, therefore, must reconstruct the past from recent recensions. They are condemned to take literally claims originally made—in language about the past—about contemporary conditions. Thus genealogies, which are " 'charters' of present social institutions," myths, which authorize political and lineage relations, undergo in oral cultures what I have earlier called modal metamorphosis—their metaphoric content is depleted; they are reduced to literal claims about the past. Only with the advent of literacy, say Goody and Watt, does a Hecateus arise to criticize the stock of Hellenic lore as "ridiculous," self-contradictory. Literacy exposes the contradictions inherent in an accretion of restructurings of the past to suit successive changed presents—the proverbial rewriting of history in every generation. The logical problem of mutual contradiction arises from preserving all the successive texts. The result is the birth of scientific skepticism.[4]

This evaluation is not wrongheaded, but exaggerated. The Greeks begin to systematize genealogy and myth at least with Hesiod, effectively in a preliterate era.[5] Still, Goody's and Watt's analysis dovetails with Cross's views. It applies to all information transmitted orally, even within a literate environment, such as ancient Israel.[6] The Pentateuchal lore, the Elijah and Elisha tales, the course of the conquest, all came to our literate historians out of the oral tradition or out of cultic metaphor, whose properties resemble those of the oral folklore.

This view is reasonably charitable: metaphor is taken literally in contexts where the distinction has no functional value—in the cult, in folklore, it little matters whether miracles occur or just what Jacob said. Some biblicists, however, adopt a more extreme line to disarticulate recollection from reality. The case is made, in fact, that Israel *could* not tell myth from history. Its classic formulation comes from G. Widengren.

Widengren observed that from Genesis forward, creation flows into ancestral lore, then into a history ending in Kings. The story is linear. But, as in Babylon, where the creation epic is unrepeatable and includes the foundation of Babylon, "myth is followed by history" without any discontinuity. Similarly, the psalms celebrate historical and mythical events side by side—creation, primordial battles, alongside mundane triumphs (as Ps. 95:5, 8ff.; 89:10ff.; 136; 148). And Israel's enemies are at once political and mythic—Egypt, for example, is identical with the monster Rahab (Ps. 87:4; Isa. 30:7; 51:9f.). Myth and history are one.[7]

Such arguments have carried weight, and now echo through the literature.[8] They demand qualification. First, that the authors of the Pentateuch did not separate myth from history does not imply that their contemporaries could not. As observed in Chapter 8, the redaction of the Pentateuch reflects precisely a historical concern in Goody's and Watt's terms: it makes of the conflation a logical, uncontradictory version of events. Indeed, even where H(Dtr) and R_{JEP} juxtapose contradictory sources, they are no less historically logical than the church fathers who (see the section in Chapter 2 entitled "The Bible Under the Microscope: Rebels for Reason") saw the contradictions, but remained certain no contradiction was there (and cf. Frontinus I.iv.9–9a).

Second, one cannot conclude from, say, J's decision to write national epic an ineptitude at historical thinking. The author of a myth communicates devotional truths, truths knowable through revelation, but not observation. So Genesis 1, for example, differs from historiography in that it is not the only or most probable portrait of creation. It makes claims of truth and validity, primarily at a thematic level, about Yhwh and cosmic order; the themes, not evidence of events, father the particulars of the reconstruction. In this account, then, the author chooses not to write history, in order to address questions that fall outside the scope of antiquarian concern. This is not evidence, however, of a cultural incapacity to address antiquarian issues.

Third, Widengren's case rests on the literature of the cult. In the temple the psalmodic cocktail of mythic and historical elements assumes the timbre of reality. Myth recurs— in Israel and in Babylon—so that the worshiper participates in the deity's primal benefices. The event of creation, like the first Eucharist, was unrepeatable. In cultic action, however, the distinction between the "historical event" and its timeless, eternal recurrence, disintegrates—it is not blurred, but transcended— and the worshiper is assumed into a sacred, ethereal dimension.

In the cult, myth denies the opposition between itself and history, or falls by definition into the category of romance. Westerners, who tote their cults around in their heads—in beliefs, in faith—therefore cling to the literal construction of sacred text. In Israel cultic action translated Rahab onto a plane of professed reality. Still, the very equation of Rahab with Egypt implies a consciousness of the distinction between them: the equation lends to Israel's prosaic struggle with a mundane foe the dimensional panoply of Yhwh's cosmogonic wars. This equation obtains in the temple, where the distinction between myth and history was irrelevant (and remains so today), and perhaps in the minds of an Israelite army (cf. Scipio's troops). But it is a local truth, like most myth: outside the temple, after the battle, its work is done, its validity attenuated. Widengren does not show that cultic convention suffused Israelite minds in every walk of life. Indeed, if it did, how did our confused Israelites produce their history of David's accession and reign, and of Solomon's succession? How did they construct a reliable account of the welfare of the Davidides in Judah—one in which the supernatural is so wraithlike in its role?

Fourth, Widengren's evidence—and Cross's, and Goody's and Watt's—can be distilled down to one point: the easy mixture of genres, of mythic and historical claims, in Israelite and other primitive literatures. Where, asks the reader, does one leave off and the other start? Answers the scholar: there is no line between them. Our problem, in sum, is that miracle and murder, myth and history, are presented in the same language, the same syntax. There is no formal difference between them.

This is the problem Thucydides addresses—that father of historical consciousness—when, in his prologue, he tags his speeches as the works of a disciplined imagination (1.22; see the sections in Chapter 10 entitled "Nonhistorical Language in DtrH: The Unhistorical" and "The Distribution of the Miraculous"). History is fictional and employs the devices of all narrative presentation. But the modern critic—Widengren, for instance—distinguishes myth from history not by its form, but by its content. It takes a twisted syllogism to conclude that the ancient Israelite could not do the same. Actualization might create confusion in this or that instance. The audience, whether Thucydides' or Hecateus', knew, nonetheless, that elements of actualization and interpretation existed on a plane different from that of factual claims.

Fifth, there is, in practice, abundant evidence that the Israelites did distinguish myth from history, fact from factitious convention. Thus inscriptions corroborate H(Dtr)'s claims about domestic and foreign affairs (see the section in Chapter 9 entitled "Concrete Evidence of Sources"). Further, H(Dtr) repeatedly cites annalistic sources as repositories of data about royal achievements, especially in building and war; nearby come notices, probably from the same sources, about all this, and plots and illnesses (the "supplementary notes"; see the section in Chapter 9 entitled "Chronicles of the Kings of Judah/Israel"). Never once does H(Dtr) appeal to these documents as sources for miracles or divine deeds— this despite a penchant for providing evidence to sustain his claims about such events (see the section in Chapter 10 entitled "Miracle and H(Dtr): 1 Kings 13"). Evidently someone in Israel managed to compile historical records without an admixture of myth—or, what is less probable, H(Dtr) isolated the purely historical from a mixed source.

Even our poor stock of Israelite inscriptions perplexes Widengren's thesis. It includes lists of names, lists of payments, dockets from the conduct of taxation or commerce, and other administrative relics. Among surviving letters, some of them military reports, is a judicial plea, which tells us nothing we should not, sensibly, deduce: a whole apparatus of private (cf. Jer. 32:10–14) and public administration was in place probably by David's, and certainly by H(Dtr)'s, time.

No one has yet suggested that the scribes who wrote or the officials who interpreted such documents lacked a sense of history or myth. Where the difference was functional—in certain literary or administrative settings—the two were kept apart; the distinction was demanded, if nothing else, in legislation against perjury, where figurative language expressing thematic truths, imitating, rather than duplicating, reality— and incidentally impugning one's mother-in-law for apostasy—was proscribed.

Myth had its immediacy outside of the quotidian world of tax receipts, law codes, and debts. Perhaps Widengren would respond that narrative history does not relate to evidence as a tax receipt to goods in hand. But both, like the trial process, involve discovering what happened in the past, in this world (Chapter 1). The very records that even van Seters concedes must ultimately underlie DtrH, such as monuments, memorials, and chronicles, presuppose an ability to differentiate the genres; even if they sometimes found Yhwh's finger in events, they cannot have skewed too sharply from the realities they purported to commemorate (see the section in Chapter 9 entitled "Limited and Occasional Sources"). The Mesha stone, like DtrH, merges theological language with historical reportage in the most delicate, correct fashion. It is no coincidence, thus, that the only Iron Age mythological text found in Israel's environs was written on the walls of a temple.[9] Myth and history belonged not just to different intellectual or economic realms, but to different spatial ones as well: they were local, restricted, genres of thought and literature.

Israel was not unique in this respect, but resembled its neighbors, as a glance at the corpus of West Semitic inscriptions will reveal. Further east, the Assyrians developed a rich historiographic tradition. Their annals sometimes refer to the past, even to distant predecessors; except to cannibalize it for imagery, however, they never refer to the mythic past. They treat the events of mundane history on a different plane from those of myth—even of myth ostensibly in human time, like the epics of Erra and Gilgamesh. Even omen texts segregate the genres. The parallel in Kings is the treatment of no event before the exodus as a historical quantity.

Mesopotamian records do differentiate types of historical literature by form. There are remains of several epics about kings: unlike the annals, they incorporate dialogue and take the form of poetry.[10] An intermediate category, in epic style, is that of "letters to the god," sent to Asshur by several neo-Assyrian monarchs.[11] The difference between the annals and the other, more elevated compositions is one of genre, and of the degree of detail and conscious actualization: the annals are generally more skeletal. Even in different editions of these, considerations of space, or interest in the gist of the king's career rather than in exact chronology, lead to the telescoping of details.[12] Too, hints such as change of person in narration (first to third or vice versa) indicate that scribes employed various sources when preparing new inscriptions.[13] That is, they reworked sources to fit the literary task at hand. The epics may bear a similar relation to the official accounts underlying the annals.[14] In sum, the scribes, writing history to an end, recognized, in effect, the difference between reductions of history and romanticizations of it. In Assyria these were different literatures—one prose, one poetic.

This general picture should surprise no one. There is evidence of a distinction in Israel as well. Even H(Dtr) is relatively free of confusion between the two genres. He introduces supernatural causation, but very rarely unnatural events. One instance is emblematic: in Judges 4 the prose author does not attribute Israel's victory to miracle. Yet what text would more easily lend itself to the interpretation that Yhwh brought a flash flood upon the enemy than Judges 5:21, "The Wadi Qishon swept them off"?

METAPHOR AND GENEALOGY—A PSEUDO-HISTORICAL LANGUAGE

All this is not to say that the Israelite distinguished infallibly between myth and history, between literal and figurative language. Cases in which poetic language was misinterpreted as literal have already been examined (Judg. 4f.; Josh. 10:13f.). A general sense of the difference does not translate into discernment in particular instances, and H(Dtr)'s heavy reliance on the oral cycle about Elijah and Elisha shows that his tolerance for the language of miracle was healthier, or, perhaps, more ingenuous, than ours.

Here the Israelite again differs little from his modern counterpart. Paul Haupt, for example, was a scholar who certainly understood the difference between metaphor and literal discourse. Yet Haupt took quite literally the poetic modes of expression in which the revelation at Sinai and the collapse of Jericho's walls were couched: they implied volcanic and seismic action, respectively.[15] Now the fire and smoke over Sinai may refract ideas of volcanic fury; Jericho's collapse may resemble an earthquake's effects. But the descriptions are metaphorical, evoking numinous, not mundane, causes. Like Haupt and like many modern religionists, H(Dtr) sometimes erred in construing the sources' metaphor; like Haupt and like Haupt's modern colleagues, H(Dtr) sometimes did not err.

What is it that leads the ancient Israelite and the modern critic alike into occasional confusion? Not, of course, the prelogical inferiority of the former (see the section in this chapter entitled "A Poet and Not a Historian"). The problem is, again, that no formal criterion marks off the theological language from the literal reportage: one can distinguish them only on the basis of their content, a criterion by which it is sometimes possible to mistake archaeological work for a hole in the ground. This is not altogether surprising: Wellhausen's great history, for example, does not formally mark off its conjectures about premonarchic or presettlement times from its more reliable narrative of the tenth–sixth centuries B.C.E. Still, some evidence that the Israelite, too, differentiated by content would, in the circumstances, be helpful.

There is one area of ancient discourse that provides a promising laboratory for controlled inquiry. This is the semantic field of kinship. In the study of ancient Israel, it has been the subject of intensive investigation for years, in social anthropology for decades.

The chief difficulty in interpreting kinship language and genealogies—a difficulty that has plagued biblical critics—is the polyvalence, the flexibility, of the terms. Deuteronomy, for example, refers to all male Israelites as brothers, an expression that can also denote covenant partners, any partners in mutual interaction ("each to his brother"), fellow Hebrews (Jacob and Esau), fellow tribesmen ("brother" Levites, as 2 Kings 23:9; probably Exodus 4:14), fellow clansmen or townsmen, or biological half- or full brothers. How does one determine, then, in the absence of formal distinctions, when this term has biological, social, or political (*KAI* 216:13–15; Amos 1:9) reference?

One thing, at least, is clear. There is no contradiction in the claims, say, that Ahab and Ben-Hadad are brothers (1 Kings 20:32f.) and that they had different mothers and fathers. The Israelite who makes such claims is hardly prelogical. Rather, the dissonance between the figurative or extended use of language and the literal truth inheres in the nature of figurative language: it answers questions about issues different from those to which the same words, used literally, are pertinent.

It would be preposterous to suggest that the author of 1 Kings 20:32f. could not distinguish political alliance from biological fraternity. Yet this is the implication of Widengren's logic. Simply, biological and geographic genealogies answer different questions. Similarly, when a Semitic scribe juxtaposes theological to literal language, metaphor to reality, the reader must be slow to conclude the scribe was confused. As in the case of the brother Israelite and the brother clansman, the reader must recognize the difference based on content.

An example illustrates the point. Ugaritic texts call the goddess Anat a "virgin" (*btlt*), which she is not. Does this sustain Widengren's position? N. Wyatt provides a reasoned perspective: Anat's virginity has nothing to do with her personal biography. It refers to "her symbolic role" in the sacred marriage: she is virginal for the purposes of cultic convention; in other contexts she is not.[16] The formal contradiction—the prelogical thought—evaporates when the components of the contradiction are placed in different frames of reference. Aristotle evinces a sensitivity to the problem in connection with kinship language. Homer's epithet for Zeus, "father of gods and man," conflicts with his literal understanding of theogony and cosmogony; consequently, he takes the genealogical language to express Zeus' supremacy in the cosmos (*Pol.* 1.1259b). Aristotle distinguishes by content alone.

Apply the same principle to the Israelite genealogies. These encode information on all sorts of different subjects, just as the term brother does—a point on which all recent studies, and anthropological research at least since Malinowski's time, coincide.[17] What does this mean in a village? Simply, in answer to one question, a family may claim descent from some eponym, A; in another connection, it will trace its ancestry to eponym B. In this way Samuel is at one point an Ephrathite (1 Sam. 1:1), donated to the shrine at Shiloh (1:24–28); where his fathering of an order of temple singers is the issue, he is a Levite (1 Chron. 6:16–28). The Levitic genealogy expresses a synchronic relationship—that of Samuel's line with Levi—in a historical metaphor: Samuel is a fictive descendant of Levi.

In the 1950s sociologists found a parallel among Arab villagers in Israel. A common practice among immigrants there, especially numerous as they were in the period before 1937, was to enter a local hamula, or expanded family, either by marriage or by some other form of alliance. This afforded legal protection and a network of readymade social and political affiliations. The newcomers, naturally enough, adopted the hamula eponym as their own; often they selected a recent, but deceased, dignitary from the adoptive hamula as an ancestor. The fictive genealogy thus has social and political meaning. Nevertheless, members of the adoptive hamula were able, generations later, to identify latecomers' descendants—usually as "sons of a slave."[18] In the village there is no confusion as to when the phrase *A, son of B* means that A is B's biological offspring, and when it means that A joined a lineage named after B or came originally from a village named B, and so on.

Villagers distinguish historical (i.e., biological) from less literal tables of generations based on content. If the "father" is a village, if a fraternal relationship is one between two eponyms, geographical or political relations are in point. The villager performs upon the genealogy the same operation Wyatt did on Anat's virginity, or Aristotle on Zeus' fatherhood: the language has moorings in a concrete setting, and cannot be taken literally, in a vacuum. What this means is that the villager is benignly tolerant of formal contradiction in the realm of kinship.

Contradiction may even be the wrong term. In one sense we may speak of the mistranslation of kinship language. Hamula-mates, for example, refer to all members of their age group as *ibn ʿamm*, "uncle's son," and to members of the father's generation as *ʿamm*, "uncle." These terms *denote* those relationships. Similarly, the word *son* in Israel may not mean "biological offspring" only, but a person or group in a certain relationship to a "father" and other "sons." Thus a villager confronting a genealogy expressing political affiliation may apply a familiarity with the referent not to distinguish between metaphorical and literal applications of language, but to determine which, among all possible kinds, of "sonship" is being described. The synchronic use of kinship language—to describe relationships among contemporary entities—would be quite as literal as its diachronic use (to describe the succession of generations).

What goes for the villager does not apply to us. Alien, imperfectly informed readers can no more reliably distinguish clan names from village names, sib names from personal, than they can divine who is "the son of a slave." When knowledge of the content dissipates, readers tend to construe genealogies literally, depleting the semantic content of the kinship language down to the level of biology.

Goody and Wyatt adduce a pertinent illustration.[19] After their first exposure to British colonialist traders, the five administrative districts of Rhodesia collapsed, through conquest and other upheavals, into four. The myth of the state's foundation therefore underwent a transformation—from a story of an eponymic king with five sons to one of an eponymic king with four sons (each the eponym of a district): the whole national genealogy was revised. Later, British administrators consulted old British records, in which the former genealogies were enshrined. They concluded that the revised genealogies, which used only existing district eponyms, were corrupt, perjured, or misremembered. As outsiders, unattuned to the kinship language, they assumed that both genealogies were biological when, in fact, both were "legal."

Confusion, in short, arises when the interpreter does not have the data presupposed by the genealogist. The genealogy, after all, does not announce formally that it is purely political or geographic: when it is used to express geographic relations, whether one mistakes it for a biological genealogy is irrelevant; it succeeds if it communicates the geographic information, regardless of the static it creates in other fields.

Parallels in biblical criticism are frequent. Thus the relationships among the Israelite tribes express the degree of their solidarity (full brother versus half-brother) and their segmental equality (each a tribe within Israel, each with clans, and so on) as geographic units.[20] The system is national: tribes are concrete only in relationship to one another.[21] Yet modern scholars persist in pursuing the prehistory of individual tribes outside the system of relationships by which they were defined, outside the confines of a people, Israel, existing in Canaan.[22] Even Wellhausen fell in with this company: Benjamin was born in Canaan, so he must have entered separately from the other tribes; the Leah group came from the south, with Joseph (who is tied to Egypt); the concubine tribes had a discrete history.[23] Wellhausen took the synchronic language of the genealogy—that of full and half-brotherhood, in which geographic relations were expressed, to have diachronic depth. Yet Wellhausen steadfastly insisted that Israel's ancestral lore had no diachronic value.[24]

Wellhausen's error in interpreting genealogy is characteristic. He did not know what kinship language presupposes—the context, the reference, of the assertions. When Eli calls Samuel "my son" (1 Sam. 3:6, 16), the irony of Samuel's role in Yhwh's blight on Eli's house (1 Sam. 2:27–36) and of Yhwh's figurative fathering of Samuel (1:10–20) is lost on a reader who takes the reference literally. Genealogy is a language in which discourse can be conducted at various levels. The reader must determine which is in point.

Samuel could be an Ephrathite, a Levite, or Eli's son. He was all three at once, both one and many. To understand this required a familiarity with Samuel's personal history and guild standing. That is, one distinguished figurative from literal language—if sometimes incorrectly—by its content. The case for the prelogical Israelite, it seems, ultimately rests upon the uninformed condition of the modern critic.

A LAST WORD: ON READING ISRAELITE HISTORIOGRAPHY

Even we, today, make the leap from language to reference, from literal to metaphoric discourse, when we read the text. We recognize the metaphor in Samuel's sonship to Eli, in the language of dual causation, in much theological language; we distinguish the conventions of presentation, such as the prophecy of Josiah's coming, from Israelite historians' reconstructions of events in the past. We do all this when we read historically. Conversely, when we read the text confessionally, as canon, we encounter difficulty in identifying these literary tropes. When we read confessionally, the distinction between language and referent is irrelevant: each claim of the text is true at each level of discourse.

The ancient audiences of the same literature did not read the books of Samuel confessionally. Hearing the stories in their original settings, they sometimes recognized that the stories mixed literal with less literal claims. For the storyteller, for the historian, it probably was not relevant whether they understood just what was romance: the fiction, the narrative as a whole, communicated the author's point. Some listeners to Greek historiography probably recognized that the speeches were concocted, supplied to order, and objected to the lack of formal distinction between the factual and the dramatization of it (hence Thucydides' qualification). This indicates that they were conscious of the limitations of the genre: it could not be narrative and altogether accurate literally.

The intention of the historian—in H(Dtr)'s case, at least in the vast preponderance of passages—is to communicate an analysis of the course of events. The listener may take the actualization, such as the dialogue, literally; this is regrettable, but not disabling. Certainly, H(Dtr) himself was prone to accept assertions from the storytelling tradition— most of his miracle accounts, for example. Yet this does not divert the historian of the monarchy from reporting, reasonably accurately, Judah's and Israel's political experience. Thus the central point remains the reconstruction. If the readers will only grasp that point, then, from the historian's viewpoint, any concerns they have as to what words were spoken, what wonders performed, what prophecies uttered, what spears chucked at whom, can be tiresome, nagging, ugly, and, above all, irrelevant.

As readers today, it is our task to get back into the mental state of the historian's ideal audience, the sophisticates who shared the historian's assumptions, and who therefore stood open to be persuaded by his logic. Where possible, we must avoid patronizing the historian as a mental prepubescent; we must read sympathetically to understand his points. Gibbon once wrote, "Any probable conjecture which tends to raise the dignity of the poet and the poem deserves to be adopted without a rigid scrutiny."[25] Any less generous posture runs the danger of *unjust* misprision.

Again, this is not to say the history is devoid of error, or inaccuracy, or, in rare instances, of downright prevarication. One cannot always, perhaps even often, get straight from it at the past it describes. But one should not mistake its use of synecdoche—of "all Israel" in Judges, of a lightning conquest—for prelogical thought or for fraud. H(Dtr) doubtless knew that the sources he was synthesizing were more narrow than the language of his presentation. He aimed to produce, however, a national history for a Josianic "Israel"—an identity—and distinctions among the parts of the premonarchic nation were dysfunctional. In general rubrics these were therefore obliterated; no pains were taken to expunge them from single stories.

H(Dtr) sometimes stumbled, through indifference or naïveté, over metaphor in his sources. The further his remove from events, the healthier was his tolerance for miracle: the hailstorm at Gibeon, the collapse of Jericho's walls, the event at the Reed Sea, can be taken as fact. Still, this is a period the confessional rehearsal of which never severed language from event. Starting from the era of the Judges, when H(Dtr) first exposes the Canaanite origins of Israelite heterodoxy, there is no spectacle, no suns standing still, no seas hurled about. The only case approaching this level of theater comes at Mt. Carmel, in a cycle about Elijah (1 Kings 18) whose penchant for the supernatural approaches that of the Pentateuch. It comes from oral sources—where distinguishing metaphor from literal language is so difficult (see the section in this chapter entitled "A Poet and Not a Historian"); it does not affect the course of the nation's fate.

To read Israel's historiography, we must allow that it stands on the far horizon of the Western tradition. The historians' idea of what leeway they enjoyed in presentation diverged from the standards of twentieth-century academic history, perhaps far more than their idea of what constituted evidence. God and history both vindicated their convictions, complementarily. Yet, for all their passion, the authors of DtrH repeatedly abandon their ideological axe-grinding to wrestle with the evidence or reconstruct the mechanics of individual episodes (Ehud, Deborah) or eras (as Solomon, the early monarchy). In all this there is no suggestion that they were any less attuned to their sources than was, say, Haupt, or the governor of New York (Chapter 1).

In his autobiography Robin Collingwood excoriates his colleagues in philosophy at Oxford. They tried, he reports, to *refute* Plato, by refuting the absolute sense of his words, taken without a context; they did not reconstruct the context for which Plato's words were meant, the questions he was trying to answer. They thus confronted Plato with logical objections irrelevant to his concerns, and made him out a fool. It was as though a man "had got it into his head that [trireme] was the Greek word for 'steamer' ": taxed with the objection that triremes did not sound much like steamships, he would respond, "That is just what I say!" The Greeks knew nothing about steamships and so were utterly hopeless at describing them.[26]

The study of Israelite historiography has long been mired in a similar condition, with Noth's the lone voice crying conviction in the steppe. Many scholars do seek unity of vision in the historiography—where vision is almost as diverse as the sources. They do so, however, at the expense of H(Dtr)'s integrity as a historian. What one must strive to understand, as Collingwood stressed, is what the ancient authors were trying to do, when their work encompassed such diversity. And, as Noth saw, the indication is that they were writing history, as they understood it. They seem to have done so in good faith. Until students of Chronicles and the Former Prophets come to terms with Noth's position, thus, their work will remain without a basis in the concrete contexts within which Israelite historians worked; it will forgo a productive dialogue with the specific historical circumstances that produced biblical historiography. It will continue to deliver up redactors and historians with no commitment to the truth of what they wrote, and with no reason not to have written versions altogether different—knaves and fools. This may be an appropriate way to approach the writing of romance. It is not the optimal starting point for research into historical writings.

The perspective defended here assumes that the historians of DtrH could and did consciously differentiate myth and history, evidence from confection, and reconstruction from dramatization; that they set out from the conviction that history vindicated their partisan biases to set down what they could learn of the events; that their antiquarian curiosity balanced the urge to censorship; that they subdued whatever was ideologically troubling more by metahistorical, editorial discourse than by falsifying concrete political developments. It is my fear and expectation that many scholars will reject this as a naive, unduly generous assessment. It is the only one that is not patronizing or condescending toward the ancient authors, the only one consonant with all the evidence examined in this book.

The method adopted in this treatment has been to separate analysis of the historians' reconstructions from analysis of their presentations—to explore the logic of two different, if interrelated, historiographic procedures separately. It operates on the postulate that H(Dtr) and his colleagues were three-dimensional human beings, not abstract, hypothetical quantities, living in a society of readers or hearers who would not tolerate outright lies or even overdone pettifoggery. This postulate may be wrong. It is the only one that, doing justice to the authors who are the object of our study, does no injustice to ourselves.

Notes to Chapter 11

1. F. M. Cross, "The Epic Traditions of Early Israel: Epic Narrative and the Reconstruction of Early Israelite Institutions," in R. E. Friedman, ed., *The Poet and the Historian* (Chico, CA: Scholars, 1983), 19.

2. The list includes R. Alter, *The Art of Biblical Narrative* (New York: Basic, 1980), 23–46; J. Barr, *The Scope and Authority of the Bible* (Philadelphia: Westminster, 1980), 5; for a convenient summary of these developments, see J. J. Collins, "Is a Critical Biblical Theology Possible?" forthcoming in W. H. Propp, D. N. Freedman, and B. Halpern, eds., *Ex Occidente Lux* (Winona Lake, IN: Eisenbrauns).

3. See, e.g., H. W. Frei, *The Eclipse of Biblical Narrative: A Study in Eighteenth and Nineteenth Century Hermeneutics* (New Haven: Yale, 1974), especially 134–36, 160f. Further bibliography in Chapter 1.

4. J. R. Goody and I. Watt, "The Consequences of Literacy," in J. R. Goody, ed., *Literacy in Traditional Societies* (Cambridge: Cambridge University, 1968), 27–68, especially 31–45. The basic insight is attested in England in the first half of the nineteenth century.

5. See already F. M. Cornford, "A Ritual Basis for Hesiod's Theogony," in *The Unwritten Philosophy and Other Essays*, ed. W. K. C. Guthrie (Cambridge: Cambridge University, 1950), 95–116.

6. See Goody and Watt, "Consequences" (n. 4), 20f. For Israelite literacy see recently, A. Lemaire, *Les écoles et la formation de la Bible dans l'ancien Israël* (Orbis Biblicus et Orientalis, 39; Göttingen: Vandenhoeck & Ruprecht, 1981). I doubt, however, whether writing was widely disseminated. The vowelless alphabet remains a cipher of the tongue; the orthography, as a recent ostracon from Khirbet Uzza with full orthography shows, did not reflect pronunciation, but was conventional.

7. G. Widengren, "Myth and History in Israelite–Jewish Thought," in S. Diamond, ed., *Culture and History: Essays in Honor of Paul Radin* (N.Y.: Columbia University, 1960), 467–90. The quotation is from pp. 484f. Widengren undergirds himself with the work of J. Hempel (pp. 472f.), whose views coincide with the ideology underlying A. Rosenberg's *Mythos des zwanzigen Jahrhunderts* and collide with those actuating Noth's work. For the history of Widengren's position, see J. A. Rogerson, *The Problem of Myth in the Old Testament* (Berlin: de Gruyter, 1974). See further on cultic metaphor, A. Bentzen, "The Cultic Use of the Story of the Ark in Samuel," *JBL* 67 (1948): 37–53; J. Pedersen, "Passahfest und Passahlegende," *ZAW* NF 11 (1934): 161–75.

8. E.g., A. Momigliano, *Essays in Ancient and Modern Historiography* (Middletown, CT: Wesleyan University, 1977), 194–96.

9. See J. A. Hoftijzer and G. van der Kooij, *Aramaic Texts from Deir ʿAlla* (HSM 31; Chico, CA: Scholars, 1984).

10. See Chapter 9, n. 31. Cf. J. van Seters, *In Search of History* (New Haven: Yale University, 1983), 92–96.

11. See on Ashurbanipal, M. Weippert, "Die Kämpfe des assyrischen Königs Assurbanipal gegen die Araber" *WO* 7 (1973): 74– 85; on Esarhaddon, R. Borger, *Die Inschriften Asarhaddons Königs von Assyrien* (Afo Beih. 9; Graz, Austria: Weidner, 1956), 68; on Sennacherib, N. Naʾaman, "Sennacherib's 'Letter to God' on His Campaign to Judah," *BASOR* 214 (1974): 25–39; on Sargon, F. Thureau-Dangin, *Une relation de la Huitième Campagne de Sargon (714 av. J.-C.)* (Paris: Geuthner, 1912). For earlier examples see the enumeration in E. A. Speiser, "Ancient Mesopotamia," in R. C. Dentan, ed., *The Idea of History in the Ancient Near East* (New Haven: Yale University, 1955), 63–67; and A. L. Oppenheim, "The City of Assur in 714 B.C.," *JNES* 19 (1960): 133–47.

12. See Chapter 8, n. 40; especially H. Tadmor, "History and Ideology in the Assyrian Royal Inscriptions," in F. M. Fales, ed., *Assyrian Royal Inscriptions* (Rome: Istituto per l'Oriente, 1981), 13–33, especially 23.

13. See A. K. Grayson, "Histories and Historians of the Ancient Near East: Assyria and Babylonia," *Or* 49 (1980): 140–94, especially 164– 68.

14. V. Hurowitz and J. Westerholz, "LKA 63" forthcoming in *Assur*. The annals are rarely suspected of wholesale distortion; cf. on Israelite redaction M. Cogan, "The Chronicler's Use of Chronology as Illuminated by Neo-Assyrian Royal Inscriptions," in J. H. Tigay, ed., *Empirical Models for Biblical Criticism* (Philadelphia: University of Pennsylvania, 1985), 197– 209, especially 55–57.

15. P. Haupt, "The Burning Bush and the Origin of Judaism," *PAPS* 48 (1909): 354–69, especially 361f.

16. N. Wyatt, "The ʿAnat Stela from Ugarit and its Ramifications," *UF* 16 (1985): 327–37, especially 331.

17. For Israel, see M. D. Johnson, *The Purpose of the Biblical Genealogies* (New York: Cambridge University, 1969); A. Malamat, "King Lists of the Old Babylonian Period and Biblical Genealogies," *JAOS* 88 (1968): 163–73; idem, "Tribal Societies: Biblical Genealogies and African Lineage Systems," *Archives européenes de sociologie* 14 (1973): 126–36; A. Demsky, "The Genealogy of Gibeon (1 Chronicles 9:35–41): Biblical and Epigraphic Considerations," *BASOR* 202 (1971): 16–23; idem, "Geba, Gibeah, and Gibeon—An Historico-Geographic Riddle," *BASOR* 212 (1973): 26–31; R. R. Wilson, "The Old Testament Genealogies in Recent Research," *JBL* 94 (1975): 169–89; idem, *Genealogy and History in the Biblical World* (New Haven: Yale University, 1977); idem, "Between 'Azel' and 'Azel': Interpreting the Biblical Genealogies," *BA* 42 (1979): 11–22; also, C. Zaccagnini, "On Gift Exchange in the Old Babylonian Period," in O. Carruba, M. Liverani, and C. Zaccagnini, eds., *Studi Orientalistici in Ricordo di Franco Pintore* (Pavia, Italy: GJES, 1983), 189–253, especially 198–202, on figurative kinship in Mesopotamia.

18. See A. Cohen, *Arab Border-Villages in Israel; A Study of Continuity and Change in Social Organization* (Manchester, U.K.: Manchester University, 1965), 3ff.

19. Goody and Watt, "Consequences" (n. 4), 30–33.

20. See B. Halpern, *The Emergence of Israel in Canaan* (Chico, CA: Scholars, 1983), 109–63, with qualifications on the status of Levi. For mixed genealogies (biological and geographical, and so on), see Malamat, "King Lists" (n. 17); Demsky, "Genealogy" (n. 17).

21. C. H. J. de Geus, *The Tribes of Israel: An Investigation into Some of the Presuppositions of Martin Noth's Amphictyony Hypothesis* (Studia Semitica Neerlandica 18; Assen, Netherlands: van Gorcum, 1976), 124–80.

22. E.g., S. Yeivin, "Toward the Number of Israel's Tribes," *EI* 14 (1978): 37f.; B. Lindars, "The Israelite Tribes in Judges," in J. A. Emerton, ed., *Studies in the Historical Books of the Old Testament* (SVT 30; Leiden, Netherlands: Brill, 1979), 95–112. Compare A. Malamat, "Die Frühgeschichte Israels–eine methodologische Studie," *TZ* 39 (1983): 1–16.

23. J. Wellhausen, *Israelitische und jüdäische Geschichte* (Berlin: Reimer, 1894), 12f., 18ff.

24. See further J. A. Soggin, "The History of Ancient Israel: A Study in Some Questions of Method," *EI* 14 (1978): 44–51.

25. E. Gibbon, "Memoirs of My Life," in *The Decline and Fall of the Roman Empire* (N.Y.: Charles C. Bigelow, n.d.), 128f.

26. R. G. Collingwood, *An Autobiography* (Oxford: Oxford University, 1970), 64.

Index